# The Canadian Public Education System: Issues and Prospects

**Edited
by
Y.L.Jack Lam**

Detselig Enterprises Limited
Calgary, Alberta

**Canadian Cataloguing in Publication Data:**
Main entry under title:
Canadian Public Education System

ISBN 1-55059-019-7
1. Education--Canada. I. Lam, Y. L. Jack.
LA412.C36 1990     370'.971     C90-091285-5

Detselig Enterprises Limited
P.O. Box G399
Calgary, Alberta T3A 2G3

Printed in Canada     SAN 115-0324     ISBN 1-55059-019-7

# Table of Contents

# Contributors

*Peter J. Atherton*, received his Ph.D. fom the University of Alberta. He is currently Dean and professor of the College of Education, Brock University. His recent research focuses on economics and educational planning.

*John Bergen* received his Ph.D. from the University of Alberta (1967) and is currently a professor emeritus in the Department of Educational Administration, University of Alberta. His current research focuses on private schools and issues in the governance of education.

*J.B. Cousins* received his Ph.D. from the University of Toronto. He is currently an assistant professor at the Ontario Institute for Studies in Education. His recent research interest is in evaluation.

*Richard Henley* has a M.Ed from the University of Toronto. He is presently a centre coordinator with the Brandon University Northern Teacher Education Program (BUNTEP). His research interests include the history of Canadian education, Native education and teacher education.

*Mark Holmes* obtained his Ph.D. from the University of Chicago. He is currently a professor in the Department of Educational Administration, Ontario Institute for the Study of Education. His current research deals with effective schools and educational policy.

*Y.L. Jack Lam* received his Ph.D. from the University of Toronto. He is currently a professor in the Department of Administration and Educational Services, Brandon University. His current research covers public education, organization-environment relationships and comparative education.

*Stephen Lawton* obtained his Ph.D. from the University of California at Berkeley. He is currently a professor in the Department of Educational Administration, Ontario Institute for the Study of Education. His recent research deals with educational finance and school retention.

*Ken A. Leithwood* received his Ph.D. from the University of Toronto. He is currently a professor in the Department of Educational Administration and head of the Centre for Principal Development at the Ontario Institute for the Study of Education. His current research covers planned change, school administrators' role in school improvement, program and personal evaluation.

*D.A. MacIver* received his Ph.D. from the University of Alberta. He is currently chairman and professor of the Department of Education at the University of New Brunswick. His current research deals with educational theory, at-risk students and comparative studies of the work of John Dewey.

*A. Wayne McKay* received his M.A. from the University of Florida and LL.B. from Dalhousie University. He is currently a professor of the Law School at Dalhousie University. He wrote and delivered papers extensively of the

*Charter of Rights,* education law, criminal law and human rights, prisoners' rights and Constitutional law.

*Lorraine O'Neill* graduated from London Teacher's College and the University of Calgary. Formerly an Ontario elementary school teacher, she is now a graduate teaching assistant and student in the Department of Educational Policy and Administrative Studies at the University of Calgary. Her present research interests include intergenerational programming and the role of volunteer grandparents within educational settings.

*Douglas Ray* received his Ph.D. from the University of London. He is currently a professor in the Division of Educational Policies, University of Western Ontario. His current research includes human rights education with special reference to the Canadian elementary school curriculum, educational policies, teacher education, and developmental education in Latin America.

*Pat Renihan* received his Ph.D. from the University of Alberta. He is currently a professor in the Department of Educational Administration, University of Saskatchewan, as well as a trustee with the Saskatoon Catholic School Board. His recent research covers administrative development and institutional image.

*Larry E. Sackney* received his Ph.D. from the University of Alberta. He is currently a professor in the Department of Educational Administration, University of Saskatchewan and the Director of Saskatchewan Educational Leadership Unit. His research interests include school effectiveness, school improvement, rural education, leadership improvement and supervision.

*Lyle Sutherland* received his B.A. and LL.B. from Dalhousie University. He is currently teaching at the Law School, Dalhousie University. His recent interest lies in school law.

*Richard Townsend* received his Ph.D. from the University of Chicago. He is currently an associate professor in the Department of Educational Administration, the Ontario Institute for the Study of Education. His research interests include politics of education and curriculum policy-making.

*D.M.A. Trider* received his Ed.D. from the University of Toronto. He is currently the assistant superintendent of Halifax Bedford. His recent professional interest is in the area of effective administration.

*Beth Young* received her Ph.D. from the University of Alberta. She is currently an assistant professor in the Department of Educational Administration. Her major research interests are related to feminist issues.

*Jonathan Young* received his Ph.D. from the University of Toronto. He is currently an assistant professor in the Department of Educational Administration and Foundations, University of Manitoba. His current areas of research include the application of ethnographic research methods to the understanding of schools in multi-ethnic settings, and teacher preparation.

*Mathew Zachariah* received his Ph.D. from the University of Colorado. He is currently a professor in the Department of Educational Policy and Administrative Studies, University of Calgary. His recent research deals with the role of education in the maintenance and change of socio-cultural systems and qualitative research.

## Acknowledgements

In compiling a book that explores the current issues confronting public education in Canada, it is crucial that the materials presented be fresh and up-to-date. My first thanks is to all contributors who responded promptly to my initial request for contributions to this book, and who put up with my numerous demands as editor.

Acknowledgements should be given to my colleagues, notably Clifford Carbno and Harold Tribe who were constantly called for assistance in providing critical comments and patient proofreading.

Last but not least is my gratitude to Jean Claeys who had the unenviable job of typing and retyping sections of this book to make it a coherent whole.

# Introduction

There is perhaps no better source from which to trace the changes in Canadian public education than the slogans echoed in the literature associated with each particular era. While such slogans are not mutually exclusive, they explicitly denote the specific concerns and thrusts that the public expects of its schools during a specific period. We denote the shift fron ensuring equal educational opportunities in the sixties, to the rising demands for accountability in the seventies, and lately, to the quest for academic excellence in the present decade.There is indeed a rigorous demand for quality output where once a mere desire for basic social justice would suffice.

With the expectations placed on the public education system, a number of questions have emerged: How do public educators fare in the present challenge? What problems are inherent in the current internal and external environments that public schools encounter? What alternatives are available?

*The Canadian Public Education System: Issues and Prospects* seeks solutions to these questions in a three-part theme. It begins with the *contextual* issues outlining the diversity of enviromnental forces that shape the public education system. It follows with the *current* issues confronted by the various levels of bureaucracy of the school system, the teaching profession and Natives. It ends with some predictions of the possible future directions that the school system might take or to which it will evolve.

Within this conceptual framework, Bergen starts with the emergence and expansion of the private schools in Canada as a major threat to the omnipotent position that the public school in this country traditionally enjoys (Chapter 1); confronting this powerful and enticing alternative, Lawton re-examines the financial conditions of the public school and identifies some of the fiscal problems it encounters (Chapter 2); Ray investigates the multicultural mandate of the public school in the context of official biligual policy (Chapter 3); McKay and Sutherland present a legalistic perspective of a new set of challenges facing public educators in enforcing order in schools (Chapter 4); and the societal quest for gender equality prompts Young to take a critical look at the public school and see how this social ideal has been materialized (Chapter 5).

Given all these challenges, public educators are saddled with the continued demands for greater uniformity of school standards. Could these demands be satisfied with the recall of the time-honored solution in the form of the public examination? Zacariah and O'Neill focus on this issue, reflect upon the Albertan experience and project some possible implications for the rest of the nation (Chapter 6). While not exausting all the environmental forces of chamge imposing upon the Canadian public school system, this section has highlighted key forces in the educational, economic, legal and social domains that constitute the current arena within which public educators have to operate.

To drive home the relative impact of the identified contextual forces, Section Two of this text follows with the exploration of various levels of bureaucracy and traces some of the proactive and reactive measures adapted by each. As well, grassroot concerns and Native education, traditionally considered as marginal to the mainstream, are documented. In the long history of the federal government's intrusion into public education, Sackney investigates its latest role and effort on the second language program as a means of cementing nationhood (Chapter 7); MacIver reviews the protocal in the policy development undertaken by the provincial government (Chapter 8); Townsend interviews school board trustees to develop an intimate look into their problems and outlooks (Chapter 9); Lam scrutinizes the front-line educators' concerns through their provincial organizations across the country to identify their startegies of coping with the changing environment (Chapter 10); and Henley and Young examine the problems, challenges and aspirations of Natives in advancing their welfare through proper education (Chapter 11).

"Where do we go from here?" seems to be a reasonable and logical question to ask. While no one really knows exactly what lies ahead, and the methodologies of accurately forecasting the future are still in an infant stage, existing phenomena, trends and data allow us to postulate, and even advocate a seemingly logical path upon which the future development of public education should travel. Given that future forecasting inevitably rests on the present phenomena, there are occasional, but unavoidable overlays in a few places to demonstrate the continuity of the likely trends.

Section Three begins with Lam's description of how the extension of the public school clientele would provide stability for the system as well as benefit the individual and the country as a whole (Chapter 12); Holmes treats the problem of future funding for private, independent schools. (Chapter 13); Atherton projects, on a more global scale, how povincial financing of public education shoud be restructured (Chapter 14); Renihan looks forward to the type and intensity of future political actions that communities will adopt for modifying the policies and decisions of official bodies (Chapter 15); and eithwood and Trider propose the kind of curriculum reform that will likely take place (Chapter 16). While Section Three pertains more to personal interpretations and extrapolation, it intends to stimulate the reader's own intuitions, reflections, discussions and further contemplation on issues raised.

Taking the three sections in a holistic perspective, the explicit purposes of the book become self-evident: it intends to inform, to provoke more personal thinking and more general discussion. In this respect, it is amiably suited for senior undergraduates as well as graduate students taking courses in education.

*The Canadian Public Education System: Issues and Prospects* draws on authors primarily from educational policy, administration and curriculum areas;

they come from the Maritime, Central and Western parts of Canada, bringing with them their particular experiences and expertise to help construct a comprehesive framework for analyzing public educational issues. While the book does not touch on all the issues facing public education, the aspiration of building such a basic framework should be achieved, in view of the wide spectrum of topics touching on the political, economic, social, cultural, legal and curriculum perspectives that are brought to bear in discussing contem- porary Canadian public education.

Y.L.J. Lam, Editor.

# Section 1:
# Contextual Issues of Canadian Public Education

# 1

# The Emergence and Expansion of Private Schools in Canada

*John J. Bergen*

In recent years, an increasing interest in private schooling has become apparent. Several provinces provide a measure of financial support to private schools. This support has caused some concern among public school boards and teacher associations, particularly during a period of decreasing enrolments and tightening budgets. The concern here is with those private schools enroling children who normally would be attending public schools which provide elementary and secondary schooling.

A private (or independent)[1] school is a school other than one under the governance of a public school board or a provincial or federal government department. The designation of *public* includes the denominational school boards of Newfoundland and Quebec, and the separate school boards of Ontario, Saskatchewan and Alberta, all of which operate under constitutional provisions and provincial statutory controls and hold privileges similar to those held by any school boards designated as being "public."

Private schools may be parochial or denominational. However, they may also be religious but interdenominational. Some are founded by churches or denominations in order to provide instruction in a particular religious doctrine. Others, generally secular in nature, are established to meet specific educational needs for which the provincial school systems have not adequately provided, such as the instruction of second languages or the education of handicapped children. Some are established in order to provide instruction from the perspective of a particular educational philosophy or methodology. Also, some elite private schools have been founded to serve the process of social selection in establishing "the individual as belonging to an appropriate group."[2] The latter schools can be afforded mainly by affluent parents.

## Historical Background

The first private school in Canada was founded in Quebec City by the Jesuits in 1635.[3] During the French Regime, the main responsibility for education was left to the church authorities who had the support of the civil administration.[4] By 1801, two types of schools were recognized in Lower Canada, "the official or Royal schools and separate or private schools."[5] However, during the early part of the nineteenth century, the public and private schools were not clearly distinguishable because the state provided grants to some of the private schools.[6]

Under early English rule, a few schools for the Protestant population were provided through private initiatives.[7] (The oldest continuing private school in English Canada was founded in 1788.[8]) Private ventures in education in the eighteenth century served mainly the children of the wealthy.[9] Even by the middle of the nineteenth century, private schools held a dominant position in the educational setting. For example, in 1847 the 25 private schools in Kingston registered 621 pupils whereas the ten common schools had 791. In 1867, the private Protestant schools of Montreal enroled 3,000 pupils while public board schools had only 750.[10] Phillips pointed out that "private initiative frequently performed a public service"[11] before local education authorities were set up, but that the "private schools in Canada became relatively unimportant after 1850."[12] However, as we shall see, this latter comment applied more to Upper Canada than to Lower Canada.

In the West, as in eastern Canada, the early schools were established mainly by missionaries and churches. Some received token support from governing councils or trading companies. The earliest schooling in western Canada was provided by the Hudson's Bay Company in 1808 for the children of its employees.[13] Stamp emphasized that

> . . . public responsibility in education is of rather recent origin in the long history of mankind. . . .The state did not emerge as the major controlling authority in education until the nineteenth century. . . . State enterprise in Canadian education grew from modest beginnings in the mid-nineteenth century to gigantic proportions in the post-World War II era.[14]

English-speaking Canadians, more so than the French-speaking, regarded education as a public rather than a private responsibility. The French had considered education "largely as a matter of family and church responsibility" until the 1960s when they "also were willing to entrust more and more of educational decision-making to the state."[15] Thus, the place and influence of religion in Canadian education is found in historical tradition and practice.

Closely tied to religion was language, the French speaking mainly Catholic, the English speaking mainly Protestant. The attempt of Strachan to gain a major stronghold in the administration of English education for the Church of England was strongly opposed by the Methodists, Presbyterians, and Baptists, and effectively by Ryerson who wanted equal rights for all denominations.[16]

Nevertheless, most Protestant clergymen were agreed that the Bible should be a textbook in the schools. The assumed objection of the Catholics to the Bible in schools and the apparent desire to continue the separate educational structures which had already evolved gave rise to 38 petitions, only one of which came from the Catholics, requesting that "separate schools" be legitimized in the terms of the 1841 *Act of Union.*[17] Ontario's separate school system was based on a separate school bill enacted in 1853.[18]

A few years later, section 93 of the *British North America Act* of 1867 gave to the provinces the exclusive right to make laws (subject to certain conditions) in relation to education "in and for each province." These conditions guaranteed Roman Catholics and Protestants rights to denominational schools in Quebec and Ontario, and were to apply also to other provinces where such schools existed by law at the time of union or were subsequently established by law. For example, those same terms were to apply to Manitoba when it was established as a province in 1870, and to Alberta and Saskatchewan in 1905.

A constitutional basis was thus laid for denominationalism in Canadian education. Certain guarantees were established for the Protestant minority of Quebec and the Catholic minority of Ontario, but for the Maritime Catholics only "as much in law as they could secure from their provincial legislatures after the union."[19] The federal government introduced the separate school principle in the Territories in legislation of 1875, which subsequently became a part of the terms of the Alberta and Saskatchewan Acts of 1905. However, Manitoba's separate schools were abolished by provincial legislation in 1890, notwithstanding the guarantees of section 93 of the *B.N.A. Act.*

Newfoundland entered the Canadian confederation in 1949. Special provisions in provincial public educational systems at that date can be generally classified as follows:

(1) Catholic and Protestant schools in Quebec;

(2) Schools for all denominations in Newfoundland;

(3) Separate Catholic elementary schools in Ontario (extended to include secondary schools in 1985);

(4) Separate Catholic or Protestant schools for grades one to twelve in Alberta and grades one to eight in Saskatchewan (extended to include grades nine to twelve in 1964);

(5) No provision for separate schools in the provinces of British Columbia, Manitoba, New Brunswick, Nova Scotia and Prince Edward Island.

However, the religious nature inherent in the Canadian public school systems was not restricted to confessional and separate schools. Stamp stated that religious exercises and instruction were a central part of the school day for nearly every Canadian young person. Such emphasis was to be expected in the openly denominational schools in Quebec and Newfoundland, and in the Roman Catholic separate schools of other regions. But it was also strong in the supposedly "public" schools, on the basis that Canada was a Christian country and the fundamental beliefs of Christianity could be imparted "without insult" to mixed classes.[20]

As late as 1944, Ontario "took formal legal steps to enhance religious education in the schools."[21] The Bible Study Committee of the Ontario Educational Association in 1942 had adopted resolutions calling for "obligatory courses in the Bible and the Christian religion in both elementary and secondary schools" and that the pupils be examined and receive credit.[22] George Drew, Premier and Minister of Education, announced in 1944 that "religious education will be offered in public and secondary schools."[23] Opposition to this course of action was expressed by Jewish leaders, the Orange Order and a fellowship of Baptists. Nevertheless, the Royal Commission on Education in its 1950 report endorsed the course of religious instruction introduced in 1944.[24] The Committee on Religious Education affirmed that Ontario society had changed from one predominantly Anglo-Christian to one which was pluralistic. Many religious denominations and sects related to ethnic groups which had come from all parts of the world now flourished in the province. "To disregard this fact would be to discriminate against large segments of the population."[25] The Committee recommended the discontinuance of the courses being offered, that opening exercises of a "universal character" be conducted, and that incidental teaching rather than formal syllabuses with respect to the "acquisition of information about the respect for all religion" take its place, and furthermore, that a formal course in world religions be offered.[26]

The Ontario story serves as an illustration of the thinking in other provinces. The *Report of the Royal Commission of Inquiry on Education in the Province of Quebec* recommended "establishing and operating, within the public sector and on an equal footing, both non-confessional and confessional education" which "best correspond to . . . the pluralism of the Quebec population."[27]

Lupul held that in Canada "there are no public schools in the sense of religiously neutral schools . . . all Canadian schools exist to produce theists."[28] For example, Bible reading and the Lord's Prayer were either permissive or compulsory in the schools of most provinces. He stressed that "Canadian parents in every province should be completely free to send their children to a Catholic, a Protestant, or a religiously neutral school."[29] To this end, he proposed a "tripartite" provincial school system which would allow for Catholic, Protestant and "neutral" schools. He assumed that the neutral school "with its emphasis on studying religion rather than celebrating the place of the Christian religion in our society," would have an appeal for atheists, agnostics, freethinkers, rationalists, Unitarians, Quakers, liberal-minded Jews, Moslems and others.[30]

# Emergence and Expansion of Private Schools in Canada

The foregoing discussion suggests at least a partial explanation for the existence and growth of private schools in most of the provinces. The preponderance of private schools in Quebec may be explained by the fact that free public schooling was not extended to the end of high school until the 1940s and that not until the "quiet revolution" of the 1960s did government initiative provide the opportunity of a high school education for aspiring youth.[31] Many of the established private schools, most of them receiving substantial government subsidies, continued to operate. Furthermore, the concurrent "separation of Church and state ... with the result that a spirit of confessionalism no longer permeates the cultural fabric of French Canada"[32] would likely tend to be conducive to the continuation of private schools in which confessionalism would continue to be promoted in contrast to the state schools which have become more "neutral" in character.

Prior to the Davis announcement that Roman Catholic separate school boards be permitted to establish the full range of elementary and secondary education as part of the public school system with full public funding beginning September 1, 1985,[33] Catholic secondary education was provided by a large number of private schools. It was not uncommon for senior secondary grades to be provided for as a "private school" operation under separate school boards. For example, in its 1974 report, the Metropolitan Separate School Board of Toronto indicated that 16 of its 20 Catholic secondary schools were the joint responsibility of the Board and of religious communities. Since September 1987, all Catholic students in such schools have become the sole responsibility of the separate school boards.

Though the education section (section 17) of the Alberta and Saskatchewan Acts of 1905 are identical, their interpretation, based on what was "in practice" by 1905, resulted in differences in school legislation in the two provinces. By 1905, a separate Catholic high school was in operation in Alberta, and separate school districts were permitted to offer both elementary and secondary education. No separate Catholic high school existed in Saskatchewan by 1905. Hence, Saskatchewan school legislation permitted the formation of only elementary separate school districts.

In 1964, new legislation was enacted allowing for the establishment of separate high school districts. Prior to this date, Catholic high schools had been established for the provision of Catholic secondary education. As in Metropolitan Toronto, some of these private school provisions were administered in cooperation with elementary Catholic separate school boards. This may explain why few Catholic private schools have existed in Alberta while more were established in Saskatchewan. Notwithstanding federal admonitions, the Manitoba government abolished its separate schools in 1890 and, subsequently, Catholic private schools, as well as those of other denominations, emerged. British Columbia has no provision for separate schools; nevertheless, a host of private Catholic as well as other denominational schools have been established over the years. The public denominational system virtually obviated the need for private schools in Newfoundland.

In Manitoba, a considerable proportion of Francophone Catholics reside in homogeneous communities in which the public schools for all intents serve as well as the separate schools in provinces such as Alberta or Saskatchewan. Some of the Mennonite communities approach total homogeneity so that their public schools virtually are "Mennonite separate schools." Similar situations may be found for parts of New Brunswick and Prince Edward Island where Catholics reside in relatively homogeneous Francophone communities. Through unofficial arrangements, certain schools are designated as Catholic in some districts of Nova Scotia.

Section 93 of the *B.N.A. Act* (now the *Constitution Act*) made no distinction between Protestant denominations, yet these may differ considerably from one another in theology and practice. Hence, it is not surprising that some denominational groups, who feel as keenly about their particular theological perspective permeating a school program as the Catholics do, would also establish private schools. From the very beginning, the Protestants of Canada were in disagreement about what the nature of religious instruction in the "public" schools should be. However, one of the major reasons for the estab-lishment of new private schools during the last several decades in most provinces may well be the secularization of the public schools.[34] Such was also the major concern expressed by private school supporters in an Alberta survey.[35] The public schools have become more like the "neutral" type of school which Lupul proposed as an option.[36] Nevertheless, Thiessen challenged the generally held view that secular public schools are religiously neutral.[37]

## Growth in the Private Education Sector

The sharp decline in the number of private schools in Quebec followed the expanded provincial provision for secondary schooling opportunities through the organization of regional units in the 1960s. With the exception of New-foundland and Prince Edward Island, noticeable growth occurred in the other provinces during the 1980s (see Table 1).

Table 2 provides a break-down in five-year periods from 1965 to 1986, showing private school enrolments by level of schooling for each province and the percentage changes during five and ten-year periods. Generally, the number of secondary pupils exceeded that of elementary pupils enroled in private schools. However, in some provinces, about the same numbers were enroled at both levels.

For most provinces, and for Canada as a whole, decreases in private school enrolment occurred from 1965 to 1976, with increases in all provinces except Prince Edward Island during the following decade. Of note are the increases which occurred in Ontario and the western provinces. In terms of the percentage

Table 1. Number of Private Schools in the Provinces, 1959-1986

| Year | Canada Total | Nfld. | PEI | N.S. | N.B. | Que. | Ont. | Man. | Sask. | Alta. | B.C. |
|---|---|---|---|---|---|---|---|---|---|---|---|
| 1959-60 | 1706 | — | 5 | 24 | 15 | 1332 | 132 | 48 | 34 | 46 | 70 |
| 1964-65 | 965 | 2 | 2 | 24 | 11 | 445 | 229 | 54 | 25 | 37 | 136 |
| 1969-70 | 1012 | 4 | 1 | 12 | 5 | 520 | 242 | 48 | 17 | 33 | 130 |
| 1974-75 | 890 | 3 | 0 | 8 | 4 | 350 | 310 | 38 | 13 | 40 | 124 |
| 1977-78 | 797 | 2 | 0 | 6 | 9 | 183 | 335 | 53 | 20 | 37 | 152 |
| 1980-81 | 971 | 1 | 2 | 10 | 17 | 183 | 438 | 53 | 30 | 42 | 195 |
| 1985-86 | 1358 | 2 | 1 | 28 | 28 | 270 | 536 | 78 | 47 | 134 | 234 |

Source: Statistics Canada reports.

Table 2. Private School Enrolment by Level and Province

|  | Grades | | | | Total* | Percentage 5-year periods | Change 10-year periods |
|---|---|---|---|---|---|---|---|
|  | Pre-elementary | 1-6 | 7-13 | Other |  |  |  |
| **Nfld** | | | | | | | |
| 1965-66 | 60 | 330 | 60 | - | 440 | | |
| 1970-71 | 60 | 250 | 420 | - | 720 | 63.6 | |
| 1975-76 | 30 | 170 | 80 | - | 280 | -61.1 | |
| 1980-81 | 20 | 150 | 100 | - | 270 | -3.6 | 14.3 |
| 1985-86 | 20 | 140 | 160 | - | 320 | 18.5 | |
| **P.E.I.** | | | | | | | |
| 1965-66 | - | - | 490 | 20 | 510 | | |
| 1970-71 | - | - | 30 | - | 30 | -94.1 | |
| 1975-76 | - | - | - | - | - | - | |
| 1980-81 | 10 | 40 | 10 | - | 50 | - | |
| 1985-86 | 10 | 30 | 20 | - | 60 | 20 | |
| **N.S.** | | | | | | | |
| 1965-66 | 330 | 2,920 | 2,050 | 70 | 5,360 | | |
| 1970-71 | 160 | 590 | 890 | - | 1,650 | -69.2 | |
| 1975-76 | 180 | 490 | 740 | - | 1,420 | -13.9 | -73.7 |
| 1980-81 | 150 | 580 | 720 | - | 1,460 | 2.8 | |
| 1985-86 | 150 | 900 | 910 | - | 1,960 | 34.2 | 39.0 |
| **N.B.** | | | | | | | |
| 1965-66 | - | 32- | 1,200 | 140 | 1,650 | | |
| 1970-71 | - | 160 | 310- | - | 460 | -72.1 | |
| 1975-76 | 30 | 200 | 190 | - | 420 | -8.2 | -74.1 |
| 1980-81 | 70 | 390 | 580 | - | 1,040 | 147.6 | |
| 1985-86 | 100 | 530 | 540 | - | 1,170 | 12.5 | 178.6 |
| **Que.**** | | | | | | | |
| 1965-66 | 6,480 | 32,720 | 44,940** | - | 84,140 | | |
| 1970-71 | 4,700 | 18,570 | 35,500 | - | 58,780 | -30.1 | |
| 1975-76 | 4,150 | 16,940 | 66,900 | - | 87,990 | 49.7 | 4.6 |
| 1980-81 | 3,960 | 17,280 | 67,520 | - | 88,760 | 0.9 | |
| 1985-86 | 2,690 | 20,660 | 71,960 | - | 95,300 | 7.4 | 8.3 |

| | | | | | | % | % |
|---|---|---|---|---|---|---|---|
| **Ont.** | | | | | | | |
| 1965-66 | 1,950 | 10,230 | 32,840 | 530 | 45,550 | -3.1 | |
| 1970-71 | 2,480 | 12,880 | 28,760 | - | 44,120 | 2.8 | 19.9 |
| 1975-76 | 3,650 | 15,240 | 35,720 | - | 54,600 | 36.1 | |
| 1980-81 | 5,230 | 19,370 | 49,690 | - | 74,290 | 2.7 | 39.8 |
| 1985-86 | 7,540 | 23,850 | 44,930 | - | 76,310 | | |
| **Man.** | | | | | | | |
| 1965-66 | 440 | 5,490 | 4,620 | 30 | 10,580 | -21.7 | |
| 1970-71 | 410 | 3,950 | 3,930 | - | 8,280 | -14.0 | -32.7 |
| 1975-76 | 340 | 2,960 | 3,820 | - | 7,120 | 18.7 | |
| 1980-81 | 370 | 3,660 | 4,420 | - | 8,450 | 12.5 | 33.7 |
| 1985-86 | 550 | 4,100 | 4,870 | - | 9,510 | | |
| **Sask.** | | | | | | | |
| 1965-66 | 40 | 40 | 2,310 | 50 | 2,440 | -36.5 | |
| 1970-71 | 40 | 110 | 1,400 | - | 1,550 | -6.5 | -40.6 |
| 1975-76 | - | 90 | 1,360 | - | 1,450 | 57.9 | |
| 1980-81 | 20 | 280 | 1,990 | - | 2,290 | 28.4 | 103.4 |
| 1985-86 | 60 | 640 | 2,250 | - | 2,740 | | |
| **Alta.** | | | | | | | |
| 1965-66 | 360 | 3,760 | 110 | 110 | 6,570 | -13.4 | |
| 1970-71 | 400 | 2,510 | 2,780 | - | 5,690 | -0.7 | -14.0 |
| 1975-76 | 330 | 2,270 | 3,060 | - | 5,650 | 14.9 | |
| 1980-81 | 280 | 2,770 | 3,440 | - | 6,490 | 101.7 | 131.3 |
| 1985-86 | 95 | 5,930 | 6,210 | - | 13,090 | | |
| **B.C.** | | | | | | | |
| 1965-66 | 890 | 15,670 | 9,910 | 100 | 25,850 | -17.5 | |
| 1970-71 | 1,010 | 12,380 | 7,930 | - | 21,320 | 8.2 | -10.8 |
| 1975-76 | 1,150 | 11,860 | 10,060 | - | 23,070 | 14.0 | |
| 1980-81 | 1,400 | 13,840 | 11,080 | - | 26,310 | 27.5 | 45.5 |
| 1985-86 | 2,550 | 16,560 | 14,450 | - | 33,550 | | |
| **Total Canada** | | | | | | | |
| 1965-66 | 10,550 | 70,060 | 101,450 | 1,050 | 183,090 | -22.1 | |
| 1970-71 | 9,260 | 51,410 | 81,930 | - | 142,600 | 27.6 | -0.6 |
| 1975-76 | 9,850 | 50,220 | 121,930 | - | 182,000 | 15.1 | |
| 1980-81 | 11,570 | 58,350 | 139,540 | - | 209,400 | 11.9 | 28.7 |
| 1985-86 | 14,620 | 73,320 | 146,280 | - | 234,220 | | |

*Totals may not agree due to rounding.
**Secondary totals for Quebec might not include students beyond Grade 12.

of all pupils in private schools, Quebec, Ontario, Manitoba and British Columbia stand out. Manitoba and British Columbia do not provide for publicly supported separate Catholic schools, which accounts for the preponderance of private Catholic schools in these provinces. The growth in Ontario has occurred despite the lack of public funding of private schooling. Though funding was introduced in Saskatchewan as early as 1966, increased enrolment did not occur until the 1980s. The immediate drop in enrolment following the introduction of funding may be explained by the extension of separate school funding to include high schools in the 1960s, which resulted in most of the previously listed private Catholic students becoming part of the publicly supported separate school system.

Though modest public funding of private schools was introduced in Alberta in 1967, noticeable growth in private school attendance did not occur until the 1980s. Only in British Columbia is a relationship between funding, introduced in 1987, and private school growth apparent. However, in the context of developments in other provinces, a causal relationship cannot be established with any degree of certainty.

The percentage of all elementary and secondary pupils in private schools during selected years from 1959 to 1988 is given in Table 3. These percentages are quite low, in spite of proportional increases in Nova Scotia and New Brunswick, for Saskatchewan and for the Atlantic provinces.

Quebec continues to lead all provinces in private school enrolments. In 1987-88, private schools in Ontario, where private schools do not receive public funding, contributed to about 27 percent of Canada's total enrolment, whereas Quebec which provides the best funding for private schools of all provinces, contributed to about 44 percent of Canada's private school enrolment. The rest of Canada contributed only about 29 percent.

The higher enrolment in Ontario's Roman Catholic private schools was due in large part to the fact that prior to 1985-86 separate schools were publicly funded to Grade 10 only. The funding of separate schools for Grade 11 in 1985-86, and for grades 12 and 13 in each of the subsequent years has brought about a substantial reduction of students classified as private school students in Ontario.

During the 15 year period, 1970-1985, public school enrolment in Canada dropped steadily (by about 18 percent). During the same period private school enrolments rose by about 64 percent. Table 4 compares the percentage changes of private and public school enrolments during each of the five-year periods from 1965-66 to 1985-86.

As shown in Table 4, the percentage changes in total enrolments in private schools differ little from that of public school enrolments; that is, if all students had been enroled in public schools, the impact would generally be less than 1 percent.

Table 4. Percentage Change in Total School Enrolments for all Provinces in 5-Year Periods, 1965-1985.

| Period | Private | Public | Total |
|---|---|---|---|
| 1965/6-1970/1 | -22.1 | 13.8 | 12.6 |
| 1970/1-1975/6 | 27.6 | -5.0 | -4.2 |
| 1975/6-1980/1 | 15.1 | -9.6 | -8.8 |
| 1980/1-1985/6 | 11.9 | -4.3 | -3.6 |

Table 3. Percent of all Elementary and Secondary Pupils in Private Schools in 1959-1988.

| Year | Canada | Nfld. | P.E.I. | N.S. | N.B. | Que. | Ont. | Man. | Sask. | Al.ta | B.C |
|---|---|---|---|---|---|---|---|---|---|---|---|
| 1959-60 | 4.3 | — | 3.3 | 3.5 | 1.7 | 8.9 | 1.9 | 5.8 | 2.2 | 2.2 | 5.2 |
| 1965-66 | 4.1 | 0.03 | 2.3 | 3.1 | 1.1 | 6.4 | 2.5 | 5.2 | 1.8 | 1.7 | 6.3 |
| 1970-71 | 2.5 | 0.34 | 0.2 | 1.0 | 0.2 | 4.8 | 2.1 | 3.3 | 0.7 | 1.4 | 4.4 |
| 1975-76 | 3.3 | 0.23 | 0.2 | 0.7 | 0.1 | 6.1 | 2.6 | 3.0 | 0.6 | 1.2 | 3.8 |
| 1980-81 | 4.1 | 0.20 | 0.2 | 0.8 | 0.6 | 7.2 | 3.7 | 3.8 | 1.1 | 1.4 | 4.9 |
| 1985-86 | 4.8 | 0.20 | 0.2 | 1.1 | 0.8 | 8.4 | 4.1 | 4.6 | 1.4 | 2.8 | 6.4 |
| 1987-88 | 4.5 | 0.20 | 0.2 | 1.0 | 0.7 | 8.7 | 3.3 | 4.7 | 1.5 | 3.0 | 6.7 |

Source: Statistics Canada

Table 5.  Private School Enrolments and Number of Schools by Affiliation.

| Affiliation[a] | Nfld. | P.E.I. | N.S. | N.B. | Que. | Ont. | Man. | Sask. | Alta. | B.C. | Total | Number of Schools | Average Enrolment per School |
|---|---|---|---|---|---|---|---|---|---|---|---|---|---|
| **Amish** | | | | | | | | | | | | | |
| 1976-77 | | | | | | 170 | | | | | 170 | 7 | 24 |
| 1985-86 | | | | | | 120 | | | | | 120 | 5 | 24 |
| **Anglican** | | | | | | | | | | | | | |
| 1976-77 | | | | | | 4,270 | 120 | | 120 | | 4,510 | 16 | 282 |
| 1985-86 | | | | | | 5,270 | 60 | | | | 5,330 | 16 | 333 |
| **Baptist** | | | | | | | | | | | | | |
| 1976-77 | | | | | | 270 | 60 | | 140 | | 470 | 10 | 47 |
| 1985-86 | 60 | 50 | 130 | 410 | | 1,390 | 130 | 80 | 300 | 40 | 2,590 | 48 | 54 |
| **Brethren in Christ** | | | | | | | | | | | | | |
| 1976-77 | | | | | | 190 | | | | | 190 | 1 | 190 |
| 1985-86 | | | | | | 170 | | | | | 170 | 1 | 170 |
| **Brethren of Early Christianity** | | | | | | | | | | | | | |
| 1976-77 | | | | | | 20 | | | | | 20 | 1 | 20 |
| 1985-85 | | | | | | 20 | | | | | 20 | 1 | 20 |
| **Calvinistic** | | | | | | | | | | | | | |
| 1976-77 | | | | | | | ? | | | | ? | ? | |
| 1985-86 | | | | | | | 270 | | | | (270) | 1 | 270 |
| **Canadian Reformed** | | | | | | | | | | | | | |
| 1976-77 | | | | | | 1,040 | 40 | | 70 | 250 | (1,400) | (12) | 117 |
| 1985-86 | | | | | | 1,350 | 50 | | 50 | 280 | (1,730) | (15) | 115 |
| **Christian Reformed** | | | | | | | | | | | | | |
| 1976-77 | | | | | | | 140 | | 1,340 | 580 | (2,060) | (12) | 172 |
| 1985-86 | | | 100 | | | 430 | 290 | | 2,800 | 4,240 | (7,860) | (12) | 655 |
| **Church of Christ** | | | | | | | | | | | | | |
| 1976-77 | | | | | | | | 170 | | 170 | | 1 | |
| 1985-86 | | | | | | | | 110 | | 110 | | 1 | |
| **General Church of New Jerusalem** | | | | | | | | | | | | | |
| 1976-77 | | | | | | 90 | | | | | 90 | 2 | 45 |
| 1985-86 | | | | | | 60 | | | | | 60 | 2 | 30 |
| **Hutterite** | | | | | | | | | | | | | |
| 1976-77 | | | | | | | | | 40 | | 40 | 3 | 13 |
| 1985-86 | | | | | | | 10 | | | | 10 | 1 | 10 |
| **Jewish** | | | | | | | | | | | | | |
| 1976-77 | | | | | ? | 5,140 | 1,060 | | 200 | 240 | (6,640) | (23) | 289 |
| 1985-86 | | | | | 6,420 | 7,500 | 910 | | 340 | 340 | 15,510 | ? | ? |
| **Lutheran** | | | | | | | | | | | | | |
| 1976-77 | | | | | | | | 480 | 400 | 90 | 970 | 6 | 162 |
| 1985-86 | | | | | | 10 | | 520 | 530 | 110 | 1,170 | 8 | 146 |

| Affiliation | Year | | | | | | | | | | | |
|---|---|---|---|---|---|---|---|---|---|---|---|---|
| Ontario Alliance of Christian Schools[b] | 1976-77 | | 60 | | 2,050 | 1,190 | 170 | 230 | 450 | 3,860 | 59 | 65 |
| | 1985-86 | | | | 2,650 | 1,610 | 320 | | 750 | 5,620 | 111 | 50 |
| Pentecostal | 1976-77 | | | | 8,570 | | | | | 8,570 | 54 | 159 |
| | 1985-86 | | | | 9,180 | | | | | 9,180 | 68 | 135 |
| Presbyterian | 1976-77 | | 10 | 100 | 50 | 10 | | | 130 | 130 | 1 | 1 |
| | 1985-86 | | | | | | | | 710 | 870 | 13 | 67 |
| Protestant | 1976-77 | | | 2,470 | 230 | | | | | (210) | ? | 120 |
| | 1985-86 | | | | 200 | | | | | 2,670 | 2 | |
| Roman Catholic | 1976-77 | | 240 | ? | 22,500 | 3,340 | 240 | 100 | 13,550 | (39,870) | 1 | 210 |
| | 1985-86 | | 370 | 78,170 | 20,470 | 3,370 | 460 | | 15,120 | 118,060 | ? | ? |
| Seventh Day Adventist | 1976-77 | | 80 | 70 | 1,210 | 60 | 90 | 700 | 800 | 3,010 | ? | ? |
| | 1985-86 | | 90 | 40 | 1,150 | 80 | 150 | 920 | 840 | 3,270 | ? | ? |
| Society of Friends | 1976-77 | | | | 170 | | | | 20 | 190 | 47 | 64 |
| | 1985-86 | | | | 150 | | | | | 150 | 84 | 51 |
| Ukrainian Catholic | 1976-77 | | | | 230 | 60 | | 110 | | 170 | 2 | 85 |
| | 1985-86 | | | | | 50 | | | | 280 | 1 | 150 |
| United | 1976-77 | | | 10 | 450 | | | 580 | | 1,040 | 2 | 85 |
| | 1985-86 | | | 50 | 600 | | | | | 650 | 2 | 140 |
| Non-Sectarian[c] | 1976-77 | 280 | 1,010 | | 10,390 | 1,380 | 430 | 3,600 | 6,470 | 23,870 | 5 | 208 |
| | 1985-86 | 250 | 1,190 | | 21,400 | 2,650 | 1,280 | 7,550 | 11,130 | 48,000 | 4 | 162 |
| Affiliation not reported[d] | 1976-77 | 10 | 10 | (90,500) | 200 | 300 | 30 | | | (90,700) | 167 | 143 |
| | 1985-86 | | | 6,220 | 3,690 | | | | | (10,320) | ? | ? |
| Total | 1976-77 | 280 | 1,330 | (90,500) | 56,940 | 7,450 | 1,580 | 7,300 | 22,580 | 188,350 | (800) | (235) |
| | 1985-86 | 320 | 1,960 | 95,310 | 76,320 | 9,520 | 2,950 | 13,090 | 33,560 | 234,260 | (1,300) | (180) |

Source: Compiled from Statistics Canada tables and provincial reports.

Notes:
[a] Estimates are placed in parentheses; a question mark indicates no available estimate.
[b] The majority of Ontario's Alliance of Christian Schools are of Christian tradition.
[c] Many of the schools reported as non-sectarian may be associated with denominations, but may regard themselves to be inter-denominational Christian.
[d] Some of the schools which did not report their affiliation may be non-sectarian or secular; others may belong to one of the listed affiliations.

From 1984-85 to 1985-86, private school enrolment in Canada dropped for the first time in 14 years, largely due to the change in Ontario's provisions for Roman Catholic separate schools.[38] During the same year, increased growth was noted only in the provinces of Alberta, Saskatchewan and British Columbia.[39]

Table 5 provides private school enrolments by affiliation and province for 1976-77 and 1985-86. However, the data given in Tables 2 and 5 must be read as close approximations. Complete data were not available for the province of Quebec. Furthermore, there is no guarantee that all private schools used the same affiliation classification for each return. It is also plausible that a number of "secular" and "non-denominational" schools were placed in the "non-sectarian" classification.

For 1985-86, the percentages of pupils attending private schools of Roman Catholic affiliation in the provinces were: Nova Scotia, 19 percent; Quebec, 82 percent; Ontario, 28 percent; Manitoba, 37 percent; Saskatchewan, 16 percent; British Columbia, 47 percent; and Alberta, less than 1 percent. These proportions relate to the absence of public supported separate schools for Roman Catholics in Manitoba and British Columbia. Though Nova Scotia does not have separate school provisions, in former years, provisions were made to designate certain schools in school districts as "Catholic." In New Brunswick and Prince Edward Island, the French-language public school districts were comprised of largely homogeneous Catholic populations, thus obviating a need for private schools. Similarly, Newfoundland's denominational school system had obviated a need for private schools.

Enrolment growths have occurred in private schools of the following affiliations: Baptist, Canadian Reformed, Christian Reformed, Jewish, Lutheran, Mennonite, Pentecostal, and the Ontario Alliance of Christian Schools. For all of Canada, about 50 percent of all private school enrolment was found in Roman Catholic Schools, about 7 percent in schools of the Christian Reformed tradition, over 6 percent in Jewish schools, and over 2 percent in each of Mennonite and Anglican schools. Each of the remaining affiliations constituted less than 2 percent of the total enrolment. Considerable growth is indicated in private schools which are listed as "non-sectarian." According to the data in Table 5, certain affiliations are restricted to specific provinces. For example, only in Ontario are Amish, Brethren in Christ, Presbyterian, and Society of Friends private schools reported. In contrast, Roman Catholic, Baptist, Canadian Reformed, Christian Reformed, Jewish, Lutheran, Mennonite, Pentecostal, Roman Catholic and Seventh Day Adventist private schools are reported in several provinces. Since 1985, the private school enrolment has dropped appreciably in Ontario as the funding of separate schools was extended to include all high school grades. As a consequence, the proportion of Roman Catholic private school students in Canada dropped to about 45 percent.

Most private schools have low enrolments. For example, for 1981 the Ontario Ministry of Education reported 479 private schools, of which only 36 had enrolments exceeding 500, 182 had enrolments between 100 and 500, and 261 had enrolments of less than 100 (of these, 25 had less than ten students).

Statistics Canada does not provide a further breakdown to show the number of schools which are not sponsored or governed by any one denomination or church. For example, for 1982, the Ontario Ministry of Education reported 26 "visa schools" which enroled 6,350 non-Ontario students — most of whom were foreign students — and which constituted about 8 percent of Ontario's private school enrolment. Another example of a non-sectarian school, though founded by the United Church, is Edmonton's Alberta College which provides high school education for more than a thousand mature students, more than 10 percent of Alberta's private school enrolment. Nor does Statistics Canada identify all private schools which provide special education for handicapped pupils, or those whose pupils attend evening classes for second language instruction. The latter, counted in the total for private school enrolments by some provinces, also attend public schools for all other instruction during the regular school day. According to Statistics Canada, there were no private schools in the Territories in 1985-86.

A Statistics Canada mimeographed report on private schools in 1977-78 listed over 200 French private schools, most of which were located in Quebec, but some of which were located in Nova Scotia, New Brunswick, Ontario, Saskatchewan, and British Columbia.

## Public Funding of Private Schools

The demarcation between private and public schools has not always been clear. Generally, as public schools became available to all, the tendency in provincial school systems has been to provide public funding for public schools only.

The province of Quebec has given substantial financial support to most of its private schools over a long period of time. The 1966 *Report of the Royal Commission of Inquiry on Education* stated that "legislation in aid of private institutions is affected by the historical and political circumstances leading up to its adoption."[40] Further, it stated that government policy must take into account " the quality of the education they impart . . . and the possible use of public funds to finance them, to the extent that they agree to share in the endeavor in offering educational services to all."[41] The subsequent legislation provided for funding up to 60 percent of the average cost of provincial schooling per student, or as much as 80 percent of the average cost if the institution is declared "to be of public interest."[42]

The 1959 Royal Commission on Education in Alberta stated that private schools were justified if they provided a "superior type of education" but

Table 6. Percent of Private Schools Revenue from Government Funds and Other Sources for 1984-85.

| Source | Atlantic Prov's[a] | Que. | Ont. | Man. | Sask. | Alta. | B.C. | Canada |
|---|---|---|---|---|---|---|---|---|
| Government Funding | 1.7[b] | 53.3 | 5.8 | 17.9 | 21.3 | 38.9 | 33.1 | 32.0[b] |
| Tuition Fees | 67.9 | 38.0 | 68.3 | 43.0 | 42.5 | 41.1 | 47.0 | 49.9 |
| Other sources | 30.4 | 8.7 | 25.9 | 39.1 | 36.2 | 20.0 | 19.9 | 18.1 |
| Percent government private school grants is of total grants for all schools | 0.0 | 3.5 | 0.1 | 0.9 | 0.5 | 1.2 | 1.6 | 1.6 |
| Percent total private schools revenue is of total public and private school funding | 0.5 | 6.3 | 3.7 | 3.0 | 1.8 | 2.2 | 4.1 | 3.9 |
| Percent of all pupils in private schools for 1984-85 | 0.7 | 8.1 | 4.7 | 4.2 | 1.3 | 2.7 | 5.8 | 4.8 |

Source: Compiled from Financial Statistics of Education (81-208), Statistics Canada.
[a] Comprising mainly Nova Scotia and New Brunswick private schools.
[b] Federal funding of second language instruction.

"without cost to the taxpayer."[43] Nevertheless, Alberta became the second province to provide direct grants to all private schools employing certificated teachers.[44] Private schools which do not employ teachers with valid Alberta certification are not eligible to receive grants.

Following a pre-election promise, the Government of British Columbia passed its *Independent Schools Act* (1977) and introduced government funding of approved private schools. A Group 1 private school, one not necessarily meeting all requirements with respect to teacher qualifications and curriculum, may receive 10 percent, and a Group 2 school meeting all standard requirements, a grant equal to 35 percent of the per pupil operating cost of the public school district in which each is located.

In Saskatchewan, a private secondary school meeting requirements with respect to program and teacher qualifications and having been in operation no less than five years, may receive government grants per student approximating those for public schools. Also, 10 percent of the approved cost of facilities is eligible for capital grants.

The 1959 Manitoba Royal Commission on Education held that "some measure of public support should be extended to private and parochial schools which provide a satisfactory standard of education."[45] Limited "shared services" were introduced in 1965 and a system of modest funding came into effect on July 1, 1978.

The 1950 Royal Commission on Education in Ontario recommended that private schools continue to be ineligible for legislative grants.[46] The 1968 Provincial Committee on Aims and Objectives of Education in the Schools of Ontario recommended that a select committee of the Legislature be established "to study in depth the position of private schools in Ontario" but made no reference to funding.[47] Financial assistance is not provided to private schools in Ontario. However, the 1985 Shapiro Commission held that the anti-discrimination provisions of the *Charter* could support an argument for the public funding of private schools being drawn into the Catholic separate schools sector by the government decision to provide full financial assistance. Shapiro recommended that private or independent schools ought to operate as "associated schools" in agreement with local public school boards, and that such schools should receive a grant equal to the average per pupil operating costs of a school under a local school board multiplied by the enrolment in the associated school.[48]

Free textbooks are the only consideration for students of private schools in Prince Edward Island. No provisions for any public funding in aid of private schools exist in New Brunswick. Since 1977, after which data the federal government no longer included grade 12 students in its calculations for post-secondary payments to the province, Nova Scotia has paid a grant of $600 per grade 12 student annually to four private schools. The denominational private schools of Newfoundland received some government assistance beginning in

1836.[49] As these were the only schools, education legislation was in relation to them. By 1920, all denominations accepted the principle of centralized administration in education with respect to matters regarding curriculum and teacher certification. The denominational schools became the public schools of Newfoundland and were centrally funded. Today, no government assistance is given to a private school unless it is the only school in a community.

Government grants were most substantial in Quebec where they amounted to about 53 percent of the revenue of private schools. The four western provinces also provide grants to private schools, but Saskatchewan provides for high school enrolments only (see Table 6). Income from student fees and all other sources is more or less inversely proportional to the amount of government assistance. That is, the more the grant, the lower the tuition fees and the amount which must be raised from other sources. Whereas tuition fees represented more than 68 percent of all income for private schools in Ontario for 1984-85, fees comprised only about 38 percent of the revenue of private schools in Quebec. "Other sources" include personal donations and subsidies from organizations and denominations associated with the schools. Government subsidy for private schooling was consistently low in comparison to the proportion of pupils in such schools. For example, in the province of Quebec, 8.1 percent of all pupils were in private schools, yet the total provincial subsidy amounted to only 3.5 percent of the cost of funding all schools in the province. For Manitoba and British Columbia, the government subsidy in proportion to the private school pupil enrolment was significantly less.

## Choice of the Private School Alternative

The freedom to choose private education has been viewed by some as a human rights issue. The 1959 Manitoba Royal Commission on Education expressed the view that:

> ... minorities have the right to dissent above all else in the education of their children, and that the majority has an unquestionable obligation not to impose upon a dissenting minority the majority view, unless it is clearly necessary in the public interest.[50]

Bullen held that:

> ... in time a level of political and social maturity may be reached where the freedom to choose schools will be valued in B.C. as the other freedoms which set aside the free democracies from totalitarian states.[51]

Writing in defence of the private school, Edmonds referred to the *Universal Declaration of Human Rights* which says "it is categorically stated that parents have the right to decide the kind of education their children should have."[52] This "right" was acknowledged in the preamble to the *Quebec Education Department Act* of 1964. In 1978, Alberta Provincial Court Judge Oliver found a parent not guilty of contravening the attendance section of the *School Act* for sending his child to a private school which had not yet been authorized by the

Minister of Education. He based his decision on the supremacy of the 1972 *Alberta Bill of Rights* with respect to the freedom of religion clause as it may apply to education.[53]

The wealthy have at all times exercised the freedom of choice in the education of their children.[54] Gossage described 51 "elitist" schools which defend their role by claiming the function of training "those already privileged by virtue of talent or birth to social responsibility."[55] Most of these schools, members of the Canadian Headmasters' Association and the Canadian Association of Independent Schools for Girls, are located in Quebec, Ontario and British Columbia. Of some 73 such schools founded in British Columbia from the 1880s to the 1980s, only eight are currently operating.[56] Most of these schools were modeled after the British boarding schools and served mostly British immigrant families. However, the elitist and expensive private schools, most of which have been around for a long time, remain a small fraction of all private schools in Canada.

Most private schools are not elitist in the economic sense. They are accessible to most families and become more accessible when government assistance allows a reduction of tuition fees. Magsino claimed that parents who patronize private schools are treated unfairly financially, relative to those who patronize public schools.[57] Nevertheless, the proportional growth of private school attendance in Ontario during the 1970s and 1980s exceeded that in all other provinces in spite of the fact that no public funding was made available.

Some denominational schools accept the children of adherents even if such families are unable to pay the total tuition fees. Some parents voluntarily make economic sacrifices when they are convinced that their children may benefit substantially by attending a private school of their choice. In a Manitoba study, VanderStoel concluded that private schools are attended "more as a result of the belief that they provide a better education than public schools, than for reasons of wealth or religion."[58]

Bezeau related that in Quebec, private schools were chosen for the values they represented, discipline and college preparatory programs.[59] Also, in private schools, decisions were being made with greater flexibility and efficiency than was possible in most public schools.[60] A private school has the advantage of being able to present a particular philosophy of education which parents by choice are able to support, whereas the diversity of parental expectations in public schools prevents the satisfaction of all parents in a pluralistic community. The private school can be characterized by a more focused direction, attention to the specific needs of an individual or of a minority group, increased discipline, a committed staff, and a more precisely defined framework of ethical values.[61]

Many parents in Alberta emphasized such matters as discipline, sound instruction in "basics," a Christian perspective, instruction in the Bible, and friendly but firm individual attention.[62] Through the private school, some parents seek to recapture the unity of home, school, church, and community which characterized many a public school in the long-gone days of the one-room country school. For example, the Holdeman Mennonites of Alberta might not have opted for the private school had centralization not taken place following the establishment of larger school divisions.[63]

In a nation-wide American study, Coleman claimed evidence of higher achievement and higher aspirations for higher education "in Catholic schools than in public schools for students from comparable family backgrounds."[64]

A major study in order to determine the consequences of funding independent schools in British Columbia found a greater degree of commitment on the part of students, teachers and parents in the private school sector than in that of the public schools.[65] This advantage of voluntarism was also noted in the report of the provincial inspector of independent schools. Also, the latter report noted a spirit of cooperation and mutual assistance between public and independent schools in a number of districts.[66]

## Public Responsibility Regarding Private Education

Private schools do not stand apart from public education. The controls are such with respect to the instructional problems, the certification of teachers, and the standards of facilities (and more so if public funds are provided) that "private" means no other than the definition used in this paper — "a school other than one under the governance of a public school board or a provincial or federal government department." Private schools are in a very real sense semi-public. Many or most of their graduates enter the public work sector and a smaller number chooses to commit entire working careers to the service of the denomination or association affiliated with the school.

On the other hand, the 1972 *Report of the Commission on Educational Planning* for Alberta warned that the growth in private schools also "might lead to an unsustainable degree of educational and social fragmentation."[67] With respect to the private schools in Quebec, Bezeau stated that they "have recruited students from all levels of society, but the upper social and economic levels are more heavily represented."[68] He indicated that, for 1973-74, 4 percent of private school students were induced to leave, 56 percent of these for academic reasons, and that 71 percent of those who left returned to the public schools.[69] Thus, the public schools were expected to pick up the pieces where the private schools failed or chose not to carry through. Bezeau also reported that the income level of parents of private school children was 41 percent higher than that of a control group.[70]

Though some private schools may draw a greater proportion of able and committed students, other private schools were established to provide services which the public school systems at the time had failed to render. Such has been most notable not only with respect to the care of handicapped children, but also for post-compulsory attendance age education of young people in parts of provinces at the time when the public school systems had failed to cover the field.[71]

Perhaps further developments in "community schools" and greater participation of parents in decisions about school programs affecting their children may increase the satisfaction of parents and reduce the tendency to flee to a private school. Also, some public school systems are attempting to increase efficiency by decentralizing a number of decisions, including the making of a school budget, to the individual school.[72]

Another possibility is the incorporation of established private schools as alternative schools by public school boards in whose districts they are located. Such an arrangement exists in Edmonton where the Hebrew private school was "adopted" as an alternative school within the public school system. As the school officially became "public," all its financial needs were met on the same basis as that of any other public school in the fear of a growing demand for alternative schools.

Thiessen argued that a monolithic system of public education necessarily violates the principle of religious freedom. He deplored the fight from public schools and the proliferation of independent alternative schools, but proposed that the "Christian public school" could be an available choice along with the "humanistic public school." He held a pluralistic public school system to be not only "logically consistent" but also to be "a moral requirement for a society which believes in religious freedom."[73] On the other hand, Miller argued that alternative religious schools in the public school system would place in jeopardy the principle of "providing equivalent educational programs for all children of a district" and the emergence of "contractually based alternative schools" not "consistent with the purpose of public education."[74]

The provincial education authority carries the obligation of providing for reasonable order and control over all education in the province, including that which occurs in private schools. A "hands-off" attitude is hardly responsible. Furthermore, it is questionable whether any private school should receive any public funding at all unless it admits every pupil who desires to enrol and who is willing to comply with the school's program. This is particularly so when public assistance is provided to such schools.

The legislation and regulations concerning private schools in Quebec and British Columbia may serve as models for other provinces. The British Columbia *Schools' Support (Independent) Act* (1987) stipulates a reasonable and responsible restriction for any private school recognized for public funding. The inspector must be satisfied that the school's program does not in theory or in practice "promote or foster doctrines of (i) racial or ethnic superiority, or (ii) religious intolerance or persecution, or (iii) social change through violent action" (section 5).

Public responsibility also concerns the cost of financing a proliferation of alternatives and reducing the efficiency of the public school system. The delivery of instructional services to small numbers of official language minority groups is costly, but the provisions of the Charter over-ride questions of cost. Federal policy governing the publication of documents jointly in both official languages, most of which are read in one of the languages only, is also costly. Decisions regarding the provision of alternatives in education are likely to be based on values held by a political majority, in addition to the criterion of cost.

A private school is always in a state of "jeopardy." When the commitment and support of its constituency is insufficient, it cannot continue its operation. Small costly public schools have been closed by their school boards. Some of these, however, survived through the efforts of their neighborhood supporters and by proving to be "good schools" in competition with other schools under the same boards. This may be as it should be. Perhaps "poor" public schools should suffer demise similar to that of "inadequate" private schools.

## Conclusion

It is beyond the scope of this chapter to make international comparisons. Suffice it to say that private schools are permitted to operate in most countries which do not have totalitarian regimes. They play a major part in countries such as Britain, France, West Germany and the United States.[75] Their traditional role is generally not seriously challenged in West European countries.

The public school as the school for all (a "common" school) appears to be a North American ideal, and as public education became universally accessible, the legitimacy of the private school's role was questioned. Whereas American private school supporters have so far carried on a persistent but unsuccessful effort to persuade legislators and the courts that public funding should be made available to them, such support has been achieved in half of the Canadian provinces. It appears that public funding of private schools in Quebec was considered to be rational in view of the heavy contribution such schools had made in that province up to the time of the modernization efforts in the 1960s. Government decisions introducing financial assistance to private schools provoked relatively little political controversy.[76] Only in Manitoba did prolonged and controversial debate take place following the favorable recommendations of the 1959 Royal Commission. A half dozen years later, the "shared services" program was seen as being directed to the individual student rather than to the private school he attended. Two decades passed before direct support to the schools was introduced.

Though these subventions have been deplored by professional and school trustee associations,[77] it appears unlikely that they will be discontinued wherever they have been introduced. It is more likely that one will see more provinces follow suit. The argument that money is being taken from public schools and given to private schools is fallacious. Private schools do not receive any share of the district property tax. Generally, they receive a per pupil grant which is a designated proportion of that given to public schools. To date, that proportion has been significantly higher in Quebec, Alberta and Saskatchewan than in British Columbia and Manitoba.

Nor do the private schools generally qualify for several other special grants, such as those for transportation and capital expenses which are available to public schools. This treatment means that private schools must continue to raise a substantial part of their income through student fees and voluntary contributions. In fact, the public school system as a whole saves money when some parents choose to enrol their children in private schools. The loss in per pupil grants suffered by public boards could be corrected by amending provincial school grant formulas.[78]

Private school supporters, on the other hand, claim an interest in receiving a measure of public funding because, as citizens of the public school district and of the province, they contribute to the revenue of both levels of government; they claim it to be equitable and ask that some of that revenue be made available to the schools of their choice. Schmeiser suggested that section 27 of the Charter may require "that we break out of our traditional modes of school financing and adopt more flexible means of accommodating those who desire different approaches."[79]

Several questions may be raised to which this chapter does not provide answers. What balance needs to be preserved between the freedom of a parent to direct to which school the child shall go and the responsibility of the state on behalf of the child to ensure the benefit of optimum opportunities? What might be the social consequences of permitting "fragmentation" of schooling through an introduction of more alternatives? To what extent will private initiatives in education provide new models of interest and value for public education? To what degree and in what manner may competition with private schools be beneficial or harmful to public schools?

Conclusive research to provide answers to such questions does not seem to exist at this time. Directions and choices appear to be primarily attributable to traditional practices and socioeconomic and political factors. The extent to which scientific research will provide answers for the decades which lie ahead remains to be seen.

Lawton conjectured that today's values of individualism and tolerance make it difficult to discuss and defend traditional practices which assumed that

> ... society has a corporate nature and that some values are better than others — or at least better serve the public interest. Instead, we depend upon a pious faith that existing institutions, including our political parties and major churches, will provide sufficient glue to hold the nation together and fend off the worst threats from ethnic and religious egoism on the one hand, and mass American commercial culture on the other.[80]

Whether a provincial legislature will pass legislation favoring the development of private schools, and whether it will make public funding available, depends on the political climate in the province as much as it does on any expressed educational or social ideologies. If the climate is conducive to change and acceptance, interest groups will continue to persuade legislators to facilitate their particular concerns.

## Notes

[1] In British Columbia the term "independent" designates a private school. In Australia, private schools are also referred to as "non-government" schools. In the American literature, private schools are frequently called "separate" schools. In Canadian context, a "separate school" is not a private school but a parallel public school established by either a Catholic or Protestant minority within an established public school district in such provinces where the choice is provided in the constitution and/or its school legislation.

[2] R.M. Stamp, quoting John Porter, *The Vertical Mosaic*, in "Government and Education in Post-War Canada," in J.D. Wilson, R.M. Stamp, and L.P. Audet, eds., *Canadian Education: A History* (Scarborough, Ont.: Prentice-Hall of Canada, Ltd. 1970), p.446.

[3] Stamp, p. 446.

[4] L.P. Audet, "Society and Education in New France," in Wilson et al., *Education,* p. 71.

[5] L.P. Audet, "Attempts to develop a School System for Lower Canada," in Wilson et al., *Education*, p. 153.

[6] Audet, p. 160.

[7] Audet, p. 149.

[8] Stamp, p. 446.

[9] C.E. Phillips, *The Development of Education in Canada* (Toronto: W.J.Gage & Co., 1957), p. 106.

[10] Phillips, p. 296.

[11] Phillips, p. 296.

[12] Phillips, p. 300.

[13] M.R. Lupul, "Education in Eastern Canada Before 1873," in Wilson et al., *Education,* p. 244.

[14] Stamp, p. 444.

[15] Stamp, p. 144.

[16] J.D. Wilson, "The Ryerson Years in Canada West," in Wilson et al., *Education,* pp. 214-240.

[17] J.D. Wilson, "Education in Upper Canada: Sixty Years of Change," in Wilson et al., *Education*, p. 210.

[18] Wilson, "The Ryerson Years," p. 237.

[19]M.R. Lupul, "Educational Crises in the New Dominion to 1917," in Wilson et al., *Education*, p. 269.

[20]R.M.Stamp, "Education and the Economic and Social Milieu: The English-Canadian Scene from the 1870s to 1914," in Wilson et al., *Education*, p. 291.

[21]S. Patterson, "Society and Education During the Wars and their Interlude: 1914-1945," in Wilson et al., *Education*, p. 380.

[22]Ontario Ministry of Education, *Report of the Committee on Religious Education in the Public Schools of the Province of Ontario* (Toronto: Ontario Department of Education, 1969), p. 11.

[23]Ontario Ministry of Education, p. 12.

[24]Ontario Ministry of Education, p. 13.

[25]Ontario Ministry of Education, p. 25.

[26]Ontario Ministry of Education, p. 93.

[27]Quebec Ministry of Education, *Report of the Royal Commission of Inquiry on Education, Part 1* (Quebec: Queen's Printer,1963), p. 63.

[28]M.R. Lupul, "Religion and Education in Canada: A Call for an End to Hypocrisy." *The Journal of Educational Thought*, 3, 3 (1969): 143.

[29]Lupul, *Journal*, p. 144.

[30]Lupul, *Journal*, p. 147.

[31]H.A. Stevenson, "Crisis and Continuum: Public Education in the Sixties," in Wilson et al., *Education*, p. 475.

[32]R. Magnuson, "The Decline of Roman Catholic Education in Quebec: Some Interpretations and Explanations," in H.A. Stevenson, R.M. Stamp, and J.D. Wilson, *The Best of Times/The Worst of Times: Contemporary Issues in Canadian Education* (Toronto: Holt, Rinehart and Wilson of Canada, Limited, 1972), p. 192.

[33]W.G. Davis, "Elementary and Secondary School Funding in Ontario," in B.J. Shapiro, *The Report of the Commission on Private Schools in Ontario* (Toronto: Ministry of Education, 1985), p. 75.

[34]For example, see the *Report of the Committee on Religious Education in the Public Schools of Ontario*, p. 75.

[35]J.J.Bergen, "The Private School Movement in Alberta," *The Alberta Journal of Educational Research*, 28,4 (1982): 315-336.

[36]Lupul, *Journal*, p. 63.

[37]J.T. Thiessen,"Is the Religious Alternative School Useful in the Public School System?" *The Journal of Educational Thought*, 17, 3 (1983): 241-244.

[38]Statistics Canada, *Educational Statistics Bulletin* 81-002, Journal 1987.

[39]One may surmise that the growth in private school enrolment might be approaching its saturation point, and that the proportion of all pupils enroled in private schools might remain fairly constant.

[40] Quebec Ministry of Education, *Report of the Royal Commission of Inquiry on Education. Part II (Quebec: Queen's Printer, 1966) p. 39.*

[41] Quebec Ministry of Education, p. 41.

[42] Government of Quebec, *Private Education Act*, S.Q. Ch. 246, (1964), ss.14-17.

[43] Alberta Department of Education, *Report of the Royal Commission on Education in Alberta* (Edmonton: Queen's Printer, 1959), p. 257.

[44] For a detailed study on the genesis and development of provincial financial support which was initiated as a result of sophisticated political activity on the part of private school interest groups, see S.L. Digout, "Public Aid for Private Schools in Alberta: The Making of a Decision," unpublished M.Ed. thesis (The University of Alberta, 1969).

[45] Manitoba Department of Education, *Report of the Manitoba Royal Commission on Education* (Winnipeg: Queen's Printer, 1959).

[46] Ontario Ministry of Education, *Report of the Royal Commission on Education in Ontario* (Toronto: King's Printer, 1950), p. 674.

[47] Provincial Committee on Aims and Objectives of Education in Schools of Ontario, *Living and Learning* (Toronto: Newton Publishing Co., 1968), p. 164.

[48] Bernard J. Shapiro, *The Report of the Commission on Private Schools in Ontario* (Toronto: Ministry of Education, 1985), p. 54.

[49] P.J. Warren, *Report of the Royal Commission on Education and Youth for the Province of Newfoundland and Labrador* (St. Johns, Nfld.: Queen's Printer, 1967), pp. 20-50.

[50] Manitoba Department of Education, p. 179.

[51] E.L. Bullen, "Freedom of Choice in Education," *Education Canada*, 18, 3 (1978): 30.

[52] E.L. Edmonds, "In Defense of the Private School," *Education Canada*, 21, 3 (1981) p. 21.

[53] J.J. Bergen, "Freedom of Education in Religious Context: The Alberta Holdeman Private School Case," *The Mennonite Quarterly Review*, 60, 1 (1981): 75-85.

[54] Bullen, p. 24.

[55] C. Gossage, *A Question of Privilege: Canada's Independent Schools* (Toronto: Peter Martin Associates Limited, 1977), p. 6.

[56] J. Barman, *Growing up British in British Columbia: Boys in Private School* (Vancouver: University of British Columbia Press, 1984).

[57] R.F. Magsino, "Human Rights, Fair Treatment, and Funding of Private Schools in Canada," *Canadian Journal of Education*, 11, 3 (1986): 245-263.

[58] L. VanderStoel, "Let's Look at Some Misconceptions about Private Schools," *MAST(Magazine of the Manitoba Association of School Trustees)*, 6, 2 (1979): 31.

[59] L. Bezeau, "The Public Finance of Private Education in the Province of Quebec," *Canadian Journal of Education*, 4, 2, (1979): 33.

[60]Bezeau, p. 37.

[61]J.J. Bergen, "Choice in Schooling," *EAF Journal of Educational Administration and Foundations,* 1, 1 (1986): 37-48.

[62]J.J. Bergen, *Private Schools in Alberta: A Report to the Task Force on Private Schools for the Alberta School Trustees' Association* (Edmonton: Department of Educational Administration of the University of Alberta, 1980), p. 49.

[63]Bergen, p. 47.

[64]J.S. Coleman, "Quality and Equality in American Education: Public and Catholic Schools," *Phi Delta Kappan,* 63, 3 (1981): 159.

[65]D.A. Erickson, L. MacDonald, and M.E. Manley-Casimir, *Characteristics and Relationships in Public and Independent Schools, an Interim Report — A Study of Consequences of Funding Independent Schools in British Columbia* (Vancouver: Educational Research Institute of British Columbia, 1979).

[66]E.L. Bullen, *Report on Independent Schools* (Victoria: Ministry of Education, 1981).

[67]W.H. Worth, *Report of the Commission on Educational Planning* (Edmonton: Queen's Printer, 1972), p. 61.

[68]Bezeau, p. 39.

[69]Bezeau, p. 34.

[70]Bezeau, p. 33.

[71]Bergen, Private Schools, p. 68.

[72]Alberta's new School Act 1988, in section 17 provides for the establishment of school councils on which the majority of the members must be parents of students. A school council may "advise the principal of the school and the board respecting any matter to the school."

[73]Theissen, p. 244.

[74]R. Miller, "Is the Religious Alternative School Useful in the Public School System?" *The Journal of Educational Thought,* 16, 2. (1982): 115.

[75]C. Podmore, "Private Schools—An International Comparison," *Canadian and International Education,* 6, 2 (1977): 8-23.

[76]J.J. Bergen, "An Examination of Private School Issues in Alberta," *The Alberta Journal of Educational Research,* 32, 2 (1986): 91-108.

[77]For example, the Alberta School Trustees' Association established a Task Force on Private Schools in 1979. Its task was to develop a guide for the Association and school boards for policy positions regarding private and alternative schools. The Task Force recommended that the Minister of Education conduct a thorough study of private schools in the province. Issues concerning private schools were addressed in R. Ghitter, *Committee on Tolerance and Understanding Final Report* (Edmonton: Alberta Education, 1984); and in Woods Gordon Management Consultants, *A Study of Private Schools in Alberta* (Edmonton: Alberta Education, 1984). Both reports recommended the continuation of provincial grants to private schools which met the Minister's criteria.

[78]J.J. Bergen, "The Private School Movement in Alberta," p. 321.

[79]Douglas A. Schneiser, "Multiculturalism in Canadian Education," in Canadian Human Rights Foundation, *Multiculturalism and the Charter: A Legal Perspective* (Toronto: The Carswell Company Limited, 1987), p. 181.

[80]S.B. Lawton, *The Price of Quality: The Public Finance for Elementary and Secondary Education in Canada* (Toronto: Canadian Education Association, 1987), p. 112.

# 2

# Current Issues in the Public Finance of Elementary and Secondary Schools in Canada

*Stephen B. Lawton*

It's December 1st. The printout of the school budget account arrives from central office. You open it and much to your dismay see the last line is in red. Seven more months of school and the budget is already exhausted. How did this happen? Why does it always happen? Why is there never enough money?

Two days later, in the Speech from the Throne, the government announces a 6.7 percent increase in provincial expenditures for education. The province will spend 19 percent of its budget on elementary and secondary education — a total in the billions of dollars. Newspaper columnists and business people are furious: why so much for schools when enrolments are declining, drop-outs are up, and recent graduates don't satisfy employers' needs?

How is it that the schools educators see on a day to day basis often seem to differ so much from those that so many outsiders see? There are no easy answers to this paradox, but an understanding of some of the underlying trends and issues may help to bridge the gap. Those issues discussed here include the push for greater efficiency in schooling, renewed concerns about equity, and the question of quality. Each of these topics subsumes a number of more specific questions including the locus of control in education — provincial, local or school level — and regional differences in the cost of education. First, though, a look at who is footing the bill.

# Passing the Buck:
# The Upward Mobility of School Board Deficits

School boards operate on the basis of balanced budgets. That is, they are generally not allowed to run deficits, particularly for operating expenses. Depending on the province and type of board, they may be allowed to issue debentures (long term debt) to pay for capital expenditures such as the erection of new buildings, but debentures may not be used to raise funds to pay for teachers' salaries, heating buildings, purchasing supplies, and the like.

On the surface, then, school boards in Canada are paragons of fiscal virtue. The $21.6 billion, or $4,373 per pupil they are estimated to have spent in 1985-86 was today's money, not that of the next generation — at least so it appears on the surface.[1] Unfortunately, reality, is far different from appearances. To see how this is so, it is necessary to locate the ultimate sources of the money that school boards spend.

According to Statistics Canada data, in 1984 the three levels of government had the following net surpluses or deficits excluding intergovernmental grants: federal, -10.0 billion dollars; provincial, +9.3 billion dollars; and local (including municipalities and school boards), -12.3 billion dollars. That is, before taking government transfer payments into account, local governments, including school boards, ran larger deficits than any other level of government! (Unfortunately, separate data are not available for municipalities and school boards).[2]

The apparent contradiction between these two images — school boards as fiscally restrained vs. school boards as fiscally incontinent — is explained by the role of intergovernmental grants. In fact, there are massive transfer payments from the federal government to provincial governments (some of which receive from the federal government about half of their total revenues), and from provincial governments to local governments, including school boards. Taking these transfer payments into account, the 1984 net federal deficit was $29.7 billion, the provinces had a net deficit of $.5 billion, and local governments had a deficit of $.5 billion.

Instead of viewing grants as the distribution of funds from upper levels of government, one can interpret the process as one of transferring deficits up the ladder — that is, of passing the buck. By the end of 1985, a lot of bucks had been passed. At that time, the federal deficit totalled about $225 billion, 90 percent of which had been incurred after 1975. The debt equalled $8,000 per each man, woman, and child in Canada and required $0.25 of each dollar of federal expenditure to pay the interest. Much of this debt has been incurred to pay current operating expenses, not to fund capital investments that will earn income in the future. This is a point not lost on those in business who, when borrowing funds for a new investment, must compete with government in the capital markets. More competition for money means much higher interest rates and higher interest rates mean lower profits — or no profits at all.

# Efficiency: Perennial Issue #1

Concern about public indebtedness has created an environment in which the issue of efficiency has blossomed into full flower. Just as concerns about energy conservation can be dated from the 1973 oil embargo, recent concerns about overall efficiency can be dated from the severe 1981-82 recession from which many provinces have not recovered.

In technical terms, efficiency in school board spending is very difficult, if not impossible to judge. According to the dictates of economics, efficiency relates to the average unit cost of producing an item of a given quality. While defining what "an item of given quality" is in manufacturing may be relatively easy, defining its meaning in education is less so. Indeed, because so many of the results in education may not be apparent for years or decades, efficiency in the educational setting is probably not definable in a complete sense. For this reason, it is usual to settle on some short-term, easily measurable characteristic as an operational definition; the most common choice is some sort of standardized test score.[3]

## *The Provincial Response*

In practical terms, the increased emphasis on efficiency has been translated into several types of provincial policies: reduced grants, expenditure limitations, increased reliance on the property tax and referenda, and wage restraint. The particular situation varies from province to province, depending not only on the tastes of the governments concerned but also, on the manner in which schools are financed.

British Columbia, as did all the provinces, made the need for efficiency a central tenant of government policy in its drive to re-establish its tradition of balanced provincial budgets. Included among its range of policies were: the transfer of the commercial and industrial tax base from the local to provincial level, thereby reducing school boards' resources; the implementation of a fiscal framework that bases the level of grants on the cost and quantity of specified inputs, such as teachers; expenditure limitations (since discontinued); salary review and roll-back legislation (since discontinued); and legislation to remove the provincial teachers' federation and its local affiliates as the sole bargaining agent for teachers. The province announced the objective of rolling back the pupil-teacher ratio (PTR) from its 1981 level of 17.3 to 1 to its 1976 level of 19.1 to 1. According to 1985-86 estimates, the goal had been achieved.

Alberta and Ontario, in contrast, seemingly have relied upon a policy of lessening the relative size of provincial grants in order to conserve funds implicitly; this practice shifts the burden onto local ratepayers, driving up the percentage of expenditures carried by property tax. Ratepayer resistance to further tax increases becomes a primary mechanism for controlling expenditures. In Alberta, the provincial share (which includes a province-wide levy on business and commercial property) has declined from 81 percent in 1974 to 64 percent in 1986; in Ontario, the provincial share has declined from 62 percent in 1973 to 48 percent in 1986.[4]

Provinces with more centralized forms of finance, such as Quebec, New Brunswick, and Prince Edward Island, have relied on a combination of tough bargaining with teachers at the provincial level, legislation (Quebec enacted an 18 percent roll-back in salaries at one point), and local referenda for any supplementary expenditures for programs not specifically covered by provincial grants. In Quebec, this covers any expenses above funds that are raised at a rate of $0.25 per $100 of evaluation or 6 percent of the operating budget; in the other two provinces, it covers all expenses above amounts provided by the provincial government.

The outcomes of most referenda are well reflected by their history in New Brunswick. Since the province assumed responsibility for funding education in 1967, only 11 referenda have been held: six for swimming pools, two for kindergartens (which are not funded by the province), and three for music programs. Only two for music programs were passed. In one of these, the "new higher cost of this supplementary requisition to the owner of property valued at $100 thousand . . . is still less than 10 cents each year."[5]

## The Local Response

At the local level, the drive for efficiency has taken a different tack. Instead of greater central control, which has tended to be the response of provincial governments, many local school boards have been considering or enacting some form of decentralized, school-based budgeting and management. As with many innovations, school-based budgeting and management is a complex concept with multiple aims and objectives. From the perspective of economics, its primary purpose is to ensure the most effective utilization of scarce resources by ensuring that the local school's own preferences are reflected in the expenditure of the budget. Uniform, centralized budgeting procedures, in contrast, almost certainly result in either the over-allocation or under-allocation of funds for specific items.[6]

Yet, the widespread adoption of school-based budgeting in diverse nations, including some states in Australia, many school boards in the United States, and some local councils in Britain, suggests there is something more. Depending on the place and time, the idea has received support from both the political left (Victoria, Australia, and Quebec during the Parti Quebecois era) and the political right (Margaret Thatcher's proposals to allow schools to collect funds directly from the national government), suggesting a popular appeal to reduce the independent power of agencies such as school boards and teachers' unions. The loss of legitimacy of these institutions was apparent in the social critiques of the sixties and seventies and the importance of keeping decisions close to the operational level is apparent in the effective schools literature. The day when "small is beautiful" may actually have arrived.

Ironically, then, increased emphasis on efficiency in schooling seems simultaneously to be resulting in greater authority at both the central provincial levels, as reflected in the imposition of expenditure limits, province-wide testing and the like, and greater authority at the school level. The powers of school trustees and central office administrators, in contrast, seem to be eroding. And, if the most recent conclusions about the greater effectiveness of smaller school boards are correct, we may see the day when city- and country-wide school boards are replaced by smaller, community-oriented school systems.[7]

### *PTR and Teachers' Salaries: The Cost Drivers*

The two key factors affecting the cost of education are the pupil-teacher ratio and teachers' salaries. In 1985-86, on a provincial basis, PTRs varied from 16.3:1 in Quebec to 20:1 in British Columbia and in the Northwest Territories. Average provincial teachers' salaries for 1982, the most recent year for which data are available, ranged from $29,400 for Newfoundland elementary teachers to $39,300 for Ontario secondary school teachers; the averages were higher in the Territories where they exceeded $40,000 in all cases.

There is evidence to suggest that, by world standards, Canadian teachers are very well paid. With salaries of elementary school teachers in major American cities serving as a baseline of 100, elementary school teachers in major Canadian cities were paid 10 percent higher in 1982 (an index value of 110) and 23 percent higher in 1985 (an index value of 123) once the relative purchasing power is taken into account. By comparison, index values for countries were as follows for 1985: Japan, 93; Germany, 85; United Kingdom, 74; Australia 101; and Switzerland, 134.8.

Even in the absence of comparative data for PTR for these same countries, it is apparent that Canadian schools are well-staffed with well-paid teachers. The social cost of maintaining our educational system is high. Education is not an industry we normally think of in competitive terms, but it is apparent that educational systems are important in the arena of international economic competition. They are important in two ways. First, money spent on them is not being spent on other modes of investment, so any funds wasted in the system lessens the nation's overall ability to compete. Second, a well-educated labor force is imperative to compete effectively. Quite clearly, pressure on educators to convince the public that the current system is cost-effective will not decline in the near future.

## Equity: Perennial Issue #2

Equity in education concerns the allocation of resources committed to the task. Key dimensions for assessing equity are related to geography, religion, and economic status. In some cases, as provinces have attempted to increase efficiency, they have allowed equity to decline. At a national level in fact, federal cutbacks in transfer payments to provinces seem to have brought about a decline in equity.[9]

A major distinction among provinces is the degree to which they have centralized financing. Historically, school boards in all provinces were financed primarily out of local resources — rate bills, property taxes, parish contributions and tuition fees. Today in Newfoundland, Prince Edward Island, New Brunswick, Nova Scotia and Quebec, virtually all funds for education are provided by provincial governments, although some local leeway exists, at least in theory, in all of these provinces. In all five provinces, teachers' salaries are bargained provincially.[10] As a result, extreme variation in educational expenditures that reflect extreme differences in wealth do not exist, at least within the public sector. One can surmise that wealthier parents may purchase educational services, such as kindergartens in the case of New Brunswick, but these expenses do not show up in provincial accounts and thus are not officially recognized as creating an equity problem.

In the remaining provinces, part or all of the property tax base remains as a revenue source for school boards. In these cases, the traditional link between school board autonomy and an independent source of tax revenue remains, although in British Columbia the recent history of expenditure controls sets it apart from the others, as does Saskatchewan's practice of centralized tripartite bargaining of teachers' salaries involving the province, trustees, and teachers.

Alberta, Manitoba and Ontario, then, have systems of school finance that permit wide differences in expenditure levels to arise. Given the declines in provincial support for education in, especially, Alberta and Ontario, this issue was highlighted by the MacDonald Commission on school finance and in Alberta it was the topic of a discussion paper, "Equity and Education Financing." Manitoba seems to have made progress in addressing the issue by implementing much of its 1983 report, *Enhancing Equity in Manitoba Schools*.[11]

Alberta's report described the equity issues that recur in Canadian provinces with decentralized, shared cost funding arrangements. With no additional equalization provided beyond the foundation grant program by the province, a school district with low property assessment is able to raise about $600 per pupil while a high assessment district is able to raise $2,800 per pupil.[12] To remedy this situation, five options were put forward: (1) to retain partial implementation of the current equity grant, which raises the low assessment revenue to $900 per pupil and has no effect on the revenue of the high assessment district; (2) to fully implement the proposed equity grant, which would raise the low assessment district revenue to $1,300 per pupil; (3) same as (2) except that other grants paid to districts of above average per pupil assessment would be discontinued and the funds redistributed to low assessment districts, thereby raising per pupil revenue in the latter to about $1,400 and decreasing that for the former to $2,600 per pupil; (4) "full non-residential tax revenue sharing, provincial taxation on non-residential assessment and school board taxation limited to requisitions on residential and farm property," a proposal that would raise the low assessment district's revenue to $1,500 per pupil while lowering the high assessment distict's revenue to $1,700 per pupil; and (5) "limited non-residential tax revenue sharing," the present arrangement as reflected in option (1) but with school boards limited in the amount they can tax non-residential property so that the province can raise its province-wide levy on non-residential assessment, thereby raising the low assessment district's revenue to about $1,450 while decreasing the high assessment district's revenue to just under $2,000 per pupil.

Option (4) above is identical to the policy adopted by British Columbia when it transferred the commerical and industrial tax base from the local to the provincial level for educational purposes. In Ontario, it was proposed by the Jackson Commission on Declining School Enrolments in 1978 and, in a modified regional form, by the recent MacDonald Commission.[13] The usual term for the concept in Ontario is "pooling" rather than "sharing," though the concepts are the same.

Who would benefit from sharing the revenue raised from property taxes on commercial and industrial assessment? The Alberta report lists school boards in each of eleven wealth categories ranging from $0 to $10,000 equalized assessment per pupil to $100,000 or over. Fifteen of sixteen districts in the two lowest wealth categories are Roman Catholic separate school districts, while 16 of the 20 districts in the top two wealth categories are public school divisions. Calgary and Edmonton public school districts fall into the $50-60,000 per pupil assessment wealth category. Clearly, greater equity would be of more benefit to Roman Catholic Schools, on the average, than to public schools. The situation in Ontario is similar, although more extreme since unassigned commercial and industrial assessment in Ontario supports public school boards, whereas in Alberta such assessment is shared on the basis of resident pupils in the coterminous boards.

Another characteristic separating the "have" and "have not" boards is geography. As the Alberta paper notes, "there has been rapid growth in the commerical and industrial sector in Alberta. However, this growth has not occurred in all parts of the province. The growth in industry has occurred primarily in areas where there are natural resources, supplies of raw materials and access to transportation routes and community facilities. Other parts of the province have not been so fortunate."[14] While the low wealth districts tend to be in rural farm areas, not all of the wealthy districts are "resource rich" in the normal use of the term. Among the districts in the top wealth category are the Banff and Jasper school districts. Parallel situations exist in all provinces, where school boards in "cottage country" have large residential tax bases and low student populations. When British Columbia removed commercial and industrial assessment from local taxations, mining-based towns such as Prince

George became welfare cases while the Gulf Islands and like areas became the nouveau riche, at least in relative terms.

In Ontario, the question of equity in finance took on more importance with the extension of funding to the secondary education in the Roman Catholic school system. This action, announced in 1984, was successfully defended by the province in the Supreme Court of Canada. As Catholic school boards expand their programs to include all levels and types of students, they will not have the resources to offer the same working conditions, salary, or PTR, as the public boards unless the province increases secondary "grant ceilings" (the equivalent in Ontario of a foundation level), provides a second level of equalization for low wealth boards, or redistributes access to commercial and industrial assessment, for which a proposal was made in April 1989.

Equity also involves the question of the use of existing secondary school facilities. In the first case of its kind, an arbitrator assigned the use of three public secondary schools (two from the Hamilton Board of Education, one of which was closed, and one from the Wentworth County Board of Education) to the Hamilton-Wentworth Catholic School Board. Though the Hamilton school board did not, to say the least, warmly embrace the decision, the arbitrator did emphasize that equity required that the province improve the facilities of the Catholic board so that they would be equal to those enjoyed by public boards and that equality should not be achieved by a process of averaging down.[15]

## The Question of Quality

Implicit in concerns over efficiency and equity in education is the matter of quality: the quality of the resources used, the quality of the educational process itself, and the quality of the results.

### Resources

Traditionally, money was considered the primary educational resource, with dollars spent per pupil assessed in relationship to various measures of effectiveness. This approach has been criticized and greater focus has been placed on the quality of the resources actually used, such as the quality of the staff, of the physical facilities, and of the students who are the object of the educational process.

The move to improve the quality of the physical facilities used in schools is especially evident in Ontario, where the issue is tied to that of equity. The completion of the Catholic system and the extension of governance rights to Franco-Ontarians has resulted in both arbitration hearings, as noted above, and court cases. In a case involving the Simcoe Board of Education, the courts held that Le Caron Ecole Secondaire in Penetanguishene, enroling 160 students in grades 9 to 13, had to be provided a facility equal to that of other secondary schools, including a gymnasium, shops and the like. Were this ruling to be applied to all French language and, by inference, to all Catholic high schools in Ontario, the cost would be in the billions of dollars.

The qualifications of teachers is of increasing importance as the teaching force ages and the number of teachers retiring each year begins to increase. Concern about the possible loss of effectiveness of older teachers was one factor that prompted the government of Ontario to offer teachers an option to take early retirement without loss of pension. At the same time, its Ministry of Education initiated a major review of the quality and kind of teacher education offered in the province so that a supply of well-qualified teachers could be assured. It is well worth noting that the qualifications of new teachers has received far greater attention in the United States where, due to a combination of more rapid growth in enrolments in some states and of lower teacher salaries, there appears to be a shortage of competent new teachers.

Complementing the emphasis on the qualifications of new teachers is renewed recognition of the importance of selecting the most highly qualified administrators. New approaches to selecting administrators, such as the use of assessment centres, are becoming widespread.[16]

Class size is an issue related to both the qualifications of teachers and facilities. The government of Ontario recently announced its intention to reduce class size in grades 1 to 3 from an average of 25 to 20 in order to improve the quality of primary education. This action will require 4,000 additional teachers and, presumably, 4,000 additional classrooms. Whether both can be supplied without compromising their quality is a question yet to be answered.

The caliber of entering pupils is also a matter for concern, in part because of the weight of the evidence that schools have a difficult time helping students overcome any disadvantages present at entry, and in part because of the shifting demographics of the student body. Again, the United States seems to be facing a much greater problem in this regard than does Canada, at least in the short run. California, for example, is expected to have members of minority groups comprise its majority by the year 2000. As well, its foreign born population is growing rapidly: California receives one-third of the world's immigration.[17] In Ontario, which is receiving much of Canada's immigration at present, school boards have become active in promoting credit courses in "parenting" through their continuing education departments and in extending education to four-year-olds by offering half-day junior kindergartens.[18] Both of these actions offer hope of improving the "cultural capital" of the children by the time they begin formal education.

## Process

The usual approach to ensuring the maintenance or improvement of the quality of the educational process is by appraising the performance of the staff. Again, Canadian provinces have not acted dramatically as have a number of states in the United States, some of which have required the testing of all practicing teachers. Nevertheless, renewed interest in staff evaluation is evident.[19] Also apparent are trends toward higher standards for graduation, and experimentation with or adoption of new types of programs.

Perhaps the most widespread of the new educational practices is French immersion.[20] Evidence favors its effectiveness though the costs tend to be higher than standard programs due, in part, to higher costs of materials.[21] To date, no formal cost-effectiveness study of different modes of French instruction (core, extended, early or late immersion) seems to have been carried out. Another popular new practice is the use of microcomputers for instruction, also a technology whose cost-effectiveness is yet to be proven.[22] Regardless of the merits of these innovations in terms of their cost-effectiveness, it is clear that both have had, to date, strong support from parents.

Several other structural or program innovations of note are the adoption of cooperative or work-study education programs at the secondary level, the creation of adult-only high schools, and the designation of special high schools. A good example of the last of these is the Ontario school board that "closed" its four comprehensive high schools in one urban area and then "opened" one academic high school for technology, vocations and business.

Implicit in the proliferation of programs and specialized schools is the provision of greater choice to parents and their children. In the jargon of the market researcher, educators are segmenting their markets and providing a variety of services for those with different tastes. Presumably, clients can "vote with their feet" and an undesired or poor quality school or program will fail due to a lack of support.

This trend toward greater choice as a mechanism for ensuring quality is evident in the increased support in some provinces for government funding of private schools. Alberta, British Columbia, and Quebec have substantially increased provincial funding for private schools in the past decade and both Saskatchewan and Manitoba provide support for private secondary schools. The 1985 Commission on Private Schools in Ontario recommended more funds for private schools in that province and, of course, the government there allowed Roman Catholic separate school boards to offer secondary education on the condition that it be open to all students regardless of religion.[23]

## Results

Several approaches have been used to assess the quality of schooling in terms of its results. One longstanding indicator of quality has been the retention rate; i.e., the percentage of students completing their high school program. The leveling off and even decline of retention rates in the past decade have focused concern on the life-prospects of youth not completing their education at a time when education seems more important than ever.[24] In 1978, the Commission on Declining School Enrolments in Ontario, in the belief that retention rates would continue to increase, indicated there was no need for particular concern about dropout rates; in 1987, the Ontario government announced a Retention and Transition Project aimed at reducing dropout rates by one-third.[25]

A more subjective measure of the caliber of school leavers is the assessment provided by those in businesses, universities, and colleges. Ken Dryden, former Youth Commissioner for Ontario, reported that employers are "only moderately satisfied with youth attitudes and personal skills, and dissatisfied with their level of basic skills."[26] Ontario universities, in recent years, have set entrance examinations to evaluate the writing skills of new students because of concerns about the writing skills of high school graduates (although the University of Toronto recently discontinued its test for budgetary reasons). As well, Ontario universities have pressed the Ministry of Education on the issue of the quality of education credits earned by students through night and summer schools.

Finally, there has been the reinstatement of province-wide testing to measure the academic performance of students in at least two provinces, Alberta and British Columbia. Ontario has made more moderate moves, including standardizing the curricula for Ontario academic credits, its former Grade 13, and by developing the Ontario Assessment Instrument Pool (OAIP). Ontario is now implementing an assessment program along the lines of the National Assessment of Educational Progress (NAEP) in the United States. This approach uses statistical sampling and cycles of testing to monitor overall progress without the cost (financial and often political) of testing every student in every school by every school board.

## Conclusion

Fiscal pressures are not new to elementary and secondary education. Why such pressures should be so evident at present given that, by most measures, schools have never been better funded, is something of a puzzle. The answer appears to be that for schools, the expectations held by parents, students, and those in agencies that receive those leaving school, have never been higher. In the past, if schools failed some students, it did not matter too much. Well paid unskilled and semi-skilled jobs were plentiful and Canada's resource-based economy could support a high level of social services. That era has passed. Our present level of services is maintained only by taking on more debt; good paying jobs are available only to those with special skills. If we are to succeed in the long run, we must choose our investments wisely and become more productive.

The challenge for educators is similar: to become more effective, to get better results, and to do so with little or no money. Competition for public funds is intense and will only grow. Health care needs are increasing with the aging population; the economy's infrastructure, developed during the fifties, sixties and seventies, needs renewal and replacement, and post-secondary educational institutions, which have been treated far less generously in the past decade than have elementary and secondary schools, are in need of new funds.

Trends identified in previous sections suggest how the educational systems in the various provinces are likely to meet this challenge. Provinces will restrain their contributions to elementary and secondary education, leaving local ratepayers to increase their contribution either through higher local taxes or through private purchase of educational services. Teachers' salaries are unlikely to increase at a rate above inflation, though salaries for beginning teachers may rise as competition for their service increases. Management will become decentralized to the school level, possibly with internal charge-back systems being used for the purchase of central services by schools. Pupil-teacher ratios will remain constant and will not decline; the costs of teachers and facilities are too great for them to be decreased significantly.

With greater administrative decentralization within school systems, school trustees will be challenged to redefine their roles, politically and economically, and to promote awareness of their contribution to the improvement of Canadian education. Unless they succeed in this, the pressure for equity and the move toward school-based management may leave them quaint vestiges of our rural past when school boards actually were school boards.

To improve quality, programs in faculties of education will likely be revised and lengthened in order to increase the quality of teacher training. However, a shortage of potential teacher candidates once the baby boom generation completes university in the next few years may make this impossible. Changes are likely to be made in the structure of schools and programs as school trustees and education officials try to satisfy all their clients — students, parents, businesses and post-secondary institutions. External measures of performance will probably be of increasing importance both to provincial governments, which monitor schools and school boards, and to schools, educators, and school boards who must prove their worth to society. Cost-effectiveness studies may be relied upon to assist in making these hard decisions.

## Notes

[1] Stephen B. Lawton, *The Price of Quality: The Public Finance of Elementary and Secondary Education in Canada* (Toronto: Canadian Education Association, 1987), Table 3, p. 92.

[2] Lawton, *Price of Quality*, p. 24.

[3] See, for example, Peter Coleman, "The Good School. A Critical Examination for the Adequacy of Student Achievement and Per Pupil Expenditures as Measures of School District Effectiveness," *Journal of Education Finance*, 12 (Summer 1986), pp. 71-96; and Herbert J. Walberg and William J. Fowler, "Expenditures and Size Efficiencies of Public School Districts," *Educational Researcher*, 16, 7 (October 1987): 5-13.

[4] Alberta Education, "Equity in Education Finance," (Edmonton: Alberta Education, October 13, 1987); Stephen B. Lawton, "Ontario's Approach: Paying

School Boards To Save," in *The Cost of Controlling the Cost of Education in Canada* (Toronto: Department of Educational Administration, The Ontario Institute for Studies in Education, August 1983), pp. 33-48.

[5] Claudette Franklyn, "Supplementary Programs in New Brunswick School Districts," *New Brunswick Educational Administrator*, 9 (November 1987): 1-5.

[6] See, for example, Brian Caldwell, "Educational Reform through School-Site Management: An International Perspective on the Decentralization of Budgeting," paper presented at the Annual Conference of the American Educational Finance Association, Arlington, Virginia, March 26-28, 1987; Fred Alexandruk, "School Budgeting Study," paper presented to the Canadian Association for the Study of Educational Administration, Winnipeg, June 1986; and Daniel J. Brown, "A Preliminary Inquiry into School-Based Management," report to the Social Sciences and Humanities Research Council of Canada. Grant number 410-83-1086, March 1987.

[7] On the relative effectiveness of different sizes of boards, see Walberg and Fowler, pp. 5-13. For a brief history of the formation of larger school boards in Canada and underlying value issues, see Stephen B. Lawton, "Political Values in Educational Finance in Canada and the United States," *Journal of Education Finance*, 5 (Summer 1979): 1-18.

[8] Stephen B. Lawton, "Teachers' Salaries: An International Perspective," in the *1987 Yearbook of the American Education Finance Association* (Cambridge, MA: Ballinger Publishing Company, 1988) .

[9] Wilfred J. Brown, "The Educational Toll of the Great Recession," in *The Cost of Controlling the Costs of Education in Canada* (Toronto: Department of Educational Administration, The Ontario Institute for Studies in Education, August 1983), pp. 1-22.

[10] Lawton, *Price of Quality*, "Chapter Five: Provincial Grant Plans," pp. 49-64. On the role of local taxation in Newfoundland, where concerns about equity remain in spite of the relatively limited role local taxes play, see P.J.Warren, *Local Taxation for Education in Newfoundland and Labrador* (St. John's, Nfld: Faculty of Education, Memorial University of Newfoundland, 1986). Nova Scotia's equity problems were addressed in the implementation of the *Report of the Commission on Public Education Finance (The Walker Report)* (Halifax: Nova Scotia Department of Education, 1981). For a discussion of the report's impact, see Eric W. Ricker, "Nova Scotia's New Deal in School Finance: *The Walker Report* as a Response to a System in Decline," in *The Cost of Controlling the Costs of Education in Canada* (Toronto: Department of Educational Administration, The Ontario Institute for Studies in Education, August 1983), pp. 65-83.

[11] The Commission on the Financing of Elementary and Secondary Education in Ontario, *The Report of the Commission on the Financing of Elementary and Secondary Education in Ontario. (The MacDonald Commission Report)* (Toronto: The Commission, December 1985); Alberta Education, "Equity in Education Finance," (Edmonton: Alberta Education, October 13, 1987), mimeographed; Glenn Nicholls, *Enhancing Equity in Manitoba Schools: The Report of the*

*Education Finance Review* (Winnipeg: Manitoba Department of Education, October 1983).

[12] Alberta Education, "Equity in Education Finance " (Edmonton: Alberta Education, October 13, 1987). Dollar figures are estimated from Figure 7, Local Tax and Equity Revenue Effect (Comparison of Options 1-5). The amounts in question would be on top of foundation levels but, apparently, would not include any supplementary taxes on residential and farm assessment, though a detailed explanation of the figure is not provided.

[13] Lawton, *Price of Quality*, p. 49. For Ontario, see *Implications of Declining Enrolment for the Schools of Ontario: A Statement of Effects and Solutions. Final Report.* (Toronto: The Commission on Declining School Enrolments in Ontario, October 31, 1978), Recommendation 100, p. 314; and *Report of the Commission on the Financing of Elementary and Secondary Education in Ontario* (Toronto: The Commission, December 1985), Recommendations 19 and 21, pp. 42-43.

[14] Alberta Education, p. 3.

[15] Stephen T. Gouge, "Reasons for Decision," in the matter of section 136x of the *Education Act*, R.S.O. 1980, c. 129, as amended and in the matter of a dispute among the Hamilton-Wentworth Roman Catholic Separate School Board, the Board of Education for the city of Hamilton and the Wentworth County Board of Education, n.d.

[16] Donald Musella and Stephen B. Lawton, *Selection and Promoting Procedures in Ontario School Boards — Research Brief: Professionalism in School Series)* (Toronto: Ontario Ministry of Education, 1987).

[17] Harold L. Hodgkinson, *California: The State and its Educational System* (Washington, D.C.: The Institute for Educational Leadership, 1986). In addition to demographic issues, Hodgkinson discusses class size, pre-school programs, and teacher supply and demand.

[18] For a description of continuing education programs in Ontario, see Stephen B. Lawton and E. Lisbeth Donaldson, *The Costs of Continuing Education in Ontario* (Toronto: Ontario Association of Education Administrative Officials, November 23, 1987).

[19] Stephen B. Lawton, E.S. Hickox, K.A. Leithwood, and D.F. Musella, *Development and Use of Performance Appraisal of Certified Education Staff in Ontario School Boards, Volume 1: Technical Report* (Toronto: Ontario Ministry of Education, 1986).

[20] Stephen B. Lawton, "French Language Programs in Anglophone Elementary Schools," *Education Canada*, 21, 1 (Spring 1981): 31-35.

[21] The Ontario General Legislative Grants (O.R. 98/87), for example, provides extra funds based on the amount of daily instruction in French and cummulative hours of French instruction.

[22] Henry M. Levin and Gail R. Meister, "Educational Technology and Computers: Promises, Promises, Always Promises," Project Report No. 85-A13, Institute for Research on Educational Finance and Governance, School of Education, Stanford University. See also, R. D. Hossack, "Cost Elements and Potential

Strategies for the Application of New Technologies," in *Background Papers: The Commission on the Financing of Elementary and Secondary Education* (Toronto: The Commission on the Financing of Elementary and Secondary Education in Ontario, 1985), pp. 203-252.

[23] Bernard J. Shapiro, *The Report on the Commission on Private Schools on Ontario* (Toronto: The Commission, 1985). Chapter 3 provides an overview of policies regarding private schools in Canada and several other nations.

[24] Ken Dryden, *Report of the Ontarion Youth Commissioner* (Toronto: Government of Ontario, 1986) .

[25] The Commission on Declining School Enrolments in Ontario, *Implications of Declining Enrolment for the Schools of Ontario: A Statement of Effects and Solutions.Final Report*, (Toronto: The Commission on Declining School Enrolments in Ontario, October 31, 1978), pp. 100-102; and Ontario Ministry of Education, "Student Retention and Transition Project Objectives,", photocopy, n.d., presented and discussed by Vincenza Travale at a meeting of continuing education coordinators of the Association of Large School Boards of Ontario, Etobicoke, Ontario, December 2, 1987.

[26] Dryden, p. 13.

[27] E. A. Hanusheck, "Throwing Money at Schools," *Journal of Policy Analysis and Management*, 1, 1, pp. 19-41.

# 3

# Multiculturalism in a Bilingual Context:
# A Current Review[1]

## *Douglas Ray*

The idea behind the twin policies of bilingualism and biculturalism (Bi and Bi) is that all Canadians must see their interests as served by and reflected in government policies and services. This generous vision was not shared by all politicians, but a majority stood behind the objective. In particular, a succession of prime ministers from 1957 to the present day have embraced the idea and supported it in their own way.

John Diefenbaker opposed discrimination, an attitude reflected in the *Bill of Rights* passed by his government in 1960. This made him wary of some of the Bi and Bi recommendations. He wanted to avoid creating "hyphenated Canadians," an idea which he feared would undermine the objectives of equal status for all Canadians and achievement on the basis of merit.[2] He believed strongly that laws should not recognize and inadvertently accentuate the differences present in any society. He feared "Balkanization."[3]

Lester Pearson took a different tack. He realized that genuine equality must be recognized and promoted in law, for in real life the existing differences were substantial and well documented.[4] His purpose in appointing the Bi and Bi Commission in 1963, obvious in the terms of reference, was to educate and create a political consensus that could overcome the fear and distrust of many Canadians. His intention is demonstrated in such phrases as the "existing state of bilingualism and biculturalism" and "two founding races." Although he also mentioned "the other ethnic groups" in the terms of reference, this was initially overshadowed by his use of the term "biculturalism" to which there was a healthy dislike. On the French side, he did not make such a mistake. He appointed to his cabinet "the three wise men" from Quebec[5] who demonstrated that Ottawa respected the views from La Belle Province.

Pierre Elliott Trudeau made his leitmotif the achievement of equal status for French and English in law, in the workplace, in cultural pursuits, in politics, and ultimately in the Constitution of Canada. Although bilingualism does not mean that every Canadian is or must become bilingual, there should be reasonable opportunities for this to happen. The growing support for the teaching of both minority and official language groups in their mother tongue in most provinces enabled most premiers to assent to the protection that was written into the *Canadian Charter of Rights and Freedoms*. Public interest is also evident in parents encouraging their children to learn both official languages. Half of the pupils are learning the second official language, spending an average of 9.9 percent of their school time in the subject. Better yet, by 1985 there were 177,824 students enroled in French immersion programs.[6]

Unfortunately, there are still numerous failures of various communities to provide public services (including education) in both official languages, and even failures of parts of the federal civil service to achieve a genuinely bilingual cadre. There is also the dubious value and high costs of programs for promoting bilingualism among adults. It is against this background that the policy of bilingualism must be assessed. It is not yet a framework that has been universally embraced.

## The Growth of Multiculturalism.

Multiculturalism grew rapidly because other ethnic groups asserted their importance to the development of Canada. They were not content to merge into one of the presumptive "founding races." At first they were accused of being obstructionists who were unwilling the accept bilingualism, insisting instead upon equal place for several language communities.[7] There was a recognition that language was a powerful — perhaps the most powerful — basis for identifying groups. And it was a feature of identity that many cultures sought to encourage in their children. In a few cultural communities of Canada, language was not a distinguishing feature, and religion or other labels represented their symbolic identity. But whatever language(s) they spoke at work or at home, many Canadians did not choose to associate themselves culturally with either English or French. For them, the *Official Languages Act* was insufficient.[8] Fortunately, some of their remedies had been reported with approval by the Bi and Bi Commission in *The Cultural Contributions of the Other Ethnic Groups*. There was broad agreement that a broader solution was only fair.

Consequently, in October 1971 Trudeau announced that:

... there cannot be one cultural policy for Canadians of British and French origin, another for the original peoples and yet a third for all others. For although there are two official languages, there is no official culture, nor does any ethnic group take precedence over any other. No citizen or group of citizens is other than Canadian, and all should be treated fairly.

The individual's freedom would be hampered if he were locked for life within a particular cultural compartment by the accident of birth or language. It is vital, therefore, that every Canadian, whatever his ethnic origin, be given a chance to learn at least one of the two languages in which his country conducts its official business and its politics.

A policy of multiculturalism within a bilingual framework commends itself to the government as the most suitable means of assuring the cultural freedom of Canadians.

Trudeau then outlined the means by which the government would introduce this policy of "multiculturalism within a bilingual framework," assisting cultural groups that "have demonstrated a desire and effort to continue to develop," to overcome cultural barriers, promote creative encounters and interchange, and to assist immigrants to acquire at least one of the official languages.[9]

The three parties represented in the Opposition warmly endorsed the policy; so, subsequent parliamentary criticism has been directed to the shortcomings of implementation rather than at the basic idea. The principle has also been supported by most provinces in legislation, particularly that affecting schools and various community support programs. The ultimate accolade was section 27 of the *Canadian Charter of Rights and Freedoms which requires that "the Charter* shall be interpreted in a manner consistent with the preservation and enhancement of the multicultural heritage of Canadians." Although section 27 is not likely to be the basis for as many legal challenges as section 15 (the equality provisions), it might be taken into account in many judgments.[10]

No policy in Canadian history has so thoroughly demonstrated that constitutionally assigning education "exclusively to the provinces" provides no barrier to the federal government's initiation of policies which impact on schooling. But language and cultural policy have less to do with the levels of government that may respond than with the needs of the Canadian population and how these needs might be served. Because of the political appeal of multiculturalism, both provincial and municipal governments have supported versions of the policy. And they have recognized that the federal government can be milked for funds while they retain the essential control.

## The Roots of Cultural Loyalties

Cultural differences have always affected Canada's internal relationships — sometimes badly and sometimes well. There are records from the time of aboriginal peoples of wars and cooperation.[11] The Europeans, Africans and Asians complicated the process but did not change the reality. The "founding races" myth comes from New France, its conquest and the subsequent rapid increase of the English-speaking populations. After 1763, the British were relatively gracious to the losers, for Catholics were entitled to be citizens, public servants, and officers in North America even before the *Quebec Act* (1774)[12] although such rights did not yet exist in Britain. The rights of the French were never seriously disputed at the time.

The *Quebec Act* guaranteed that these rights would be respected in the future,[13] and that document serves as a constitutional guarantee for Quebec and French rights. And these rights were not assumed to be limited to Quebec, so there were important misunderstandings that still surfaced in Canadian debate. Were the Acadians exiled for fear of their military menace to Halifax, or because they had the best farm land which those across the peninsula wanted?[14] French-speaking and Catholic Metis in Manitoba and Saskatchewan were promised lands enough for their needs,[15] a promise that still seems to be unfulfilled.[16]

Many settlers experienced their tragedies before arriving in Canada, and they were essentially physical or political refugees. Of course, they endured grievous pioneer conditions without developing a sense of injustice. However, when faced with the additional burden of minority status, obliged to forsake some valued aspects of their culture in exchange for the rights of being "Her Majesty's subjects living in Canada," and of sharing only the tail end of the gradually improving opportunities that were produced by the labors of various peoples, they were outraged.[17] This minority status was more resented than their temporary poverty, their soddy shacks, and their toil-worn hands.

## Migration and Modernization

There were many opportunities to start again in Canada. The newcomers had much in common despite their various origins and periods of arrival. Something like refugee status was common to some of the French and, in particular, the Acadians;[18] the lower ranks of British veterans;[19] the Scots uprooted by enclosures;[20] the famine-driven Irish;[21] escaped slaves from the United States;[22] the German minorities of the eighteenth and nineteenth centuries (who usually came from other lands);[23] the Ukrainians who settled much of the West;[24] the Chinese and Indians who came as indentured laborers;[25] British orphans;[26] the displaced Baltic refugees after 1945;[27] job seekers from the then destitute South Europe after 1945;[28] the Hungarians after 1956;[29] the East Africans seeking refuge from Idi Amin or displaced by racism in Kenya;[30] the Caribbean and Mexican workers of recent times;[31] boat people from Vietnam;[32] and refugees now arriving from Nicaragua. The list is not complete for the past, and it will be extended by future developments.

Some settlers came with nothing and in poor health, but very often they were among the most vigorous and creative persons in the lands of their birth, and they were therefore envied and had sometimes been persecuted mercilessly by their neighbors and governments with "a better idea" for them to follow. These persons were often particularly fearful and resentful when their Canadian neighbors assumed they would be subservient.

Gradually, the premium upon labor and farmers was replaced by a demand for business acumen and the capacity to provide jobs. During the quarter century of rapid expansion of the Canadian economy from 1945 to 1970, many of the skilled workers and intellectual leaders were foreign born, for Canada could not meet its own requirements. Mass selective migration was the answer.[33] As much of the world was the source of the required population, more diversity among Canadians was quickly noticeable. (See Table 1). Soon it was obvious that the "two founding races" had been joined by a third group, now numbering almost one third of the population, and in some communities larger than the founders. The third group was no longer in a mood to accept compulsory subservience to either of the founders, although they accepted the obligation of learning one or both official languages. Many of the leaders from this third force intended to preserve their cultures in Canada, and their urban life styles made this task easier than it had been for farming[34] and bunkhouse conditions.[35]

The successive arrivals altered the Canadian population over the decades. Pre-Confederation Canada (now Quebec and Ontario) was more or less evenly French and British, the Atlantic colonies were mostly but not exclusively British, for Acadians, Germans, Blacks (who were English speaking) and Indians were important also. British Columbia was a wild assortment because of the gold rush just before the colony entered Confederation. The prairies were settled quickly by migrants from Ontario and the Maritimes, immigrants from the United States, and thousands attracted by land companies in Europe.[36] This land boom coincided with the arrival of the railroads: the CPR was finished in 1885, but northern lines continued building until after 1914. Among the famous immigrant settlers were the "men in the sheepskin coats," for Clifford Sifton wanted only settlers who were likely to survive and prosper in the tough conditions of western homesteading.[37] Peasants from Eastern Europe were ideal.

Although early life in Canada placed a premium on physical ability — paddling or portaging a canoe, swinging an axe or pick, or cooking for 30 laborers every day[38] — many of the early immigrants were learned, and there were some of genius. These natural leaders determined which of the valued traditions of their civilizations would be preserved within Canada, and even taught to others.[39] Their early efforts were usually directed to those who knew their language or followed their religion, to the securing of their roots so that the plant might grow in new soil. At first, cultural survival depended mainly upon their own efforts, for the official policies of many provinces were to assimilate minorities.

Fortunately, a measure of religious toleration enabled cultural groups to survive around their prayers and sacred books.[40] However, there was also plenty of bigotry, with the worst abuse meted out to non-Christians (traditionally Jews but now often Sikh and Islamic peoples). But mistreatment among Christians was also possible, as witnessed by Mennonites,[41] Hutterites[42] and Doukhobors,[43] Seventh Day Adventists in Quebec,[44] and others. Perhaps the most infamous religious discrimination was directed against the religions of Native

Table 1. French and English Canadians, and Foreign Born

| | Canadian Born | | Foreign Born | | | | |
|---|---|---|---|---|---|---|---|
| Year | Fr. Cdn. | Eng. Cdn. | Brit. | American | European | Asian | Other |
| 1931 | 2832 | 5137 | 1185 | 344 | 714 | 61 | 3 |
| 1951 | 4068 | 7082 | 933 | 282 | 802 | 37 | 6 |
| 1961 | 5123 | 10270 | 1017 | 284 | 1468 | 58 | 17 |
| 1971 | 5794 | 12473 | 1193 | 319 | 1685 | 120 | 79 |
| 1981 | | | 878 | 302 | 1291 | 312 | 403 |

Sources: (1) F.H. Leacy, ed., Historical Statistics of Canada, second edition (Ottawa: Statistics Canada, 1983), calculated from Tables A185, A261, A264, A304, A305, A323-25 and A326; (2) Statistics Canada, Canada's Immigrants (Ottawa: Supply and Services, 1984), Table 12; and (3) Walton O. Baxhill, The Citizenship Characteristics of the Canadian Population: 1981 Census (Ottawa: Supply and Services, 1986), Table 4.e.

Canadians, where missionaries and the laws combined to make illegal some traditional beliefs.[45]

Eventually, most newcomers became well acquainted with some aspect of the better life in Canada, but sometimes it took generations.[46] Part of the process of learning to get along with their neighbors, to respect them and work with them, was undertaken in schooling, and some in the joint activities that were necessary in developing their community. There were also many friendships that resulted in marriages with persons of other origins, a proportion that is hard to imagine except in the United States or Latin America. This statistic (available in any Canada yearbook) shows why *multi*culturalism is very acceptable to many Canadians.

## The Failure of Assimilation.

For more than a century, there were few exceptions to the policy of assimilation that was urged upon all Canadians — except those of "the two founding nations." When schools were established by the state, they were regarded as ideal vehicles for this objective, and their net reached wide enough to catch all but a few languages[47] and a few religions.[48] In a few moments of extremism, there were even thoughts of rolling back the promises of the *Quebec Act*. Lord Durham, as Governor of both the colonies of Canada (now Quebec and Ontario) recommended imposing English to achieve linguistic unity. Although the British government rejected this suggestion, the Canadiennes have never forgotten nor forgiven.[49] Scott nearly accomplished anglicization in the schools for the Indians near the turn of the century.[50] J.T.M. Anderson, as school inspector, later Minister of Education and eventually Premier of Saskatchewan, largely succeeded in his broadly aimed "Canadianization" objectives.[51] Other provinces were similarly oppressive culturally, but times change. The assimilation policies of Manitoba were not effectively challenged for nearly a century, but have recently been ruled contrary to the *Manitoba Act* of 1870, and schools are among the institutions that are now being adjusted to respect minority rights.[52]

## Minority Official Language Rights: An Assessment
### *English in Quebec Schools.*

For two centuries, English has been required in secondary education in Quebec, and for many years it has been taught as a second language in elementary education for all children in Quebec. As a result, most Canadians fluent in both official languages have been from Quebec, and spoke French as their mother tongue.[53] The opportunity for education *through English* is limited by Bill 101 to reflect:

(1) Family origins (a parent who had attended English schools in Quebec;

**Table 2. Changes in the Population through Migration**

| Interval | Canada | Atlantic | Quebec | Ontario | Prairies | B.C. |
|---|---|---|---|---|---|---|
| 1931-41 | -92 | -8 | -2 | +77 | -73 | +82 |
| 1941-51 | +169 | -92 | -12 | +305 | -267 | +231 |
| 1951-56 | +598 | -31 | +96 | +377 | -26 | +135 |
| 1956-61 | +482 | -59 | +109 | +308 | +18 | +105 |
| 1961-66 | +259 | -104 | +64 | +237 | -78 | +140 |
| 1966-71 | +464 | -27 | -42 | +369 | -44 | +222 |
| 1971-76 | +493 | +27 | -19 | +235 | +60 | +199 |
| 1976-81 | +232 | -18 | -146 | +52 | +190 | +165 |
| 1981-86 | +260 | -15 | -36 | +233 | +7 | +64 |

Sources: F.H. Leacy, ed., *Historical Statistics of Canada* (Ottawa: Statistics Canada, 1983), data A339-350; and Statistics Canada, Quarterly Estimates of Population of Canada (various years).

(2) Continuity (a child who had started education in English schools in Quebec could finish such education);

(3) Cohesiveness (all members of the family had the right to attend the same school system);

(4) Compassion (persons temporarily resident in Quebec were normally exempt from the rules); and

(5) Aboriginal Status (children of Native persons were exempt).[54]

This means that although English families can send their children through school and university in English (with French taught as a second language), French families and those of neither English nor French mother tongue (Allophones) do not have this right. The hardships now occurring for the English school systems have more to do with declining enrolments and fiscal stringency than with political oppression, and Quebec's firm stand on French in the schools affects mostly the Allophone community where many families would prefer to send their children to English schools for the economic opportunity thereby possible. This argument is being addressed by vigorous upgrading of the French business and economic programs available in Quebec universities. In summary, for the English of Quebec, their regular school system and the prestigious English universities offer among the best education in Canada, with a much better program and financing than is available to their French counterparts in any other province.

Because of several aspects of Quebec's 'maitres de maison' policy, some Anglophones, Allophones, and a great many businesses left Quebec for other provinces and for the United States, contributing significantly to the growth of Toronto and Calgary. Because the policies have now been softened or reversed (but English is still not an official language of the province, and is partly restricted in the private sector), those most offended are now willing to accept their new reality or have left the province (see Table 2).

## French in Ontario Schools

Franco-Ontarions make up almost half the total Canadian French speaking population outside Quebec. They are found not only in their old settlements near the Ottawa River, but in Northern Ontario, Penetang and Essex county, and increasingly in the great cities. Their identification with the French of Quebec and other provinces has been eroded by assimilation into the English speaking work force and through marriage into the Allophone or Anglophone family structures.[55] Until the 1970s, there was little prospect for complete education in French for these children.

Although repeated suggestions by Trudeau that Ontario should make French an official language were regularly rejected, the Peterson government may bend. Several of the necessary public services are already available in French. The 1985 *Education Act* dropped its demanding requirements for "sufficient numbers" of pupils before French families had the right for their children to be educated in French. For the non-French population, access to French is improving. More French courses are now taught, more immersion programs are introduced, more French teachers are being hired in an era when teachers of English find jobs scarce. Although the regulations for Ontario require French for grades 4 to 8, plus two credits in high school, many parents and most boards have even higher expectations.[56]

# Parallel Official Languages
## *New Brunswick and Manitoba*

Because they are theoretically bilingual provinces, both New Brunswick and Manitoba now operate parallel school programs in English and French, and parents have their choice of schools wherever numbers warrant. There are institutions for higher education in French, but these are not equivalent in the variety of courses and programs to those available in English, and particularly not in graduate specialization.

New Brunswick and Manitoba introduced the official minority second language (for example French to Anglophone or Allophone children) in elementary grades, require instruction in it for several years, and regard it to be an important academic subject at the heart of the secondary school program. The necessary teachers and materials are priorities, despite the general efforts to control the costs of education. Even though there are important and highly publicized "English only" groups in both provinces, the governments have shown no sign of changing policy, and the majority of the population apparently believes in a bilingual future.

## *Minority Treatment in the Other Provinces*

Other provinces have not made French an official language for purposes of instruction, so it is not yet a right of Francophone parents. Nevertheless, the courts have supported instruction "wherever numbers warrant," justified on the basis of the *Canadian Charter of Rights and Freedoms*. Nova Scotia and Alberta have traditional enclaves where French schools operate, and immersion schools exist in all the larger population centres. In both provinces, there are French institutions of higher education, but their position is tenuous because of their relatively small size. In many communities, a few classes of French students are offered in the regular schools where the children are strongly affected by the Anglophone environment of the school. Judging from previous experience, assimilation is a likely consequence.

The situation in the remaining provinces and the territories is worse, for the size of their French populations is even smaller, and is now probably below the critical mass for sustaining services in French. Although there are few citizens willing to argue for minority language rights in these locations, parents want the best for their own children and recognize that good language programs are important. French will continue to be the most important of these second languages, but will not be a language of instruction except in immersion schools.

## Heritage Languages and Heritage Schools

The heart of cultural identity may be language, but not every Canadian is identified with English or French, even though almost all can communicate in one of these tongues. Heritage languages (in Canada) are neither official nor aboriginal. They were carried in the hearts of migrants and their descendents, they formed the core around a number of social, cultural, historical and political aspirations. Until the last generation, these struggles for linguistic survival were intensely difficult and usually unrewarding, for most ministries of Education were intent only on providing unified systems.[57]

Since they had no ministerial support, advocates taught their heritage to their children as a duty, often without authorization nor qualification. Sometimes the classes were very small, but several communities developed private *heritage schools* with significant success.[58] Ideally, instruction in the language led to its use for instruction in some other subjects, typically those that convey the heritage through culture (music, family studies, art, history, and especially religion).

In the schools of a few enthusiasts, instruction in the heritage language may occupy half the total day, the remainder being used to teach official languages and use them for instruction in (for example) mathematics and science.[59] Most research has shown that the children sacrificed nothing in their mastery of English and other subjects. Instead, they gained a knowledge of another language and culture, and they gained in self assurance.[60]

## Modest Heritage Language Programs

Few cultural groups advocate going so far, but most state schools offer heritage languages to the children whose parents press for the programs, and in some cases there are dozens of programs offered. Mastery of the language is an uncertain outcome, for the teachers are not always both fluent and well trained, and sometimes neither. (See Table 3). Equipment and books may be sparse and the students may not be particularly enthusiastic. Nevertheless, the programs are usually regarded as important and successful. In most provinces they are regarded as equivalent to official language instruction — not rivalling these in numbers of students, but catering to specific needs.

In Ontario, heritage languages offer no school credit, may be taught by non-certified teachers, and may not be taught during school hours. Usually there are after school or Saturday courses, but in Toronto heritage languages were squeezed into the day by adding an appropriate amount to the total instruction

Table 3. Language Continuity for Selected Non-Official Languages, Canada and the Provinces, 1981.

| | Italian | German | Ukrainian | Chinese | Aboriginal |
|---|---|---|---|---|---|
| Canada | 68.6% | 31.7% | 33.1% | 83.5% | 78.0% |
| Newfoundland | 37.5 | 26.9 | 33.3 | 84.8 | 58.5 |
| P.E.I. | 60.0 | 24.1 | 50.0 | 69.0 | |
| Nova Scotia | 44.0 | 24.4 | 14.2 | 68.4 | 90.5 |
| New Brunswick | 44.0 | 31.5 | 27.6 | 81.8 | 85.0 |
| Quebec | 75.1 | 36.5 | 54.9 | 84.3 | 88.0 |
| Ontario | 69.1 | 34.2 | 41.6 | 86.1 | 76.0 |
| Manitoba | 59.3 | 42.5 | 34.0 | 85.9 | 78.8 |
| Saskatchewan | 43.8 | 21.9 | 32.4 | 76.1 | 76.6 |
| Alberta | 51.8 | 30.4 | 26.0 | 85.7 | 70.5 |
| B.C. | 48.4 | 25.0 | 17.9 | 80.1 | 47.0 |
| Yukon | 16.6 | 22.4 | 7.0 | 78.6 | 27.3 |
| N.W.T. | 69.6 | 12.2 | 7.1 | 85.7 | 85.6 |

Source: Statistics Canada, *Language in Canada* (Ottawa: Supply and Services, 1985), Table 5.

time. This drew the ire of other teachers, for if a course is not recognized for credit, it should not be allowed to interfere with the normal timetable.[61] The Ontario government has not reversed the "no-credit" policy, but it now requires all boards to offer heritage languages of demand to the parents entitled to expect them.

## Conclusion

The ideal of multiculturalism is that all Canadians should come to understand the richness of the Canadian heritage, should respect all members' contributions to this richness, and should welcome further contributions from a variety of sources. This ideal has its limitations, for some traditions are forbidden by Canadian laws, and may not be welcomed by the majority who follow their own set of practices. Not all customs can be allowed just because they have existed for centuries (e.g., slavery, infanticide, suttee, duelling) not even if they are backed by one of the great religious books.[62] Multiculturalism, therefore, challenges Canadians to think through their allegiances, to examine the justifications for them, to make their traditions live in the community and evolve rather than be applied slavishly or mechanically.

The problem is that the potential for diversity overwhelms both the teacher and the citizen, for few individuals understand all the idiosyncrasies of their own beliefs, or necessarily hold them dear. Since to *respect* all the other revered traditions of Canada's diversity is virtually impossible, the appropriate start for the schools is to insist that prejudice is always wrong for logical and academic reasons, and if it leads to harmful actions, it may be unlawful. For example, the Ontario government has proposed a race relations policy[63] that is being progressively extended and interpreted for school purposes.

Then comes the challenge of selecting *which* facts and experiences would be most useful for a particular situation. The following list provides guidelines that aid in the acceptance and promotion of multiculturalism:

1. Know thyself and thy family.
2. Know thy neighbors and some of their roots.
3. Make acquaintances who are:
    (a) religiously different;
    (b) linguistically different; and
    (c) nationally different.
4. Sample, tolerate, appreciate, and (if you like) assimilate.
5. Accept that others may not agree with you.

While it is not easy to establish absolutes, teachers can provide thier students with information about historical roots and current intellectual justifications for the necessary selections. Beyond that, students, not their teachers or parents, are ultimately responsible for shaping their own lives. For example, they can decide how far to follow the teaching of their ethnic or religious group, and they ultimately make the personal decisions about when to disagree.

## Notes

[1] I would like to acknowledge the insightful suggestions of two of my friends and colleagues: Maryann Ayim and Judson Purdy.

[2] "When you talk about "two nations," that proposition will place all Canadians who are of other racial origins than what is wrongly described as English and French in a secondary position. All through my life, one of the things I've tried to do is bring about in this nation a citizenship which was not dependent on race or color, or blood counts or racial origin, but a citizenship whereby each and every one of us is a Canadian. I'm not going back on six or seven strong today, in a position that we're trying to build strong and united." Reported in Peter C. Newman, *Renegade in Power* (Toronto: McClelland and Stewart, 1973), pp. 159-160.

[3] John G. Diefenbaker, *One Canada*, Volume 3 (Toronto: MacMillan), p. 248.

[4] The most famous study of inequality of power and rewards in Canada, published shortly after the Bi and Bi Commission began its work and before it had released any publication, was that of John Porter, *The Vertical Mosaic: An Analysis of Social Class and Power in Canada* (Toronto: University of Toronto Press, 1965). Several research studies conducted for Bi and Bi documented massive inequality which could be associalted with language or ethnicity (See for example, the two volume study *The Work World* (Ottawa: Queen's Printer, 1969).

[5] Pierre Elliot Trudeau, Marc Lalonde, and Gerard Pelletier. In fact, several other important Quebec politicians were attracted to the strategy, including Jeanne Sauve, Eric Kierans and Jean Cretien, all of whom served in Trudeau's cabinets.

[6] Commissioner of Official Languages, *Annual Report, 1985, Part V — Youth, Languages and Education* (Ottawa: Supply and Services, 1985), Appendix B.

[7] Isajiw Wsevold, "Special Presentation," in *Multiculturism as State Policy* (Ottawa: Canadian Consultative Council on Multiculturalism, 1976), pp. 169-171.

[8] This case is put eloquently by Manoly R. Lupul in *Ukrainians Canadians, Multiculturalisn, and Separatism: An Assessment* (Edmonton: University of Alberta, Canadian Institute for Ukrainian Studies, 1978), pp. 153-167.

[9] Pierre Elliot Trudeau, *Parliamentary Debates* for October, 1971 (Ottawa: House of Commons).

[10] Gordon Fairweather, "The Constitution and Multiculturalism: A Closer Look at Section 27," *Multiculturalism*, 11,1 (1987): 15-19.

[11] Arthur C. Parker, *Parker on the Iroqois, with the Code of Handsome Lake*, William N. Fenton, ed. (Syracruse: Syracruse University Press, 1968).

[12] Hilda Neatby, *The Quebec Act: Protest and Policy* (Scarborough: Prentice Hall, 1972), p. 11.

[13]Neatby, p. 50.

[14]Thomas R. Berger, *Fragile Freedoms: Human Rights and Dissent in Canada* (Toronto: Clarke Irwin, 1981).

[15]Joseph Kinsey Howard, *The Strange Empire of Louis Riel* (Toronto: Swan Publishing Company, 1963).

[16]Berger.

[17]W.J. Eccles. *The Canadian Frontier, 1534-1760* (Albuquerque, New Mexico: University of New Mexico Press, 1969).

[18]Berger.

[19]Susanna Moodie, *Roughing it in the Bush* (Toronto: McClelland and Stewart, 1923).

[20]John Prebble, *The Highland Clearances* (London: Martin Secker and Warburg, 1963); and John Kenneth Galbraith, *The Scotch* (Boston: Houghton and Mifflin, 1964).

[21]Cecil Woodham-Smith, *The Great Hunger* (New York: Harper and Row, 1962).

[22]Daniel G. Hill, *The Freedom Seekers: Blacks in Early Canada* (Agincourt: The Book Society of Canada, 1981).

[23]Multiculturalism Directorate, *The Canadian Family Tree: Canada's Peoples* (Toronto: Corpus, 1979).

[24]Manoly R. Lupul, ed., *A Heritage in Transition: Essays in The History of Ukrainians in Canada* (Toronto: McClelland and Stewart, 1982).

[25]Graham E. Johnson, "Chinese-Canadians in the 1970s: New Wine in Old Bottles?" in Jena Leonard Elliot, ed., *Two Nations, Many Cultures: Ethnic Groups in Canada*, (Scarborough: Prentice Hall, 1983), pp. 393-411.

[26]Kenneth Bagnell, *The Little Immigrants: The Orphans Who Came to Canada* (Toronto: MacMillan, 1980).

[27]Multiculturalism Directorate.

[28]Oster D. Chimbos, *The Canadian Odysseys: The Greek Experience in Canada* (Toronto: McClelland and Stewart, 1980); and A.V. Spada, *The Italians in Canada* (Ottawa: Riviera, 1969).

[29]Multiculturalism Directorate.

[30]Multiculturalism Directorate.

[31]Multiculturalism Directorate.

[32]Multiculturalism Directorate.

[33]Freda Hawkins, *Canada and Immigration Policy: Public Policy and Public Concern* (Montreal: McGill/Queens University Press, 1972).

[34]Myrna Kostash, *All of Baba's Children* (Edmonton: Hurtig, 1977).

[35]Edwin Bradwin, *The Bunkhouse Man: The Story of Work and Pay in the Camps of Canada, 1903-1914* (Toronto: University of Toronto Press, 1972).

[36]W.L. Morton, *Manitoba: A History* (Toronto: University of Toronto Press, 1977).

[37]Clifford Sifton, "The Needs of the Northwest," *Canadian Magazine*, 20, 5 (1903).

[38]Bradwin.

[39]J.S.Woodsworth, *Strangers Within Our Gates* (Toronto: University of Toronto Press, 1972).

[40]Stewart E. Rosenberg, *The Jewish Community in Canada* (Toronto: McClelland and Stewart, 1970).

[41]Frank H. Epp, *The Mennonites in Canada, 1786-1920: The History of a Separate People* (Toronto: University of Toronto Press, 1974).

[42]Berger.

[43]George Woodcock and Ivan Avacumovic, *The Doukhobors* (Toronto: Oxford University Press, 1968).

[44]Berger.

[45]Chief John Snow, *These Mountains are Our Sacred Places* (Toronto: Samuel Stevens, 1977).

[46]Kostash.

[47]Apart from English and French, German was one of the few languages recognized for instruction in Ontario, Manitoba and Nova Scotia. That right was lost because of animosity after 1914.

[48]Catholic and Protestant often were treated as alternatives for public funding. Newfoundland allowed six denominations to share in public funds, and everywhere some religions sought refuge in private schooling.

[49]Denis Moniere, *Ideologies in Quebec: The Historical Development Policy* (Toronto: University of Toronto Press, 1981), pp.112-118.

[50]Brian Titley, "Duncan Campbell Scott and Indian Education Policy," in J. Donald Wilson, *An Imperfect Past: Education and Society in Canadian History* (Calgary: Detselig, 1984), pp.14-153.

[51]These were spelled out in his University of Toronto thesis, later published as J.T.M. Anderson, *The Education of New Canadians* (Toronto: J.M. Ent and Sons, 1918).

[52]Joseph E. Magnet, "A New Deal in Minority Language Education," in Micheal E. Manley-Casimir and Terri A. Sussel, eds., *Courts in the Classroom: Education and the Charter of Rights and Freedoms* (Calgary: Detselig Enterprises,1986), p. 106.

[53] Statistics Canada, *Language in Canada* (Ottawa: Supply and Services, 1985).

[54]Heather Lysons-Balcon, "Minority Language Educational Guarantees in the Canadaian Charter" in Ratna Ghosh and Douglas Ray, eds., *Social Change and Education in Canada* (Toronto: Harcourt Bryce & Javanovich, 1987), pp. 155-166.

[55] Jacques Lamontagne, "Minority Official Language Education: Where Can It Be Secure?" in Douglas Ray and Vincent D'Oyley, eds. *Human Rights in Canadian Education* (Dubuque: Kendall Hunt, 1983), pp. 176-197.

[56] Commissioner of Official Languages, pp. 36-40.6.

[57] Manoly R. Lupul, "Ukrainian-Language Education in Canada's Public Schools," in Manoly R. Lupul, ed., *Heritage in Transition*, pp. 215-243.

[58] R.S. Pannu and J.R. Young, "Ethnic Schools in Three Canadian Cities: A Study in Multiculturalism," *Alberta Journal of Educational Research*, 26, 4 (December, 1980): 247-261.

[59] Some schools with traditions of offering heritage instruction preceded Multiculturalism policy, and included Mennonite, Hutterite and Jewish communities in many provinces. Recently, the programs have also been associated with Ukrainians, Islamic and Sikh populations. The numbers may expand beyond current levels.

[60] Manoly R. Lupul, "Multiculturalism and Canadian National Identity: The Alberta Experience," in Alf Chaiton and Neil McDonald, eds., *Canadian Schools and Canadian Identity* (Toronto: Gage, 1977), pp. 105-175.

[61] Geraldine Gillis, "The Expectations of the Teaching Profession," in Ghosh and Ray, eds., *Social Change and Education in Canada*, pp. 28-37.

[62] John Kehoe, "Strategies for Human Rights Education" in Ray and D'Oyley, *Human Rights in Canadian Education*, pp. 68-109.

[63] Ontario, *The Development of a Policy in Race and Ethnocultural Equity* (Toronto: Ministry of Education).

# 4

# Making and Enforcing School Rules in the Wake of the *Charter of Rights*

*A. Wayne MacKay and Lyle Sutherland*

The making and enforcing of school rules have always been important and difficult aspects of the educator's role. Maintaining an orderly teaching environment is a statutory duty in all Canadian jurisdictions in addition to being a vital part of the teacher's *in loco parentis* role. As a corollary to the duty to maintain discipline and order, there must the power vested in the education authorities to make rules and enforce them with appropriate forms of discipline. Sometimes the power to discipline students is expressly stated in the relevant education statutes. Other times, such power must be implied from the statutory duties imposed on teachers and administrators or even derived from the *in loco parentis* doctrine.

Educators, when making and enforcing school rules, are acting as agents of the state and not as mere delegates of the parents. While there are rare occasions in which a teacher acts strictly *in loco parentis* when enforcing rules and promoting order, he or she acts on behalf of the state. This fact is crucial because parents and their delegates act in a private capacity and, thus in the majority view, escape the restrictions of the *Charter of Rights*.[1] Meanwhile, the Minister of Education, departmental officials, school boards, school administrators and teachers are subject to the *Charter of Rights*, as public actors on behalf of the state.

The *Charter*'s arrival on the school scene has caused concern and confusion among educators. These feelings have been particularly acute among school administrators who are on the front lines of rule enforcement. In the past, the individual school principal was given broad discretion to make and enforce rules within his or her school and there was little chance of challenge to this exercise of authority. Similarly, school boards were given broad authority to manage students within the school districts. As school systems grew in size, however, education became more centralized so that provincial and even national authorities eroded the local autonomy of both the principals and the school boards. The one-room school, run by the local community, was the epitome of the older *in loco parentis* structure. Cut off from the parental community, the larger modern schools were emanations of the state and the educators accountable to provincial authorities.

Thus, local educational authorities felt a loss of power even before the arrival of the *Charter*. In addition to provincially imposed restrictions upon local decision-makers, principals and teachers faced parents who were less inclined to impose order in the home and more inclined to challenge school authorities. Parents also experienced an increased alienation by the various levels of school administration and authority. This alienation contributed to a new "rights" consciousness among parents and students, replacing the former deference to school authorities. This phenomenon has been extended by the *Charter* which gives both parents and students a powerful tool by which to challenge the schools. It has also been argued that the *Charter* will result in the imposition of national restrictions on school authorities and thus extend the centralizing process one step further.[2]

In summary, the *Charter* may be the final stage in the erosion of local authority, but it did not begin the process. Legally, statutory authority has replaced the common law concept of *in loco parentis* as the core of educational authority. Provincial education departments have eclipsed local school boards and principals as the primary policy-makers. Finally, parents and students, who are more willing to challenge the schools, have been given a new weapon in the form of the *Charter of Rights*.

It is little wonder that educators feel under siege. Faced with the possibility of challenge from either higher political authorities or the courts, some school boards and administrators have abdicated some of their authority. Efforts to maintain order in the schools have diminished in some cases. If the administrators abdicate, the front-line teachers are left to their own devices and a sense of abandonment. Students, as the consumers of education, have the most to lose from this process. Therefore, educators need not abandon the disciplinary aspect of their task but learn to exercise it in accordance with the new *Charter* standards. The process should be one of accomodation rather than abdication. What follows is a modest proposal in that direction.

## Educators: Different Roles and Capacities

The appropriate response to the restrictions of the *Charter* will partly depend on the role being played by the particular educator. It makes a difference if the person is an education department official, school board member, administrator or teacher because each performs a different role. To further complicate things, each of these people can be involved in rule-making and enforcement at different levels in the hierarchy: department official for the province, board member for the school district, administrator for the school, and teacher for the classroom. Thus, it is useful to talk more generally about the different disciplinary roles.

The school rule process can be broken into three phases:

(1) Making Rules.

(2) Enforcing Rules.

(3) Penalizing for Breach of Rules.

Given this breakdown, the school can be viewed as a microcosm of the larger political structure:

(1) Rule-making is a legislative function.

(2) Rule-enforcing is an administrative function.

(3) Penalizing is a judicial function.

All rungs of the school hierarchy are involved in rule-making at different levels. Department of Education officials and school board members spend most of their time in policy formulation and the drafting of rules. School administrators and teachers are the primary rule enforcers and, in some respects, resemble a school police force. Finally, it is school administrators and school board members, as well as committees composed of both, who normally sit in a judicial capacity and determine the penalties for a breach of a particular rule. The compartments are far from water-tight as teachers and administrators also may get involved in rule formulation or the assessment of penalties. It is important to consider which of the three rule related functions is relevant to a particular set of facts because there are different *Charter* considerations for each function.

## Rule-Making: Content Consistent with the *Charter*

At the rule-making level, the major *Charter* concern is with the actual content or substance of the rules. One example is a school rule which treats particular individuals or groups differently. It is common practice to discriminate between students on the basis of age by having more restrictions on elementary students than those in high school. Not all discriminations are suspect. Indeed, most rules discriminate in some way between different groups of people. However, as the Supreme Court of Canada has indicated in *Andrews* v. *Law Society of British Columbia* and *R*. v. *Turpin*, many acts of discrimination, in a general sense, will not produce a violation of section 15 of the *Charter*.

An interesting example of discriminatory rules which will be examined in light of the equality guarantees in section 15 of the *Charter* is the package of special rules applied to children with physical or mental disabilities. It has generally been accepted that students with mental or physical disabilities must be treated differently in order to give them a fair opportunity to learn. The supporters of special education classes and other forms of separate treatment argue that this is a kind of affirmative action needed to achieve equality, rather than a violation of section 15 of the *Charter*. On the other hand, the proponents of integrating the disabled argue that such discrimination on the basis of mental or physical disability is inherently suspect and violates the letter and spirit of section 15 of the *Charter*. This issue will be addressed in the courts as one of the early applications of the *Charter* to the substantive rules governing education.

Another example of how the *Charter* can be used to challenge the content of school rules is the application of the fundamental freedoms in section 2 of the *Charter*.

2. Everyone has the following fundamental freedoms:
   (a) freedom of conscience and religion;
   (b) freedom of thought, belief, opinion and expression, including freedom of the press and other media of communication;
   (c) freedom of peaceful assembly; and
   (d) freedom of association.

Many school rules will in some ways restrict the above quoted rights. The most notable case to date involving this section is *Zylberberg et el.* v. *Sudbury Board of Education*,[3] in which a group of parents successfully challenged a school board policy requiring schools to hold religious exercises each day. The parents lost the preliminary because the court found participation in the exercises to be voluntary (i.e., parents were able to have their children excused from the exercises). However, the Ontario Court of Appeal found that "voluntariness" meant nothing to young children who would feel singled out if they were excused from the classroom. They held that children are acutely sensitive to classroom norms and peer pressure, and this would serve to coerce religious minorities contrary to their rights under the *Charter*.

Freedom of speech and association are yet to be tested in the classroom. However, the banning of slogans on T-shirts or buttons, the banning of gay rights meetings, and the removal of books from school libraries are a few examples of rules which could violate section 2. All such rules will not disappear because of the *Charter*, but they will have to be defended under section 1 as a reasonable limit on rights. In the American cases, the critical test is whether the restriction on rights is necessary to promote and maintain order in the school, but a full examination of that would be another article on student rights.[4]

There is another avenue open to school officials who wish to defend a rule which appears on the surface to be discriminatory. They can seek to justify the rule under section 1 of the *Charter* which states:

1. The *Canadian Charter of Rights and Freedoms* guarantees the rights and freedoms set out in it subject only to such reasonable limits

proscribed by law as can be demonstrably justified in a free and democratic society.

The burden of showing that a particular rule is a reasonable limit on a *Charter* right rests squarely with the state agent who made the rule or seeks to apply it.[5] In the school context, this means the school board, school administrator, department official or teacher. Furthermore, the burden is a heavy one as the rule-maker must "demonstrably justify" the rule as a reasonable one in a free and democratic society. In order to meet such a test in courtroom litigation, the school official will have to bring forth some convincing evidence as to why the rule is necessary and why its objective could not be achieved without violating a *Charter* right. The Supreme Court of Canada has set a further requirement for section 1 that the means used to sanction a particular behavior be reasonable and proportional to the ends sought.[6] In most cases, this will mean the presentation of empirical evidence and expert educational opinion. This will be an expensive and time-consuming process and educators should pause and ask whether they feel that strongly about maintaining the rule in issue.

What are the standards of reasonableness? This is another complex question. In section 1 of the *Charter* the only reference point is "free and democratic societies." This has led some judges to look at the situation in other countries such as the United States and the United Kingdom. In other cases, judges have considered international standards as well as those which have been traditionally accepted in Canada. An important question is whether judges will also look to more localized standards be they provincial, school district or individual school. Reference to these local standards will allow the greatest diversity, and allow schools in St. John's, Newfoundland, or Vancouver, British Columbia, to escape national *Charter* standards, which will frequently be set in Ontario.[7] Courts are unlikely to allow a fully localized approach but they are likely to take some account of regional differences.[8]

Another limitation on the use of section 1 of the *Charter* to justify a rule which appears on its face to violate a *Charter* right is that it must be "proscribed by law." At a minimum, this means that the rule must be clear enough to allow students to understand when their conduct would violate the rule. The rule must be communicated in a clear and accessible form. In practical terms, this means that school board and school rules must be in written form and publicized in some way.[9] The safest course is to have the rules codified and distributed to both parents and students at the beginning of the school term. Secret policy memoranda and oral rules may be a thing of the past.

The phrase, "proscribed by law," may also be a window through which judges will import American doctrines of vagueness and overbreadth. In the United States, these doctrines have been important devices for limiting the substantive content of rules and policies.[10] The general idea behind the doctrine of overbreadth is that a rule which limits a right should be no more intrusive of the right than is necessary to achieve its goal. If a rule is too broad, it should be struck down and replaced with a narrower one. Vagueness as a constitutional doctrine can best be summarized by the following quote from an American case:

> It is a basic principle of due process that an enactment is void for vagueness if its prohibitions are not clearly defined. Vague laws offend several important values. First, because we assume that man is free to steer between lawful and unlawful conduct, we insist that laws give the person of ordinary intelligence a reasonable opportunity to know what is prohibited so that he may act accordingly. Vague laws may trap the innocent by not providing *fair warning*. Second, if *arbitrary and discriminatory* enforcement is to be prevented, laws must provide explicit standards for those who apply them. A vague law impermissibly delegates basic policy matters to policemen, judges, and juries for resolution on an ad hoc and subjective basis, with the attendant dangers of *arbitrary and discriminatory application*. Third, but related, where a vague statute "abut[s]" upon sensitive areas of basic First Amendment freedoms," it "operates to inhibit the exercise of [those] freedoms." Uncertain meanings inevitably lead citizens to "steer far wider of the unlawful zone . . . than if the boundaries of the forbidden areas were clearly marked." (emphasis added)[11]

It is evident from the above quotation that there are both substantive and procedural aspects to the doctrine of vagueness. It is used, however, to attack the substantive content of the rule in issue. In the Canadian context, the vagueness doctrine has been employed by judges to strike out conditions in probation orders for young offenders. In one recent case,[12] a youth court judge held that a probation order which required the youth to "live with mother and obey rules and curfew" was too vague to be enforceable. Similarly, school rules which allow suspension for "immoral conduct" may be too vague to be enforced if a student were to challenge his or her suspension.

How should educators respond to these *Charter* challenges? If rules are too specific and leave no room for discretion it can lead to different kinds of problems. For example, in the case *C.T.* v. *Board of School Trustees* (Langley), a thirteen-year-old girl was automatically suspended for the remainder of the school year for possession of a narcotic.[13] The parents challenged the suspension and at trial the judge held that the girl had not been given proper notice of the rule, and therefore the suspension was not in accordance with fair procedures. The British Columbia Court of Appeal held that the student had to be 15 to receive notice according to the regulations. However, they overturned the suspension on the grounds that a mandatory policy could not be applied to remove the statutory discretion granted to school officials.[14]

The *Charter* was not argued in this case. However, the decision of the trial judge would be fortified by an argument under the procedural guarantees of section 7. *C.T.* v. *Board of School Trustees* (Langley) is an example of the difficulty that schools may run into if their rules are too specific and do not allow for some degree of discretion. There should be a happy medium where rules are flexible enough to leave some discretion in the hands of the administrator, but specific enough to allow students to know what conduct is in breach of the rule. School rules should be re-examined with the following question in mind: Does this rule tell the student what conduct is unacceptable? Of course, if the rule is not written or in some way available to the student, it does not meet the test.

Another question which must be asked is whether the content of the school rule is itself in violation of a *Charter* right. If that question is answered in the affirmative, a second question arises. Is this rule sufficiently important for education purposes that we should attempt a section 1 reasonable limits justification? The problems with mounting a section 1 defence are discussed above and these should be considered. If educators consider the rule important, they should, nonetheless, be willing to defend it and not fold up their tent merely because a *Charter* challenge has been raised. In many cases, a thoughtful review of rules will allow educators to avoid any conflict in the first instance, by "cleaning their own house." Being proactive rather than reactive is the key to avoiding *Charter* challenges.

We began this section by using discriminatory school rules as examples of *Charter* violations. Since most *Charter* rights apply to students as well as adults, there are many other sections which a rule restricting students may violate.[15] Procedural matters such as the right to "fundamental justice" in section 7 of the *Charter*, the right to be free from "unreasonable searches" in section 8 or the legal rights contained in section 9, 10 and 11 may be offended by the procedural content of a particular school rule. In summary, school rules must be examined in light of the *Charter*, made accessible to students and defended where they are educationally sound. However, it is not possible to list in detailed form every possible ground for suspension.

# Enforcing Rules:
## Due Process in the School Context

While rule-making is fairly distinct from the other two categories, the line between administratively enforcing the rule and judicially setting the sanction is much less clear. This is largely due to the fact that the same people are often involved in enforcing the rule and deliberating on the penalty. In the larger society, there is a clear line between the police who enforce the laws and the judges who handle the sentencing. In the school setting, the principal may be the person who makes the rule, enforces it and penalizes those who break it. Often there is no clear line between these different roles.

In the next section on penalties for breach of school rules, we shall focus on whether the penalty itself violates some provision of the *Charter*, as well as examine the investigative procedures of school personnel in light of the *Young Offenders Act*. The thrust of this section will be the unconstitutional application or enforcement of rules. Some confusion arises from the fact that rules are sometimes intended to be enforced by administrative procedures and on other occasions by the criminal law. Thus, the educator's role becomes a blur of school discipline and police procedures.

It is easy to think of school rules which in their content do not violate the *Charter* but could be applied in such a way as to be unconstitutional. A rule which states that no student or teacher may smoke in class does not discriminate on its face. If the rule is only applied to males or only applied to students, then there may be grounds for an equality challenge. This is a problem of application and not content.

A more likely problem is the procedure by which rules are enforced. While many provinces have adopted a detailed procedural code, other provinces such as Manitoba, Newfoundland, New Brunswick and Prince Edward Island give students very few procedural rights. Quite apart from the fact that these provincial disparities may lead to claims of regional discrimination, some of the provinces appear to fall short of the fundamental justice guarantees contained in section 7 of the *Charter*. This section reads as follows:

> 7. Everyone has the right to life, liberty and security of the person and the right not to be deprived thereof except in accordance with the principles of fundamental justice.

This is an important section of the *Charter* which has been interpreted by the Supreme Court of Canada as having both procedural and substantive content.[16] This means that it may be used to challenge both the content and the procedure of government action. Thus, it could be used as the basis for a vagueness challenge to the content of a rule as discussed in the previous section or the nature of a penalty as will be explored in the next section. It also imposes a constitutional form of Canadian due process.

In applying section 7 to the school context, we are assuming that education is encompassed within the phrases of "liberty and security of the person."[17] There could also be simple cases of detention in the school context which would attract section 7 procedural protections. Essentially, schools may not deprive a student of her "liberty" (i.e., education) without following some form of due process. There is not space to properly explore the meaning of due process in the school context[18] but it should be emphasized that it is less than full court procedure. Those provinces which have a detailed code of procedures for suspension would likely meet the section 7 standard with the possible exception of those that allow only for *post facto* hearings for the student. In some cases, a pre-suspension hearing may be appropriate even if it is only an informal discussion in the principal's office. Those provinces with no procedural guarantees are unlikely to meet the section 7 standard.

The necessity of due process in the school is illustrated by a Nova Scotia case in which a teenage girl was suspended from high school and placed in a private school by the Children's Aid Society because she was allegedly "unmanageable" under section 55(1) of the *Children's Services Act*.[19] The court held that this placement violated section 7 of the *Charter* because the girl was not provided with the dates, locations, and specific instances of her alleged "unmanageability" to allow for a proper defence. It is a commonly held principle of fundamental justice that accused persons have the right to know the case against them.

In a more recent decision, the New Brunswick Court of Appeal upheld the expulsion of a student who had violated the school's no smoking rule for the third time.[20] On the first infraction, he and his parents had been informed of the rule, and on the second he had been suspended for three days. The student was expelled by the principal for the third infraction, and this decision was supported by the school board at a meeting attended by neither the parents nor the student. The student obtained an interlocutory injunction to force the school board to reconvene and consider the matter with proper representations.

The board met a second time, examining affidavits from students and teachers and allowing the student, his parents, and his lawyer to make representations; the expulsion was upheld. The student appealed further to the Queen's Bench for reinstatement and damages, but the action was dismissed. This decision was appealed and dismissed by the Court of Appeal which held that the interlocutory motion should never have been granted because the student did not have a "real prospect of succeeding" at trial. In spite of this final ruling, which is based primarily on the legal complexities of interlocutory motions, this case underscores the requirement for school boards to act fairly and in accordance with the principles of fundamental justice when they are suspending students. If the school board had initially put procedures in place which accorded with section 7 of the *Charter*, they might have avoided time-consuming and costly litigation.

Student records provide a less obvious example of enforcement problems. They are only a form of discipline in the sense that undesirable conduct can result in a negative notation on the record. The possible consequences of such notation for future employment are great. Accordingly, questions of student and parent access to these records are significant. Only Ontario, Saskatchewan, Alberta and the Yukon expressly address the question of access to student records. For many other jurisdictions it is a matter of school board or even school policy. Furthermore, when rights of access are given, they are given to parents or students who have reached the age of majority.[21] This aspect of the content of such rules, whether in the form of a statute or policy guideline, may lead to a *Charter* challenge on the basis of age discrimination. There are other difficult procedural matters in relation to student records, such as, the access of the non-custodial parent in a separated or divorced situation. Student records raise many issues of privacy beyond the scope of this article.[22]

# Investigation Procedures:
# Search, Detention and Questioning

Investigation procedures such as detention, questioning and search and seizure are an integral part of enforcing rules in the school. The application of the *Young Offenders Act* and the *Charter* have a dramatic effect on these common procedures because they serve to blur the lines between the role of the educator and the role of the policeman. This confusion of roles occurs in situations where the school rule overlaps with the criminal law. Instances of theft, possession of or trafficking in narcotics, vandalism, and assault, are all examples of where this role confusion may occur.

Section 3(e) of the *Young Offenders Act*[23] affords young persons a "special guarantee" of their rights under the *Charter*. This includes section 24(2) of the *Charter* which allows the courts to exclude evidence that is gathered in a manner which violates the rights of an accused. Therefore, if a young person is improperly searched or questioned, any evidence gathered may be held inadmissible and could result in an acquittal. Prior to 1984, these issues would not arise because the previous *Juvenile Delinquents Act*[24] contained very little protection for the rights of young people. It is clear that these restrictions apply to police officers, but the more difficult question is whether they should apply to school officials acting in a police capacity.

There are three different capacities in which school authorities can act:

(1) *In Loco Parentis* (delegates of the parents)

(2) Educational State Agents

(3) Police State Agents

Subject to complex arguments about the breadth of state action, it is likely that the administrator in the private school is acting *in loco parentis* and thus may escape the restrictions of the *Charter*. A principal in search of evidence that will be used strictly for school discipline purposes is acting as an educational state agent. These cases rarely pose difficulties. The real problem is the principal in search of illegal drugs, which if found could result in a criminal charge, as well as whatever penalties are provided for breach of the school rule. If the incriminating evidence is passed along to the police, the principal may be seen as acting for the police as well as the schools.[25] He or she is a double agent.

The guarantees against unreasonable search and seizure are contained in section 8 of the *Charter* and are given special emphasis for young persons pursuant to section 3(e) of the *Young Offenders Act*:

8. Everyone has the right to be secure against unreasonable search or seizure.

Search powers provide a good launching pad for a discussion of the various capacities in which school disciplinarians may act. If a principal is conducting a search to determine whether a student has broken a rule about smoking, is he or she acting in the same capacity as the principal who is searching student lockers for illegal drugs? What happens if the principal, while searching for cigarettes, discovers marijuana?

This latter question has been answered by the United States Supreme Court in *New Jersey* v. *T.L.O.*[26] In that case, a principal found marijuana in the purse of a fourteen-year-old girl while he was looking for cigarettes to prove that the girl had violated the school's no smoking rule. The Supreme Court held that the constitutional protections against unreasonable searches applied to school officials. However, they felt that a lower standard of reasonableness should be applied to schools than police officers. The Court allowed the evidence to be admitted because they found that the search was not overly intrusive given the age of the student and the significant drug problem in New Jersey schools.

A similiar position has been adopted in Canada by the Ontario Court of Appeal in *R.* v. *J.M.G.*[27] In that case, a principal searched a student's socks after being informed by another student that J.M.G. was in possession of narcotics. The principal found marijuana and the student was charged with possession. Grange, J.A. upheld the search as reasonable, although he did not spell out whether the authority to search stemmed from the common law doctrine of *in loco parentis*, or as an implication from the statutory duty to maintain order and discipline. The latter is the more realistic analysis and the one that allows the student to call in aid the *Charter* protections against unreasonable searches.[28]

There is a further potential for trouble where the student does not cooperate in the search or even physically resists. What are the limits on the execution of the search? In *R.* v. *Morrison*[29] the Ontario Court of Appeal upheld a strip search of an adult woman charged with theft and the possession of stolen property. However, the search was conducted at the police station in the presence of a female officer and incidental to a lawful arrest. Unless there is some element of imminent danger or urgency, it would not seem appropiate for school personnel to be strip searching young offenders. Further, if the student physically resists the search, then the police should be involved to handle the matter. A principal certainly has a responsibility to maintain discipline and order in his or her school, but crime control is the job of law enforcement agencies and should be left in their hands whenever it is practicable to do so.

Another common type of search in schools is the locker search. Although there is some debate over the rights of students to "exclusive possession" of their lockers,[30] it is unrealistic to expect the courts to declare lockers "out of bounds" for school personnel. The crux of the problem is that lockers create an expectation of privacy on the part of the renting student, and some consideration ought to be given to this expectation.[31]

In the United States, students have been held to have exclusive possession of lockers vis-a-vis other students, but not to have such exclusivity over the locker as against school authorities.[32] A simple course of action for schools is to dispel any notion of privacy by notifying the students at the beginning of each school year that their lockers are school property and may be subject to search at any time. It should be noted that the power to search lockers does not include the right to conduct blanket or "dragnet" searches.[33] There must be some reasonable suspicion that searching a particular locker will turn up evidence.[34]

Another important investigative tool for enforcing school rules is the detention and questioning of students. Section 10(b) of the *Charter* covers detention:

10. Everyone has the right on arrest or detention . . .

(b) to retain and instruct counsel without delay and to be informed of that right . . .

If an educator, acting as an agent of the police, detains a young person for questioning he may be required to comply with the requirements of section 10(b) of the *Charter*.

In *R. v. J.M.G.*, Grange, J.A. examined the applicability of section 10(b) of the *Charter* to principals, and concluded that there was no need to inform students of their right to instruct counsel upon detention. His reasoning, however, is far from satisfactory. First, he assumed that the principal was acting in an educational capacity, despite the fact that the police had been called both before and after the detention. In the *R. v. J.M.G.* situation, criminal charges were clearly contemplated. Grange J.A. was not clear on whether a school official should ever adhere to the section 10(b) *Charter* warning except to concede that in "serious" cases a principal should either comply with the *Charter*, or involve the police.

Justice Grange further clouds the issue by claiming that students are in a "constant state of detention" while in school and therefore it is impossible for them to be detained within the meaning of section 10 of the *Charter*. This likens the school setting to a prison and clearly violates the established principle in the United States that students do not shed their constitutional rights at the schoolhouse gates.[35] The approach of Grange, J.A. is unacceptable because it does not adequately protect the individual rights of the student who faces the same consequences whether the investigation is conducted by the principal or the police.

The question still remains of how best to detain a child for investigation while maintaining the integrity of his or her *Charter* protections. The courts are yielding to the discretion of educators in these situations, even though it is inconsistent with the special protections afforded to young offenders under section 3(e) of the *Young Offenders Act*. Most educators welcome this administrative discretion because they are not prepared to inform children of their "rights" upon every detention. We would recommend, however, that school officials take a pro-active stance in this area and set guidelines that are consistent with the *Charter* protections. If the purpose of the detention is to enforce an in-house rule, then no warnings or legal counsel should be required.

If criminal proceedings are contemplated, however, then the young person should be informed as to the nature of the allegation, and at least be permitted to contact a parent before any further investigation takes place. In some cases, he or she should be allowed to contact a lawyer. It is necessary to maintain order and discipline. However, schools also serve as a microcosm of society at large. There is, therefore, an educational as well as legal basis for offering protections guaranteed by the *Charter of Rights.*

Under ordinary circumstances, questioning students about their conduct is common school practice and does not present a problem. If the discussion suddenly turns into an admission of criminal conduct, there are requirements under the *Young Offenders Act* that should be considered. Section 56 sets out conditions which must be met if the statements are to be admissible in court for the purposes of a criminal charge.

The first important feature of this section is that it applies to "persons in authority." In *Rothman* v. *The Queen*,[36] the Supreme Court of Canada interpreted the statutory phrase "persons in authority" (in a different context) to be a subjective test. Therefore, if teachers are regarded as persons in authority by their students, they will be similarly regarded by the law. "Authority" is not used in the colloquial sense, but must involve a belief by the accused that the person can influence the course of a prosecution.[37] In *R.* v. *H.*[38] both the Youth Court and the Alberta Queen's Bench agreed that teachers are persons in authority for the purpose of section 56(2). It is reasonably certain that courts across Canada will reach the same conclusion.

If statements given by a student are to be used later in criminal proceedings, and if school officials are persons in authority, they will have to be aware of the requirements under section 56(2). The first criteria, under subsection (a) is that the statement be "voluntary." This term has a long and complicated legal history. However, it is sufficient for the purposes of this discussion to treat this as meaning that statements must be given "without fear of prejudice or hope of advantage exercised or held out by a person in authority."[39] In the school setting then, threats of after school detentions or promises that "things will go easier if you just tell the truth," may render statements inadmissible in later criminal proceedings.

The second criteria, as set out in subsection (b), is more problematic because it forces educators to act like police officers in "reading a student his or her rights." Unlike the debate over informing students of their right to instruct counsel upon detention, the *Young Offenders Act* is clear that a student must be informed of his or her rights under subsection (b) if a statement is to be used as evidence. It is important to note that the student is to have these rights explained in language which he or she understands. Studies in the U.S. have shown that children do not fully understand or appreciate their rights when given in a "Miranda type" warning.[40] Therefore, it would be advisable for school boards to draft a proper format to be used in schools for advising students of their rights.

The final significant impact of section 56(2) lies in subsection (c). This subsection allows a youth to consult with a parent, counsel, relative, or "other appropriate adult" before making a statement. This raises the difficult and time consuming problem involved in contacting one of the individuals named in the section. However, if the student has been detained and legal consequences are contemplated, there should have been an attempt to contact an appropriate adult.

It raises another problem if the student chooses a teacher to be the "other appropriate adult." A recent amendment to the *Young Offenders Act* sets out that persons consulted under paragraph 56(2)(c) are not persons in authority for the purposes of this section.[41] Statements made to a teacher acting in this capacity may therefore be admissible against the accused without the protections included in section 56(2)(b) of the *Act*. Teachers should be particularly careful when asked to consult with a young person under section 56, so that they are not put in the awkward position of betraying the confidence of the student. If a lawyer is consulted pursuant to paragraph (c) then the conversation is protected by solicitor and client privelege, however this privelege does not extend to a consultation between a teacher and student. We would suggest that teachers should not act as advisors under this paragraph where the young person may be subject to serious criminal consequences.

The area of questioning students brings the importance of delineating between criminal and in-house investigations into sharper focus. Section 56 leaves little room for discretion on the part of educators; it comes into operation immediately if any of the statements given by the accused are to be used as evidence against him or her.[43] This reinforces the argument presented earlier that educators should develop different procedures when handling young offenders than those normally practiced when enforcing school rules.

# Penalizing for Breach of Rules:
# The Constitutional Limits of Punishment

While most sanctions could be challenged as infringing a liberty or security interest under section 7 of the *Charter*, judges will not ban all forms of discipline in the schools. Thus, suspensions, fines, and the recording of negative comments in the form of student records are likely to be acceptable so long as they are enforced fairly. Similarly, detentions are likely to be acceptable if they are not so long in duration as to constitute cruel or unusual treatment under section 12 of the *Charter*. Some jurisdictions, such as British Columbia, have solved this problem by establishing, in their regulations, statutory maximums (e.g., 30 minutes) on detentions. The critical *Charter* section is section 12:

> 12. Everyone has the right not to be subjected to any cruel and unusual treatment or punishment.

Most penalties could be administered so as to violate the cruel and unusual provision. However, the concern of this section will be penalties which by their substantive nature could violate section 12. The most logical candidate for concern is corporal punishment.

The first question to be considered is whether section 12 of the *Charter* applies to the schools at all. In the United States, the American cruel and unusual provision was not applied to the schools.[43] This decision has been criticized extensively, and for reasons elaborated elsewhere[44] we think that section 12 of the *Charter* will be applied to Canadian students. Other than Newfoundland which permits corporal punishment and British Columbia which bars it, statutes and regulations in Canada are silent on the topic.[45] Corporal punishment is handled usually in the form of school board or school policy. It is likely that corporal punishment will be struck down as contrary to the *Charter* but it may take many years and more than one trip to the Supreme Court to produce this result.

In Nova Scotia, section 12 of the *Charter* was used to strike down the critical truancy provision of the *Education Act*.[46] Family Court Judge Roscoe found that the procedures followed did not meet the requirements of "fundamental justice" in section 7 and the indefinite sentence to a reformatory violated section 12 of the *Charter*.[47] As a response to this decision, the Nova Scotia government amended the *Education Act*[48] to take truancy outside the criminal context altogether. It is a matter for Social Services and truancy may be one factor in a child protection proceeding. This process of court challenge followed by legislative reform may become a familiar pattern for changing rules with unfair procedures and excessive punishments.

# Conclusion

By way of conclusion, we present a current legal development in suspending students which illustrates a classic dilemma between protecting a young person's *Charter* rights and maintaining a safe and orderly environment in the schools. This dilemma has arisen from two recent cases in which schools have taken disciplinary actions against students charged, but not yet convicted, under the *Young Offenders Act*. There is no clear correct course of action in these situations that will reconcile all of the interests involved.

The first case[49] arose in a Saskatchewan school where three students had been charged, but pleaded "not guilty" to allegations of sexual assault. In response to these charges, the school placed the youths on "short bounds" restrictions, which required them to go immediately to their classroom upon arrival and remain there for the duration of the day except to attend physical education classes, and to move through the halls with the permission of a staff member. The parents challenged these restrictions. However, MacLellan J. found this to be a valid exercise of the school board's power to "exercise general supervision and control over schools" pursuant to section 91 of the *Education Act.*[50]

The second case[51] occurred in Ontario, where four youths pleaded not guilty to charges of forcible confinement and sexual assault. They were subsequently suspended by the principal of the school. The Peel County School Board upheld the suspensions and moved to have the students expelled. However, they initiated an application to the Ontario Supreme Court to determine whether the proposed expulsion hearing would offend section 38 of the *Young Offenders Act*, which prohibits the publication of the indentity of a young offender. Justice Reid held that the expulsion hearing could not proceed because it would inevitably lead to the publication of the identities of the accused, as well as prematurely stigmatize the youths as "guilty." Reid J. stated further:

> This comes distressingly close to condemnation without trial. The principal seems to have assumed that the students were guilty simply because they were charged. That is wholly contrary to the fundamental principle of our system of justice. Everyone is presumed innocent until found guilty by due process of law. Had the principal not jumped to the conclusion that the students were guilty he would have had no basis for ordering their suspension.[52]

There are two important principles in conflict in both of these cases. The first principle is that school authorities should suspend children who are suspected of criminal conduct so that other students in the school are not put at risk. The second is that everyone has the right to be presumed innocent, and children in particular should not be stigmatized as "guilty" when they may in fact be innocent. Although the Ontario case focused on protecting the identity of young offenders, the presumption of innocence was the more significant issue in that case.

There are no simple answers to the questions which arise when a student is charged with a serious criminal offence. Section 7 of the *Charter* protects the rights of children to receive an education and not to be deprived of that right except in accordance with principles of fundamental justice. Furthermore, section 11(d) guarantees the presumption of innocence. On the other hand, there are good public policy reasons for limiting these rights where school children are potentially at risk, and section 1 of the *Charter* allows school authorities to create reasonable limits.

We would suggest that placing "short bounds" restrictions on students such as those used by the school in Saskatchewan may be an appropriate compromise, but this is far from definitive. There are a number of variables to be considered in each case, including the character of the students involved and the seriousness of the offence with which they are charged. Regardless of the manner in which schools deal with a particular case, it is important that school boards develop written policies for implementing discipline procedures so that the procedures can be defended under section 1 of the *Charter* as limits which are "prescribed by law." School boards should also be sensitive to the need for protecting the identity of young offenders wherever possible.

The meshing of statutes, regulations and policies was difficult even before the *Charter*. The additional challenge of the *Charter* in the discipline process has sent some educators scurrying for cover. However, the number of actual *Charter* challenges have been few. There is still time for the educators to put their own houses in order before the courts require them to do so. A careful in-house review of rules, procedures and penalties may prevent legal action and give educators a greater sense of being in control of their own destiny. Action is better than reaction.

# Notes

[1] There is some debate about whether the *Charter* applies to the private as well as the public sector but the majority of cases and academic comment suggest that it will only apply to agents of the state. This is also the literal reading of section 32 of the *Charter of Rights* which defines its applicatiuon.

[2] M.E. Manley-Casimir and T.A. Sussel, "The Supreme Court of Canada as a National School Board," *Canadian Journal of Education*, 11, 3 (Summer 1986): 313.

[3] *Zylberberg* v. *Sudbury Board of Education* (1986) 55 O.R.(2d) 749 (Ont. Div. Ct. ); rev'd October 3, 1988 (Ont. C. A.) [not yet reported].

[4] W. Mackay, "The Canadian Charter of Rights and Freedoms: A Springboard to Student Rights," *Windsor Yearbook of Access to Justice*, 4 (1984): 174. The exact elements of student rights change with the times. A boy recently won the right to wear earrings in school as the result of a Manitoba Human Rights Commission ruling. B. Gory, "School Lifts Ban on Earrings for Boys," *The Globe and Mail* (January 7, 1986).

[5] *Southam* v. *Hunter* (1984), 55 N.R. 241 (S.C.C.).

[6] *R.* v. *OAKS* (1985) 24 C.C.C. (3d) 321 (S.C.C.).

[7] H. Brun, "The Canadian Charter of Rights and Freedoms as an Instrument of Social Development," in C. Beckton and W. Mackay, eds., *The Courts and the Charter* (Toronto: University of Toronto Press, 1985), pp. 1-36. He emphasizes that the bulk of *Charter* cases have been litigated in Ontario.

[8] The trial division of the British Columbia Supreme Court has decided that local community standards are relevant to a consideration of lifestyle restrictions placed on a teacher. However, it is not yet clear whether this would be directly applied to an argument under section 1 of the *Charter*: see *Abbotsford School District 34 Board of Trustees* v. *Shewan and Shewan* (1986), 70 B.C.L.R.40 (S.C.T.D.) [This case is currently under appeal to the B.C. Court of Appeal].

[9] *Ontario Film and Video Appreciation Society* v. *Ontario Board of Censors* (1983), 147 D.L.R.(3d) 58 (Ont. Div. Ct.); aff'd. (1984), 5 D.L.R. (4th) 766 (Ont.

C.A.). This case insisted that a policy manual be written and made public before it could be used as a section 1 justification.

[10]M. Manning, *Rights, Freedom and the Courts* (Toronto: Edmond-Montgomery, 1983), pp. 168-192. He provides more detail on the American experience and its application to Canada.

[11]*Grayned* v. *City of Rockford*, 408 U.S. 104 (1977), at 108-109, per Marshall J.

[12]See *R.v. P.D.F.* (1987), 57 C.R. (3d) (Ont. Prov. Ct.).

[13]*Taylor* v. *Board of Trustees (Langley)*, (December 17, 1984) (B.C.S.C.); rev'd. *B.C.T. and J.T.* v. *Board of Trustees (Langley)* (1985), 65 B.C.L.R. 197 (C.A.).

[14]Both of these cases have been summarized by Judith Anderson. For a more thorough description see J. Anderson, "Board's Pupil Suspension Policy Declared Invalid," *Canadian School Executive*, 4, 8 (1985): 19-22; and "Pupil Suspension Policy Reviewed," *Canadian School Executive*, 5, 7 (1986): 18-20.

[15]There is some question as to the exact age at which a child is entitled to exercise *Charter* rights; this depends largely upon the nature of the right. For example, freedom of expression might only be available to high school students, whereas equality rights may be claimed by a disabled child at any age: see also Romulo Magsino, "Students' Rights in a New Era," *The Canadian School Executive* (November, 1983): 3.

[16]*Reference Re Section 94(2) of the B.C. Motor Vehicle Act* (1985), 24 D.L.R. (4th) 536 (S.C.C.).

[17]This is an argument that I have made elsewhere. W. Mackay, "Public Education in Nova Scotia: Legal Rights, Fleeting Privileges or Political Rhetoric" (1984), 8 *Dal. L.J. 137;* see also A. Wayne Mackay and Gordon Krinke, "Education as a Basic Human Right: A Response to Special Education and the Charter", in *Canadian Journal of Law and Society,* 2 (1987): 73.

[18]For a more detailed discussion see note 1.

[19]See *RE M.B.* (1984), 65 N.S.R. (2d) 181 (N.S. Fam. Ct.).

[20] *Mazerolle* v. *Keith Coughlan et le District Scholaire No.7* (1987), 83 N.B.R. (2d) 389 (N.B.C.A.).

[21]W. Mackay, *Education Law in Canada* (Toronto: Edmond-Montgomery, 1984), pp. 62-64. I discussed the topic of student records as one aspect of parents' rights. The possibility of using freedom of information statutes is also discussed here.

[22]E. H. Humphreys, *Privacy in Jeopardy: Student Records in Canada* (Toronto: OISE Press, 1980), explores some of these issues.

[23]R.S.C. 1980-81-82-83, c.110.

[24]R.S.C. 1970, c. J-3.

[25]This may seem obvious to some, however, in an American case, *Rellnier* v. *Lund* (1977), 483 F. Supp. 223 (U.S.Dist. Ct. Texas), an entire fifth grade class was strip searched to find an individual who had stolen three dollars. The search was ruled "unreasonable" by the court.

[26]*New Jersey* v. *T.L.O.* 105 S. Ct. 733 (1985).

[27] *R.* v. *JMG* (1986), 54 C.R. (3d) 380 (Ont. C.A.).

[28] A. Wayne Mackay "*R.* v. *JMG* Case Comment: Students as Second Class Citizens Under the Charter," (1987) 54 C.R. (3d) 390

[29] *R.* v. *Morrison* (1987), 35 C.C.C. (3d) 437 (Ont. C. A.).

[30] Lyman Robinson, "The Charter and Searches and Seizures in Schools," in T. Wuester and A. Nichools, *Education Law and the Charter of Rights and Freedoms* (Vancouver: B.C. School Trustees Association, 1986) pp. 90, 97.

[31] Robinson, p. 98.

[32] *People* v. *Overton* (1967), 229 N.E. (2d) at 598.

[33] *R.* v. *Heisler* (1983), 7 C.R.R. 1 (Alta. Prov. Ct.). This did not involve a locker search but it is a precedent for the illegality of dragent searches.

[34] For a thorough and thoughtful approach to all kinds of searches in schools see Charles Avery and Robert Simpson, "Search and Seizure: A Risk Assessment Model for Public School Officials," in *Journal of Law and Education*, 16, 4 (Fall 1987): 403.

[35] See *Tinker* v. *Des Moines Independent Community School District*, 21 L.Ed. (2d) 733 (1969), at p. 737.

[36] *Rothman* v. *The Queen* (1981), 59 C.C.C. (3d) 30 (S.C.C.).

[37] *R.* v. *A.B.* (1986), 50 C. R. (3d) 247 (Ont. C. A. ), at p. 258. see also Nicholas Bala, "Questioning of Young Suspects"(1986), in 50 C.R.(3d) 260.

[38] *R.* v. *H.* 43 Alta. L.R. (2d) 250 (prov.Ct.); Alta. Q.B. June 26, 1986 [unreported]: see *School Law Commentary*, 1, 1.

[39] Bala and Lilles, *The Young Offenders Act Annotated*,(Don Mills; Butterworths, 1986) cite *Ibrahim* v. *The King*, (1984) A.C. 599 (P.C. ) at p. 609 for this proposition.

[40] A.B. Ferguson and A.C. Douglas, "A Study of Juvenile Waiver," *San Diego Law Review*, 38 (1970).

[41] See *Y.O.A* section 56(6), c.32, s.38.

[42] In *R.* v. *H.[supra].*, four students confessed to having stolen a sum of money from a teacher. They were originally told that there would be no consequences if the money was returned. However, when the principal heard the confessions he called the police and the youths were charged with theft. The confessions were excluded and the youths consequently acquitted because the principal had not informed them of their rights pursuant to section 56 of the *Y.O.A.*.

[43] *Ingram* v. *Wright* 430 U.S. 651 (1977).

[44] A.W. Mackay, *Education Law in Canada* (Toronto: Edmond-Montgomery, 1984), pp. 83-85.

[45] See (British Columbia) *School Act Regulations*, B.C. Regulation 436/81, section 14; and (Newfoundland) *Schools Act*, R.S.N. 1970, c.346, s.84.

[46] R.S.N.S. 1967, c.81, c.99.

[47] *R.* v. *B.M.* March 19, 1985 (N.S. Fam.Ct.)

[48]Bill No. 76, 1st Reading April, 1985. It eventually passed all three readings and became law.

[49]*H. et al.* v. *Board of Education of the Shamrock School Division no.38 of Saskatchewan* (1987), 57 Sask. R. 188

[50]The sole ground relied on by the applicant was that the school board had acted in excess of the powers granted by s.91 of the *Education Act.* (see *H. et al., p.190*).

[51]*Re Peel Board of Education et. al.* (1987), 59 O.R. (2d) 654 (Ont. H.C.J.).

[52]*Re Peel Board of Education, supra.,* at p. 661. see also Judith Anderson, "Expulsion Hearing Contrary to Young Offenders Act," in *Canadian School Executive*, 7, 4, p. 23, at p.5.

# 5

# Not There Yet:
# Women in Educational Administration

*Beth Young*

In the past two decades, there has been an increased interest in the status of women in Canadian society and in the nature of women's participation in that society. Much speculation and rhetoric has surrounded and sometimes obscured the scholarly work and practical achievements in this area. Nonetheless, accomplishments there have been. And, there continues to be disturbing anomalies and frustrations. All of this holds true for the field of education and, specifically, educational administration.

## At Present

In the *Report of the Commission on Equality in Employment,* Abella expresses concern about the concentration of women in a relatively small number of occupations compared to the "heterogeneous occupational structure" characteristic of the male labor force.[1] This pattern is duplicated even within the dominantly female basic education sector. Abella notes that there are more women who hold administrative positions in the publicly funded, basic education sector than in most other areas. Even so, men hold a wider variety of positions related to teaching than do women, and men occupy those positions in greater numbers.

In 1987-88, nearly 20 percent of all principals and almost 25 percent of all vice-principals in English-speaking Canada were women.[2] The majority of these administrators were employed in elementary schools. While these figures represent slight increases over previous years, it must be remembered that about 60 percent of all full-time teachers are women. Viewed from this latter perspective, only 3 percent of the women teachers held positions as principals and vice-principals compared to 10 percent of the men teachers. Moreover, the representation of women in administrative positions decreases dramatically at the level of senior central office positions.[3] These data confirm that Abella's observations still hold true some years later.

Canadian women educators tend to be involved in providing instruction, managing classrooms, and making decisions with respect to individual students; but they are not involved in the management and policy-making that affect the world of the classroom. That is, women most frequently deliver rather than administer public school education. They occupy very few of the appointed positions that have been the principal organizational means of rewarding merit and cooperation; providing alternative challenges to those of classroom instruction; and offering formalized, substantive opportunities to make decisions and influence policy beyond the parameters of the individual classroom.

Nixon points out that this situation has been well known and thoroughly documented for some time.[4] People in positions of power and influence, not to mention academics, have stated their support for an "egalitarian ideal,"[5] but concrete progress has been slow. Explanations abound, but the question remains: "Given the attention over the last decade to the objective dimension of discrimination (i.e., the disparity in numbers), why has there been so little change?"

## In the Past

Reynolds emphasizes the importance of coming to understand the historical social processes through which women's and men's roles in education became defined.[6] She says that we should ask "not only why so few women have become school administrators, but how it is that this has happened."[7] Working from that perspective, some scholars have discussed the development of the conventional split between women in the classrooms (especially the elementary ones) and men in the administrators' offices.

Mah traces the development of the split in the late nineteenth century.[8] With the growth in population and the introduction of compulsory schooling, many teachers were needed. Women were increasingly available for those jobs, as they themselves demanded and were grudgingly allowed access to more education and were, at the same time, being relieved of various domestic duties (and of a significant social role) because of industrialization and technological advances. Women were also the logical candidates because teaching was regarded as a suitable role for them, while other options were opening up for men. Indeed, within the limited number of socially acceptable options, teaching did offer women some degree of independence, status and satisfaction. The pay remained low — lower for women than for men — but women were generally expected to move on to motherhood within a few years anyway. And, it was the very qualities of the good mother that were thought to make women the most suitable teachers for young children. Working with those children was preparing the women for their maternal role.

Danylewycz and Prentice caution against overly simplistic interpretations of the "feminization of teaching" during the nineteenth century, stressing the importance of taking into account "regional differences" and "ideological complexity."[9] They note that research which takes as its focus the experiences (expressed through their own writings) of the women teachers demonstrates the variety of experiences and tasks encountered, often in shockingly inadequate physical facilities. They stress, however, that teaching school did provide some Canadian women with a "liberating" opportunity to find employment on the western Canadian frontiers, and/or as a transition to other professional and political roles. Nonetheless, they document an overall pattern of increasingly segregated (by grade and lower pay) and externally controlled work for the women who were teaching in Canadian schools.[10]

Mah and Oseen describe the differential treatment of women teachers with regard to their behavior off the job, as well as on it.[11] While there were regulations about the behavior of men teachers, they were less restrictive than the attitudes and policies that governed women's participation in Canadian schools through the late nineteenth and first several decades of the twentieth century. For example, a woman's marriage was often grounds for dismissal from her teaching position (and, certainly, pregnancy was). Oseen points out that the Edmonton Public School Board maintained its (illegal) policy requiring women to resign continuing appointments upon marriage until World War II. At that time, faced with a challenge by three newly married women teachers — and in combination with a severe shortage of teachers — the school trustees reluctantly agreed to allow the married teachers to continue teaching.

Even so, the maternal, woman-as-nurturer image was used as an argument against women administrators. It was thought that women could not discipline older children, so they were not fit to teach older children or to manage schools. Meanwhile, as schools became more bureaucratized, the feminine virtue of compliance had made women good employees, while men chose occupations that afforded them more independence, status, and income. Those few men who remained in education were then especially valued as managers, exercising the necessary discipline and authority within the schools and relating to the influential (male) members of the community.

As Nixon puts it, "The tradition of women as teachers and men as principals and superintendents was well entrenched in Canada by the end of the nineteenth century."[12] Therefore, even during the expansionary decades of the 1960s and the 1970s, men were generally regarded as the most suitable candidates for administrative positions. Awareness of women's absence from such positions gradually increased, but the number of women holding administrative positions did not change appreciably.[13]

## Canadian Research and Publication in the 1980s

Canadians have contributed in significant ways to the writing and research about women in education. Canadian writers in the 1980s have brought various perspectives to their reviews of the existing theory and research related to the issue of women in educational administration. While much of the research surveyed in their reviews is American, some published Canadian work is included. In the following subsection, "Overviews," articles by Reynolds,[14] and by Gaskell and McLaren[15] offer a general introduction to research on "women in management" and on "women in Canadian education." Three reviews, by Swiderski,[16] Nixon,[17] Fullan[18] and his associates, address more specifically the question of "women in educational administration." The subsequent section, "Additional Canadian Research," presents some examples of Canadian research from the 1980s that were not included in the reviews just summarized. These studies do elaborate on some of the scenarios and issues described in "Overviews." The research was conducted in Ontario and in Alberta.

## Overviews

Reynolds offers us a feminist critique of the 1970s research related to women's careers in management and education.[19] She uses certain much-publicized recent books on women in management as examples of works that "do not seem to question the rules of the game by which the women they studied have played or even the rules by which they as researchers are playing," that accept conventional definitions of success, and that emphasize "fitting in" regardless of the costs to the women concerned. Reynolds contrasts those works — cast in what is often termed the "liberal feminist" mode — with the more radical approach of some subsequent works.[20] These latter writings introduce and argue for different values, such as the "ethic of caring," the engagement of the researcher with and for women, and the "outsider's" perspective on organizations. Reynolds suggests that research with this more radical orientation will ultimately benefit both women and men in education because it introduces a greater range of human values, experiences and organizational practices.

Reynolds points out, though, that "gender inequality will not disperse without struggle and that the processes that perpetuate inequity may be very difficult to see and even more difficult to change."[22] Gaskell and McLaren echo Reynolds sentiments.[23] They note that most "recent feminist thought suggests that a new synthesis needs to be created for everyone, a synthesis that allows both male and female experiences to be seen in their variety, to be valued, and most importantly, to be rethought."[23] They argue that both educational and feminist research share a concern with the linking of theory to practice, a commitment to "changing practice" for the better.[24] In spite of that compatibility, gender issues have achieved no prominence on the Canadian educational research/publication agenda. These authors speculate that the "continuing dominance of men in positions of authority in education" may partly account for the lack of attention to gender issues, in spite of the expressed concern and even commitment of individual men to such matters.[25]

Swiderski is pragmatically concerned with the entry, survival and advancement of women in educational administration.[26] She bases her article on data from Statistics Canada and on a review of some 40 articles.

With respect to the "entry" issue, she discusses three factors. She notes that sex-role stereotyping, if not as pervasive as it was two decades ago, still influences our images of women, their capabilities and their behavior. Existing studies also point to continuing discrimination against women in administrative roles, even in the face of research demonstrating that women are effective administrators. Finally, Swiderski asserts that women's own reluctance to apply for administrative positions is a major obstacle. She attributes this reluctance to a lack of self-confidence, "low expectations of success," and a lifestyle preference for classroom teaching because of its adaptability to domestic responsibilities. She cites the need for more female mentors, sponsors and role models for women; and also for awareness-raising, training and placement assistance.

Regarding the "survival" of those women who do enter administration, Swiderski comments on a number of personal and professional realities. She mentions the negative attitudes of colleagues — male and female — that women administrators may encounter. As well, many women face the necessity of juggling domestic and paid work responsibilities, even when they have supportive husbands. Then too, women encounter the difficulties of "fitting in" and gaining peer acceptance as women in a men's world. Swiderski recommends a planned and incremental task orientation, together with the recognition that an "outsider" perspective may promote development as an "androgynous" (situation appropriate rather than stereotypically masculine or feminine) administrator. As to advancement beyond entry-level administrative positions, Swiderski stresses the importance of sponsorship and access to largely or exclusively male networks. These are the keys to information and to the opportunity to display one's competence and develop additional skills.

In her article, Swiderski provides a comprehensive (and daunting!) checklist of the attributes and strategies that will enhance the probability of success (conventionally defined) for aspiring and practicing women administrators.[27] Among these are commitment, self-confidence, flexibility, good interpersonal and communication skills, appropriate academic credentials and a career plan. In addition, individuals should make their ambitions known, be "part of" their staffs, seek and sustain good contacts throughout the system, and volunteer for committee/task force/leadership training opportunities. Finally, women should be actively supportive of other women. Swiderski concludes that women require a combination of ability, desire and opportunity if they are to move in greater numbers into school administration and move on at all to senior administrative positions.

Nixon's framework is somewhat more theoretical and critical.[28] She classifies the literature as providing explanations based on an "equity through understanding" approach and on an "understanding discrimination" approach. She states that research within the former category was conducted with the belief that once the reasons for the small number of women administrators were uncovered, relatively superficial remedies could and would be instituted. She provides a historical Canadian perspective on the traditional split between women-as-teachers and men-as-administrators. She also cites the literature on socialization, the perceived "costs" of administration, women's "inadequate" professional preparation and experience, and the lack of female role models and mentors.

Noting that all these explanations and proposed remedies did not in fact result in any substantive changes to the numbers of women administrators, Nixon goes on to examine more directly the question of overt and covert discrimination.[29] She asserts that, while overt discrimination is no longer socially or legally acceptable, much more subtle forms of discrimination have become recognized as pervasive influences. She refers to theoretical models and standards in practice (for example, some stereotypical, competitively oriented notions of a good leader) that have been developed on the basis of conventional male experiences, then applied to women as the measures of their suitability for administrative positions. She suggests that, as a result of such complex and sometimes subtle factors, women have experienced "role, access and treatment discrimination."

In addition to the aspects of the problems described by Swiderski, Nixon mentions the influence of social reproduction on recruitment efforts, selection criteria, anti-nepotism policies, and the redefinition of positions. She observes, as well, the way in which role expectations operating as social constructions of reality may act to filter out some candidates. Not only are many women ignored or rejected because of the entrenched values, but women who do not accept those values are faced with rejecting the administrative opportunities that might be theirs within existing organizational frameworks.

Fullan, Park, Williams, and their research associates, Allison, Walker and Watson,[30] organize a review of the literature by decades, distinguishing between the work done in the 1970s and that of the 1980s. They divide the approaches taken in the 1970s into three categories: the "socialization and sex-role stereotyping studies," the "discrimination" approach and the "organizational research." They note that each approach has provided somewhat different explanations and remedies (cf. Swiderski's and Nixon's presentations).

Fullan et al. go on to identify the themes that have emerged in the work of the 1980s. They note an overall decrease in the volume of publications on the subject and an emphasis on strategies to "redress the imbalance" between the numbers of women and men administrators.[31] These authors observe that some research on the "experiences and attitudes of women administrators" has been done. They also note the emergence of a stronger "radical feminist" voice in approaches to the question of women in administration. It is this radical feminist critique that queries existing organizational arrangements, proposing alternatives that are based on values such as caring and collaboration, and incorporating a recognition of the need to achieve a better balance between paid work and "other" (personal, family, community) commitments.

Like Swiderski, Fullan et al. mention the "androgynous administrator" as a potentially helpful approach to the re-conceptualization of the able school administrator.[32] However, they recognize the limitations of that (essentially individualistic) proposal. They assert the need to re-think "the nature of educational organizations and their work arrangements" more generally.

Fullan and his associates move beyond Swiderski's orderly careerism and Nixon's radical pessimism to a hopeful assessment that change is occurring, albeit slowly.[33] And, they support their optimism by identifying some factors that will contribute to change. They argue that women's aspirations and expectations are increasing, that women have had the opportunity to develop leadership skills and capacities in recent years. The pool of well qualified women is larger than ever before. The statistics these authors cite indicate that there are more and more women in entry-level administration roles, and that these new women administrators are very different from their predecessors. Moreover, there is greater public and institutional concern about organizational hiring and promotion policies and practices, and the emphasis on "instructional leadership" in education will favor women with strong classroom and curriculum backgrounds. Finally, there will be openings because of the coming wave of retirements at all levels of education organizations.

Those authors are addressing themselves specifically to the situation in Ontario. While many of the same factors exist elsewhere in Canada, the particular socio-political contexts for those factors vary from province to province. Whether or not the insights of Fullan et al. have application outside Ontario is a significant question to carry into the 1990s.[34]

## Additional Canadian Research

Reporting on a poll of Ontario female public school administrators, Ridler observes that women teachers are taking leadership training and seeking out related volunteer activities in greater and greater numbers.[35] The respondents in this survey considered "demonstrated leadership in school-related activities" to be the most important factor contributing to their appointment as administrators.

Willis and Dodgson document the influence of mentors on the careers of Canadian women educational administrators.[36] During interviews, the study participants indicated that mentors had exerted a substantial influence on their careers, although the extent of that influence was only evident in retrospect. Participants said that mentors acted as role models, sponsors, teachers, guides and eventually, in many cases, friends. In turn, many of the respondents became mentors to other colleagues. The authors note that, when they presented these findings in workshops to senior administrators, many "had never really considered the potential in mentoring" as a form of human resource development for their school systems.

In her study of selected male and female principals employed by an urban Ontario school board, Reynolds uncovers differences and similarities in the experiences of those who began teaching before 1950 and those who began teaching after 1950.[37] All agreed that it was socially acceptable for them to become teachers and much less acceptable for them to be principals. They themselves had rarely encountered women principals. Indeed, the initial administrative appointments received by the women participants in this study were to "marginal" settings, such as vocational, problem, and all girls' schools, or the appointments were part-time or temporary.

Women from the earlier decade viewed it as a foregone conclusion that men would be the administrators. Those women did, however, receive encouragement to apply for administrative positions from male teachers and administrators. They received support in their teaching activities from their female teacher-colleagues, but were unable to find a comparable support group as principals because there were so few women in that role. Once appointed, they were initially doubtful of their ability to do the job and attributed their appointments to working hard and being "in the right place at the right time." They functioned as the "only woman" in their peer groups. They regarded career and marriage as two mutually exclusive directions in life: these women were single.[38]

Women in the post-1950s were more active about considering the possibility of an administrative appointment and seeking it out in the face of obstacles. They received encouragement for their administrative ambitions from male and female colleagues, family members and housekeepers. They saw their appointments as being linked to a change in societal attitudes, and they described the beginnings of women's support networks as part of their experience. Once appointed, they felt the pressure of being role models for other women. They also experienced guilt about their professional/family role conflicts even though these women were of varied marital and family status.

In a recent conference paper, Reynolds reviews a number of pertinent research projects done by graduate students in Ontario.[39] The projects include a school climate survey; a survey of perceptions about the administrator selection process; interviews regarding the barriers encountered and the coping strategies of some women administrators; and a comparative interview study documenting the attitudes and experiences of administrators, aspiring administrators and teachers who did not aspire to administration. This collection of studies shows that women and men often had different perceptions/experiences of school leadership, of the barriers to and sponsorship for promotion, and of coping strategies.

Reynolds also notes the existence of one study surveying and comparing several affirmative action programs.[40] As she correctly points out, much of the Canadian research related to the subject of women in educational administration is being done by graduate students. That work does enrich our understanding of the issues, but little of it sees the light of publication or any other form of widespread dissemination.

In a western Canadian M.Ed. project, Kimmel surveyed female school administrators in an Alberta school district regarding mentors.[41] Most of the respondents indicated that they had been assisted by one or more mentors (male or female), and that they in turn had acted as mentors to other women. Some respondents felt that formalized mentoring programs should be implemented, among other initiatives to promote employment equity.

Porat interviewed female principals in southern Alberta.[42] She describes the "haphazard" career development of the participants in her study, who tackled new tasks and positions for their intrinsic interest and potential to enhance personal and professional growth. These women focused initially on developing their expertise as classroom teachers and continue to focus (more than men principals, in their opinion) on classroom activity and people in their roles as principals. Porat notes the various problems cited by these women principals. She adds that "all women do not experience these problems in the same way," nor do they all indicate that they have experienced the same problems.

This theme of diversity is illustrated in a recent M.Ed. study by Warren on the role socialization of some women principals.[43] From her interviews with selected women principals and assistant principals in an Alberta school district, Warren draws out four themes. She notes the chance elements in the early career development of the women, up to and including their selection as school administrators. For some of the women, this stage was followed by an increasing realization of the need to plan ahead and make choices. Warren also observes a continuum: some women actively adapted to their administrative roles by "asking questions, seeking out strong mentors, joining networks and profiling themselves," while other women were passive and, consequently, isolated in their administrative roles.[44] There is a comparable continuum of "knowing and not knowing" their formal and informal organization at the district level.

Finally, Warren notes the key role of the school principal in encouraging administrative aspirations, providing prospective women administrators with opportunities to gain a wide variety of experience, and then writing positive recommendations.[45] The women in this study felt that the principals to whom they were assigned as assistant principals acted as influential role models and, sometimes, sponsors.

These women criticized their school district for failing to provide adequate training for neophyte administrators. They felt that the "system" was over-dependent on the informal socialization networks and processes to which the women often had limited access. Indeed, the participants in this study encountered all the negative effects of being a woman in a non-traditional role that have already been described in this chapter. Warren comments that, as she reflected on her findings, her first reaction was that "things had not changed much since I first entered administration 11 years ago."

My own recent study describes anecdotally the careers of some western Canadian women with doctorates in educational administration.[46] The life-story narratives illustrate the complex relation between choice, chance, and opportunity in career development. Readiness to capitalize on opportunities is an important feature of these careers. Some anecdotes also show the impact of chance (as defined by the study participants) remarks, of unexpected job openings, and of role re-definitions that fostered "widening horizons" for these women. There were also situations in which these women tested out certain types of jobs and decided they did not want them. As well, two women described organizations that were, for them, "nurturing environments," which provided a combination of support and challenge conducive to professional development.

With respect to our usual notions of a "career" and of "success," I made several observations.[47] The "competing urgencies" of paid work, academic studies (usually part-time) and family responsibilities are apparent in the lives of these women. Just as choice and chance are interwoven, so are the personal and the professional in these women's stories. The women are "late bloomers" according to traditional (male) career norms of achievement. They provide some models of "flexible success," which is characterized by interruptions in paid work, part-time paid work, fulfilling lateral moves, and slower hierarchical progression, if it occurs at all.[48] These women's stories show us ways to re-define certain key concepts that have traditionally been defined according to some men's experiences of careers.

## Proposals for Change

The research that has just been summarized has implications for organizational structures and practices, as well as for individuals. What follows is a synthesis of the recommendations for change that have been made by Canadian writers.

The recommendations fall into several categories. First, there are suggestions for actions that individual women might take in order to enhance their own careers and, if they aspire to them, to increase their chances of achieving administrative appointments within educational organizations as they are currently structured. Those recommendations have already been outlined in the summary of Swiderski's article. Then, there are suggestions for incremental changes in the policies and practices of organizations that will further enhance the opportunities for women to enter and achieve in administration. Finally, there are recommendations for a more radical conceptual and practical re-orientation that might encourage wider options for both women and men in the future.[49]

## Changes in the Policies and Practices of Organizations

(1) Offer awareness workshops/conferences for interested women teachers (prospective administrators) and for incumbent (male and female) administrators who set policy for and manage administrator selection processes.[50]

(2) Offer diverse and equitably distributed opportunities for both women and men to develop and demonstrate their talents. For example:

(a) Increase the use of task forces, cutting across organizational levels and bridging the isolation of individual teachers;

(b) Offer special assignments, "bridging appointments," acting positions, boundary spanning roles to promising individuals;

(c) Make the role of vice-principal a worthwhile training experience.

(3) Make principals aware of their key role in recruiting and developing potential administrators.

(4) Investigate/exploit the potential of mentors and mentoring programs. For example:

(a) Provide workshops on mentoring for senior administrators, and for interested women;

(b) Make systematic attempts to identify and reward individuals and groups who informally fulfill mentor functions;

(c) Establish formal mentoring programs.

(5) Institute an affirmative action program, with components such as awareness workshops, non-sexist language policy, a clear and sound promotion policy, incentives for women to take leadership training, and hiring targets.[51]

(6) Provide institutional support for women placed in positions through affirmative action, to reduce the effects of isolation and the resentment of colleagues.

(7) For all new administrators, offer a thorough program of orientation and inservice training. Such a program would reduce reliance on the informal network from which women are more often excluded than their male counterparts.

(8) Encourage the development of more "androgynous" administrators, women and men who exhibit a wider range of behaviors, whether they be stereotypically "masculine" or stereotypically "feminine" behaviors. The point is that the behavior is appropriate to the situation.

## Re-Orientation on a Wider Scale

(1) Redesign professional work to accommodate other dimensions and demands of life, especially as they relate to family and leisure. For example:

(a) The teaching day and year might be regarded as an enlightened norm because it permits the possibility of balancing professional and personal/family responsibilities. Seeking such a balance should not be regarded as an absence of true professional commitment;

(b) Priorities vary with the individual and throughout life. Organizational options could better accommodate these varying priorities. Well designed part-time and shared jobs could be made more widely available and accorded higher status. Re-entry after time out for child-bearing and care-giving should be made as easy as possible, given the social importance of such responsibilities. Moreover, "fast track" norms for the achievement of certain positions by certain ages should be scrutinized. Later entry into administration, for example, is another way to reduce the concurrent pressures of paid and family work to more sequential roles;

(c) Daycare centers could be set up in schools.

(2) Revise substantially our notions of what constitutes a "career" and of suitable roles for women and for men, thus increasing the options for everyone.

(a) A career might be defined as a series of paid work opportunities to apply what one has learned (from previous paid work, family, community, and leisure activities) in the past. "Success" then depends on access to interesting new opportunities that are not necessarily associated with upward mobility. Indeed, opportunities for varied assignments within any one formal role designation might be built in.

(b) Crossover assignments of men to positions traditionally held by women and vice versa would help.[52] In education, this might mean assigning more men to teach kindergarten and more women to administer high schools.

(c) Recognize experience in care-giving roles as good preparation for administrative work. Many of the skills acquired, such as juggling competing demands, negotiating, and nurturing are transferrable to the administrator's office.

(3) Re-structure governance and administration, at least at the school level. Rotate administrative jobs by electing or appointing administrators for

limited (and not immediately renewable) terms; use seniority as one criterion for selections. A more collaborative, less hierarchical, form of governance would result.

## Changing? The 1990s and Beyond

So much for what has been proposed, in various contexts, primarily by academics. What action has been and is being taken by practitioners? In 1986, the Canadian Education Association surveyed 255 school boards across Canada regarding their "programs and services . . . to women employees or women in the community."[53] Seventy-two school boards responded, with 42 of them describing such programs. The great majority of the programs mentioned in the Canadian Education Association report are located in Ontario and Quebec:[54] the report is a valuable compendium of formal initiatives. Meanwhile, these scenarios from four provinces depict some of the contrasting situations across English-speaking Canada.

### *Alberta*

In Alberta at the time of writing, there are very few formal initiatives underway. According to statistics provided by Alberta Education for the 1988-89 year, 28.6 percent of the province's assistant superintendents and 5.1 percent of the superintendents were women (all in small jurisdictions). So were 24 percent of the vice-principals and 16.5 percent of the principals. While all four categories show some increase, the most substantial change has occurred at the assistant superintendent level.[55] There are no systematic government initiatives related to this under-representation of women in the administrative ranks.

In early 1989, the Alberta Teachers' Association established a task force to "study the issue of women in administration and propose remedies for the situation."[56] The results of a questionnaire survey undertaken as part of the task force's mandate indicate that 5 percent of the school jurisdictions have an employment equity policy of some kind.[57] About one-third of the responding boards publish their procedures and criteria for administrator selection. The task force, struck in early 1989, reported to the ATA Provincial Executive Council in early 1990. It has recommended the establishment of a standing ATA committee, a conference and workshops on women in education, including administration. If the task force recommendations are accepted by the Annual Representative Assembly in March 1990, the ATA will then be urging school boards to find ways of increasing the number of women appointed to administrative positions.

### *Nova Scotia*

In Nova Scotia, statistics show that 75 percent of the province's educational administrators are male.[58] Approximately one of every five principals is a woman, as is one of every four department heads.[59] An Affirmative Action Directive to Nova Scotia School Boards was issued by the Minister of Education in 1984. It was largely ignored.[60] In 1988, the Minister of Education, the Nova Scotia Teachers' Union and the Nova Scotia School Boards' Association issued a joint statement urging the appointment of more women to administrative positions in education and proposing a program of affirmative action to achieve greater employment equity.[61] However, that proposal has not been systematically translated into formal initiatives at the school district level, nor has the government imposed any sanctions for non-compliance or provided funding for implementation.[62] Nova Scotia school boards apparently remain free to interpret or reject the joint proposal at their discretion.[63]

## British Columbia

In British Columbia, 1987 statistics indicated that 15 percent of the province's school principals were women.[64] Through the efforts of the British Columbia Teachers' Federation, issues relating to women in education were given quite a high profile in British Columbia education circles through the 1970s and early 1980s.[65] Nonetheless, in 1988, the Royal Commission on Education was moved to note the continuing under-representation of women in administrative positions. The Commission recommended that school boards and the Ministry of Education implement hiring practices that "give explicit attention and emphasis to the *potential* (my emphasis) appointment of females . . ."[66]

One response to this concern was an initiative undertaken through the Principals' Institute at the University of Victoria.[67] The Institute, under the directorship of Dr. Yvonne Martin and with funds made available from two provincial ministries, organized a conference on "Women in the Principalship." The conference had several objectives. The sessions were intended to raise the awareness and aspirations of the female participants regarding the principalship as a career option. As well, there were skill development sessions. Finally, it was hoped that women who aspired to administrative positions would find the seeds of a province-wide network at the conference.

Selected school districts in British Columbia were invited to propose an appropriately qualified nominee for the conference, based on stated criteria. While some districts did not respond to the invitation, many did — there were many more nominees than could be accommodated. The women who were then chosen to attend the conference reacted very positively to the experience, even though much needed "follow-up and support networks"[68] were not part of the overall scheme. Some of the conference participants have since been appointed to administrative positions. Plans were laid for two more regional conferences to be held in the fall of 1989.[69]

## *Ontario*

By contrast with the preceding scenarios, in Ontario, Ministry of Education policies regarding pay equity and employment equity have been introduced and are currently being implemented on a widespread basis.[70] Statistics indicate that 17 percent of the province's elementary school principals and 11 percent of the secondary school principals were women in 1987.[71] The Ministry has stated to the school boards that there should be a minimum of 30 percent women throughout all levels and types of jobs in Ontario school systems by the year 2000, and a target of 50 percent.[72] To this end, the Ministry established an Affirmative Action Incentive Fund, which has now been in existence for five years. Once a school board has adopted a general affirmative action/employment equity policy with respect to its women employees, money from the Incentive Fund is made available to assist with the implementation of the policy. The Equal Opportunity/Affirmative Action Unit of the Ministry of Education administers the program. While the Ministry has thus far provided incentives for boards to undertake affirmative action, it has not identified any sanctions for failure to achieve the desired objectives. Nonetheless, the scene is set for "employment equity/affirmative action . . . to be one of the most important issues that [Ontario] school boards have to deal with in the future."[73]

# Conclusion

This brief "Cross-Canada Checkup" on the status of women in educational administration illustrates a dominant feature of Canadian public education — variation from province to province. Given the legislative framework(s) for Canadian education systems, such diversity is hardly surprising. The *Canadian Charter of Rights and Freedoms* does provide one nation-wide thread in the education fabric. However, as Nixon points out, the Charter insists on formal equality[74] but does not deal with the question of substantive equality (or equity, as some would label it). Therefore, even the enforcement of the *Charter* (through court decisions, over a long period of years) is unlikely to erase provincial differences of approach to employment equity in education. The structures of opportunity for women educators will continue to differ from province to province and, no doubt, over time.

A concerted combination of scholarly work, practical initiatives, and inter-provincial communication among concerned individuals and groups is underway (for example, the Canadian Teachers' Federation annual Status of Women conference), but will likely take on a higher profile during the next decade. Educators in one province will naturally look to the experiences of their colleagues elsewhere in Canada as they negotiate and re-negotiate formal policies, organizational practices, and patterns of daily life. The danger is that the high sounds of rhetoric may be drowning out the silence of inaction in some provinces. Elsewhere, even the rhetoric sounds rather faintly.

Change is occurring, but at a distressingly slow rate in some parts of Canada. The question, even now, is this: Will the change consist largely of "fitting more women in" to administrative positions as they are currently structured? Or will the change involve the re-formulation of the structures themselves, introducing more humane, balanced options for both the women and the men educators in our Canadian schools?

## Notes

[1] R.S. Abella, *Report of the Commission on Equality in Employment* (Ottawa: Supply and Services Canada, 1984), p. 62.

[2] Statistics Canada, *Education in Canada: A Statistical Review for 1987-88* (Ottawa: Supply and Services Canada, August 1989), p. 197.

[3] Statistics Canada, p. 196.

[4] M. Nixon, "Few Women in School Administration: Some Explanations," *The Journal of Educational Thought*, 21, 1 (1987): 63-70.

[5] Nixon, p. 63.

[6] C. Reynolds, "The State of Research on Women in Education," *The ATA Magazine*, 65, 4 (1985): 44-46.

[7] Reynolds, p. 46.

[8] H. Mah, "Women's Struggle for Acceptance," *The ATA Magazine*, 65, 4 (1985): 20-24.

[9] M. Danylewycz, and A. Prentice, "Revising the History of Teachers: A Canadian Perspective," *Interchange* 17, 2 (1986): 135-146.

[10] Danylewycz, pp. 135-146.

[11] Mah, pp. 20-24; and C. Oseen, "Right to Both Husbands and Jobs Not Easily Won," *The ATA Magazine*, 65, 4 (1985): 26-27.

[12] Nixon, p. 64.

[13] K. Porat, "The Women in the Principal's Chair," *The ATA Magazine*, 65, 4 (1985): 10-15.

[14] Reynolds, pp. 44-46.

[15] J. Gaskell, and A. McLaren, "Introduction" in J. Gaskell and A. McLaren, *Women in Canada* (Calgary: Detselig Enterprises, 1988).

[16] W. Swiderski, "Problems Faced by Women in Gaining Access to Administrative Positions in Education" *Education Canada* (Fall, 1988): pp. 24-31.

[17] Nixon, p. 64.

[18] M.G. Fullan, P.B. Park, and T.R. Williams, with associates P. Allison, L. Walker and N. Watson, *The Supervisory Officer in Ontario* (Toronto: Ministry of Education, 1987).

[19] Reynolds, pp. 44-46.

[20] Reynolds, p. 45.

[21] Reynolds, p. 46.

[22] Gaskell and McLaren, "Introduction."

[23] Gaskell and McLaren, p. 11.

[24] Gaskell and McLaren, p. 13.

[25] Gaskell and McLaren, p. 14.

[26] Swiderski, pp. 24-31.

[27] Swiderski, p. 26.

[28] Swiderski.

[29] Nixon, p. 64.

[30] Nixon, p. 67.

[31] M.G. Fullan, P.B. Park, T.R. Williams et al., *Supervisory Officer.*

[32] Fullan et al., p.227.

[33] Fullan et al., p. 30.

[34] Fullan et al., p. 30.

[35] Fullan et al. p. 231.

[36] O. Ridler, "Women in Educational Administration: The Ontario Scene" *Orbit,* 15, 3 (1984): 10-12.

[37] H. Willis and J.Dodgson, "Mentoring of Canadian Women in Educational Administration," *The Canadian Administrator,* 25, 7 (1986).

[38] C. Reynolds, "Schoolmarms and Tokens," *Orbit* (February 1988): 5-7; and C. Reynolds, "Men and Women Principals," *Reporting Classroom Research,* 15, 3 (1986): 1-3.

[39] Reynolds, "Schoolmarms," pp. 5-7.

[40] C. Reynolds, "Man's World/Woman's World: Women's Roles in Schools" *Women's Education des Femmes,* 7, 3 (1989): 29-33.

[41] C. Reynolds, *Some New Directions for Research on Affirmative Action.* Paper presented at "Focus on Leadership" conference (Toronto, March 31, 1989).

[42] S. Kimmel, *Women in Administration: The Calgary Board of Education Story* M.Ed. thesis, University of Calgary (May, 1988).

[43] K. Porat, pp. 10-15.

[44] J. Warren, "The Role Socialization of Female School Administrators," unpublished M.Ed. thesis, University of Alberta (1989).

[45] Warren, p. 120.

[46] Warren, p. 131.

[47] B. Young, "Not Finished Yet: The Stories of Four Women's Careers in Education," unpublished Ph.D. thesis, University of Alberta (1989).

[48] Young, p. 226.

[49]These points are a synthesis of the comments and recommendations made in the literature that has aleady been reviewed in this chapter, except where an additional source is noted by a specific citation.

[50]M. Maloney, "Tapping the Potential Through Affirmative Action," *AVISO*, 3, 1 (1987): 9-10; and M. Nixon, "An Old Problem: Will New Approaches Come?" *The ATA Magazine* (March/April, 1989): 41-43.

[51]M. Maloney, pp. 9-10.

[52]R. Schlesinger, "Towards More Appropriate Roles for Women" *The Canadian School Executive*, 7, 9 (1988): 12-14.

[53]Canadian Education Association, *Especially for Women: Programs and Services Offered by School Boards* (Toronto: CEA, 1988), p. 5.

[54]Canadian Education Association, p. 5.

[55]Data provided by Dr. John Berger, Policy and Planning Secretariat, Alberta Education, in a private communication, November 6, 1989.

[56]A. Luniw, "Low Numbers of Women Administrators to be Examined," *The ATA News* (January 30, 1989): 3.

[57]Communication with Dr. John Berger, Policy and Planning Secretariat, Alberta Education, October 20, 1989.

[58]Maloney, pp. 9-10.

[59]A.L. Berard, "Redefining Role Models in School Administration," *AVISO*, 4, 1 (1988): 14-15.

[60]M. Maloney, "Guidelines Aren't the Answer," *AVISO*, 4, 2 (1989): 6.

[61]The Hon. R.C. Giffin, "A Message from the Minister," *AVISO*, 4, 1 (1988): 2.

[62]Maloney, "Guidlines."

[63]Communication with Dr. David MacKinnon, Acadia University, November 8, 1989.

[64]Private communication with Dr. Yvonne Martin, University of Victoria (statistics quoted from the Ministry of Education).

[65]See, for example, *The B.C. Teacher*, October/November 1984.

[66]Reported in Nixon, p. 41.

[67]Nixon, p.41.

[68]Nixon, p. 43.

[69]Private communication with Dr. Yvonne Martin, October 16, 1989.

[70]M. Pierce, "Employment Equity in School Boards," *Ontario Education*, 20, 2 (1988): 24.

[71]Ontario Ministry of Education, *The Status of Women and Affirmative Action/Employment Equity in Ontario School Boards: Report to the Legislature by the Minister of Education* (Toronto: Ministry of Education, 1988).

[72]Ontario Ministry of Education, "Foreword."

[73]Pierce, p. 24.

# 6

# The Re-introduction of Public Examinations in Alberta: School Context, Reasons, Implications

*Mathew Zachariah and Lorraine O'Neill*

A school teacher plays many roles in his or her professional life: representative of society (inculcates moral precepts); resource person (possesses and dispenses on personal knowledge and skills); referee (settles disputes among students); detective (discovers rule breakers); and role model (possesses traits which pupils may imitate).[1] These roles sometimes complement each other and, at other times, are in conflict. Sensitive, professionally competent teachers in Canadian schools are aware of two other roles that are almost always in conflict: nurturer (helps students develop confidence to master new subject-matter and develop new attitudes, values, etc.) and judge (gives marks and grades).

Canadian teachers sometimes envy teachers in other countries whose main responsibility is to prepare students "to sit for" examinations organized by other agencies (e.g., a ministry of Education) at the conclusion of one or two important grades (such as the examinations at the end of the "Sixth Form" in England or the "Tenth Standard" in India). Teachers in these countries also give tests and quizzes as well as conduct examinations for diagnostic and evaluative purposes. But, they and their students primarily focus on the "really big" examinations conducted by external authorities.

No one knows students better than their teachers. No one knows better than the teachers what and how they have taught the topics in the curriculum. If students know that their teachers will also be their markers, they will pay close attention to the teaching which can help improve both teaching and learning. These are only three of the arguments of those who maintain that teachers should be completely responsible for grading students in every grade of the school system.

If teachers are given complete responsibility for grading students, they may not be as conscientious in their work as when they know that a public examination will test their students and thus indirectly, the teachers themselves. Therefore, one or two strategically placed public examinations can help promote good teaching. Public examinations help provide a minimum standard that all schools in a province must meet. The results of such examinations provide a more objective measure of the academic competence of the most able, the average and the below average student than the idiosyncratic evaluations of teachers. These are only three arrows in the quiver of those who attack complete control by school teachers over tests and grades.

After 36 uninterrupted years of dominating Alberta politics, the Social Credit party was defeated in 1971 by the Progressive Conservative party led by Peter Lougheed. Recognizing the political significance of school education and the apparent public concern about the quality of schooling, the Lougheed government supported the continuation of the work of the Commission on Educational Planning. This commission was appointed by the previous Social Credit government in 1969 by an Order-in-Council under the *Public Inquiries Act* under the chairmanship of Walter H. Worth.

In 1972, the government of the province of Alberta published the Commission's report on the future of Alberta Education, *A Choice of Futures? A Future of Choices* — popularly known as the *Worth Report*. Among other things, the *Worth Report* set before Albertans the vision of a "person-centred society" and pleaded for a new direction for formal education to help bring about such a society. The Commission, for instance, endorsed wholeheartedly what it perceived as "the growing demand for personalized learning leading to self-actualization at all levels of recurrent education. . . "[2] Rod Evans rightly points out that the Commission report emphasized the leading part the educational system can play for bringing about significant changes in society instead of just reinforcing existing dominant values and beliefs.[3]

Public examinations tend to test students on information transmitted to them in books and by teachers who follow a traditional curriculum. Given the perspective of the *Worth Report,* we can understand why the second of the Commission's "top-ten" proposals was " abolition of grade 12 departmental examinations."[4] In 1973, the Government of Alberta abolished the grade 12 departmental examinations. (The grade 9 departmental examinations had been abolished in 1967. They were called " departmental examinations" because they were conducted by the provincial department of education.) Yet, in 1984, departmental examinations (to be defined in the next section as public examinations) were re-introduced as compulsory diploma examinations. Why were compulsory public examinations abolished in 1973? Why were they re-introduced in 1984? What does the concern for standards that led to the re-introduction signify for formal education? This essay will attempt to answer these questions. One of our major conclusions is that the compromise worked out in the mid-1980s was a very good one indeed.

## Preliminary Definitions

A 1985 Government of Alberta publication re-iterated the distinctions, as outlined in the *Junior/Senior High School Handbook* published earlier, between schooling and education as follows:

> While the goals of schooling outline the responsibilities of school staffs in promoting learning, the goals of education are a shared responsibility [of the community].[5]

A goal of schooling is to "develop competencies in reading, writing, speaking, listening, and viewing." Note the broader and general nature of a goal of education: "to develop intellectual curiosity and a desire for lifelong learning."[6]

Education is a very broad term. In its most general sense, it encompasses notions of *means* ("One needs education to get ahead in society"): *process* ("She is now learning to understand the concept of numbers without seeing objects"); *personal goals* ("With his Bachelor's degree, he has completed his education"); *social goals* ("We need to produce citizens who are familiar with computers"); and *interaction* ("I learn better with teacher X than with teacher Y"). For our purposes, let us define education as a life-long means as well as interaction by which more established members of a society *transmit* selectively the values, skills, attitudes and knowledge they deem important to newer members of that society. Those who acquire such education use the values, etc., sometimes to help *transform* themselves and their environment, including the more established members.

Some scholars and practitioners have distinguished between three types of education: informal, formal and non-formal education.[7] What distinguishes formal education (schooling) from informal (e.g., a mother teaching her baby to use a fork) and non-formal education (e.g., courses in " Art Appreciation," "How to Manage Your Money") is formal education's highly structured as well as hierarchical nature, its removal of knowledge from immediate contexts as well as uses, and its direct link with certification of immediate or (if there is further study) eventual employment.

## Schooling

Schooling for the masses is, in world history, no more than a century and a half old. Among other things, the major characteristics of mass schooling are:

(1) Age-graded classrooms:

(2) Separation of most knowledge from its immediate context thereby making it more abstract;

(3) The packaging and teaching of such knowledge in the form of discrete subjects or disciplines;

(4) The assessment of the acquisition of knowledge and skills by teachers or by external examiners;

(5) The open as well as hidden promotion of attitudes, beliefs and values approved by the dominant economic, political and cultural elites;

(6) A tendency to take over some of the functions of other social institutions (such as the family and the church); and

(7) The sorting, certifying and selecting of young people for future occupational and social roles.

Ideally, schooling should promote education both within and without schools. Yet, who hasn't heard comments such as these? "I have never let my schooling interfere with my education" or "Schooling prostitutes education." What these comments reveal is the tension between schooling and education. There have been persons such as Ivan Illich who, in *Deschooling Society* (1972), passionately argued for dismantling the institution of schooling, but they have been a small minority. Most of the practitioners of and writers on education have tried to reform schooling itself to foster genuine education. To do so, they have proposed that: pupil's interests be stimulated, their intrinsic motivation be harnessed, school hours and curricula be flexible, schools work closely with other social institutions, teachers be guides instead of imposers of knowledge, assessment focus not on externally imposed criteria but on the progress the pupil has made in comparison to his or her own past achievement, and that the link between schooling and employment be broken.[8] Such proposals have implications for other aspects of schooling: for example, such innovative flexibility means educational administration needs to be decentralized and that schools must share their power with other social institutions.

Although the *Worth Report* did not recommend deschooling Alberta society, its vision of a "person-centred society" and many of its recommendations revealed that it accepted some criticisms of deschoolers and also shared the temper of the sixties. It wished to promote personally liberating and socially unifying education within schools.

## Public Diploma Examinations

Assessment is necessarily an inherent part of any type of teaching and learning. Formative assessment takes place in the course of school teaching and is concerned with whether the teacher is effectively communicating knowledge, skills, values, etc., and whether the pupil is learning such knowledge, skills and values at the requisite pace and depth of understanding. Summative assessment differs from formative assessment in two respects: as the term itself implies, it occurs at the conclusion of a unit or course of study and the emphasis is almost exclusively on the pupil. Examinations are, almost always, formal summmative assessments. As Patricia Broadfoot points out, examinations perform three functions for schools: they *attest* that the pupil has (or has not) attained a particular standard; *predict* the pupil's probable future performance; and, *evaluate* him or her in relation to the achievement of comparable peers.[9]

Public examinations are even more formal assessments. By way of evidence for this greater formality, we may note three points: pupils become candidates for such examinations; elaborate and strictly enforced rules surround the conduct of the examinations; and, typically, the examiners are not the teachers. The departmental examinations (until 1973) and the current diploma examinations of Alberta are public examinations as defined above.

## Comprehensives

Comprehensive examinations, a volatile topic at the beginning of the 1980s, were to be part of a major evaluation program announced by Education Minister David King in the fall of 1980. Scheduled to begin in January of 1983 and to be administered province-wide to grade 12 students, they were intended to certify the degree of academic achievement attained by "well-motivated" and "achieving" students in four major discipline areas (language arts, mathematics, history and the social sciences, and the physical and biological sciences). King argued that comprehensives would provide a broader range of evaluations for the use of employers and post-secondary institutes. Unlike the old departmental examinations, compulsory until 1973, comprehensives would be optional and provide students passing them an additional credential — a Comprehensive Education Certificate Content Test would be cumulative, covering curricula through grades 10 to 12.

## The Abolition of Public Examinations in Alberta in the Late 1960s and 1970s

In Alberta, the question of how student progress should be evaluated has been an increasingly controversial issue. Perceptions about changes in Alberta society fuelled the controversy. The 1959 *Report of the Royal Commission on Education in Alberta* — known as the (Donald A.) *Cameron Report* — cited the changing role of the farmer, for example, to manager, businessman and expert. He needed specialized knowledge in science, mechanics and business. Rapid technological changes meant that agriculture would require fewer but better educated people in the future. The report pointed to the shift in occupations from unskilled labor, as required in many aspects of coal mining, to more highly trained workers in the growing oil and gas industry. Representative sampling of Alberta manufacturers indicated a further demand for highly skilled workers and managers. The business sector had complained loudly to the commission that many of their new recruits were deficient in communication and computational skills.

The general public had a perception that schools were emphasizing social adjustment and personal achievement in terms of peers at the cost of intellectual training and excellence based on set standards. More women were entering the working world and the educational system needed to respond to their needs, said the *Cameron Report*.

In formulating a response to these changes, the *Cameron Report* had to balance three considerations: the central importance of teachers in the educational system, the demand for "good products" (namely, qualified, committed, future workers) and the fact that a compulsory, tax-supported, school system catering to almost all the children in the province could not promote only a narrowly academic curriculum.

The *Cameron Report*'s recommendations took cognizance of these three considerations. Its four recommendations were:

(1) Improve the qualifications of future teachers;

(2) Increase the salaries of qualified teachers to encourage higher professional, committed behavior;

(3) Promote in schools a deeper study of basic subjects such as English, mathematics, science, social studies and other languages, especially French; and

(4) Recognize and provide for the wide range of interests and capacities of pupils with appropriate curriculum and teaching methods.

The subsequent discussion and selective implementation of the *Cameron Report*'s recommendations tended to emphasize (1), (2) and (4).[10] The Alberta Teachers' Association was probably very influential in this development as the ATA sought for higher recognition as a professional organization. The abolition of grade 9 departmentals in 1967 was an outcome of such an emphasis. Grade 12 compulsory examinations hung on until 1973.

The 1960s were a period of great economic growth in Alberta. The government had veritable *embarras de richesses*. Unemployment was mainly sectoral and marginal; indeed the economy needed more people. People were attracted to Alberta both from within Canada and elsewhere. The sixties was also a period which saw the emergence of human capital theory: it viewed formal education as transforming people into human capital by embodying in them knowledge and skills that can promote economic growth.[11] The human capital theory strengthened the voices of those who argued that schooling was promoting economic growth directly and indirectly and that, therefore, it ought to receive more priority in state funding. The Commission on Educational Planning, which began work in 1969, shared in this very positive evaluation of the good effects of formal schooling as is evident in its publication known also as the *Worth Report*.

Curiously, the *Worth Report*'s central theme took for granted that economic expansion was likely to continue indefinitely in Alberta. Since Alberta was assured of abundant wealth, it seemed to say, we could create a new caring community in which persons could pursue the unprecedented flowering of the human spirit. The *Worth Report* was infused with an optimistic belief in the possibility that human beings can create new, humane institutions. It argued that Alberta society ought *not* to strive for second-phase industrial society characterized by conformity, puritanism, material acquisitions, hierarchical structure, authoritarian relations, competition and values about exclusive ownership of resources. Instead, the people of Alberta should work toward a society where individualism, sensualism and flexible structures would promote equal relationships, cooperation and values about social ownership of resources.[12] We are unable to offer a convincing explanation for a Conservative government supporting a commission that produced the *Worth Report* with its humane, radical (almost socialist) viewpoint. ("The temper of the times" is a general, if vague, explanation. That temper was reflected in the Hall-Dennis Report, *Living and Learning* (1968), sponsored by another Conservative government in the province of Ontario).

Soon after the publication of the *Worth Report*, openly or quietly, individuals and groups expressed criticism of its perspectives and specific recommendations: for example, Alberta's university spokesmen vigorously opposed the unflattering comments about universities in it.[13] The *Worth Report* did not result in many significant changes in Alberta's educational system. But, it can claim one unqualified success: in 1973, compulsory departmental examinations were abolished in Alberta. Specifically, in 1973, the Department of Education announced that every "qualified" senior high school in Alberta was to be accredited to assign final marks in all courses for all student, and that the grade 12 government examinations would no longer be compulsory.

## The Reaction

In retrospect, it is clear that the *Worth Report* was not representative of the views of the majority of Albertans or of the government in power. Barely three years after the abolition of the grade 12 public examinations, observers noted the beginnings of a "Back to Basics" movement.[14] Many factors contributed to this reaction in the later 1970s which became very pronounced in the early 1980s.

### External Factors

There were three very important factors external to the school system. First, there continued to be economic expansion but its rate had decreased.[15] At about the same time, enrolment in schools began to decline,[16] stimulating governments to seek ways to curtail burgeoning education budgets.[17] Second, the phenomenon of unemployment among youth, a persistent long-standing problem in many other parts of Canada and the world, became a reality in Alberta too. Third, the public perception that standards in schools had worsened continued to persist. Reporting on the results of a Gallup Poll undertaken in April 1979, the Canadian Education Association Task Force on Public Involvement in Educational Decisions, in its first Report noted:

> There should be widespread concern on the part of educators that according to several categories of the total sample, the standard of education has worsened. This attitude may be a continuing feeling, originating in the back-to-the-basics movement, that school graduates are incapable of writing clear prose or performing straightforward mathematical computations. Then again, this opinion may be substantiated by evidence of lack of competence by school graduates in work situations![18]

It might be appropriate to note that a similar 1984 poll showed virtually the same results: in 1984, 34.1 and 38.7 percent of the sample for all of Canada had opined that standards had improved or worsened respectively; in 1979, the respective percentages were 36.3 and 40.0.[19] In the prairies, the percentages of those who believed that standards had improved or worsened were almost the same in 1979, but in 1984, 38.4 percent of the sample had opined that standards had improved. In contrast, 33.4 percent believed them to have become worse. Yet, the back-to-the-basics movement was gathering supporters in the prairies too.

It is noteworthy that the gathering storm against a lack of standard did not find expression in all important documents of the period. The 1975 Organization for Economic Cooperation and Development (OECD) *External Examiner's Report on Educational Policy in Canada* devoted some 67 out of a total of 334 paragraphs to the topic of equal educational opportunity in schools, but not one paragraph exclusively focused on evaluation (let alone public examination) of pupils.

Indeed, even in 1980, Arthur Kratzmann, Timothy C. Byrne and Walter H. Worth in their report "born of a collective bargaining dispute between the Calgary Board of Education and its teachers"[20] — entitled *A System in Conflict* — emphasized almost exclusively process variables in school teaching and learning: "the quality of education is a product of the relationship between a student and his teacher," they quoted with approval.[21] The evaluation of students was barely touched. But others, particularly Peter Lougheed, the Premier of Alberta, began speaking publicly and often about the necessity to redefine the goals of Alberta's educational system and to end the Legislature's traditional abdication of the topic.[22] One concrete outcome of the government's concern was the 1976 formation of the Minister's Advisory Committee on Student Achievement (MACOSA) by Lougheed's Minister of Education, Julian Koziak, to advise the Minister on appropriate action to be taken.[23]

## *School System Factors*

Let us begin with historical factors. In Alberta — as in all the other provinces — governments have controlled and regulated curriculum and conducted public examinations for a long time.[24] The late George S. Tomkins, perhaps the foremost scholar on curriculum policy in English Canada said:

> The thrust towards curriculum centralization that was so apparent across Canada by 1980 could be viewed as representative of the normal state of affairs, with the decentralization of the preceding fifteen years viewed as aberrant.[25]

Evidence, particularly from the United States, pointed clearly to the fact that schools, by providing equality of opportunity, cannot overcome inequality of conditions (e.g., in the home background) and cannot ensure equality of results that a true meritocracy promises (because, for instance, of the leverage that upperclass parents can exercise to get the best jobs for their children). To conservative educational theorists, this was a matter of *deja vu*. Liberal and radical theorists concluded from such evidence that inequality in society must be confronted much more directly, and some of them rediscovered the importance of schools equipping children from economically poor (or otherwise disadvantaged) backgrounds with basic skills with which they can compete for available jobs.[26] Thus, the *provision* of and *access* to equal educational opportunity emerged again as policy objectives at the cost of emphasis on background *conditions* and equitable *results*.

The clamor that school systems be more accountable for their performance to the taxpayers who foot the bill was also a factor. If schools would only delete irrelevant frills, the argument went, and emphasize the fundamentals (e.g., the four Rs: Reading, 'Riting, 'Rithmetic and Right Conduct) we could get a better education for lower costs.

B.T. Keeler, Executive Secretary of the ATA, referred to another factor:

> The argument runs as follows: since the demise of departmentals, there has been "grade inflation" (a higher proportion of passing marks in grade 12 subject . . . departmental examinations were good predictors of university success and the teacher-assigned grades lack this predictive ability.[27]

Keeler cited a University of Alberta study to show that such assertions were unfounded. We will mention two of the six findings. Grade inflation had not increased the number of persons pounding the gates of universities for entrance; indeed the percentage had dropped from 40 to 22. There was "a higher correlation in 1977 between matriculation grades and university grades than . . . when departmental examinations were used."[28] Such evidence notwithstanding, there was a widespread view that students entering post-secondary institutions were not as well-prepared as earlier.

A final factor was the desire to identify and encourage intellectually gifted children within the public school system. There was widespread perception, based on documents such as the IEA (International Association for the Evaluation of Educational Achievement) studies on mathematics achievement in the 1980s, that the public school system was not challenging the most intellectually gifted children in Canada to do their best.[29] Many concerned individuals asserted that the lack of challenge was frustrating to these students and that their inadequate intellectual development in schools was a loss to society.

One MACOSA (mentioned earlier) study addressed the question: What has happened to the quality of education since compulsory grade 12 examinations were dropped in 1973? The study by F. Dumont concluded that schools across the province were employing widely differing criteria and standards, that during the period 1973 to 1977 students had been getting noticeably higher grades ("grade inflation") and that "the general feeling was that achievement in mathematics and science has remained constant or had improved, but . . . achievement in English was lower." The study also noted the superintendents' claim that the public had little confidence in education, especially regarding basic skills . . ."[30] The committee (MACOSA) advised that achievement tests be developed using a matrix sampling procedure to establish benchmarks and that the mandatory departmental examinations not be re-implemented.

## The Harder Report

The Government of Alberta's first clear signal of a change in school policy could not have been more different from the *Worth Report*. The *Worth Report* was the culmination of millions of dollars worth of expenditure. Its tone was messianic; its recommendations were sweeping. The 325+ page document was printed on art paper in all the colors of the rainbow. In contrast, Jacob Harder's "Alberta Education and Diploma Requirements: A Discussion Paper for the Curriculum Policies Board" (revised Fall 1977) was a 68 page dry-as-dust technical document printed on ordinary yellow office paper. Yet, it had apparently created something close to apoplexy among several influential members the Alberta Teachers' Association.[31] Rod Evans observed that "the emergence of the *Harder Report* provides evidence that the liberalism and progressivism of Worth is under serious challenge by those elements in society who reserve for education far more passive and conservative expectation."[32] Of the *Harder Report*'s 10 recommendations, numbers 4, 5, 6 and 7 anticipated the policies implemented with some modifications in 1984. They were that: systematic monitoring be carried on in all school systems; four check points be mandated . . . at the end of grades 2, 5, 8 and 11; students must pass competency levels and if they do not pass, their advancement be delayed until, with special attention, they achieve competency; and the option program become more restrictive in favor of compulsory electives.

In the wake of the *Harder Report*, the criticisms of public examinations that appeared in professional publications repeated many of the arguments presented in 1960s for their elimination: that such examinations discriminate against the working class and favor the middle class pupils; that they do not measure significant and valuable learning; that they do not predict future academic or occupational success with any degree of precision; that they create unnecessary anxiety among teachers and students, and that the extreme expenditure incurred in conducting them could be put to better use in the schools.[33] Suggested better uses included the development of diagnostic tests, useful tools in the teaching-learning process and a test item bank made available to teachers. The government meanwhile was concerned about quelling public discontent over falling standards aroused by regular media reference to the business sector's complaints about ill-prepared new employees. In the fall of 1980, Education Minister David King announced a major evaluation program, the first phase of which was to include achievement tests, diagnostic tests and optional comprehensive examinations to evaluate students at the end of their high school careers. Further phases would also evaluate teachers, school systems and programs over a five to six-year period.[34]

The proposed program received accolades from significant segments of Alberta's post-secondary system. But it aroused heated debate at the ATA's Annual Representative Assembly (ARA) in the spring of 1982. Arguments that the government would undermine teacher autonomy, lead to test-oriented courses, and could be the first step toward mandatory departmental examinations, formed the basis on which a resolution was passed that year that the Association oppose the administration of the exams under their proposed format (i.e., comprehensive in nature and optional).

On Thursday, November 11, 1982, the ATA publicly announced its position. Within an hour after the announcement, the Minister's office responded which ended with a six-page statement ending with a definitive edict: "The comprehensive examinations will be used in January 1983." King accused the ATA of using "students — and the future of students — as a weapon" in abandoning the cooperative model for a confrontational model while failing to appreciate the need to establish the grounds for public confidence in the quality of education.[35] Determined not to be outmaneuvered, the teachers' provincial organization was committed to demonstrating its cohesiveness and strength of purpose.

Arthur Cowley, ATA president, commented that "the comprehensive examinations as currently conceived are an insult to the professional integrity and competence of teachers." He criticized the whole idea of external examinations declaring the "evaluation should be a part of the educational process and not independent of it."[36] Comprehensives covering subject matter from grades 10 through 12 would be unfair to students transferring to Alberta schools from outside the province. Additionally, an accurate assessment of the students' learning would not be possible because, Cowley argued, "the examinations cannot measure the human development component that the Alberta curriculum has contained for many years." Furthermore, the raw scores which would be recorded on the students' transcripts would serve little purpose. The teacher who taught them would be the most competent judge of students' progress in all aspects of the curriculum. Cowley concluded that "if teachers need assistance with implementing this function, then it is the responsibility of Alberta

Education and school boards to provide the opportunities for such inservice education."[37] The Edmonton Public School Board supported the ATA's resolution by recommending that boards in the province boycott the examinations set for January and June of 1983.

At their fall convention, the Alberta School Trustees (ASTA) added further support to the teachers. The trustees' concern with the comprehensive centered on who should take them and what bearing they should have on a student's final transcript. Although ASTA had consistently supported mandatory examinations for *all* grade 12 students, they opposed "voluntary testing of the top 30 to 50 percent of students" on the grounds that such "does not appear to meet the public's concern or wishes."[38] The trustees passed a resolution to urge the government to defer the program "until a clearly stated rationale is developed and appropriate examinations prepared."[39] Such a delay would provide time to prepare an alternative program.

Opposition by the ATA, the Conference of Alberta School Superintendents (CASS), the Alberta School Trustees Association (ASTA), and the Edmonton Public School Board posed a formidable barrier to the implementation of King's student evaluation package without serious revision.

In a statement released in December 1982, King reiterated that the optional exams scheduled for January and June of 1983 would proceed. However, he indicated that a revised mandatory comprehensive examination program would be announced in the spring of 1983.[40] That same month the Provincial Executive Council (PEC) of the ATA established the ATA's Task Force on High School Student Evaluation to make a major review of the Association's position on high school student evaluation. By spring 1983, the Task Force presented its findings to PEC. Several recommendations were developed based on the apparent consensus of opinions. They were that examinations should:

(1) Be specific to the course offered at the grade 12 level;

(2) Count for up to one-half of the students' final mark;

(3) Be restricted to language arts, social studies, mathematics and science;

(4) Provide a basis for making comparisons of students marks; and

(5) Provide a means of assuring that students who receive a diploma have attained a level of competence in the basic skills (reading, writing and computation).

The High School Diploma Examination Program was the final product conceived as the best resolution of this contentious issue in that it recognized the right of the government as representative of the public to monitor the effectiveness of the educational system and met the government's need for a system of public accountability. At the same time, the program gave provincially administered examinations more meaning since they could be used for more than just benchmaking purposes.

The ATA scored a decisive victory in blocking optional comprehensives. When presented to the Education Committee of the Government Caucus, the Task Force recommendations received wide support. Education Minister, David King, announced the new student evaluation program on May 31, 1983 — called High School Diploma Examinations — which was implemented in January 1984.

The examinations are conducted in Grade 12, three times a year because of the semester time-table. The students are examined in English 30, English 33, Social Studies 30, Mathematics 30, Biology 30, Chemistry 30 and Physics 30. The examination format is predominantly multiple choice. The exceptions are the examinations in English 30 and 33 where students are required to write essays.

Since 1984, the transcripts for regular students have carried the results of the diploma examinations, the teacher assessments and a "blended" grade. The "blended" grade gives equal weight to the diploma results and the teacher assessment. Mature students have the option of their transcripts recording either only the diploma examination results or the blended grade as defined above. To receive credit, a student must make at least 50 percent as a final mark in a course (in line with an earlier revision of the criteria of 40 percent for passing a course).

Alberta Education from 1984 on has taken the responsibility for issuing high school diplomas. (This responsibility, we may recall, had been transferred to "qualified" senior high schools in 1973.)

# Impact of the Re-introduction
# of Public Examinations on Schools

Monitoring of pupil achievement by external agencies has resulted in a number of changes in school policies and practices in other places. In the absence of research information on Alberta, we may extrapolate these findings for the province. (Several Alberta school teachers have affirmed — on the basis of their observation and experience — that the following five changes have occurred in Alberta also.)

In the senior grades, teachers have changed their teaching procedures and strategies to emphasize formal tests and examinations. In other words, the emphasis has shifted from process variables in teaching and learning to product variables to some extent. During the teaching act, teachers may tend to devalue the natural motivation of pupils ("I won't be able to complete this topic if I discuss your question") and heavily promote extrinsic motivation ("you will appreciate this later"). Teachers have perceived a necessity to assign more "homework" to pupils to ensure minimum competence in basics. There has been an increase in the tendency to emphasize criterion-referenced tests (i.e., established standards of competence constitute the yardstick) more often than norm-referenced tests (i.e., the performance of one individual is compared to the performance of others in similar situations). Teachers often promote memorization at the expense of demonstrating understanding through relationships or application.[41]

Public examination results appear to have increased the awareness of the public about differences in modal scholastic achievements for different schools. The partial separation of the teaching and evaluation functions has probably prodded lazy teachers to be more effective in the classroom since the results of public examinations inevitably raise public questions about the standards of teachers and schools. Such separation can, on the other hand, reduce pressure on conscientious, sensitive teachers who often find it difficult to manage their roles as both nurturers and judges, since anonymous persons become partly responsible for the latter role.

However, public examinations do give the public the message that teachers and schools are being asked to be publicly accountable. The public, while acknowledging the inevitable elitism of public examinations, generally supports them because "they are also one of the principal bastions of egalitarianism (in an unequal and competitive society) by providing for equality of opportunity and a much fairer basis for selection than that of family wealth and nepotism which they have typically replaced."[42]

## Conclusion

There are school systems in many parts of the world — for example, in India and Japan — where compulsory, public examinations completely dominate the content of the curriculum, the teaching strategies and teacher-pupil relations throughout the school years.[43] The joys of innovation, discovery and intrinsic motivation are difficult to promote in such systems. On the other hand, the assertion that entrusting to teachers the complete responsibility for pupil evaluation results in some deterioration of discipline and standards is, in our view, valid. The ideal resolution is to ensure that teacher assessment and public examinations complement each other and are included in the evaluative statements about pupils. Alberta now has such a policy (50 percent for diploma examinations; 50 percent for teacher assessments and a blended grade).

One important distinguishing characteristic of formal education, let us recall, is its link through certification to future jobs. There is no likelihood — in Alberta or elsewhere — that the link will be severed in the near future. In this context, large sections of the population are likely to view public examinations as legitimate and credible ways to assess what pupils know. Such perceptions become quite credible as research data reveal the very low scholastic achievement in some subjects of North American children and youth in contrast to students in places such as Japan and Taiwan. Such perceptions also take on a sense of urgency when our children have to compete with children from other countries in the "global marketplace" in the coming decades.

Do public examinations tend to undermine — instead of complement — the relationship between schooling and education? The answer is a qualified "yes." Schools generally reflect and reinforce existing socioeconomic relationships; they cannot take the lead in reconstructing society. Unless the nature of the economy and politics changes significantly, the nature of schooling will not change. Therefore, in Canada and other areas of the world where some form of centralist tradition in education exists, public examinations are here to stay.

## *Notes*

[1] Roland Meighan, *A Sociology of Educating* (London: Holt, Rinehart and Winston, 1986), pp. 39-40.

[2] Alberta, *A Future of Choices, A Choice of Futures*, report of the Commission on Educational Planning, Walter H. Worth (Commissioner) (Edmonton: L.S. Wall, Queens Printer, 1972), p. 229. See also, *Worth Report.*

[3] Rod Evans, "The Pendulum Swings," *ATA Magazine*, 59, 3 (March, 1979): 8-11.

[4] *Worth Report*, p. 300.

[5] *Worth Report*, p. 5.

[6] *Worth Report*, p. 43.

[7] Phillip Coombs and Manzoor Ahmed, *Attacking Rural Poverty: How Nonformal Education Can Help* (Baltimore: Johns Hopkins University Press, 1974), p. 8.

[8] See Mathew Zachariah, "Standards in Education: A Plea for a Broader Perspective," *Loyola Journal of Social Sciences* (India), 1, 1 (July, 1987).

[9] Patricia Broadfoot, "Comparative Perspectives on the Reform of Examinations" in Keith Watson, ed., *Issues in Education* (London: Croom Helm, 1987) p. 8.

[10] Lorraine R. O'Neill, "Findings and Impact of Two Royal Commissions on Education: Alberta 1959: British Columbia 1960," unpublished paper, Robin Martin, ed. (1986).

[11] Mathew Zachariah, "Lumps of Clay and Growing Plants: Dominant Metaphors of the Role of Education in the Third World," *Comparitive Education Review*, 29, 1 (February 1985).

[12] *Worth Report*, p. 32.

[13] See also Zachariah, "Is There a Plan" in "A "Choice of Futures," *Journal of Educational Thought*, 7, 2 (August 1973): 121-127.

[14] K.M. Kryzanowski, "The Pendulum Swings," *ATA Magazine*, 58, 1 (1977): 407; and Fred Whitworth, *Basic Education and Much More* (Ottawa: The Canadian School Board Studies Trust, 1977).

[15] Jaques Bernier and George S. Tomkins, eds., *Curriculum Canada II* (Vancouver: Centre for the Study of Curriculum and Instruction, 1980), p. 32.

[16] Margaret Gayler, *A Review of Canadian Education*, 2nd edition (Toronto: The Canadian Education Association, 1978).

[17]Bernier and Tomkins, p.32.

[18]Canadian Education Association, "Speaking Out: The 1984 Poll of Canadian Opinion on Education," results of a poll conducted March/April 1984 by the Canadian Gallup Poll Ltd. under the direction of the CEA (Toronto: CEA, 1984), pp. 58-59.

[19]Canadian Education Association, p. 27.

[20]Arthur Kratzmann, Timothy C. Byrne and Walter H. Worth, *A System in Conflict*, a report to the Minister of Labour by the Fact Finding Commission (Edmonton: Alberta Labour, 1980), p. 1.

[21]Kratzmann, p. 4.

[22]Kryzanowski, p. 40.

[23]*ATA News*, 17, 5 (November 8, 1982): 4.

[24]P.J Atherton, P.J Hanson and J.F. Berlando, *Quality Education, What Price?* research monograph no. 16 (Edmonton: Alberta Teachers' Association, 1969), p. 39.

[25]Tomkins, p. 151; and Andrew S. Hughes, "Curriculum 1980: The Centralization of Authority," in Bernier Tomkins, *Curriculum Canada II*, p. 23.

[26]"In short, our school system neither levels nor educates The two objectives, egalitarianism and intellect [should] be separated, and that the schools be left free to address . . . intellectual concerns while the state attacks inequality more directly." Christopher Lasch quoted in University Council of British Columbia. Ad Hoc Committee on Accessibility to Post-secondary Education, *Report*, (1977), p.vii.

[27]B.T. Keeler, "Teacher Testing vs. Departmental Examinations: New Evidence," *ATA Magazine*, 58, 4 (1978): 31. Keeler was Executive Secretary of the Alberta Teachers' Association at that time.

[28]Keeler, p. 31.

[29]R.A. Garden, "The Second IEA Mathematics Study," *Comparitive Education Review*, 31, 1 (February 1987): 47-68.

[30]Verner Richard Nyberg, "Educational Standards in Canada," in Leonard L. Stewin and Stewart J.H. McCann, eds., *Contemporary Educational Issues: The Canadian Mosaic* (Toronto: Copp Clark, 1987), p. 116.

[31]*St. John's Calgary Report*, "Can Jake Harder Restore Standards to Alberta Schools?" 1, 44 (January 20, 1978): 21-25.

[32]Evans, p. 11.

[33]Norm Goble, "Neo-Conservativism: Back to Privelege," in *ATA Magazine*, 61, 2 (1981): 52-55.; and Broadfoot, 1987.

[34]*ATA News*, 17, 10 (February 7, 1983): 1.

[35]*ATA News*, 17, 6 (November 22, 1982): 1.

[36]*ATA News*, 17, 5 (November 8, 1982): 1.

[37]*ATA News*, 17, 5 (November 8, 1982): 1.

[38] *ATA News*, 17, 6 (November 22, 1982): 1.

[39] *ATA News*, 17, 5 (November 8, 1982): 4.

[40] *ATA News*, 17, 8 (January 10, 1983): 1.

[41] Fred Whitworth, *Basic Education and Much More* (Ottawa: The Canadian School Board Studies Trust, 1977), p. 58.

[42] Broadfoot, p. 9.

[43] See Mathew Zachariah, "Standards on Education: A Plea for a Broader Perspective," *Loyola Journal of Social Sciences* (India) 1, 1 (July 1987): 66-70.

# Section 2:
# Current Issues in Canadian Public Education

# 7

# Federal Intrusions into Education through Immersion and Second Language Programs

## L.E. Sackney

"English and French are the official languages of Canada and have equality of status and equal rights and privileges as to their use in all institutions of the Parliament and government of Canada."
(Constitution Act, 1982, section 16(1))

Ours is a country which recognizes two official languages. The issue of language rights has been hurried in and out of the spotlight by the government, sometimes with bewildering rapidity.

In the Canadian framework, what is generally understood as language rights is the freedom to choose the official language in which one will receive certain government services, educate one's children, or if necessary, be heard before the courts. This seems simple enough. Where the waters get muddied is in deciding where, how, and to whom these rights apply, or if indeed they are rights at all and not privileges which may be granted or withdrawn by governments as they choose. There is also the added question as to who shall pay for these services. Finally, we must reckon with the fact that language rights are caught up in the politics of national unity and federal-provincial disputes over the distribution of powers.

Caught up in this debate are boards of education who must deliver the educational services to the students. This sometimes histrionic climate obscures how much is at stake for the official language minorities when it comes to defining and implementing the language principles by which we intend to live.

At present, as the country engages in language instruction, French immersion and minority languages have seized center stage. Through no fault of its own, immersion and minority language instruction has a tendency to disrupt more established or traditional educational formats.[1]

The push for second language competence and minority language rights has implications for educational policy and planning at the provincial and local level that cannot be ignored. Furthermore, the federal government, as an important and interested partner of improved second language teaching is implicated in the search for solutions.

The purpose of this chapter is to examine some of these jurisdictional issues and their implication as the federal government attempts to promote immersion and minority language programs in the schools of Canada. In particular, the emphasis will be on the inroads that the federal government has made into an area of provincial and local board jurisdiction. In order to better understand the jurisdictional issues, the current status of second language training and the types of programs that are currently available, will be addressed first.

## Patterns in the Delivery of Minority Language Programs

There are many methods of organizing and delivering minority language education. In general, they consist of variations of the following:

(1) **French school.** This term is used to describe a school in which French is the language of instruction for all subjects except English as a second language (the reverse is true in Quebec). All or most of the students are French-speaking and the language of work and play is French. This is the program that is requested most often by the various Francophone groups outside of Quebec.

(2) **Mixed school.** This term is used to designate schools where part of the student body is French-speaking and receives instruction in French; the other part is English-speaking and receives instruction in English. This pattern exists in those localities where the number of students does not warrant the establishment of two schools. In some cases, boards by policy prefer the two schools to cohabit one building.

(3) **Bilingual school.** This is a school where some subjects are taught in French, others in English. The proportion of teaching time devoted to instruction in French may vary greatly.

(4) **Immersion school.** These schools are organized for the purpose of teaching French as a second language to students whose mother tongue is not French. In these schools, some or all of the subjects are taught in French. In many provinces, the pattern is for instruction to be 100 percent French in kindergarten and decreased to 50 percent of the instructional time by the end of Division One. Some school systems offer early, intermediate and late immersion programs. Although this type of program is intended for students whose mother tongue is not French, in some instances it is the only French language instruction available to French-speaking students.

(5) **Core or French as a Second Language (FSL).** In virtually all provinces, core French or French as a second language (FSL) is offered. This pattern is most typical of sparsely populated rural areas (especially in the West).

(6) **Extended French.** Another pattern of offering French is to teach French as a second language plus one additional subject, usually social studies, also taught in French. Some school jurisdictions offer early, intermediate and late extended French (e.g., Edmonton public schools).

(7) In all provinces there are areas in which no instruction in the minority language is offered. In many instances students may attend classes in the minority language in neighboring communities.

(8) Finally, in many places, because of the sparse distribution of the minority language population, students receive minority language instruction by boarding away from home.[2]

## Enrolment in Minority Language Programs

One indicator of the state of minority language education in the provinces is to examine the enrolments in these programs. The Commissioner of Official Languages collects this data from Statistics Canada on an annual basis. Table 1 provides the second language enrolments by provinces.

It is evident from Table 1 that the enrolments in second language programs have been increasing in the past decade. In 1986-87, immersion accounted for 4 percent of the English-speaking students (approximately 200,000 students).

Minority language education programs are provided in Table 2. These enrolments and the number of schools have, on the other hand, been dropping during the last decade.

In 1986-87 there were 259,165 minority students enroled in 1,010 schools as compared to 444,942 minority students in 1,197 schools in 1970-71. In part, the decrease in enrolments reflects the drop in the number of students and schools in Quebec as a result of Bill 101.

### *Public Attitudes*

What is the public attitude towards second and minority languages? Although it is difficult to say with any precision the degree of acceptance or rejection of the concept, the 1985 *Annual Report* of the Commissioner of Official Languages indicates:

(1) A substantial majority of Canadians favor, in principle, the proposition that Canadians should be able to receive government services in either language;

(2) A similar majority also hold that effective minority and second language education in English and French should be a Canadian birthright;

## Table 1. Second Language Enrolment in Public Schools, by Province

(Commissioner of Official Languages, Annual Report, 1986, pp. 212-215)

| | Total school population | Elementary[d] (Core) | | | Secondary[d] (Core) | | | French Immersion | | | |
|---|---|---|---|---|---|---|---|---|---|---|---|
| | | School population having English as the language of Instruction (French in Quebec) | Second language[c] Enrolment | % | School population having English as the language of Instruction (French In Quebec) | Second language Enrolment | % | Enrolment | Schools offering Immersion | Total number of schools | Total Second Language Enrolment |
| **Newfoundland** | | | | | | | | | | | |
| 1977-78 | 156,63 | 93,623 | 33,585 | 35.9 | 62,270 | 34,111 | 54.8 | 95 | 3 | 706 | 67,791 |
| 1985-86[c] | 142,332 | 73,700 | 36,687 | 49.8 | 66,536 | 37,692 | 56.6 | 2,015 | 25 | 607 | 76,394 |
| 1986-87[b] | 139,371 | 70,722 | 36,325 | 51.4 | 66,085 | 41,183 | 62.3 | 2,328 | 26 | 600 | 79,836 |
| **Prince Edward Island** | | | | | | | | | | | |
| 1977-78 | 27,491 | 13,284 | 7,351 | 55.3 | 13,034 | 8,332 | 63.9 | 541 | 7 | 72 | 16,224 |
| 1985-86[c] | 24,996 | 10,534 | 6,089 | 57.8 | 11,458 | 7,379 | 64.4 | 2,492 | 21 | 69 | 15,960 |
| 1986-87[b] | 24,763 | 10,381 | 6,027 | 58.1 | 1,253 | 7,368 | 65.5 | 2,692 | 21 | 70 | 16,037 |
| **Nova Scotia** | | | | | | | | | | | |
| 1977-78 | 198,097 | 100,529 | 30,025 | 29.9 | 91,545 | 58,839 | 64.3 | 127 | 3 | 613 | 88,991 |
| 1985-86[c] | 172,614 | 86,164 | 47,357 | 55.0 | 80,456 | 53,572 | 66.6 | 1,859 | 23 | 553 | 102,788 |
| 1986-87[b] | 170,800 | 84,500 | 46,000 | 55.4 | 80,800 | 54,500 | 67.5 | 1,800 | 23 | 550 | 102,300 |
| **New Brunswick** | | | | | | | | | | | |
| 1977-78 | 162,229 | 49,019 | 29,563 | 60.3 | 56,930 | 37,887 | 66.6 | 3,179 | 34 | 482 | 70,629 |
| 1985-86[c] | 141,332 | 37,737 | 28,876 | 76.5 | 42,517 | 28,486 | 67.0 | 14,530 | 100 | 436 | 71,892 |
| 1986-87[a] | 140,400 | 37,000 | 28,500 | 77.0 | 40,900 | 27,600 | 67.5 | 16,400 | 110 | 430 | 72,500 |
| **Quebec \*** | | | | | | | | | | | |
| 1977-78 | 1,232,678 | 571,069 | 211,296 | 27.0 | 456,486 | 456,176 | 98.0 | No English immersion programs exist | | | 667,472 |
| 1985-86[c] | 1,059,445 | 586,244 | 238,569 | 40.7 | 338,521 | 331,759 | 96.0 | | | | 570,320 |
| 1986-87[a] | 1,065,500 | 610,000 | 244,000 | 40.7 | 330,000 | 323,000 | 98.0 | | | | 567,000 |
| **Quebec \*\*** | | | | | | | | | | | |
| 1977-781 | 1,232,678 | | | | See Table 2 | | | 17,800 | n/a | 2,765 | 17,800 |
| 1985-86[c] | 1,059,445 | | | | | | | 18,006 | n/a | 2,549 | 18,006 |
| 1986-87[a] | 1,065,500 | | | | | | | 18,200 | n/a | 2,600 | 18,200 |
| **Ontario** | | | | | | | | | | | |
| 1977-78 | 1,943,064 | 1,206,205 | 650,136 | 53.9 | 607,940 | 220,369 | 36.2 | 12,764 | 160 | 4,742 | 883,269 |

| Region / Year | | | | | | | | | | | |
|---|---|---|---|---|---|---|---|---|---|---|---|
| **Ontario** | | | | | | | | | | | |
| 1977-78 | 1,943,064 | 1,206,205 | 650,136 | 53.9 | 607,940 | 220,369 | 36.2 | 12,764 | 160 | 4,742 | 883,269 |
| 1985-86[f] | 1,769,074 | 1,023,912 | 655,133 | 64.0 | 566,155 | 241,078 | 42.6 | 87,819 | 737 | 4,840 | 984,030 |
| 1986-87[a] | 1,745,000 | 998,500 | 647,000 | 64.8 | 558,000 | 248,300 | 44.5 | 97,000 | 850 | 4,800 | 992,300 |
| **Manitoba** | | | | | | | | | | | |
| 1977-78 | 221,408 | 110,831 | 42,576 | 38.4 | 100,707 | 41,376 | 41.1 | 1,667 | 13 | 724 | 85,619 |
| 1985-86[f] | 199,013 | 92,974 | 47,930 | 51.6 | 87,979 | 40,464 | 46.0 | 12,581 | 67 | 713 | 100,975 |
| 1986-87[b] | 199,200 | 91,000 | 48,200 | 53.0 | 88,700 | 41,700 | 47.0 | 14,300 | 75 | 710 | 104,200 |
| **Saskatchewan** | | | | | | | | | | | |
| 1977-78 | 216,716 | 110,382 | 4,928 | 4.5 | 104,543 | 48,469 | 46.4 | 407 | 2 | 971 | 53,804 |
| 1985-86[f] | 202,560 | 107,706 | 20,034 | 18.6 | 87,682 | 40,207 | 45.9 | 5,965 | 43 | 933 | 66,206 |
| 1986-87[b] | 205,000 | 108,000 | 21,000 | 19.4 | 88,800 | 41,300 | 46.5 | 6,900 | 45 | 930 | 69,200 |
| **Alberta** | | | | | | | | | | | |
| 1977-78 | 439,804 | 216,656 | 52,435 | 24.2 | 215,899 | 58,903 | 27.3 | n/a | n/a | 1,367 | n/a |
| 1985-86[f] | 448,339 | 226,844 | 56,835 | 25.1 | 201,081 | 64,238 | 31.9 | 19,017 | 121 | 1,520 | 40,090 |
| 1986-87[a] | 448,300 | 222,500 | 59,000 | 26.5 | 203,000 | 65,000 | 32.0 | 21,300 | 135 | 1,530 | 145,300 |
| **British Columbia** | | | | | | | | | | | |
| 1977-78 | 527,769 | 305,574 | 75,740 | 24.8 | 220,894 | 84,069 | 38.1 | 1,301 | 15 | 1,610 | 161,110 |
| 1985-86[f] | 485,777 | 275,560 | 76,042 | 27.6 | 193,981 | 98,367 | 50.7 | 15,590 | 123 | 1,549 | 189,999 |
| 1986-87[a] | 469,300 | 268,000 | 75,000 | 28.0 | 181,800 | 100,000 | 55.0 | 17,700 | 130 | 1,545 | 192,700 |
| **Yukon** | | | | | | | | | | | |
| 1977-78 | 5,394 | 3,545 | 1,346 | 38.0 | 1,849 | 939 | 50.8 | n/a | n/a | 23 | n/a |
| 1985-86[f] | 4,554 | 2,594 | 1,058 | 40.8 | 1,681 | 953 | 56.7 | 247 | 1 | 25 | 2,258 |
| 1986-87[b] | 4,805 | 2,739 | 1,187 | 43.3 | 1,733 | 968 | 57.0 | 291 | 1 | 25 | 2,466 |
| **Northwest Territories** | | | | | | | | | | | |
| 1977-78 | 12,717 | 8,801 | 2,100 | 23.0 | 3,916 | 1,100 | 28.1 | n/a | n/a | 70 | n/a |
| 1985-86[f] | 13,470 | 9,409 | 2,275 | 24.2 | 3,811 | 1,435 | 37.7 | 250 | 3 | 74 | 3,960 |
| 1986-87[a] | 13,644 | 9,500 | 2,380 | 25.1 | 3,920 | 1,550 | 39.5 | 224 | 3 | 75 | 4,154 |
| **Total** | | | | | | | | | | | |
| 1977-78 | 5,143,535 | 2,789,518 | 1,141,081 | 40.9 | 1,936,013 | 1,050,570 | 54.3 | 37,881 | 237 | 14,147 | 3,114,975 |
| 1985-86[f] | 4,664,475 | 2,533,378 | 1,216,885 | 48.0 | 1,681,853 | 945,922 | 56.2 | 180,345 | 1,265 | 13,068 | 2,342,852 |
| 1986-87[a] | 4,626,109 | 2,512,842 | 1,215,419 | 48.4 | 1,654,991 | 953,481 | 57.6 | 199,111 | 1,419 | 13,865 | 1,367,01 |

a Statistics Canada estimate.
b Preliminary figures supplied by the Department of Education.
c Does not include students for whom the regular language of instruction is English in Quebec and French in the other provinces and territories.
d Includes grades K to 6, except Ontario (K-8); British Columbia and the Yukon (K-7).
e Includes 7-12, except Ontario (9-13); Quebec (7-11); British Columbia and Yukon (8-12).

f Figures revised since publication of the 1985 Annual Report.
* Students in Quebec having French as a first language.
** Students in Quebec having French as a second language.
n/a: no figures available.
Notes: In previous years the information shown above was presented in two separate tables, numbered 8.3 and 8.4.
Source: Statistics Canada, Elementary and Secondary Education Division.

# Table 2. Minority Language Education Programs

Enrolment in programs designed to provide education in their mother tongue (English in Quebec and French elsewhere), to members of the official-language minority groups, grades in which offered and number of schools where offered, for each province and territory, 1970-71, 1985-86 and 1986-87.

(Commissioner of Official Languages, *Annual Report*, 1986, p. 216).

| | Enrolment | Grades | Number of Schools |
|---|---|---|---|
| **Newfoundland** | | | |
| 1970-71 | 185 | k-10 | 1 |
| 1985-86[c] | 181 | K-10 | 2 |
| 1986-87[b] | 236 | K-11 | 4 |
| **Prince Edward Island** | | | |
| 1970-71 | 796 | 1-12 | 7 |
| 1985-86[c] | 512 | 1-12 | 2 |
| 1986-87[b] | 484 | 1-12 | 32 |
| **Nova Scotia** | | | |
| 1970-71 | 7,388 | p-12 | 32 |
| 1985-86[c] | 4,135 | p-12 | 22 |
| 1986-87[a] | 3,700 | p-12 | 18 |
| **New Brunswick** | | | |
| 1970-71 | 60,679 | k-12 | 196 |
| 1985-86 | 46,548 | k-12 | 154 |
| 1986-87[a] | 46,100 | K-12 | 154 |
| **Quebec** | | | |
| 1970-71 | 248,855 | K-11 | 519 |
| 1985-86[c] | 116,674 | K-11 | 392 |
| 1986-87[a] | 107,300 | K-11 | 370 |
| **Ontario** | | | |
| 1970-71 | 115,869 | K-13 | 381 |
| 1985-86[c] | 91,188 | K-13 | 359 |
| 1986-87[a] | 91,500 | K-13 | 360 |
| **Manitoba** | | | |
| 1970-71 | 10,405 | K-12 | 49 |
| 1985-86[c] | 5,497 | K-12 | 32 |
| 1986-87[a] | 5,200 | K-12 | 32 |

| | | | | |
|---|---|---|---|---|
| Saskatchewan | 1970-71 | 765 | K-12 | 12 |
| | 1985-86[r] | 1,207 | K-12 | 17 |
| | 1986-87[a] | 1,300 | K-12 | 18 |
| Alberta | 1970-71 | n/a | n/a | n/a |
| | 1985-86[r] | 1,397 | K-11 | 10 |
| | 1986-87[a] | 1,500 | K-12 | 12 |
| British Coumbia | 1970-71 | - | - | - |
| | 1985-86[r] | 1,646 | K-11 | 34 |
| | 1986-87[a] | 1,800 | K-12 | 37 |
| Yukon | 1970-71 | - | - | - |
| | 1985-86[r] | 32 | 1-5, 8-10 | 2 |
| | 1986-87[b] | 42 | 1-6, 8-9 | 3 |
| Northwest Territories | 1970-71 | - | - | - |
| | 1985-86[r] | - | - | - |
| | 1986-87[a] | - | - | - |
| Total | 1970-71 | 444,942 | | 1,197 |
| | 1985-86 | 268,899 | | 1,027 |
| | 1986-87 | 259,165 | | 1,010 |

[a] Statistics Canada estimate.
[b] Preliminary figures provided by the Department of Education.
[r] Figures revised since the publication of the Annual Report, 1985.
n/a: no figures available.
Notes: In previous years this information has been published in table B.5.
Source: Statistics Canada, Elementary and Secondary Education Division.

(3) Somewhat more tentatively, many Canadians are weary of futile and over-emotional linguistic sparring between the provinces, school systems and the federal government; and

(4) Many Canadians would like to see some practical justice in the near future.[3]

Thus, while it appears that the majority of Canadians have reconciled bilingualism and minority language rights, such is not the case with politicians at all levels of government.

## Minority Rights and Francophone Aspirations

Section 23 of the *Charter of Rights and Freedoms* confirmed the minority rights of the French outside of Quebec and the English in Quebec to have their children educated in the minority language. The *Act* states:

> Citizens of Canada (a) whose first language learned and still understood is that of English or French linguistic minority population of the province in which they reside, or (b) who have received their primary school instruction in Canada in English or French and reside in a province where the language in which they received that instruction is the language of the English or French linguistic minority population of the province, have the right to have their children receive primary and secondary school instruction in that language in that province.[4]

According to the *Charter*, eligible parents have the right "where the number of children so warrants, to have them receive that instruction in minority language facilities provided out of public funds."

Of the ten provinces, New Brunswick comes closest to full compliance with section 23 of the *Charter*. Most provincial education laws either fail to mention language rights at all (Newfoundland or British Columbia), contain restrictive clauses (Prince Edward Island), or permit, but do not require, school boards to establish programs in languages other than English without clearly identifying what constitutes a French-language program (Saskatchewan and Alberta).[5]

Thus, while minority language rights are guaranteed in the *Charter*, provincial governments have been slow to make language provisions in the education Acts. Local boards have been even more reluctant to make provisions for minority language education. The various annual reports of the Commissioner of Official Languages (1979-87) makes continual reference to the lack of educational provisions for Francophones. Due to the lack of response by governments and boards, the Francophones have resorted to the courts. Le Comite de Parents pour l'Ecole Francoise is a typical case. After various attempts by the Society to establish l'Ecole Georges Bugnet, under the umbrella of either Edmonton Public Schools or Edmonton Separate Schools, they took the Alberta government to court. The judge in the Bugnet case found that the *Alberta School Act* was in conflict with the *Charter* to the extent that this right was omitted. Moreover, the court ruled that l'Ecole Bugnet had the right to publicly funded education in a facility managed by a Francophone school board.[6]

This scenario is being replayed in many other provinces. In Saskatchewan, the recent Trembley Case (1985) and Mercure Case (1987) have served to reinforce minority rights. Frustrated by the lack of response from provincial governments and local boards, the various Francophone associations have resorted to the courts in order to obtain their minority rights. In the majority of the provinces, the only schools their children can attend are immersion schools. However, they argue that immersion schools do not satisfy their language and cultural needs. The language of the playground tends to be English, the French is usually poorly taught, and the program does not provide for cultural aspects of the language. They use research (e.g., Cummins[7]; Fishman[8]; Skutnobb-Kongas[9];Stern[10]; Swain[11]) to substantiate their arguments.

Recently the Francophone associations across Canada have also been lobbying for their own school boards, because they feel their needs have not been well served by the English school boards. Thus, groups such as the Commission des Ecoles Fransakoises argue that only when they control their own education will true equality of rights exist.

Judges have so far struck down certain sections of provincial education acts. They have gone further and stated that provincial legislators have a duty to amend their current laws to make them consistent with minority constitutional rights to education. What is not clear is how and where these services must be offered. For example, there has been no definition to date of the concept "where numbers warrant." How can sparsely populated rural school divisions provide minority language programs when the major urban centers are having difficulty in providing programs? The scattering of potential French language students among numerous rural school divisions makes the implementation of French minority language programs highly problematical, let alone providing parents the degree of control that the judges deem necessary. The next few years should see some major developments in this area.

## Immersion and Second Language Programs

The issue of providing immersion and second language programs is a contentious one for school boards and provinces. In some provinces, and especially in western Canada, boards have been reluctant and slow to provide immersion and second language programs because of the "heatedness" of the debate. At the same time, we have witnessed a number of court cases whereby parents have attempted to pressure school boards to provide French immersion programs. In Saskatchewan, for example, the Canadian Parents for French took the Weyburn School Board to court in an attempt to obtain immersion instruction.[12] And although the parents were unsuccessful, the Weyburn School Board did establish a core French program for Kindergarten to Grade Six.

A somewhat different situation occurred on Vancouver Island's Saanich Peninsula where a dispute occurred between the parents of children enroled in early immersion and the Board. In April, 1986, the Board voted to phase out the French immersion in elementary schools. The Board regarded French immersion, in which 600 of the districts' 6,300 students were registered, as an "administrative nightmare."[13]

At the same time, the demand for immersion programs and second language programs has been growing (see Table 1). In some cities (e.g., Calgary, Vancouver, Edmonton) parents have had to line up all night in order to register their children in French immersion classes.

The increased interest in immersion programs has caused numerous problems for school boards. In cities, these programs tend to be located in middle and upper class neighborhoods. In some cases, these programs have seriously jeopardized the viability of the neighboring schools or the regular English programs where the two programs share the same facility. Moreover, the students that do remain in the regular English program tend to be of lower ability level.

Depending on where the immersion schools are located, it is often necessary to bus many children to these schools. This, in turn, causes problems in that it decreases the enrolments in some neighborhood schools to the point of school closure. There is, in many provinces, also the added cost of transportation which is not provided for. Moreover, there are instances where two families reside in the same neighborhood and their children attend the same school, but one is in French immersion and the other is in the regular program, resulting in the French immersion children being transported, but not the English program students. All of these issues tend to cause tension in the community.

For some parents, teachers and specialists, the immersion programs represent elitism in education. Furthermore, they see these programs draining resources that could be used by the schools to improve other programs and services.

For many rural school divisions, immersion programs are even less viable. The avenues open to them are core and extended French programs. The Commissioner in the 1985 *Annual Report*[14] points out that 90 percent of all students taking French as a second language, and virtually all French-speaking students studying English as a second language, are in core programs. Furthermore, their research as well as that of OISE (e.g., Cummins[15]; Fishman[16]; Stern[17]; Swain[18]), shows that these programs are not highly effective in developing fluency in a second language. Added to the difficulty is the high drop-out rate experienced by students in these programs. One wonders how well these programs serve the needs of students and whether genuine equity exists for all students.

Each year brings new proof, both in research results and in the performance of thousands of students, that immersion programs can ensure students a high level of competence in their second language at no risk to their mother tongue.[19] Yet, school boards have all too often been reluctant to meet this demand. One has to wonder why. Are there antediluvian prejudices among trustees and administrators? Perhaps for some, some of the time, but not to any great extent. Olson and Burns[20] in their study revealed that in many school jurisdictions a policy and planning vacuum exists. Their contention is that both in the long and short run, this may pose a greater threat to innovative language teaching than the prejudices of the past.

## Teacher Supply

The expansion of immersion and core French has not happened without a considerable degree of pressure on the capacity of the school system to supply qualified teachers and new facilities. In every province there is a shortage of teachers. In Saskatchewan, for example, it is estimated that approximately 100 teachers per year will be required to meet the increasing demand.[21] Thus, existing teachers will have to be retrained or new ones hired. This, of course, means that some teachers will be dislocated or declared redundant.

Although most provinces have attempted to recruit teachers from outside the province, school boards are finding the task difficult or impossible. A number of school boards in western Canada have been recruiting French teachers from Quebec, sometimes with less than desirable results. Some teachers have come to western Canada only able to speak French and have found it difficult to adjust to an English speaking community. Added to the problem is that some of these same teachers are fluent in French, but are not good teachers, and thus the added dilemma.

The availability of qualified teachers is bound to have a major impact on the long-term success of the program and the rationalization of the teacher training programs. It is apparent that all stakeholders, boards, governments and universities must grapple with this issue.

## Financial Commitment

No one can deny that second language programs are expensive. During the period that provinces have been receiving formula payments, most have voiced a determination to improve minority and second language education. Their credibility would be greatly enhanced if their commitment was deeper than the federal pocket book. Ottawa, on the other hand, must accept the fact that a pullback in funds could seriously threaten a fragile situation.

In none of the English-speaking provinces is the level of educational services for minority groups equal to what the English-speaking majority enjoy.[22] Fragile second language programs are in drastic need of federal and provincial support.

Since immersion programs receive federal support for the most part from the same formula budget as minority language programs, a larger proportion of the money is being spent to support French second language programs for Anglophones and a professionally smaller share is being allocated to support Francophones studying in their first language. Of the federal money spent in 1986, over one-third of the $210,000,000 was destined for second language instruction, while less than two-thirds was designated for minority language education.[23] Moreover, the federal government, for its part, has not increased the amount of money being spent on languages in the past few years.

The provinces, for their part, are not too proud to accept large amounts of federal money, but they are equally not shy about claiming exclusive rights to manage their own educational systems. For the consumer the question is how good a job are they making of it? Moreover, how effectively are they coordinating their minority and second-language programs to take advantage of each other's expertise? Through the Council of Ministers, one occasionally sees items on minority and second languages (e.g., Council of Ministers).[24] The Commissioner of Official Languages has over the years commented on the lack of an effective information network on curriculum evaluation, learning assessment materials, tests developed in French, French language teacher training programs and sharing of research results.[25]

## Other Languages

One would be remiss without mentioning the impact of other languages on educational systems. As language groups have become more numerous, both in terms of the languages spoken and the number of their speakers, the teaching and learning of languages other than English and French have also grown.

Heritage language classes and other language bilingual school programs have overtaken the traditional second language courses found in schools. Each of the prairie provinces has bilingual schools or programs involving the main languages spoken there. Alberta was the first province to make provisions (1977) for bilingual other languages. Saskatchewan and Manitoba followed in 1979. Bilingual programs exist in Ukrainian, German and Hebrew in all three prairie provinces. In 1983-84, Alberta had 2,647 students registered in other bilingual programs, while Saskatchewan had 1,691 students and Manitoba 1,294 students.[26]

In Ontario, funding has been provided to school boards since 1977 to teach heritage languages up to two-and-a-half hours per week outside the regular five-hour school day. This provision allows for three possibilities: instruction on weekends, after regular school hours, or teaching integrated into a school day which has been extended by a half-an-hour.

Proponents of heritage language programs have seen promotion of heritage languages as academically advantageous for minority students, as a means of increasing cohesion and communication within the families, and as a means of expanding the social and cultural horizons of all students. Opponents, on the other hand, have seen heritage language teaching as socially divisive, excessively costly, and educationally retrograde in view of minority students need to learn English.[27]

Researchers (e.g., Cummins[28]; Morrison[29]; Swain[30]; Stern[31]), however, seem to agree that bilingual minority language students perform better in later stages of their schooling as a result of their heritage language experiences. In this regard, a number of provinces have been offering heritage language opportunities for native students in an attempt to increase their success and retention rates.

In Ontario, funding has been provided to school boards since 1977 to teach heritage languages up to two-and-one-half hours per week outside of the regular five-hour school day. In the city of Toronto some school boards offer in excess of 26 heritage language programs.

Edmonton Public School Board in 1984 operated six (Native, Ukrainian, German, Hebrew, Arabic and Chinese) bilingual programs. Their estimate was that it cost upward of $150,000 to initiate a new program. Much of this money was designated for translating and acquisition of materials.[32] Furthermore, many of these costs continued as the program expanded through the grades.

Part-time teaching of languages after school and on weekends is at present funded partly by the federal government's Multicultural Program and provincially by "heritage" or "ancestral" language programs. In 1984-85, funding amounted to $4,000,000.[33] Unfortunately, if we believe in multiculturalism within a bilingual country, much greater effort, financial and material, will be required.

## Post-Secondary Education

Universities are presently confronted by a lack of funds. Given these constraints, they find it difficult to expand or increase efforts in second language areas. However, that is not to say that much more cannot be done. Canadian universities have been recalcitrant with regard to the long overdue reinstatement of a second language entrance requirement. The Commissioner in his 1985 report indicated that of 60 institutions, three universities and three bilingual faculties required some level of second language standing for admission and only two institutions required it from all students for graduation.[34]

Stern in his report concluded that universities can, and in effect do, exercise enormous influence on all other phases of education in a given field of study. Universities have the power to give shape and substance to a view of society in the particular field of learning. He further adds:

> What we are talking about is ensuring that Canadians who aspire to the highest levels of education, and potentially to positions of leadership in our

society, are being attuned to the linguistic environment in which they will be called upon to act.[35]

Moreover, universities need to address the needs of Francophone students. There are few opportunities for these students to train in their own language in post-secondary institutions.

Finally, universities need to deal with the issue of second language teachers. Programs need to be put in place whereby qualified teachers will be trained to take their place in the schools. At the University of British Columbia, 36 teachers per year are being trained where immersion enrolments are increasing at the rate of 2,000 students per year. Similar situations exist at the University of Saskatchewan and the University of Regina.[36]

Another problem faced by teacher training institutions is that many have contracted funds for the training of teachers. Thus, they are not clear as to what will happen with the funding when the contracts expire. Federal and provincial governments need to clarify these issues in light of the pressures being felt by universities.

## Language Opportunities

Even though more and more Canadians agree that facility in both official languages is something they want and need, access to worthwhile language learning opportunities is far from assured for many Canadians. In fact, access is rapidly becoming the issue in second language learning. The Commissioner of Official Languages in his 1985 report stated:

> It is more than tantalizing to be told of the benefits of bilingualism and not to be able to learn the other language, because courses are unavailable, available but full, or are offered up to a certain grade, or in a distant location with no transportation. The unfortunate fact of the matter is that what might seem a clear-cut right to have one's children instructed in their second official language is virtually non-existent.[37]

Many rural boards still balk at the introduction of programs, other boards provide no transportation or charge a fee for it, and still others are limiting access by opting for late rather than early immersion programs to save money. Some trustees, under pressure to trim budgets, are looking to improved core or extended French programs as a cheaper alternative to early immersion.

It is baffling that educational authorities, with all the research on language learning at their disposal, still appear to consider a two or three-year exposure to some 30 minutes of language instruction per day as adequate training. Optional courses, on the other hand, suffer from "on-again off-again" participation.

The federal-provincial agreements on official languages have been extended until 1988. However, the Commissioner[38] argues that "too little money is being spread too thin, and minimum funding does not begin to match the rise in demand." He goes on to add:

The problem is that one source of funds must be all things to all people. Not only are all minority and second-language programs in the elementary and secondary school systems competing for those limited funds, but from the same pot must also come support for universities and community college programs, teacher training, adult education, student bursaries and fellowships, and the monitor program. Thus, a province using the funds to meet demands for one activity must often shortchange another, like pulling up a short blanket to cover one's shoulders only to suffer from exposed feet.[39]

In summary, much greater cooperation between governments is necessary if we are to ameliorate these concerns. The federal government, for its part, may well have to take a more muscular attitude towards negligent provinces. This is not an easy stance, but in some cases necessary.

## The Importance of Immersion and Second Languages

If we truly believe in the importance of bilingualism, then it is mandatory that language opportunities be provided for all students. Otherwise, the rhetoric becomes hollow.

There are negative factors associated with an assimilation policy. Instead of a peaceful integration of minorities, we are beginning to see that educational, psychological and social problems are not a failure inherent in the ethnic group, but are more or less caused by feelings of assimilation, regardless of whether or not it is deliberate or unintended policy by the majority.

Tove Skutnobb-Kongas[40] in his study argued that cultural assimilation and structural incorporation of linguistic minorities is a dangerous path to follow. The advantages far outweigh in favor of equality of language opportunities for these groups. He argues that the task of the school should be to give minority children a command of the mother tongue as they would get in a school in their native land.

For the majority, knowledge of the second language is useful for building a stronger Canada. An appreciation of French will lead to a better understanding of Quebec's concerns. Nation building can only take place in an environment of understanding and mutual support.

Furthermore, we are moving towards a global society. Canadian students are much less fluent than their European and Asian counterparts with regard to languages. If we are to be participants in a global sense, then knowledge of other languages is crucial.

It is imperative that the notions of equity, fairness and opportunity be afforded to all the children of Canada. Considerably greater cooperation at the local, provincial, and national level must be forthcoming if we are to achieve such goals.

# Conclusion

To date, a torrent of words and no end of exertion have gone into the debate over constitutional language rights. We now have to ask ourselves whether we have made any difference.

The expectations that have been created are unlikely to be met unless we accept and put into practice the fundamental principle of equality, the right of minorities as well as majorities to decide what kind of education is best for their children. Hurdles put in place by various levels of government need to be removed.

More human and financial resources are the first prerequisite for providing a first rate education. We should be aiming in each province at a comprehensive structure for minority and second language education.

In this regard, the various stakeholders have an important part to play. Universities are not giving the lead expected of them in language education. They need to: reinstate second-language requirements; develop language programs to benefit graduates for Canadian and world realities; and adopt language learning to enhance our understanding of our cultural diversity.

School boards for their part need to engage in policy and planning efforts that indicate the importance of immersion and minority language programs. Too many immersion programs are set-up on an adhoc basis, with little attempt to define linguistic objectives desired. At the secondary level, many immersion students are not challenged in their language competence.[41] In many instances, what they acquired at the primary level is merely maintained, or even allowed to slip back at the secondary level. Moreover, principal leadership needs to be strengthened. They are the ones who must provide the leadership and direction to the programs.

Additionally, school boards must ensure that quality teachers are provided in the schools. This means that some teachers will have to be retrained and new ones hired. But more than anything else, school boards must rationalize the delivery of services. Long and short range planning is a must.

Provincial governments, on the other hand, need to develop comprehensive curriculum and policy guidelines for boards. In addition, they need to: establish meaningful, functional second-language standards; develop appropriate curriculum and the necessary expertise and classroom materials; and make parents and students aware of the value of second language skills. Inter-provincially, the Commissioner of Official Languages[42] contends that the Council of Ministers needs to share linguistic curriculum, tests and curriculum materials, and the results of research efforts.

In terms of federal-provincial relations, further progress in minority and second-language education in Canada is hampered by under-financing and federal-provincial wrangling. The federal government needs to increase the funds available for these programs, develop a national information center and clearinghouse on languages, and promote quality language programs across the country. More than anything else, it needs to ensure that Canadians have access to the languages and services that are provided for in the *Act*. Perhaps the Commissioner of Official Languages best captures the essence of the issue in the 1981 annual report:

> Not only is it here to stay but also it is a mode of education that stands to forge its way into existing school structures at an ever increasing pace. As a result, there is much to be gained by becoming responsible partners in these new demands, rather than remaining passive reactors.[43]

Only the future will tell how successful we have been.

## Notes

[1] Commissioner of Official Languages (1987), *Annual Report 1986* (Ottawa: Minister of Supply and Services Canada, 1987).

[2] Council of Ministers of Education, *The State of Minority Language Education in the Ten Provinces in Canada* (Toronto: Council of Ministers, 1978); Commissioner of Official Languages, *Annual Report 1981* (Ottawa: Minister of Supply and Services Canada, 1982); and Commissioner of Official Languages, *Annual Report 1984* (Ottawa: Minister of Supply and Services Canada, 1985).

[3] Commissioner of Official Languages, *Annual Report, 1984.*

[4] *Canadian Charter of Rights and Freedoms, Constitution Act* (1982). As enacted by the *Canada Act,* (U.K.), section 23.

[5] Commissioner of Official Languages, *Annual Report 1987.*

[6] Commissioner of Official Languages, *Annual Report 1986.*

[7] J. Cummins, *Heritage Language Education: A Review,* language and literacy series (Toronto: OISE Press, 1981).

[8] J. Fishman, "Minority Language Maintenance and the Ethnic Mother Tongue School," *Modern Language Journal,* 65 (1980): 167-172.

[9] T. Skutnobb-Kongas, *Language in the Process of Cultural Assimilation and Structural Incorporation of Linguistic Minorities* (Rosslyn, Virginia: National Clearinghouse for Bilingual Education, 1979).

[10] H. Stern, *Issues in Early CORE French* (Toronto: OISE Report, 1982).

[11] M. Swain, "Time and Timing in Bilingual Education," *Language Learning,* 3 (1981): 1-15.

[12] Commissioner of Official Languages, *Annual Report 1984*, p. 180.

[13] Commissioner of Official Languages, *Annual Report 1985* (Ottawa: Minister of Supply and Services Canada, 1986), p. 182.

[14] Commissioner of Official Languages, *Annual Report,* p. 183.

[15] See note 7 above.

[16] Fishman, pp. 167-172.

[17] Stern.

[18] Swain, pp. 1-15.

[19] F. Morrison, *Longitudinal and Cross-Sectional Studies of French Proficiency in Ottawa and Carleton Schools* (Ottawa: Ottawa Board of Education Research Center, 1981).

[20] P. Olson and G. Burns, *Politics and Planning in French Immersion* (Toronto: OISE Press, 1981).

[21] Commissioner of Official Languages, *Annual Report 1986*; and Commissioner of Official Languages, *Annual Report 1985*.

[22] Commissioner of Official Languages, *Annual Report 1985*.

[23] Commissioner of Official Languages, *Annual Report 1985*, p. 177.

[24] Council of Ministers.

[25] See the various Commissioner of Official Languages reports from 1981-87. These comments are made in every report.

[26] Commissioner of Official Languages, *Annual Report 1985*, p. 177.

[27] J. Cummins, *Heritage Language Education. A Review* (Toronto: Ministry of Education, 1983).

[28] See note 27 above.

[29] Morrison.

[30] Swain, pp. 1-15.

[31] Stern.

[32] Edmonton Public Schools. Various board reports prepared during 1983-84.

[33] Commissioner of Official Languages, *Annual Report 1985*, p. 186.

[34] Commissioner of Official Languages, *Annual Report 1985*, p. 189.

[35] Stern, p. 81.

[36] Commissioner of Official Languages, *Annual Report 1984*, p. 198.

[37] Commissioner of Official Languages, *Annual Report 1984*, p. 185.

[38] Commissioner of Official Languages, *Annual Report 1984*, p. 185.

[39] Commissioner of Official Languages, *Annual Report 1984*, pp. 185-186.

[40] T. Skutnobb-Kongas, "Language in the Process of Cultural Assimilation and Structural Incorporation of Linguistic Minorities," paper published by the National Clearinghouse for bilingual Education (1979), 20 pp.

[41] Commissioner of Languages, *Annual Report 1984*, pp. 185-186.

[42] Commissioner of Official Languages, *Annual Report 1984*, pp. 187-186.

[43] Commissioner of Official Languages, *Annual Report 1980* (Ottawa: Minister of Supply and Services, 1981), p. 48.

# 8

# Policy Development
# in Provincial Government

## Don MacIver

The writers of the *OECD Report on Canadian Education* (1979)[1] expressed surprise at discovering that, with the exception of Quebec, there was little variation in educational policy and practice across Canada. On consideration, this claim merely emphasizes the truth of Robert Redfield's assertion that different observers of social situations see different things, but that each observation may be valid and contribute to an understanding of the whole.[2] Thus, the OECD reporters in their snapshot of the provinces saw similarity in that curriculum development tended to be highly centralized in each province; that 12 years of education was becoming the provincial norm; and that Canadians seemed to have a penchant for writing reports on education which were then left to gather dust.[3]

On the other hand, those who have labored in the field of Canadian education over many years see a different picture. An intimate knowledge reveals ten different provincial systems, two territorial systems and a variety of approaches to Native education, all loosely coordinated and monitored by the federal government and the Council of Ministers of Education. To the close observer, the systems reveal major differences varying from support for private education in British Columbia to the non-support and complete absence of all private education in Newfoundland; or from an entirely secular system of education in three Maritime provinces, to a complex amalgam of a religiously run but a provincially controlled system in Newfoundland. There are a gamut of differences relating to such key issues as language policy, integrating the handicapped, alternative schools, funding and vocational education.

The many differences reflect regional issues and differing approaches to policy development and practice. Lawson and Woock (1987) indicate that the policy process involves four components:

(1) The emergence of issues and identification of problems;

(2) Policy formulation and authorization;

(3) Implementation; and

(4) Termination and change.[4]

Once local issues are identified and the policy-making process is initiated, three accompanying principles that legitimize policy-making have been discussed by Murray Thomas. They are:

(1) The creation of education laws and the increased involvement of courts in educational policy-making;

(2) The use of research and experts; and

(3) The introduction of participatory decision-making.[5]

It seems that the suggestions of Lawson and Woock on the one side and Thomas on the other, are complementary. For example, French language policy is a matter of critical concern in New Brunswick where about one third of the population is Acadian. It is not considered such a serious issue in those provinces where the French are a small minority. Consistent with Lawson and Woock, emerging issues are defined differently in various parts of Canada and, consistent with Thomas, the process of the legitimization of policy is critical. The process in each province may have differences, especially with regard to participatory decision-making. Thus, the definition of the problem and the way it is legitimized establishes provincial differences in policy-making and acceptance while common institutional characteristics maintain a certain uniformity amongst the provinces.

While these comments may state the obvious, the fact is that policy-making and implementation is sometimes bungled and sometimes effective. This paper is an attempt to explore these differences in the small province of New Brunswick. While the smaller provinces may have certain idiosyncrasies, the fact of their smallness may be helpful in elucidating the problem of policy-making in larger provinces. As with the study of science, the study of simpler organisms may shed light on more complex structures. Perhaps the better analogy is with classical studies which have been justified because the study of Ancient Greece and Rome ". . . is the history of the world writ small."

## Policy, Legislation and the Courts

Historically, Ontario has had the greatest influence on educational policy-making in Canada since before Confederation. Ryerson set the pattern with a series of education laws which nullified Strachan's early efforts to establish a kind of English system of education in Upper Canada. Ryerson was a shrewd politician who dominated the educational scene in Ontario for four decades from about 1830. By the time of Confederation, Ryerson's stamp on education in Ontario was indelible. It was established by law and the laws were indefatigably enforced. Ryerson's astuteness as a politician was apparent in his willingness to compromise when he had to, as with the separate schools issue, so that when his legislation became law, it was readily accepted by the powerful majorities.

The pattern of dependence on legislation which, for English Canada, started in Ontario, influenced the rest of the country and it had an impact on New Brunswick. The complexity of the religious-ethnic makeup of New Brunswick prevented a simple arrangement and even inhibited the kind of compromise that Ryerson made in Ontario. The initial New Brunswick legislation (the *Common Schools Act* 1871) eventually produced the Caraquet Riots after the courts, including the Judicial Committee of the Privy Council in London, failed to satisfy English-speaking and Acadian Catholics.[7] Where the legislation and the courts failed, the Riot succeeded because after the disturbances, a secret agreement was made with the Catholic community and the mainly Protestant legislature in which traditional rights of the Catholic population were safeguarded.[8]

Much has been written about the Caraquet Riots so the topic will not be pursued here but it certainly drove home the message that legislation and the courts, while the prime mode of legitimization in Canada, do not have the last word when traditional rights are transgressed. Since the 1875 Caraquet Riot, New Brunswick educational legislators have heeded the warning and legislation has reflected the views of the powerful majorities so that it has been, in general, acceptable.

The thesis that legislation and the courts legitimize educational policy was tested early in New Brunswick and found wanting but the lesson was well learned. The *Charter of Rights* has introduced a new element into the mix and while the courts have, since the late nineteenth century, legitimized policy, it is difficult to predict the part that the courts will play in the future development of educational policy given the precedent of the Caraquet Riot. The decisions of the Supreme Court in Ottawa on matters of human rights may be no more welcome in the hinterlands than the decision of the Judicial Committee of the Privy Council.

The statement that legislation and the courts legitimizes educational policy is confirmed in the Canadian context. It is possible to cite an exceptional case in New Brunswick but the prestige of legislation and the courts has contributed greatly to the respect in which educational policy is held.

## Research and Experts

In a sense, Ryerson was one of the first and, in a historical context, one of the greatest authorities in Canadian education. He was not a researcher in the contemporary sense but he was more familiar with the upper Canadian situation than anyone else of his day. He was familiar with the American (Massachusetts) reforms and he studied educational systems in Europe. From this research developed the Ontario system which influenced Canada, east and west. Thus, Canada has a long tradition of paying attention to the experts and heeding their research.[9]

Probably the most famous of the contemporary statements by a group of educational experts, in the sense of producing reaction, was the *Hall-Dennis Report* (1968).[10] This colorful, MacLuhanesque document reflected exactly the tenor of the times and it was 20 years before there was a major Ontario response to its own creation. The contrast between the *Hall-Dennis Report* and the Radwanski response[12] is both depressing and remarkable. The *Hall-Dennis Report* exuded optimism and discussed education for the leisure society which will be produced by contemporary technology. The Radwanski rebuttal smacks of the grey suited men of Bay Street and the author writes of little else but work. If there is to be any benefit from technology it is to profit corporate Canada not to shorten the working week or increase the leisure possibilities of the poor.

The educational policy implicit in the *Hall-Dennis Report* was far too liberating and the changes which took place in Ontario education in the early 1970s as a result of the Report were soon modified or assimilated by the conservative tradition.

The point is, however, that the *Hall-Dennis Report* did more than influence Ontario as it seemed to have had the effect of producing a spate of reports across Canada. These reports varied from a look alike version in Alberta[12] to the little known but interesting *McLeod-Pinet Report* (1973)[13] in New Brunswick. The *McLeod-Pinet Report* was more attuned to the conditions and attitudes of New Brunswick than *Hall-Dennis* was to Ontario. *McLeod-Pinet* was a confirmation of the very considerable reforms that had taken place in New Brunswick in the 1960s following the introduction of the *Equal Opportunities Act* (1967). It was this *Act* which brought New Brunswick a *de facto* secular system of education and which eventually ensured an equitable distribution of funding across the province.

None of these changes were produced without careful and thorough research and reference to expert authority. The research was a justification for the legislation which established and legitimized educational policies. Research, however, does not always clearly support one side or the other in a policy issue as the two examples discussed below will illustrate.

## Participatory Decision-Making

Effective participatory decision-making seems to have come into its own in urban centres like Toronto during the late 1960s. When the public system was established, local committees were deeply involved in their schools but by the late fifties, however, meaningful local involvement was more a "sop to cerebus" than significant involvement. For example, in Alberta during the 1950s, towards the end of the spate of school consolidations, senior government officials, the local school superintendent and local principals would appear at some village hall to explain the advantages of consolidation (i.e., the closing of a school), and to hear the arguments of the people. In general, the procedure was *pro-forma* and the consolidation went ahead regardless of local opposition.[14]

By the late 1960s, community groups in urban centres like Toronto were learning how to organize and to bring pressure to bear on the government and school boards. The presentation of a brief by the Park School Community Council in November, 1971,[15] was one of the pressures that finally made the Metropolitan Toronto Board of Education responsive to the needs of inner-city children. The recognition was manifested in a shift in resources, an increased sensitivity to inner-city community needs, and in subsequent years, the development of alternative schools. There is no question that the process of participatory decision-making was critical in the developments subsequent to 1970 in Toronto.

Since the student discontents of the late 1960s and early 70s, during that brief period when bureaucracies became sensitive to those they served, the pattern of participatory decision-making has become widespread. Unobtrusively, it has become part of the policy-making process in small provinces like New Brunswick. Issues related to the environment, health care, urbanization, transportation and education, have all been subjected to scrutiny and change by the involvement of the general public. It is becoming apparent that while governments are quite prepared to steamroll through programs of their liking, they will respond to well organized public pressure groups.

The main players in policy-making in Canada are the provincial departments of education, teachers' associations, trustees and university faculties of education.[16] The positions adopted by these players are nevertheless mediated by the general public and when there are conflicts amongst the main players or amongst the experts, the general public plays a key role. Frequently the decisive factor after all the arguments are heard is the economic one. That is, unless there is considerable public outcry, the solution eventually adopted is the most economical as seen from the perspective of short-term costs.

The main players indicated by Lawson and Woock interact in various ways and the public is frequently called upon to influence the final legislation which will legitimize the educational policy in question. In a province like New Brunswick, the interacting groups are few, they are familiar with each other and the lines of demarcation amongst the groups are clear. There is close communication amongst, for example, the executive members of the New Brunswick Teachers' Association, the senior levels of the Department of Education, the executive of the School Trustees and senior members of the Faculty of Education. There is a great deal of informal participatory decision-making before important matters reach the stage of public decision-making.

When one group, usually the Department of Education, ignores the informal network, then negative consequences are almost inevitable.

In contrast to an almost familial pattern of participatory decision-making, large provinces have huge bureaucracies, sometimes a number of teachers' and trustees' organizations and many universities. The inertia of large bureaucracies slows down decision-making; the necessity to accommodate all parties and to ensure everyone has a say diffuses the policy and this added complexity of size may result in a policy that is not clear cut. There are some positive elements in such complexity in that individual principals and teachers may have leeway to interpret a policy and to adapt it to meet local circumstances.

The comparative simplicity of participatory decision-making in small provinces will be illustrated in considering the development of specific policies in New Brunswick. What should be noted is that even in a province where the policy-making is regarded as the epitome of simplicity, the processes involved may be prolonged, repetitive, circumlocutory and acrimonious. Perhaps acrimony is more likely to accompany policy-making in a small province where personalities are not likely to be muted by the formalities of large bureaucratic organizations.

## Policy Successes

When policies are developed and implemented successfully, little is heard about them and most policies in education tend to be of this kind. The general success of most policies results in considerable attention being directed towards those that prove difficult to introduce because of resistance from some group or groups. Usually the interest group that most resists departmental policies is the teachers' association. When the Department of Education is careful and respects the informal network, policies that deal with sensitive issues can be introduced. In the province of New Brunswick, two policies dealing with potentially explosive issues will be explored briefly, in order to show how the precautions taken by the Department enabled smooth policy introduction.

## Policy on AIDS

The North American tradition that schools should respond to the problems of society that influence youth is apparent with regard to the problem of AIDS. The issue was identified in New Brunswick and elsewhere by public health groups and was given high profile by the press. Hence, the first criteria cited by Lawson and Woock[17] is satisfied. The second requisite of Lawson and Woock, which is effective policy formulation was satisfied and at the same time legitimized by research and experts.[18]

The implementation of the AIDS policy was legitimized by participatory decision-making. Public hearings were organized, authorities presented their cases and debated the issues and as a result of these meetings, the Department of Education and the Fredericton School Board developed a curriculum that involved the cooperation of teachers, representatives of the public health groups, trustees and departmental representatives. The program was piloted in selected districts and was widely introduced into the English system in New Brunswick in the fall of 1989 with hardly a complaint.

The introduction of the AIDS policy in New Brunswick covered the components of effective policy-making discussed by Lawson and Woock and these components, except for reference to the courts, were legitimized in the fashion suggested by Thomas. Given the sensitive nature of the issue and the fact that New Brunswick is a very conservative province in sexually related matters, such as AIDS, the successful implementation of this policy reveals the careful observation of all aspects of policy-making and implementation.

## Expert Opinion and Public Opinion in Policy-Making

One of the more serious difficulties in policy-making occurs when the experts, who are familiar with the best available data, hold a conflict of opinion with parents, teachers, and/or trustees. This may be defined very loosely as a conflict between science and democracy and such a situation has occurred in recent years in New Brunswick in the area of physical education. In addition to the disagreement amongst the various groups there appears to have been the distinct impression that the physical education problem was not a matter of urgency so that it was possible to be leisurely in considering the issues involved.

In the early 1970s, the departmental authorities responsible for physical education introduced ideas about physical education programs designed to have a lifelong impact on the lives of students. The program emphasized individual sports and reduced the emphasis on competitive team sports. In particular, the new policy proposed more opportunity for physical activity for all and less emphasis on select competition. This concept was resisted by many of those who were teaching physical education because some teachers and coaches had a strong personal commitment to team sports and many schools had a tradition of success in competitive sports. At one level the ensuing debates over curriculum change revealed classical bureaucratic delaying tactics; i.e., desultory discussions, meetings, reports, conferences, studies, reviews, pilot projects and great attention to minority concerns. These were tactics more typical of a large, rather than a small, system.

At another level, whether by chance or design, a learning process was operative since learning probably accompanies any bureaucratic procedure that is not designed to be systematically obfuscatory. As far as the physical education curriculum was concerned, the experience proved to be useful and effective. Evidence regarding the efficacy of lifelong physical education programs accumulated throughout the 1970s. University programs in physical education, building on fitness research, pressed for a broader based approach to games and sports in the schools. Concurrent with all these activities was heavy federal government investment in advertising about "Participaction" which was aimed at convincing the public of the importance of lifelong physical activity.

Gradually, the new research, new graduates in physical education, and the persistence of an ever-growing number of advocates, persuaded virtually all administrators in New Brunswick schools to switch to the new program. It was a slow process taking more than a decade to accomplish, but ultimately the program was accepted and there were no serious confrontations between those who made policy and those who carried it out. On the negative side, it took an exceedingly long time to introduce the new program, but whether it could have been introduced at all if it had simply been imposed, is open to doubt. Also, given that morale is so critical in the climate of the school, a curriculum unacceptable to the majority of teachers would have a negative impact on the process of education. So while such discursive methods of policy development appear slow, sometimes unconscionably so, in the long run where there are definite obstacles to be overcome, a careful persistent approach will establish educational policy.

## Policies with Problems

When educational policy in New Brunswick is discussed, the tendency is to look to the courageous decision taken in 1972 to introduce French immersion programs to the English school system in Canada's only officially bilingual province. Curiously, resistance to this policy *per se* has not been great, but arguments about detail have been common and persistent.

Once established as a bilingual province, New Brunswick was assured of financial support from the federal government in the development of its language policies. The implementation of the language policy in schools was slow and cautious because the Department of Education was aware of the traditional sensitivities of the French and English. Ambitious, upwardly mobile parents were anxious to avail themselves of the immersion programs so that in some situations there was a greater demand for immersion places than could be satisfied. Features such as extra financial support, influential parental support and careful planning, ensured substantial support for the French language policy.

One problem with the implementation of this policy was that in a period of minimal demand for teachers, Acadian teachers were employed to teach in English language schools at the expense of unilingual English-speaking teachers. This situation has now eased as more young people whose first language is English prove capable of teaching French. In addition, the demand for teachers has grown so that direct competition between Anglophone and Francophone teachers for the same position has diminished.

A more lasting problem relates to the makeup of French immersion classes in contrast to unilingual English classrooms. The ambitious parent could be assured that immersion classes would be self-selected and comprise the brighter children of that age group with the obvious implication that the unilingual classes would be made up of the poorer pupils. This situation has improved to some degree but many teachers in English unilingual classrooms believe that problem children in immersion will sooner or later end up in the unilingual program. This situation may well be compounded with the policy of integrating handicapped children into classrooms, an issue discussed below.

There have been conflicts amongst authorities that relate to the best time to introduce immersion programs: i.e., at grades 1, 4, 7, or even later. This has led to localized conflicts on occasions, but such conflicts have tended to peak at board elections and to subside afterwards. This pattern characterizes the immersion program in New Brunswick. The general policy has been well accepted and effectively implemented but the sensitive nature of the issue has produced a fairly constant series of minor eruptions.

This discussion of the introduction of a policy that held potential for considerable dissension but which, in fact, was implemented quite smoothly, will serve as a useful background to a policy that has proved to be very troublesome. On the surface, the policy of integration, the placing of learning disabled and/or physically handicapped children into classrooms ought to have produced few difficulties; unfortunately, it has produced many.

Perhaps it was because integration appeared to be such a "motherhood" issue that things went wrong in the development and implementation of this policy. After all, who could possibly complain about integrating children with special needs into classrooms. This obviously humanitarian act had something else going for it; namely, that it appeared to be a money saving device. With humanitarianism and economics in its favor, the rapid introduction of the policy of integration into the schools was irresistible to government.

The rapidity with which this policy was developed may be illustrated by the historical background provided by the Special Committee on Social Policy Development (1989).[20] The resultant government report stated that a study into special education was initiated by the government in 1981. In May, 1982, Premier Richard Hatfield promised that his government would integrate special-needs children into the regular school system. Public hearings were held from February to April, 1983, and in September, 1983, a government report recommended that special-needs children be served by the public schools. In December, 1985, the major centre for serving severely disabled children, the Dr. W. F. Roberts School in Saint John, was closed. In June, 1986, the Legislature passed Bill 85 establishing the principle of school integration. It should be noted, however, that according to the *Sixth Report*, when Bill 85 became law, the Advisory Committee to the Minister of Education had yet to develop a statement on the principle of school integration.

In sum, public hearings were held in early 1983 and the recommendations that special-needs children attend public schools were made in late 1983. The major institution for special-needs children was closed in 1985 while Bill 85 which confirmed the integration of special-needs children did not become law until June 1986. Given this time-line, only two full school years have elapsed since the process of integration was introduced to the school system with the force of law.

During these two years there has been a flurry of workshops for teachers and the main provincial university has introduced required courses in special education but these efforts will not yet have had the necessary impact. Hence, the complaints from teachers that they are not prepared to deal with integrated children. This hurried preparation is probably one reason for the complaint that teachers' morale is low and even the casual visitor to the school system will note the pressure due to the added responsibilities placed on teachers by integration. It is little wonder that the *Sixth Report* which was produced to review the progress of integration, as a result of rumblings from teachers and parents stated that the province of New Brunswick should

> improve their programs to enable them to better prepare teachers for the education of exceptional students. Furthermore, the Committee recommends that the Minister of Education address the need for increased professional development for teachers through in-service programs and primarily at the local level.[20]

The *Sixth Report* points out that "the Committee, however, came to realize that the system was not adequately prepared for these giant steps in integration."[21] This statement is verified consistently in the *Sixth Report*. For example, the Committee recognized the inadequacy of support services, including speech/language pathologists, physiotherapists, psychologists and so on. They recommended more financial support for the whole system because of the added burden of the integrated student and the need to train all para-professionals and to extend the teacher aide classification.

While the concept of integration was fully endorsed, the absence of a precise meaning to the term "integration" was noted in the following recommendation

> that the Minister of Education reconcile the differences in the interpretation and implementation of Bill 85 and provide strong and clear directives to all School Boards regarding the processes required to fulfil the spirit and intent of the said Bill; and furthermore that the Minister review and bring into effect modifications or revisions in the guidelines and/or statement(s) of principles to interpret Bill 85 consistently to ensure the rights to education for all children in New Brunswick.[22]

In the interests of successful policy-making, it is in this area of defining the meanings of "integration" that enormous care will have to be taken. Experts differ amongst themselves about the meaning of integration and teachers will be required to act in situations that, in effect, are created by the definitions. The extra training, and the extra resources of all kinds will be of little avail unless there is common agreement about the meaning of the term.

In the context of policy-making, the problems associated with integration have been recognized. The initial policy formulation and implementation appears to have been rushed and insufficient time was available for participatory decision-making. Implementation was handicapped by insufficient resources (human and material) and proper training programs were not carried out. It would seem that all of this is understandable because the process of integration is so obviously a humane and timely act and except for those who are authorities in the field, it would seem that the process of integration could have been accomplished *without* systematic and sophisticated preparation. Everyone is now aware that more resources, more training and clarification of the meaning and process of "integration" are necessities.

The *Sixth Report*, which is an interim report based on an initial analysis of over 250 submissions from the public and interested organizations, has set the policy-making process on integration back on the track of legitimization by giving participatory decision-making a high profile. There is still a need to listen to what the experts say and to study the research on integration. To diminish the conflicts between interest groups within the province, it is essential that experts who have a variety of views on integration be heard and that the variety of opinions involve the spectrum of views that exist outside, as well as within, the province.

In sum, the policy on integration was introduced without a sufficient understanding of the complexity of the issue. As a result of a variety of pressures from interest groups, the Sixth Committee encouraged public participation and has raised the probability that the further implementation of the policy will be successful. There is more work to be done which will involve the authorities on integration as well as the continued participation of the various interest groups. Finally, and perhaps above all else, a full explanation of the concept of integration, when it is defined, needs to be widely communicated throughout the system.

## Conclusion

The critical feature of policy implementation and change is its legitimation. Lawson and Woock have indicated the steps involved in policy development and Thomas has argued that unless there is proper and effective use of the experts and the involvement of participatory decision-making, the implementation of the policy will run into difficulties.

The policy on AIDS in New Brunswick and the policy on physical education were shown to have been legitimized in the fashion argued by Thomas. The French policy was also legitimized in the fashion indicated, but ran into a number of localized problems that were overcome in part because of the careful policy-making that characterized the introduction of French immersion programs from the seminal stages of the policy.

The last policy considered was that of integration and it has been argued that this policy was prematurely introduced and insufficient attention was paid to both the experts and the need for participatory decision-making. Following a hefty dose of participation involving a committee of the New Brunswick Legislature, the process of legitimation may now be back in place but careful and fair use of expert advice remains necessary.

Finally, little has been said about legitimation of policy in the courts. There is no question of the authority that the courts possess but the Caraquet Riots revealed that the authority of the courts is not quite absolute. This reference, however, has not been lost on education policy-making in New Brunswick which, in general, has reflected the wishes of the large majority of the population. The resort to the courts is a last resort and fortunately the appeals system provides ample time for consideration and reconsideration by all parties. While justice delayed is usually regarded as justice denied, in sensitive cases of educational policy-making, careful preparation which may lead to a delay in justice being served, may be essential to ensure that justice will be served at all.

## Notes

[1] OECD, *Report on Canadian Education* (Paris: OECD, 1979).

[2] R. Redfield, *The Human Community* (Chicago: University of Chicago Press, 1961), pp.17-32.

[3] OECD.

[4] R.F. Lawson and R.R. Woock, "Policy and Policy Actors," in R. Ghosh and R. Ray, eds., *Social Change and Education in Canada* (Toronto: Harcourt Press, 1973), pp.133-4.

[5] M. Thomas, *Politics and Education* (Oxford: Pergamon Press, 1983).

[6] There had been legislation related to local options before the *Common Schools Act*.

[7] T. Murphy, "The Emergence of Maritime Catholicism," *Acadiensis Reader*, volume 1 (Fredricton: Acadiensis Press, 1988), pp. 68-88.

[8] G. Stanley, "The Caraquet Riots of 1875," *Acadiensis Reader*, volume 2 (Fredricton: Acadiensis Press, 1985), pp. 78-95.

[9] C. Phillips, *The Development of Canadian Education* (Toronto: Ryerson Press, 1958).

[10] E. M. Hall and L.A. Dennis, *Living and Learning* (Toronto: Department of Education, 1968).

[11] G. Radwanski, *Ontario Study on the Relevance of Education, and the Issue of Dropouts* (Ontario: Ministry of Education, 1973).

[12] W.H. Worth, *A Choice of Futures* (Edmonton: Government of Alberta, 1972).

[13]G.E.M. MacLeod and A. Pinet, *Education and Tomorrow: Report of the Minister's Committee on Educational Planning* (Fredriction: Department of Education, 1973).

[14]The author was present at such a meeting in Blueridge, Alberta, in March 1960.

[15]G. Martell, *The Politics of Canadian Education* (Toronto: Larimer & Co., 1974) pp. 39-64.

[16]Lawson and Woock, pp. 133-42.

[17]Lawson and Woock.

[18]M. Thomas, *Politics and Education* (Oxford: Perganon Press,1983).

[19]Social Policy Development, *Sixth Report of the Special Commission Committee* (New Brunswick, 1989).

[20]*Sixth Report*, p. 10.

[21]*Sixth Report*, p. 11.

[22]*Sixth Report*, p. 9.

# 9

# With the Board in Mind:
# Trustees Look at Issues and Prospects

*Richard G. Townsend*

A board of education is a modern version of the bell rope that once, eons ago, dangled in front of the private school. Anyone could tug it, day or night, whereupon the schoolmaster would come out to inquire, "What's wrong?" In North America, as education became a responsibility of the state and as schooling came to be regarded as too important to be left entirely to professionals, elected and appointed laymen on boards of education also began responding to those who claimed that schools could be easily improved.

Over the past decade, in conversations averaging an hour in length, I have "tugged at" 144 board members across Canada.[1] They are a fairly well-educated elite, almost 75 percent of them being college or university graduates. This chapter is an inventory of the issues and prospects expressed by them, no trustee being quoted more than once. Sections below deal with the relationships with constituents, employees and others in the educational arena (the provincial governments, fellow-trustees, et al.). But first, the focus is briefly on what they assert is the prime purpose of the school system — teaching and learning.

## Boards and the Educational Process

Sometimes grave disappointment sets in among those who are interested in classroom instruction. As one chairman comments:

> A few years ago at each meeting, we had a half-hour set aside when a superintendent, supervisor, department head, or coordinator would share with us something about education. . . . Actually, I always found it a relief to talk about the real heart of education. It beats talking about property management. . . . Most of the Board, though, found these sessions objec-

155

tionable. They didn't like to sit around and talk about teaching. They liked sticking to business.

Despite such avoidance of pedagogy by some, numerous other trustees are very willing to discourse on the educational programs and products. To be sure, not one of those interviewed cites the scholarly literature, whether on questioning strategies, problem-solving emphases in math, or effective schools, and the prospects they enunciate are not as sophisticated as those treated in this book's chapter on curriculum. Yet board members do appear to have some basic if implicit understanding of what they think of as good education.

According to John Stuart Mill, a function of a legislative body is to criticize the executive, and trustees in this study occasionally rise to that function. For instance, the quality of secondary education, that hot issue of the eighties, catches condemnation from about 20 board members — tougher marking and more required subjects definitely are wanted. A Nova Scotian blames teachers for high-school graduates not being able to think, write, or do math properly. Most of these board members seem to welcome the recent initiations of provincial exams and other tightenings of curricula.

Trustees, of course, can also be fairly specific about programs they do favor. Consider this example from the West:

> We had a struggle over integrating handicapped kids. Parents were split right down the middle. Some parents said, "No, those kids should be put in a special school where they are not laughed at or ridiculed or kicked around." Other parents said, "No, life is life, facts are facts, and let them go with the others." Administrators were split too. "If you integrate them, you will lose them," most said, "and we won't be able to give them that one-on-one [attention] that research says is important." We [trustees] thought some of the parents [of children without learning disablities] would scream "Get those cripples out of here." There were enough of us on the Board who felt it was well worth the time and money to give it a try.... The amazing thing now is that the children in the school are just overwhelmed by these kids — they help them dress and cross the street. There's a good feeling.

"We support effective teaching," another chair in the East says in characterizing her long-time commitment, "even if our teachers don't always think so."

This report is not the place to critique the pedagogical competence of elected officials, so much as it is to suggest that trustees may be becoming sophisticated about curriculum. About a tenth of those I interviewed seemed to value receiving, in advance of board meetings, staff documents about the niceties of teaching and learning. Contrary to conventional wisdom which has many trustees rooted in an academic past, these officials seized the chance to read through and to frame questions about brand-new curricula. Invited to speak at greater length about this, these trustees saw teachers as pedagogical experts but not as ones who invariably had "all the right answers."

In the view of politicians in my survey, while educators might be the right ones to decide on the tactical forms and sequencings of new programs — the best age to begin immersion, whether tutorials or simulations are the best formats for computer learning, the texts to use for whole language, and so forth — educators' professional standards ought to carry great weight in implementation but might not be appropriate to deciding if immersion, computers, or whole language should be introduced in the first place. A proportion of trustees claimed such strategic choices for themselves. In effect, many of the trustees were saying: "It's good to heed professional school people once you decide on a curriculum, but these folks aren't the only ones you should listen to when you decide on a curriculum or not."

## Relationships With Constituencies

In describing their experiences in educational governance, those interviewed reveal their attitudes toward the citizens they represent. Let me try to sort out those attitudes into two trilogies of board-constituency relations.

### *Trilogy 1*

Perhaps the most familiar distinction[2] to describe the outlook of politicians is one that suggests three possibilities — independence (where the official relies on his or her own convictions in deciding issues), loyalty to the grassroots (where the official is the delegate for her or his constituency), and a politico sentiment (where the official borrows from the independent and grassroots etiquettes on the basis of what he or she thinks appropriate for given situations). As it happened, no Canadian board member in this study used those very terms, yet these three orientations turn out to be consistent with the contexts of many interviewees' remarks.

More than 20 percent project themselves as autonomous decision-makers, strong enough to make their own unpressured judgments. They see the ideal role of the public in educational policy-making as (1) voting and thereby choosing leaders and (2) showing interest in issues. They are quick to claim that they are not being pushed around by interest groups, e.g., "I don't believe in compromise. I promote my position, and if my constituents like it, they'll re-elect me; if they don't like it, they won't."

Over 50 percent of the trustees go somewhat further to envisage an activism for citizens — the latter should phone with concerns, file briefs and otherwise make their views known to individuals on their board; as more than one person interviewed recalled, trustees frequently make reference at board meetings to being "in touch" with such community sentiments. These trustees will welcome, but claim that they do little to actively seek, specific opinions from citizens on educational goals or particular issues. Indeed, sometimes these independent-minded trustees speak of the public with a trace of pessimism and paternalism. The next speaker is a woman from Alberta:

> [As a Board member] you have to speak out [on what needs to be done] and just because you say something once, that is not enough because people are not necessarily listening . . . you have to say it over and over again. After a while, the public begins to understand and agree with what needs to be done.

On the other hand, the grassroots trustee is more open to being regularly advised by the rank-and-file — individually or in advisory groups — who give their taxes, time, and children to schools. As a British Columbian says, "My constituency is made up of those who see education as an instrument for social reform and upward mobility. I'm perceived as someone who's a vehicle for the ambitions of underprivileged children to be achieved." "Sure, I represent my ward," a somewhat similar trustee from Ontario tells me, "I have to look after their interests. If I'm wrong, the other trustees will outvote me." From another: "It's the folks who have the influence. They'll let you go for a bit, but when they reach the end of their string, look out!" Officials who articulate this populist disposition like to indicate that their antennae are out for the genuine voice of the community; thus, narrow-based demands for change are suspect. For example, a Saskatchewan trustee does not want to isolate herself from change, yet she is wary of catalysts who arise "out of nowhere" with no visible backing. They may be unqualified and uninformed:

> Delegations? There are always individuals who don't speak for any community at all and [who] give the impression they have a big following. That's when the board member has to inquire as to whom the petitioner represents. You know, the petitioner may be speaking only for himself . . . and not know a thing. . . . We need more delegations that genuinely reflect broad community feelings. The better organized they are, the better for us. . . . Makes our job easier.[3]

From the tenor of their complete conversations, a rough estimate of between 15 and 18 percent of the trustees interviewed perceive of themselves — at least in part — as tending to be stalwart voices for their grassroots, i.e., "By and large, I want what my community wants." None go so far, though, as to propose that citizens sit in on Board-teacher negotiations, a proposal occasionally bruited about in the U. S. back in the late 1970s.[4]

The rest, surely no more than 12 or 13 percent, appear to be politicos, picturing themselves as trying to span that gulf between independent thinking and constituency-catering. To walk this tightrope may appear to require equivocation and waffling, yet politcos may be presumed to have an internally consistent rationale: if not to represent all interests in sizeable communities, they may try to defuse conflict by keeping everybody somewhat placated. Thus, a Manitoban declares:

> We have a predominance of middle-class people like myself on the Board. We can afford the time and don't need the money. The job doesn't pay enough to attract people from the working class. . . . We have our eye out for our youngsters' needs, sure, but I'm also enough of a public servant to push for what the working class would push for — if they were on the Board.

The only board member in my study to allude to violence speaks of representation in two senses — of the accountability that stems from election, and of having a similar social background to one's electorate. Still, as he also indicates while speaking of his need to depart from common interests he has with those voters, no irrevocable link appears to exist between this politico's upbringing and issues that attract his support:

> My community [in New Brunswick] is one tough community. They've burned people out of their homes over an issue. . . . The only reason I can "buck" them on a few issues is that I am one of them. The thing is, I've paid my dues. I come from the same background as they do.

Less common in the scholarly literature about board members are stances that can be arrayed on a continuum of change. Let me venture one such spectrum now, of (1) preservationists, (2) those who would change schools as circumstances change, and (3) agents for modestly changing the schools and, thus, modestly changing society.

## Trilogy Two

The largest number of trustees, perhaps as many as 70 percent, primarily portray themselves as interpreters of local values and as preservationists of community distinctiveness. They talk of battling a strong and single-minded educational establishment with professional or wider-than-local values. Hence:

> The provincial government [in Prince Edward Island] transports kids out to new high schools out in the country. We have nothing around those schools except trees and football fields. The government was wrong to phase-out schools. They were centres of village life.

> I'm concerned about the notion that one shouldn't confine oneself to rural Newfoundland. It's felt that if you're going to be a success, you have to go to St. John's or Toronto. It's beneath you to go into the fishing industry or any of the old trades. That's how teachers talk. Teachers put down blue collars and small places.

If these board members are saying that educators should recognize the worthy aspects of a locale, the next one articulates the view that students ought to learn that the community's conflicts are authentic expressions of interactions among the various aspects of the community:

> There's a demand for labor history. In my area, there's the tradition of a strong trade union, of militant struggle against absentee management. . . . of solidarity among workers and the cooperative building of credit. Everybody in _____ doesn't side with management.

"Remember the locales' ethnic diversities," other board members say. For them, the dominant white Anglo-Saxon community needs to set restraints on its freedoms so minorities can move toward equal circumstances. Listen to these pleas for a revived cultural democracy:

> We transgressed the rights of the Natives in the 1950s, abolishing a Native curriculum in Labrador. Today we want the same for Indians as we have for ourselves — the right to keep a culture. Most Indian children don't speak

> their native Cree, Ojibway, any of the original languages. [It's] time we gave them their languages back.

> We caused disruption in strongly matriarchal families by not having classes where children could learn more about their families' heritages. Though immigrant fathers and children got out of the house, mothers didn't go out without chaperones. . . . Our English-only programs undermined the fabric of those families.

> Ukrainians at one time had an excellent school system in rural Manitoba. It was destroyed by the provincial government's school inspectors [reducing everything to a common denominator]. . . . Now we need to recoup some of that loss.

This respect for a common past, something of a foil to the isolation and disorder of the city, is found among urban as well as small-town or rural trustees. (My respondents did not suggest that tightly-knit communities can exist within the big city, or that village life can include the class divisions and anonymity of the metropolis, or that the so-called harmony of villages can be an imposed one.)

Some board members, not numerous but among the longest-serving, fall into a middle ground for change. They argue for schools to be changed along with changing circumstances. What attracts some of them to board service is the sense that they are helping to make schools different from those in which they, as children, learned:

> Prejudices one acquires from teachers as a young person are difficult to unlearn as an adult. . . . We've got to sensitize teachers so they won't spread misunderstandings . . . [like] my teachers [in Britain] did about Irish history.

In addition, calls for faster rates of adjustment between schools and today's communities are associated with changes in demography and migration:

> Older teachers in some schools work for a long time and the situation changes around them. The community changes, but they don't.

> Back in 1950, the community [outside Toronto] was white, Anglo-Saxon, Protestant. Period. Since then, it's changed dramatically in terms of population composition. Still, many trustees are totally unaware of that. Remarkable! They come from areas which are not ethnic [or foreign] in background and their relationships are such that I don't think they ever see those people. They react as if it were the same way "back when." It's really strange because if you say, "We have a changing system and so we had better deal with the particular issue that 40 percent of the population are Caribbean students and that we have only Anglo-Saxons on staff," everybody sort of sighs and goes on to the next [agenda] item. I tried once to make a pitch for an inter-community kind of organization, and I was accused of trying to use racial differences as a political gimmick. Imagine!

Old-fogeyism, in the sense of reverence for the status quo, also is a clear enemy for those board members who want schools to revise their programs to train high-school students for brand-new jobs that are now opening up in the community and beyond. Another call is for Saskatchewan students to have more of a world view — social studies should be geared more to "the global village we've become." A trustee in B.C. wants systems to start giving orientations for "new" parents "out there," especially those who are single parents and those who are culturally different. A Newfoundlander wants more connections between the children and growing numbers of senior citizens.

While most trustees are not skeptical of change in general, only a tenth or so of those interviewed talk as if they might fit into a third category of inclinations toward change, those who are actively interested in promoting incremental reform; at best, they would change 5 or 10 percent of the whole system, nothing more.[5] Usually those who relish this sort of problem-solving see themselves as bringing in a new policy or practice that directly affects children (such as more equipment for science classes or programs above provincial minimums) instead of a shift that primarily affects educators, e.g., term-appointments for principals or sabbaticals for teachers.

Whatever their focus, many of these change-agents worry about straying too far from what is acceptable. Here's a Nova Scotian who is more explicit about this than others:

> It isn't easy to implement a decision if it goes against public opinion, but at times we have to. When we built our new school, we had opposition from the public. They complained about the tax bill, but sometimes [as a Board member] you have to lead, some things you can't leave up to the public. . . . They don't have the whole story.

One trustee indicates that even if parents had the "whole story," they may not be the most appropriate choosers. In a conservative farming community, she is willing to stick her neck out for an updating of health education:

> Sex education is not being taught in the home. No matter how open or upfront or modern you are as a parent, you're still uncomfortable talking about the nitty-gritty of sex. You could be young, a true swinger, but you still find it uncomfortable. That all goes back to when you were growing up. You could talk about sex with friends, but you could never picture your parents having a wild relationship. . . . I'd feel more comfortable telling adolescents across the street than I would feel telling mine. That's the main reason why sex ed. should be in the schools. The schools are removed from the situation. They can be more factual and direct. The student asks more questions of the teacher than the parent.

Other gladiators for change, focusing on different human potentialities, try to serve as brokers between the school system and their constituencies:

> It's fine for me as a trustee to hire an art teacher, a music teacher, and that's the end of it — I've done my job, basically. But if I haven't been able to talk to parents of that community, and have them whole-heartedly get behind the idea that the Board has, and that the teaching body has, for broadening the base of education, the program is going to fail. Well, then it's a problem of my going out into the community, taking the time to sell the idea to the people who elected me.

A theme tying together many board members as reformers is that citizens often lack a stock of education-relevant facts. So, they say, it's up to board members to access and then to disseminate relevant information. Another theme is distrust of major change. The trustees I interviewed would have critics shout less and listen more.

## Contract Relationships with Employees

Bargaining with teachers need not be conflictive — a chair in B.C. as well as a chair in Ontario say they can work at great depth during negotiations to improve communications and find common causes. Through bargaining, they see patterns being set for shared responsibility in decision-making.

These two officials are alone, however, in saying a positive word about the process and outcomes of collective bargaining. Indeed, when many other trustees from one province meet with trustees from another, reportedly they exchange "horror" stories about provincial teachers' associations and the direction they exert over local affiliates. Rather simply, I'm afraid, a number depict teachers as grubbers who want more pay to do less work. Union leaders are said to be more radical than the rank-and-file. "Why can't teachers' contracts be settled as simply," a Prairie trustee asks, "as our secretaries' and custodians' [contracts]?" A couple of board members tell me that because they have experience dealing with unions in the private sector, they understand the negotiating process for schools.[6]

According to some trustees, up to now, bargaining is a no-win situation for provincial governments. In provinces where teachers enjoy the right to strike (i.e., in every province except Manitoba), one or two interviewees argue that since bargaining has not furthered harmonious relations between board and staff, that right should be abrogated. Others retort that any provincial government that so abrogated would create an election issue of the first rank; educators are too accustomed to those arrangements to change anything that fundamental. In those places with provincial-level bargaining for teachers, several interviewees still blame their provincial legislators for initially "giving away [local] management rights" by authorizing central-level negotiations. These trustees, usually old-timers, assert that they felt more responsive to their communities before teachers' salaries, teaching conditions, staffing procedures and routines for staff development were set by provincial contracts.

A further distinction can be made among bargaining practices in different provinces. Quebec is an example of *two-tier* bargaining where salaries as well as pupil-teacher ratios are handled at the central level, with working conditions and staff development being worked-out at local levels. There, education ministries are expected to give negotiators more support (e.g., non-aligned consultants to help both sides arrive at contractual settlements), and not just before the contract expires. On this, one commissioner (a Quebec trustee) implores, "Why shouldn't negotiations be in progress months before?" Next, in the four provinces with *local-level* bargaining, on occasion, ministers are blamed for not stepping in soon enough to settle local strikes. And when ministers or ministries do try to step in, in one trustee's perspective:

We've had government-imposed contracts that have tied us in knots, and that take far too much of people's time. Our margin of flexibility in dealing with people has been very much reduced. Teacher-student relations have become more and more difficult to organize.

If this study's interviewees had any new ideas for more effective formats to achieve labor peace, they did not pass them on to me. Only one speculated freely, suggesting that his province should set up a tripartite tribunal to settle staff problems. Besides equal representation from boards and teachers, administrators would then have a separate say, presumably because their concerns would not be altogether consonant with either of the two other entities. That is, as controllers of resources, superintendents and principals seem to want more discretion than many teacher unionists are comfortable with; at the same time, as supervisors of personnel, administrators want higher salaries for teachers — since that hike kicks into gear the boosting of their own salaries. Or so declared this one speculating chairperson.

Around the country, certain trustees are looking at the steps taken in 1987 by the B.C. provincial government, requiring teachers to belong to a college of teachers for their professional development. Such professional interests are now split from bread-and-butter matters, Victoria now giving teachers the choice of bargaining either as a non-union association or as a certified union. The British Columbia Teachers' Federation (BCTF) "would appear," in the Minister's words, "to be a logical contender" for local associations to affiliate with. Worried that implementation of the new Bill 20 would destroy teacher solidarity, BCTF leaders say their significant programs "will not be able to continue." Those interviewed wondered whether this approach would "work" in their own province, and — for that matter — how the College of Teachers approach would work even in B.C.

## Other Relationships in the Arena[7]

By way of capturing a further sense of the issues facing those who serve on boards, I asked my population of trustees, "What is the least appealing aspect of your involvement in educational policy-making?" Highlights appear next from what they had to say about *intra*personal conflict (tensions within themselves), *inter*personal conflict (disputes with other individuals) and inter-organizational conflict (especially between levels of government).

### *Intrapersonal Conflicts*

A major disappointment that respondents say they have to learn to live with is that only about 20 percent of their budgets can be allocated, the rest going automatically for salaries. Some newcomers to boards had assumed that they would have more fiscal significance than they do in the educational arena, and their slight amount of budgetary leeway prompts many members to question the point of their role. As a New Brunswicker said, "I felt I had taken something out of the community and I should give something back. However, I find [as a trustee] that when it comes to money, the bottom line, I don't count for very much."

Relatedly, a number of trustees report that policy-making also can be boring, thanks to requirements that they endorse technical routines such as tendering and copyright regulations. Tediousness also sets in discussions of details of the school plant — of expansions, architectural styles, asbestos problems and pavings of parking lots. An Ontarian jests that a kind of Parkinson's Law is operative: the less important the issue, the higher the frequency of intense discussion and haggling. Often, administration is scorned:

> In terms of educational substance, most of the things that people think are educational issues could be handled by my ten-year-old daughter. I can sleep through three-quarters of a board meeting . . . I sit on the Board because I believe that certain things have to be done, but most of what we do is gutless.

Several board members profess to be irked by poor working conditions they endure. They see their pace as hectic, often having to make decisions too quickly with insufficient data. Notably, those on large boards regret having to forego moments with their families or the necessity of having to cope with heavy workloads, reading through staff documents and serving on many board committees (a handful of urban trustees claimed service on as many as six of seven committees). What further upsets certain trustees is the seeming emptiness of some of their impacts; before election and from a distance, the member's role had somehow seemed more profound, meatier. Or easier. In any event, members do not envisage those drawbacks to their role changing substantially — although one suggests that she and her peers are likely to become more adept at information-processing.

## Interpersonal Conflicts

Another grounding for the reply about "least appealing aspects to the role" is the conflict that surfaces when people express divergent opinions and act out power struggles. Assuredly, conflicts of this ilk can take their intrapersonal tolls, but the emphasis here is on disagreements that erupt between board members and citizens, fellow-trustees, and educators.

Uncharitable actions and attitudes of a sniping public strike some board members as inappropriate. Members do not expect slavish attention from the citizenry, but generally they look for public interest *before* issues are settled. Too often, as a woman from the Prairies remarks, people "make a fuss *after* we've made a decision [about which] they didn't even try to reach us."

Several trustees insist that they do not appreciate noisy groups — and these officials perceive too many noisy groups blocking bus routes and taking other direct and collective actions — at the expense of quieter citizens who wait their turn for official consideration in question periods and in private meetings. Others fret that so few parents and ratepayers communicate their wishes to board members. For instance, a Maritimer mentions that "Often, I have to second-guess all our wordless citizens. That worries me."[8]

Board members also irritate each other. As might be expected, some do not admire the working styles of their colleagues. More specifically, some are seen as not carrying their weight, e.g., "Sometimes there isn't even another trustee who has read the report of staff. They're not conscientious in doing their homework." Other peers are perceived as overly constraining: "They expect Board matters to be discussed only at Board meetings, when everyone knows that members discuss problems over the phone all the time" (prior to meetings). A Toronto lawyer says he resents fellow-trustees who work at the Board office 40+ hours a week: "There's enough of these trustees that they work out all the problems while the rest of us have day jobs. They bug the hell out of administrators."

Elsewhere, a number chaff at the conservativeness (but, curiously enough, not the progressiveness) or the parochiality of colleagues who "can't see beyond their noses." Thus, a teacher-trustee finds the farmers, businessmen and mothers on his Board difficult to convince about what's desirable for schools (at least about his view of what's desirable). Urban-rural splits also emerge, as do money-spending and money-conserving alignments. As well, in Manitoba,

> Many on our Board are "pro-teacher" instead of "pro-kid" and it's impossible to bring the pro-teacher side to our point of view. Changes frighten board members who don't want teachers on their backs.

Several trustees indicate that such differences are unlikely to vanish. A number, however, attach a positive value to the diversity among those on boards — allegedly and idealistically, the expression of differences enables members to make their way through the political maze to the adoption of policies that help one element of the overall community without hurting another.

> Male chauvinism surfaced in central Canada where, in the midst of gruff reflections about work with colleagues on Board committees, one businessman-trustee observed, apparently in all seriousness, "I don't understand why they appointed Mrs. _____ to our Building and Maintenance Committee. What do women know about property maintenance?"

For only a fraction of trustees with whom I spoke, the least pleasant side of educational governance is working with uncooperative school people. In the estimate of this small band of board members, educators are stingy in generating alternatives and in circulating information. The nub of a Quebec trustee's ire, for instance, is that the administration will not share minutes of meetings of parents' committees with her. The flash point for several other members is the politicking of administrators; by way of example, one points to a coalition-building director in Ontario who "slides in a few points, more than what we agreed on, and who changes a few lines in a report just to make a few more trustees happy." A Quebec commissioner looks forward to annual meetings where "we don't have to meet with the administration." She reasons that when board members are by themselves, they can accomplish more of what *they* care about. Yet another trustee is angered by the "blackmail" of an Albertan superintendent who threatens to resign if his recommendations are not 100 percent accepted. Once policies are adopted, a few other board members suspect that those policies are not really being implemented at the school level. In this vein, a Manitoban finds:

> Teachers as a group do not accept change although they are supposed to help the child adjust to change themselves. Teachers are very inflexible. I hadn't realized this before I went on the Board. Now I sometimes think that if every teacher could retire after 15 years, we could have a truly dynamic system.

In other conversations that touch upon disharmonies in board life, several trustees reveal a view of change that is imposed by them from the top — staff are perceived as recalcitrant receivers of directions and not necessarily 100 percent faithful implementers in the policy process. A possible antidote to this sour perception would be for these trustees to spend more time in the schools discussing programs and problems with principals and teachers, but none of my respondents alluded to undertaking such a touching-base on education's front lines.[9]

## *Inter-organizational Conflict*

Support exists for letting non-school groups use school facilities, although trustees acknowledge (and shrug off) that teachers complain about the messy blackboards and askew seats that may be left behind. Aside from discussions of such open schools, a plaintiff quality appears in remarks about Board interactions with other public agencies. An example from the West:

> We have continual interference from county councilors who feel for some reason that they are better citizens than we are [on the Board]. In rural areas, one person is elected for a whole municipal and school area, and it's much easier for that person to see a hole in the road than a hole in the educational system.

Others hold that schools must retain political-administrative independence from other agencies in the community for "the trade-offs would be scary. It would be roads against education, roads against social services. There wouldn't be enough votes for education, politicians and administrators in other departments being what they are.

Belief in locally controlled schools is so considerable that by far the most frequent and intense complaints and fears revolve around the intrusiveness of the provincial government and its "controlling" ministers and bureaucrats. Over 40 percent of the board members in this study believe these provincial sources to be the most influential source in education — ahead, say, of local boards, interest groups, educators, the electorate, the media, university faculties, academic scribblers and ecclesiastical interests.[10] "I'm just a rubber stamp for the provincial government," one chairman scowls. Another sees trustees as buffers for provincial authorities who do not want to encounter the political "trouble" of assuming total responsibility for schooling.

In turn, however, trustees are not above faulting specific provincial actions in domains besides collective bargaining. Ministers get poor marks for their curricula (if anything, provincial guidelines are seen to inhibit local initiatives), their restrictions on personnel (the Ministry is painted as insular for only certifying as supervisors those who have taught within the province), their attempts in Quebec to reorganize boards (abandoning denominational boards for linguistic ones) and their policy on capital construction. For example:

> One day I asked my child where he ate lunch [at elementary school]. He said "in the science room." He said it was the only place to eat. I decided to visit the school and found it was in such a mess that I couldn't believe they had kids going there. It was a disaster area . . . I became involved with other parents to get a new school. It took us four years of bucking the Minister and the Deputy Minister. They told us, "Yes, you can have the school," [and] "No, you can't have the school," etc., etc. We kept the fight going and finally we got it.

Provincial inaction or "dilly-dallying" is faulted by board members too. For instance, board members in a prairie province imply that the functionaries in the Ministry are putting red tape in the way of localities because they interpret the Minister as wanting to stall in decision-making.

An incident of provincial-local conflict — that all the recent interviewees referred to with concern — is the dissolution of the Vancouver and Cowichan boards by British Columbia's Social Credit government. In 1982, that government had passed the *Education (Interim) Finance Act* removing the rights of boards to levy taxes on eight of nine classes of property and determine their own needed level of expenditure. When it appeared that those boards had failed to comply with the Minister's directive to cut expenditures, their elected trustees were dismissed from office and an official trustee was appointed for each system. Next, five of the 18 trustees took the case to court, but the judge ruled that "school boards are not above the law." At the time of the next election, trustees returned to office in both systems, but not before trustees and various polls expressed great malaise over the fragile autonomy of local government, the aloofness of the official trustee and a growing insolence of senior administrators, the loss of parent and citizen input through consultative committees that had been developed and the loss of trustee representation. The Minister could have taken other steps than suspend the boards for such a long period, trustees insisted.[11]

The conflict is not simply over the amount of money but over the limited discretion that local authorities have with money at hand. Of course, a short argument can be made for Ministry controls, if not Ministry rigidities. Bluntly put, the case is that the administrative centre (i.e., a ministry) upholds standards that mean-spirited or bigoted minds at the periphery (i.e., local boards) might decide to ignore. No trustee in this study, however, is so blunt as to allude to this rationale or to this characterization of local individuals. In fact, several intimate the opposite — that local officials are so discriminating that they will not tolerate low standards or narrow-mindedness. In some ways too, those on the firing line at the board level are perceived to be abreast of the latest educational ideas, sometimes well ahead of "bureaucrats" at provincial headquarters. And, if mistakes do occur at the periphery, in the view of a chairman from Saskatchewan, it is in spite of central's coordination.

The accusatory nature of many trustees' remarks about ministries appears associated with trusteees sensing that they and their province-wide associations politically are weak and not especially effective counterbalances to their legislatures or organizations (syndicates, federations, associations) for educators. A pair of chairmen, in different regions, volunteer that their board associations should combine with other groups (e.g., political parties, teacher groups) to press for changes in their ministries' fiscal provisions and attitudes.

## Relationships with Political Parties

In keeping with the exhortatory literature on school boards, the majority of the members I interviewed emphasize the importance of trustees being part of one team. This means being an effective "corporate" member, listening to others, responsibly expressing one's own views, and finding solutions that do not relate to the public interest. In some trustees' views, this membership means participating in a division of labor, suspending judgement on the broad range of issues, because much of the real deliberation goes on in committees and committee members like to have their work ratified. In the end, corporate membership also means working through the group and respecting the ultimate decisions that the board as a whole has made.

In this perspective, trusteeship also means interpreting the whole community as one's constituency, rationalizing specific needs of any one group against overall needs of the entire system. The specters of individualistic trustees, of in-fighting, and of discrepant public interests in education are *not* welcomed. In fact, these images are almost resented by most trustees I spoke with. A special sneer is awarded to those colleagues who would politically maneuver for factional gains or for gains that advance a single ward's interests ahead of the whole system's.

To a handful of urban trustees, however, shifts toward competition in governance would increase electees' links with electors, thereby also increasing board members' claims to being legitimate representatives. This handful of trustees pictures the essence of democracy as teams of leaders striving over time for public support through different policies. As they see it, the concerted power that exists at the provincial level in ministries of Education and cabinets is dangerous without the competition in ideas that can be aggregated and articulated by civic parties (which might be aligned on issues with federal or provincial parties).

These competition-prone trustees portray themselves as bridging the gap between the board and the people. They reason that if the characteristics and preferences of communities become much more heterogeneous, challenges will be mounted against a unitary "one-best" way of delivering education (a "we-know-best" disposition that a few trustees think exists in their systems today).

In the face of cultural differences, parents will make demands for their own kinds of schools; conservative, liberal and socialist interests in education — or some other combination of orientations — will be identified. Party activity along those lines thereafter will grow beyond its open presence today in Vancouver, Calgary, and Toronto, and its backstage presence in other communities. Once they defeat candidates of opposing outlooks, "new wave" board members will have a feeling of responsibility to adopt what they campaigned for. Voters will use the platforms of these civic networks as yardsticks to gauge how well their representatives delivered on their promises. Non-partisan board members gradually will diminish, or so say this study's smattering of political party-minded trustees — in what is as much a wish as a prediction.[12]

In the years ahead, some possibility may well exist for such partization. To be sure, the board member who keeps party politics out of education will continue to make vital contributions, particularly if she or he establishes credibility by becoming informed, by developing some expertise, by pragmatically and periodically helping the board set working objectives. "When I first became a trustee," one such well-regarded chairperson told me, "I was shy, naive, and intimidated by the administration and by trustees who had been on the Board for almost forever. I had to build up my confidence, learn how to research, learn how to work with the system librarian, how to tap the ideas of members of boards in other jurisdictions, how to find out what you need to back up arguments. . . . I didn't need then, and I certainly don't need now, a political party to do my thinking."

## Conclusion

A final question that I asked the 144 trustees for this report was "Who should have the most influence in educational policy-making?" To their board members' credit, most responses were consistent with the general thrusts of their preceding comments about various issues in education. About a third put their weight mostly behind more say for local boards, with less control by the provinces. Primarily leaning towards more participation by parents and the public were almost 10 percent. Less autonomy for local administrators was the top recommendation of another 10 percent, while a reduction of the influence of teachers' unions was contemplated by perhaps 7 percent. About 5 percent sought some reorganization of their board's own operations, through more influence for local administrators, overhauled procedures for committees, or even (in two cases) special staffs for trustees. If we discard an additional 5 percent who responded vaguely or not at all, we are left with roughly 30 percent who championed no clear change, or at least no such change was on their mind when we talked.

One intriguing feature of this list of impressions is its conservatism. Examples of this moderation are suggestions that the power of provincial mandarins be constrained and that parents should be allowed to serve in a non-voting capacity on board committees. No one outside Quebec championed that province's arrangement for a parent to sit in a non-voting capacity on a board's executive committee. No support is evident either for an idea consistent with the decade's talk about teacher empowerment, i.e., teachers should be represented on boards to articulate student and staff interests. More revolutionary trustees might have urged, for example, the replacement of city-wide boards with neighborhood councils, protection of "whistle-blowers" in the educator ranks, the forming of more single-member wards for trustees, school-site budgeting, the provision for representation of key minorities, and the establishment of interactive computer networks to provide opportunities for citizens to obtain information and express opinions on curriculum methodology.

Also of note, no one appears so dissatisfied with the ethnic or social-class background of the influentials in educational policy-making that they repudiate the legitimacy of current political arrangements for schools or for Canada. At many boards, as several intimated, the "rank" authority of the board may give way to the "technical" authority of the educator, and a paramount need of governance may be to find a workable balance between educator initiative and board control — yet fresh blueprints for structural, process, or personnel change are not emanating from this study's trustees.[13]

Since this was a very limited but broad study, we must not overgeneralize from it. In other circumstances, interviewees might react differently. But at least in the views of this one group of 144, no single redistribution of influence and no wholesale reform in governance are called for. Input into educational policy-making is proceeding adequately, but more power for local boards would be just fine, thank you.

## Notes

[1] This study was partially supported by the Finance and Governance Project, with a grant to OISE from the Ministry of Education, 1989. One-hundred and thirty-seven of the 144 were nominated as highly influential by administrators from every province attending two leadership courses at Banff; the seven others were board chairs I subsequently and recently met in leadership roles at various conferences around the country. While making no claim that the 137 are a representative sample of Canadian trustees, I do hold that this selected population is reputed (by selected administrators) to be among the more politically significant of board members. I draw upon different data and report altogether different findings on this group in *They Politick For Schools* (Toronto: OISE Press, 1988). For another approach to the perceptions of some Canadian trustees,

see the Ontario work of Harold Jakes, "How Successful Was Their First Year in Office?" *Ontario Education* (May-June, 1984): 3-7. And for a good but terse overview of educational governance in Canada, see Edward S. Hickcox, "School Boards," *The Canadian Encyclopedia* (Edmonton: Hurtig, 1985): 1649-1650.

[2]See for instance, Hannah Pitkin, *The Concept of Representation* (Berkeley: University of California Press, 1967).

[3]The danger from writing-off the "out of nowhere" spokesperson is well-described in Paul E. Peterson, "Community Representation and the Free Rider," *Administrator's Notebook*, 22, 8 (1974): 1-4.

[4]See for example, Seymour Sarason et al., *The Community At The Bargaining Table* (Boston: Institute for Responsive Education, 1974). Also absent from the board members' comments is any mention of the finding, discerned by C. Lopate et al. in "Decentralization and Community Participation in Public Education," *Review of Educational Research*, 40, 1:135-150) that students tend to achieve more in school when their parents are involved in that school's life. Presumably, parents' participation in school outreach activities promotes their youngsters' positive attitudes toward learning.

[5]Instead, they are more interested in being where the action is (the great drama, fun and influence of policy-making), in communicating their board's needs to the community, in fulfilling their citizenship duty (sometimes following in the footsteps of relatives who had been board members) and the sociabilty and conviviality that comes from problem-solving with fellow board members.

[6]Four considerations have been raised in this paragraph, and I acknowledge that my last 2 responses, below, resemble a unionist's perspective. (1) Whether union leaders are more "radical" than their membership is an empirical question; I suspect that the answer varies from union to union, year to year. (2) As far as I can tell, the deprecators of teachers' bargaining insufficiently appreciate the difficulties that teachers are having in delivering ministerially-mandated programs for individual-plan students (which may take 15 percent of their time), special education students (which may take another 15 percent of their time), and regular students (the 28 other students in a class). (3) As a result of many rounds and years of negotiations in the public sector, pay, conditions of work, and fringe benefits for clerical and blue-collar positions have been set. Fairly easily, those levels are transposed to comparable posts in educational systems. (4) I am not persuaded that because a businessperson-trustee has experience in working with a steelworkers' union, she or he necessarily grasps the unique milieu from which spring the demands of classroom teachers. On that special world of teachers, see the Canada-wide work by William A. Marcotte, *A Comparative Analysis of Certain Aspects of Teachers' Contracts* (Toronto: Council of Ministers of Education, 1984).

[7]Over the past decade, several scholars, especially Thomas B. Greenfield in "Organizational Theory as Ideology," in *Curriculum Inquiry*, 9 (1979): 97-112; and Richard Bates in "Administration, Culture, and Critique" in T. Sergiovanni and J. E. Corbally, eds., *Administrative Leadership and Organizational Culture* (Urbana: University of Illinois Press, 1983), have argued that attention to educational organizations can de-emphasize the importance of individuals who

inhabit those enterprises. These academics insist that those at the top of hierarchies may only see one of *many* realities in the school system. I accept their general point that preoccupation with organizational goals, divisions of labor, structures and processes can accompany inattentions to meanings, aspirations and interests of particular human beings who contribute to schools. In that spirit, I extend their notice of individuals embedded in school-oriented organizations to those who serve on boards. (That said, I should add that Greenfield's work deserves still-closer notice in governance studies.)

[8]That the public often abstains from involvement in school governance has been noted as well in H.J. Tucker and H. Zeigler, *Professionals versus the Public: Attitudes, Communication, and Response in School Districts* (New York: Longman, 1980), a study of 11 school districts (10 American, 1 Canadian). Only 10 percent of all board discussions that the researchers monitored had demands that had been made by citizens; in some districts, citizens' inputs were as low as 1 percent of the agenda. For a Canadian explanation of the rise of parental participation in early childhood services in Alberta, see W. R. Dickson, "Involvement By Decree: Citizen Involvement in Education By Legislative Mandate," paper given to the Canadian School Trustees Association Congress on Education, 1978.

[9]Of late, certain Ontario trustees, often female and retired men, have reported such discussions. They also acknowledge doing volunteer work in classrooms, serving as mediators in school disputes, and even acting as evaluators of classroom practices. For administrators who don't want trustees in their hair, this involvement is of course an issue. "In a recent publication of the Ontario Public School Boards Association, see John Davis' interesting "Trends in the Trusteeship," *Education Today* (November-December, 1989): 14-15.

[10]In *Schoolman and Politics* (Syracuse: Syracuse University Press, 1962), Stephen Bailey et al. found academic scribblers in the U. S., such as those who write for learned journals, to be influential. The perception about the subsidiary influence of ecclesiastical interests is contrary to the finding of Frank MacKinnon in "Big Engine, Little Body," *Canadian Provincial Politics*, (Scarborough: Prentice-Hall, 1978): 222-247; MacKinnon's observation is that religious associations "precipate or paralyze official action by threatening to intervene."

[11]For an account of other steps the Minister might have taken, see Norman Robinson, *Report of School Board Dissolution Commission* (Burnaby: Simon Fraser University, 1985). Through this document and a number of others this decade, Robinson (as Commissioner) has invented a memorable genre for commenting on crises of educational governance.

[12]The argument for this particular view is more judiciously presented in Valerie Nielsen and Norman Robinson, "Partisan School Board Elections: New Evidence to Support The Case For Them," *Administrator's Notebook*, 29, 3 (1980-81): 1-4.

[13]On board-administrator transactions, see Michael Awender, "The Superintendent-School Board Relationship," *Canadian Journal of Education*, 10, 2 (Spring, 1985): 176-198. Other Canadian research along the "control" portion of these lines has been initiated by P.J. Renihan and F.I. Renihan, in a paper

presented at the annual conference of the American Association of School Administrators, 1979. Among these brothers' findings from a study of 21 boards in British Columbia: the more decisions made by a board, the less important they tend to be; boards with more trustees tend to make higher-level, corrective-type decisions in the area of finance and business management. In the U.S., discussion on the interplay between elected and administrative officials has recently been revitalized by James H. Svara, "Dichotomy and Duality: Reconceptualizing the Relationship Between Policy and Administration in Council-Manager Cities," *Public Administration Review,* 45 (January-February, 1985): 221-232.

# 10

# Concerns and Priorities of Canadian Teacher Organizations: Revisitation of Militancy Models[1]

## Y.L. Jack Lam

In the eighties, few students of politics of education entertain any lingering doubt that education can be insulated from the intense political activities of all concerned individuals and groups. Foremost in the list of organizations that attain quasi-official status in terms of their involvement and the final shaping of educational policies are teacher organizations in the country. It seems self-evident that front-line educators, who are instantly affected by whatever action the provincial government adopts in education, are most sensitive and eager to claim a share in every stage of the educational decision-making process.

Conceptually intertwined at times, there are two global trends that tend to complicate the life of teachers and activate politicization of teacher organizations. First and foremost is the upsurge of accountability movement propelled by the public's acute awareness of shrinking resources and their desire to optimize performance of all public sectors and to maximize their investment returns. As Campbell[2] earlier noted:

> In all public sectors we are being challenged to look anew at public needs, to plan progress to meet those needs and to recognize our structure and procedures to more effectively implement such programs . . . such a demand becomes . . . a dominant theme of the environment of every public situation, including school.

From the resource dependency perspective[3] which aptly describes the relationship between the public at large and the educational system it supports, the school as an organization is most vulnerable to the growing complexities of its external environments — be they political, economic, social or cultural. There is every evidence these days that almost all educational legislative acts,

175

funding priorities, resource allocation and curriculum reform are outcomes of intense struggle, strategic lobbying and eventual compromise among diverse special interest groups. However, by the very nature of its conservatism and non-litigious tradition of the Canadian society compared with its southern neighbor,[4] differences are, with a few exceptions,[5] conventionally mediated through lengthy negotiation rather than more radical means. To this extent, earlier observation by Greenhill[6] that the external context of the public education is less "turbulent" remains valid while Carlson's version of the public school system as primarily a "domesticated enterprise" immune from scrutiny and justification for its existence should be modified. External constraints both on the operation of the school[7] and on classroom instruction[8] are, nonetheless, real and should be brought into consideration if the activism of the teaching force is to be clearly understood.

The second global trend that fosters activism among the teaching profession is intimately related to the fundamental societal changes that are slowly but surely transforming the role of the school and the public educators. In the face of the decline of church influence upon the young and the breakage of a traditional family structure resultant from divorce and remarriage, the vital roles of preserving the cultural heritage, preparing the young for the challenges of life, providing the basic educational skills and moral attitudes, vacated by the two time-honored social institutions are now firmly in the hands of the teachers. Indeed, tracing the job evolution of teachers over the past four decades, Lam observed:

> Barely recuperating from broad strokes of experimentation both in terms of curriculum materials and teaching strategies (in the sixties), teachers . . . were expected to be therapists of academic ills; they were expected to inculcate moral justice and humanity in the young; to keep up with instructional technological advances as in the use of micro-computers to help combat social problems like drug abuse, venereal disease (AIDS), alcohol problems, sexual abuse, broken families, malnutrition, abortion, and racial prejudice.[9]

Accompanying such an expansion of teachers' roles are the growing complexity and congestion of curriculum and high expectation of the public on school effectiveness in accomplishing these roles. Inherently, both the *external* demands and *internal* working environment are transformed into testing grounds of a teacher's very survival. The critical questions one should pose are: (a) How does the teaching profession cope? and (b) What seem to be the critical areas of concerns presently identified by the profession in face of these constant challenges and what are the coping strategies?

To the first question, one can speculate that coping strategies could be segregated in terms of individuals and groups (or organizations). On the individual basis, one can anticipate, as the prevailing organization theory advocating environmental determinism suggests,[10] the primary mode is that of on-going adaptation and adjustment. Judging from the morale and sense of calling among the teaching profession,[11] one has to assume that the rate of successful adjustments must be high. However, the rising tolls of job-related stress and job-burnout as documented in the growing literature on this topic[12] suggest the high price the teaching profession is paying in the process of adjustment. The second common coping strategy is to solicit assistance from their professional organizations. Indeed, the list of inservice agenda and the concerns either raised in the annual meetings or documented in the teachers' research publications register thorny issues that teachers encounter in the adaptation process.

At the organizational level, on the other hand, the strategies in dealing with potential challenges take on a far more aggressive stand. Backed by the treasuries and human resources of the gigantic teacher organization, the political institutionalization of public educators display intense advocacy and militant behaviors which Bacharach and his associates[13] conceptualized appropriately as a strategic choice of a collective action within a specific context. Discussion of specific strategic choices adopted by the various teacher organizations in Canada is therefore best made with references to the unique external milieus that each provincial teacher organization responds to and this will be examined closely in the sections that follow.

Prior to the examination of the strategic actions taken by the teachers' organizations, the manifested concerns and priorities must be scrutinized. The lack of a national educational system necessitates such an investigation on a province-by-province basis. Reference to the literature on labor militancy should also be made as a basis for ascertaining the compatibility between the theoretical development and the political realities in public education. This will facilitate further expansion and modification of our conceptual framework.

## Newfoundland

Aside from the persistent effort of increasing benefits and improving working conditions for the membership at large, the Newfoundland Teachers' Association indicates[14] that excessive workload, updating teachers' skills in subject areas such as core French and French immersion, and the general problem of high drop-out rate are the three areas of their major concern.

Apparently, the provincial effort of consolidating classes and subjects results in a much heavier workload for teachers in this province than before. Additionally, in line with the national bilingual policy,[15] the teaching of a second official language in curriculum has been aggressively pursued by the federal government in terms of incentive grants. This creates problems for teachers in a province which is mainly English-speaking. Calls for assistance has translated core French and French immersion instruction into an inservice program that receives top priority attention from the teachers' association. As to the third problem, high drop-out rate, it is at first sight a general educational if not social and economic issue. Nonetheless, the high attrition rate must be the root cause for class and subject consolidation that necessitate the current comprehensive approach.

Recognition of the root problem and the end result has greatly shaped the strategies adopted by the Teacher Association. They have designed, and are in the process of implementing, a network involving leading commercial companies and educational agencies to look into the attrition problem. They have secured support from the business sector to promote and fund a program to reduce the number of dropouts. They have appealed to the Faculty of Education, Memorial University to set up an external review committee to ensure a greater match between the supply and demand of teaching personnel in this province.

## *Prince Edward Island*

In outlining the current concerns and priorities, the Teacher Federation identifies two issues related to working conditions, three issues related to professional development and one issue pertaining to membership welfare.[16] In terms of working condition issues, the Teacher Federation is most concerned about adequate human and material resources in the process of integration of children with special needs. They also demand an increase in guidance and library services in schools. In terms of professional development issues, the Federation hopes to improve the quality of inservice training, to encourage school-based staff development programs, and to expose the membership to research in effective schools. In the area of membership welfare, they hope to develop and implement with other agencies a comprehensive employee assistance program.

Like a number of other provinces, the integration of exceptional children into the regular classes and the recognition of the fact that under the *School Act*[17] they have a right to an educational program that allows them to develop to their potential, poses great challenges to the teaching profession at the time when new curriculum demands more services in the regular classroom. Further, the dramatic reductions of guidance and library services in the past eight years have created additional problems for the school.

In conjunction with the increasing demands on the job, there are two other factors that prompt inservice to be on top of the Teacher Federation's agenda. First is the recognition that many of the teachers have been in the profession for over two decades since their initial training. Secondly, quite a few, in the course of re-deployment, have been entrusted with subjects with no previous training. Both necessitate continuous upgrading of staff to achieve effective schooling.

To accommodate the aging of the teaching force in the province, to deal with problems of stress and burnout on the job, to prepare teachers who intend to take early retirement, the Teachers' Federation is looked upon to take initiative to bring about a comprehensive employee assistance program.

In examining the course of action planned by the Department of Education, it is surprising to note a large overlap between the Teachers' Federation and the provincial government. Perhaps the relatively small size of the province and the resultant simplistic political structure allows the advocacy role of the teacher organization to take on a conciliatory and cooperative format.

## Nova Scotia

The current agenda of the Teachers' Union in this province[18] places heavy emphasis on professional development in response to the aging teaching profession and curriculum changes. Membership welfare concerns are also intimately related to inservice activities. In terms of working conditions, mainstreaming and some aspects of special education are top concerns. With respect to general education, high school curriculum, vocational schools and AIDS in the school are top priority issues.

Other than the desire for the revamping of vocational programs in line with the push for changes in the community college system, the Nova Scotia Teachers' Union shares many similar concerns with other Maritime teacher organizations. In the context of strategies which the Union attempts to implement, there is a general impression that the Union single-handedly attempts to deal with the issues identified. The development of programs such as the I/D/E/A, principals' inservice, the teaching effectiveness program, the employee assistance program and the retirement counselling seminars are good examples of the Union's initiatives. Likely what is viewed as internal is undertaken by the teacher organization. What appears to be brought about by the external is co-optation as in the case of Prince Edward Island Teachers' Federation.

## New Brunswick

From the list of items identified by New Brunswick Teachers' Federation, it seems that improvements in class size, reduction in the number of combined classes or multi-grade classes and increased preparation time for teachers are the common concerns of English and French teachers in this province.

From the perspective of the New Brunswick Teachers' Association, two additional issues have emerged to be of paramount importance. The first is the growing legal complexity surrounding teachers' behaviors in school. A second and a more perplexing concern is the mainstreaming of students with special needs.[19] In contrast to the government's claim that the integration process is proceeding on target, the survey conducted by the Teacher's Association tends to show it is otherwise.[20] There is a general fear that any gains made by the special needs students are at the expense of the regular ones when there are insufficient resource personnel and structural support for the present effort.

In terms of coping strategies, the teachers' organizations in this province tend to follow the general pattern accepted by teachers' organizations in the maritime provinces. Mainly, they attempt to lobby with the government for some types of relief and additional support and, at the same time, provide internal assistance to their members. Such an assistance is rendered in a diversity of ways: pamphlets (as in the case of dissemination of legal advice), and inservice in areas of membership's concerns and negotiation. Broadly speaking, teachers' organizations assume the traditional role of an active advocacy for their membership, hoping the emerging issues can be effectively tackled.

## Quebec

While very different in orientation and interests, the three provincial teachers' associations in Quebec, the Centrale de l'Enseignement due Quebec (CEQ), the Provincial Association of Protestant Teachers (PAPTO), and the Provincial Association of Catholic Teachers (PACT), seem to be presently preoccupied with similar sets of concerns: job security, rights of teachers to be involved in educational policy-making, support in adapting to curriculum change and serving pupils with learning difficulties. Similar to teacher organizations in other provinces, they are searching for ways to reduce the stress which an aging teaching profession is experiencing and for a means to improve the quality of educational services.[21] Sensitive to various social issues, CEQ has been actively involved in Peace education, advocating prevention of dropout, and social equality. [22]

Parallel in many respects in terms of their concerns with teacher organizations in other provinces, the strategies employed by the teacher associations in this province are by far one of the most militant in the country. Indeed, with the unionization of the profession in the sixties, the relationship with the government has been strained. Study sessions, rotating strikes, full strikes, and establishing solidarity with other public sector employees have punctuated the entire educational development. Fully aware of its power both as an employer and the final arbiter of labor relations, the government's actions (e.g., Bills 25 and 111) reflect both the uncompromising attitude of a domineering boss and the lucid inclination to extend and exert control over the teaching profession. Hopeful signs of conciliation, with greater flexibility and more realistic expectations, however, seem to have returned to parties in the public education system in the last few years.

## Ontario

Fragmented by sex, culture, religion and level of school (elementary/secondary), the five teacher organizations in Ontario are united into a supra-educational labor organization, the Ontario Teacher's Federation (OTF). Given that this is an umbrella institution of different affiliated teacher organizations, it is not surpising that the list of concerns[23] approved by OTF Board of Governors is lengthy and all inclusive. They range from maintaining and improving the quality of education, membership welfare issues, liaison with the Canadian Teacher Federation and the international assistance program to monitoring and influencing government policies. When comparing this list with the year before, the priority list remains the same. This suggests a necessity to scrutinize specific issues within the broadly defined framework if current and urgent concerns are to be segregated from the perpetual concerns. More critically, the power patterns of the teacher organizations need to be briefly examined if the major thrust from the teaching profession is to be understood.

In brief, from the analysis of Townsend,[24] the Ontario Teacher Federation (OTF) is externally the badge-wearer among the teacher federations, exercising sanction power in dealing with the government. Internally, it assumes the role of a "broker" mediating the diverse interests expressed by the autonomous affiliates.

The Women Teachers' Association of Ontario is a quietly effective group promoting women's issues (affirmative action, pay equity, community involvement, concerns for battered children). They also support a new teacher's certification program that prevents members from being bumped by secondary teachers.[25] The Ontario Public School Teachers' Federation, the male elementary teachers' organization, is by far, the least aggressive. It is more concerned about extending membership to elementary women teachers and least concerned about "rocking the boat."

On the other hand, historically the best educated, the male-dominated Ontario Secondary School Teachers' Federation actively assumes a forward policy in dealing with the government. With substantial resources, it can muster its drive for the very priorities without diluting its energies across the entire policy environment. To this extent, its concerns assume a higher profile and at times overshadow the concerns of other teacher organizations in the province. In the five-point agenda presented by this federation,[26] this affiliate seems to be obsessed with the government decision (Bill 30) to extend funding to separate secondary schools, precipitating as the leaders of teachers, fear of dual public systems competing for shrinking tax dollars.

In terms of strategies, the Ontario Secondary School Teachers' Federation, with its vigilant staff and "economic juggernaut,"[27] is the most militant group, defying openly at times that it will not implement Ministry plans it disagrees with. This Federation, in conjunction with the other groups[28] has challenged the said Ontario law in the Supreme Court of Canada. While the litigation has not been successful, it leads the nation by being the first teachers' organization in taking the legal action against a provincial government.

## Manitoba

Four items are identified as top priorities by the Manitoba Teachers' Society for the presidents of local teacher associations.[29] These include education finance, improvement to the province's *Public Schools Act*, public relations and the move to provincial bargaining.

In education finance, teachers are most concerned with the implementation of an earlier government's commitment to raise the level of provincial support to 90 percent. In his critical review of Education Support Grant provided by the previous Progressive Conservative government, Nicholls[30] proposed the elevation of government support and was readily accepted by all the three parties in the province. To date, the Progressive Conservative Party is back in power. However, such a suggestion has not been put into practice and regional disparity remains a serious problem in financing public education.

As for other issues, the proposed amendment to the *Public Schools Act* aims at updating employer-employee relations which become obsolete in the context of the evolutionary changes in the general labor legislation. As to the public relations issue, the Society attempts to launch a series of activities to project to the public a positive image of teachers and their problems, particularly the funding constraints that the public educators face. The push for provincial bargaining is an attempt to resolve the growing problems with the existing mode of local level negotiation. After many defeats at the annual general meetings, the proposed format of province-wide bargaining is a compromise with an opt-out clause for those who still feel uncomfortable with this approach.

Given the fact that the teachers' society has explicitly preferred binding arbitration to strike, the general approach is that of active participation in all aspects of educational decision-making, and rigorous lobbying efforts to preserve the interests of teachers. To date, the Society has achieved considerable success with the government at the expense of, at times, a special interest group within its organization, such as the principals' association.

## Saskatchewan

The Saskatchewan Teachers' Federation raises four issues which are closely related to the general funding restraint adopted by the government as their major areas of concern.[31] With the exception of decision-making in education, other issues such as program development, education funding, and quality of education issues are strikingly familiar to those raised by other teachers' organizations in the prairie provinces.

Beneath the policies and resolutions presented to the Minister of Education, is a profound concern of the teacher organization for the "cutback" mentality of the government. On the issue of decision-making in education, the teacher organization is actually worried that the drastic reorganization of the Department of Education will result in a major reduction in the leadership and support services available at the provincial level. In the funding issue, the Federation is concerned that the decline of provincial support is forcing local taxpayers to pick up a greater share of K-12 educational costs. In the program development issue, the concern is focused on the slow-down in the implementation of the recommendations of a five-year study.

In the "quality of education" issues, the Federation initiates four new policies.[32] With the exception of the first proposed policy in child abuse and neglect, which is fundamentally a social issue, the remaining three are either direct or indirect attempts to ensure "job security" for teachers. In dealing with the French education staffing, there is a two-prong emphasis of training French language teachers from within the province (as opposed to transportation of teachers from other provinces) and of preventing erosion of the existing program and teaching positions by expansion of French education. In regulating private schools, the Federation stresses that only those holding valid Saskatchewan teacher's certificates should be allowed to practise in private schools. In the policy dealing with teacher associates, care has been shown to delineate their responsibilities so as to avoid school boards from confusing their role with that of the teacher. The professional development agenda is therefore geared toward preparing teachers to cope with change.

Similar to the general strategies adopted by the Manitoba Teachers' Society, the teachers' federation of this province has professed to honor the tradition of shared decision-making involving all the major partners in the educational enterprise. In the climate of economic uncertainty, it seems that the Federation continues to adhere to the tradition of political activities like lobbying to safeguard their interest.

## *Alberta*

In quite a few respects, the Alberta Teachers' Association is facing the same situation as the Saskatchewan Teachers' Association: government cutbacks. Of the six areas approved by the Provincial Executive Council,[33] one underlies the overall concern of the financial situation in Alberta (which prompts the government to adopt a stringent measure in funding); two pertain to actions dealing with the government; and the remaining three pertain to the promotion of member services, professional development and teacher welfare.

Topping all other concerns is the Association's basic position that there should be "no more cuts" by the provincial government in funding the school system. The retrenchment of teaching positions in the province is far greater than that projected by the Association so that the organization's own financial situation is strained. The two areas pertaining to government reflect the Association's effort to strengthen its influence on the government's decision and will be elaborated on in connection with the teachers' organizational strategies. In the member services, the more notable effort is to ensure that teachers' interests are adequately represented in the process of revising the

*School Act* and related legislation. The professional development program encompasses a wide range of activities: development of the Association Instructors' Corps, setting up new curriculum inservice, dealing with the French immersion issue, organizing Francophone teachers' conferences, planning job fairs, improving administrators' inservice, and monitoring the impact of inservice educational grant removal on local PD activity. In the protection of teachers' welfare, emphasis is placed on improving the pension plan, preventing contract stripping and publicizing the effect of government fiscal policies on education.

Reference to the strategies adopted by the Association shows that a comprehensive plan of action is in place. In essence, there are two categories of strategies — one gears toward the government and one toward the public. With respect to the government, the Association has created a new position in its structure, an executive secretary whose tasks apparently are to coordinate all efforts in extending influence on the government. It has devised a PR program for the government's consumption. It has initiated a formal orientation program for MLA contacts. It has provided support for locals in the development of lobbying skills. In legislative terms, it has monitored the revision of the *School Act* and other bills affecting the interests of teachers. In addition, despite strong opposition, it has continued to push for a *Teaching Profession Act* that would greatly enhance the autonomy of the profession in much the same line as the medical and legal professions.

In the realm of winning the public, the Association has increased its liaison with other groups soliciting support for education. It has assisted members and locals in expanding or developing public relations programs. Further, it plans to increase provision of columns and radio clips for local media. It intends to start evaluating the advertising program.

Through all these efforts, the Association attempts to reverse the tide of funding cuts and restore full provincial support. Whatever the outcome, the systematic organization and campaigning skills of the teacher organization have indeed reached a high degree of sophistication and maturity within the traditional political framework.

## British Columbia

While the agenda of the 1987 British Columbia Teachers' Federation touch on many of the familiar issues: professional ethics, rights and standards, programs for affirmative action, bargaining rights, public relations, pensions and teacher welfare,[34] the preparation of this chapter has caught the Federation in the midst of intensive struggle for its very survival.[35] The immediate crisis was brought on by the action of the government in the spring 1987 when Bills 19 and 20 became provincial law. In brief, the legislation makes it illegal for principals or vice-principals to belong to the British Columbia Teachers' Federation. Furthermore, it creates a college of teachers to which all teachers, principals, vice-principals, supervisors, directors and superintendents would be required to pay annual dues to belong. In this sweeping legislative act, not only is the Federation being dismembered, but the very legitimacy of its continued existence is questioned.

Apparently, in passing these bills, the government has capitalized on the latent and manifested tension that exists between teachers and middle-ranged management — the school principals and vice-principals — which is by no means unique to this province.[36] Indeed, in the natural course of the growing professionalism of school administrators, many principals and their deputies in various provinces are no longer content to be relegated as a special interest subgroup within an organization with overwhelming teacher interest.

As countermeasures, aside from appealing to other organizations (including Canadian Teacher Federation) for support, the BCTF is instructing 75 local teacher associations to be certified under the *Industrial Relations Act* as locals of the Federation, while the Federation will attempt to influence the forthcoming elections to the governing council of the new teachers' college so as to ensure that the Federation nominees will constitute a majority on this council.

From the longitudinal political perspective, the action of the Social Credit government represents a new high in a series of blows between the B.C. Teachers' Federation and the Social Credit Party. Governed by the tradition of a labor-union orientation, BCTF has been among the foremost militant teacher organizations in the country. Its political strategies have trespassed the framework within which most of the Canadian teacher organizations operate (i.e., lobbying government and winning public support for educational issues). Instead, in the past ten years, teachers in this province have been deeply involved in voting at the local and provincial levels.[37] While the voting behaviors of teachers have been governed more by individual political ideologies than *en bloc* directed by the teacher organization, they have emerged to be a powerful group capable of determining the outcome in case of close elections.

In 1986, quite a few teachers went one step further by turning themselves into candidates. Indeed, in the 1986 provincial election, teachers comprised the second largest single occupational group among the candidates running for political office. Modelled after their American counterpart, the Federation has established political action committees involved in raising money for their own candidates or those deemed favorable to the interests of teachers. The present struggle with the government may represent the climax of tests of wits and will between two hostile parties. Meanwhile, however, the militancy of the British Columbia Teachers' Federation has reached another new height.

## Summative Observations

This panorama of the concerns of teachers' organizations reveals more similarities than differences, despite diverse provincial structures and political climates. The problem of funding public education, more a reflection of the Canadian general economic condition than a specific provincial government's doing, continues to plague the nation's public school system. The expansion of teachers' roles necessitated by the fundamental social changes, as depicted in the beginning section, has indeed translated into curriculum and adjustment problems (stress and burnout) for teachers, resulting in general demands for teacher organizations in the country to provide more inservice support.

The response strategies adopted by the teacher organizations, on the contrary, display significant regional differences. In general, the Maritime teachers' organizations seem to work closely with the provincial governments and the pattern resembles that of co-optation. Teacher organizations in other provinces, however, share considerably different perspectives with their governments. Response strategies, however, should at least be classified in two different categories. There are those whose activism is confined to the traditional political framework (e.g. public relations activities, lobbying and job actions). Falling into this category are the teacher organizations in Manitoba, Saskatchewan, Alberta and, to some extent, Quebec.[38]

There are still others whose political actions have gone beyond the realm within which teacher organizations operate. Included in this category are the Ontario Secondary School Teachers' Federation that litigates against its provincial government in the Supreme Court for extending funding to the separate school system, and the British Columbia Teachers' Federation that exercises the electorial punches against the governments, provincial and local, that do not profess to protect teachers' interests. By running their own candidates in the election, BCTF has emerged as a one-issue political party that has heralded a new stage in the development of militancy of Canadian teachers.

## Revisitation of Militancy Models

In revisiting the prevailing conceptual models of labor militancy to assess which framework best describes Canadian teachers' response patterns to external challenges, the four models identified by Schutt[39] need to be examined.

The first model describing labor militancy is the *economic* model. In essence, it posits low pay as a source of discontent which breeds aggressive job actions. The second framework, the *incongruency* model, emphasizes the desire of workers for greater control at the work place leading to a latent and manifested conflict between autonomous-independent orientation of the professional worker on the job and the subordinate-dependent reality of the organizational structure. The third, the *social-background* model, stresses that the background characteristics of employees may influence perceptions and the framework of reference in situations for which no clear occupational norms exist. The last one, the *political* model, propounds that the political context to which union members are exposed on the job influences the degree of support they have for militant actions.

By reference to the concerns of the Canadian teacher organizations, it is true that collective bargaining remains a top priority, and while teachers at times go on strike for salary issues, it is doubtful that "low pay" is the primary source of aggressive job actions. True, distributive bargaining (competitive behaviors designed to influence the proportionate allocation of scare resources) remains the most predominant type of negotiation between teachers and employers.[40] Collective bargaining from the Canadian teachers' perspective in recent years is not so much as to rectify the "low pay," as in the case of their American counterparts, but to prevent deterioration in the relative level of salaries.[41] The *economic* model is therefore very inadequate as a conceptual framework for explaining Canadian teachers' militancy.

The *incongruency* model, at first sight, provides a more viable theoretical explanation. Indeed, with the continued upgrading of teachers' expertise, either through government regulations[42] or inservice activities, and their perceived inadequacy of resources in accommodating the additional demands of their profession, teachers' assertion of greater control over working conditions overshadows their concern for salary increment in many of their recent negotiations with employers. From a historical and longitudinal perspective, teachers' recognition of the importance of having some control over working conditions has evolved in three overlapping stages. First, is the assertion of classroom autonomy, which leads to clash with administrators' tasks of supervision and the present tension between teachers' and principals' organizations. Second, is the assertion of improvement of the overall conditions of work, which hardens their confrontation with the school boards who claim infringement of managerial perogatives. Third, is the preservation of the general welfare of teachers against constraining environments which necessitates one type of political action or another in dealing with their boss — the provincial government. By the very restriction of the *incongruency* model to an organizational context, this conceptual framework alone is once again insufficient to account for the political actions of teachers' organizations on the global scale.

The *social background* model which dominates others in governing empirical research[43] is by nature a micro-sociological analysis of individual characteristics to explain propensity of militant actions. Age, sex, race, socioeconomic background, educational level, ideology and degree of specialization,[44] to name a few, are some of the most common characteristics cited in this approach to make a prediction on militancy. Accepting the basic premise of this approach to be correct, we might begin to assert, for instance, that the aging of the Canadian teaching force accounts for rising activism for protecting their welfare. We might cite the Ontario Secondary School Teachers'

Federation, historically the most specialized and the best educated in Ontario and still dominated mainly by males, as by far the most vocal and aggressive. We might resort to teachers' ideology in B.C. to forecast their voting patterns. By the same token of citing cases, we become fully aware of the limitation of this approach. Short of empirical evidence of the influx of blue-collar family background teachers that incite the union-mentality of teachers' organizations,[45] we cannot attribute socioeconomic factors to militancy as we have done with other professions. That the Ontario Women Teachers' Federation is by far a more effective political body than the male-dominated Ontario Public School Teachers' Federation casts doubt on the utility of using single traits to map militancy.

In short, by their very nature, most teacher organizations in the country are not organized by individual traits, and the actions of teacher organizations are best described as the strategic choice of a collective action. Therefore, the *socio-background* model is ill-suited to delineate the proper parameter for us to interpret teachers' group activities.

The fourth model that emphasizes that the *political* context on the job will govern the degree of support for militant actions seems to be verified, as the general patterns of teachers' organizations across Canada are compared. Given parallel issues, the Maritime teachers' organizations, by the very nature of their less-militant environment are the least militant groups in the country. Those that reside in the intermediate level of political environment, as in the case of the Prairie teachers' organizations, tend to react with medium intensity of political actions. Quebec teachers' organizations, one time the most militant, seem to take on a more reconciliatory stand when their political environment tends to relax. Those that operate within the most complex and intense political environment, as in the case of Ontario and British Columbia, seem most inclined to adopt the most radical and the most uncompromising actions in dealing with the identified adversaries. By accepting the premise of the political model as correct, we seem to be endorsing the recent theoretical framework of environmental determinism which assumes that organizations (in this case, teachers' organizations) continue to adapt and adjust to external changes.

There is, however, a fundamental flaw in this conceptualization. By stressing the omnipotent roles of environmental forces and by relegating teachers' organizations to one of passive reaction rather than aggressive proaction, the political model has failed, notably, to accommodate the recent actions of B.C. Teachers' Federation which has taken initiative in restructuring and remodelling its external environment. While the risk of such action is abundantly clear and its effectiveness remains to be seen, the political model presently described becomes somewhat outdated.

No existing models of militancy, in retrospect, suffice to provide a comprehensive interpretation of the spiral activism of Canadian teachers' organizations in their quest for preserving teachers' interests. New or modified paradigms are urgently needed to bridge conceptualization and the empirical reality of teachers' collective militancy.


## Notes

[1] Acknowledgement is made to all teachers' organizations in the ten provinces for providing the basic material for this chapter.

[2] R.F. Campbell, "Organization and Environment: A Critique," a paper presented at the annual American Educational Research Association meeting in February 1971.

[3] H.E. Adrich, *Organizations and Environments* (Englewood Cliffs, N.J.: Prentice Hall, 1979).

[4] Such a comparison is drawn by W.M. Bridgeland, R.G. Townsend and E.A. Duane, "Power Patterns among Michigan and Ontario Teachers' Lobbies," *Urban Education*, 20, 4 (1986): 363-379.

[5] See litigation initiated by Ontario Secondary School Teachers' Federation and other groups against the provincial government's Bill 30 in G. Dickinson "Toward Equal Status for Catholic Schools in Ontario: the Supreme Court of Canada Examines Constitutional Issues," *Canadian and International Education*, 16, 2 (1987): 5-23.

[6] C.J. Greenhill, "Central Office Officials in the Politics of Education," in J.H.A. Wallin, ed., *The Politics of Canadian Education*, 4th Yearbook (1977).

[7] Y.L.J. Lam, "Relationships between Setting, Size and School Environmental Characteristics," *Administrators Notebook*, 31, 9 (1985).

[8] Y.L.J. Lam, "Patterns and Constraints of External Environment on Teaching," a paper submitted for publication, 1987.

[9] Y.L.J. Lam, "The Changing Roles of North American Teachers in the Eighties," *Education and Society*, 2, 1 (1984): 91-96.

[10] J. Pfeffer and G. Salancik, *The External Control of Organizations: A Resource Dependence Perspective* (New York: Harper & Row, 1978).

[11] Y.L.J. Lam, "Teacher Professional Profile: A Personal and Contextual Analysis," *Alberta Journal of Educational Research*, 28, 2 (1982): 122-134.

[12] B. Hiebert, *Stress and Teachers, The Canadian Scene* (Toronto: Canadian Education Association, 1985).

[13] S. Bacharach *et al., Strategic Choice and Collective Action: Organizational Determinants of Teacher Militancy*, technical report 143 (Washington, DC.: National Institute of Education, 1983).

[14] Documents provided by Newfoundland Teachers Association, 1987.

[15] In 1971, the Canadian Parliament adopted the Bilingual official policy for the country.

[16] Documents provided by Prince Edward Island Teacher Federation, 1987.

[17] P.E.I. Department of Education, *A Plan of Action for Education* (Charlottetown: P.E.I. Department of Education, 1987).

[18] Documents provided by Nova Scotia Teachers' Union, 1987.

[19] Document provided by the New Brunswick Teachers' Association, 1988.

[20] New Brunswick Teachers' Association, *Report on a Survey of Classroom Teachers on the Integration of Special Needs/Exceptional Pupils* (Fredericton, N.B.: New Brunswick Teachers' Association, 1988).

[21] N. Henchey and D. Burgess, *Between Past and Future: Quebec Education in Transition* (Calgary, Alberta: Detselig Enterprises, 1987).

[22] Document provided by Centrale de l'Enseignement due Quebec, 1987.

[23] Documents provided by Ontario Teachers' Federation

[24] See Bridgeland, Townsend and Duane.

[25] Document provided by Ontario Women Teachers' Federation, 1988.

[26] Documents provided by Ontario Secondary School Teachers' Federation, 1987.

[27] See Bridgeland, Townsend and Duane.

[28] Dickinson, pp. 5-23.

[29]. Manitoba Teachers' Society, *MTS Update*, 6, 3 (1987): 1.

[30] G. Nicholls, *A Summary of Recommendations from the Report of the Education Finance Review* (Winnipeg: Deptartment of Education, 1983).

[31] Documents received from the Saskatchewan Teachers' Federation, 1987.

[32] Document received from the Alberta Teachers' Association, 1987.

[33] See note 32 above.

[34] Documents received from the British Columbia Teachers' Federation 1987.

[35] See note 34 above.

[36] The tension between the Manitoba Teacher Society and Manitoba Principal Association has been high and the writer and two principals were asked to compile a report, *Status of MAP: A Critical Review*(1984) to consider whether the principals'association should break from the teachers' organization.

[37] N. Robinson and N. Stuart, "The Political Punch of Teachers," *The Canadian Administrator*, 26, 5 (1987).

[38] This is meant to describe the Quebec's general educational landscape rather than the traditional strategies employed by the teachers' organizations.

[39] R.K. Schutt, "Models of Militancy: Support for Strikes and Work Actions among Public Employees," *Industrial and Labor Relations Review*, 35, 3 (1982): 406-422.

[40] J. Fris, "Militancy and Accommodativeness in Teachers' Negotiations: Two Ontario Surveys," *The Canadian Administration*, 16, 1 (1976).

[41] Indirectly from P.J. Atherton's research, "Collective Bargaining: Its Impact on Educational Cost," a paper presented at the Annual Meeting of the American

Educational Research Association, Montreal, Quebec, April, 1983. One notes that the intent of teachers' negotiation is to prevent deterioration in the relative level of salaries rather than reacting against "poor pay."

[42]The Manitoba government, for instance, has increased the teacher certification to two years of training for all university graduates.

[43]See for example, J. Bruno and I. Nelken, "An Empirical Analysis on Propensity for Teachers to Strike," *Educational Administration Quarter*, 11, 2 (1975): 66-85; and D.N. Snarr, "Strikers and Non-strikers: A Social Comparison," *Industrial Relations*, 14, 3 (1975): 371-74; and Schutt, pp. 406-422.

[44]Schutt, pp. 406-422

[45]See literature review by Schutt, pp. 406-422.

# 11

# Indian Education in Canada: Contemporary Issues

## Dick Henley and John Young

The aspiration of Indian control of Indian education, articulated in the National Indian Brotherhood's policy paper submitted to the federal government in 1972 and further developed most recently in the Assembly of First Nations' 1988 document *Tradition and Education: Towards a Vision of Our Future*, remains in large part unfulfilled, and the quality of schooling available to Indian children continues to be, by almost any standard, dramatically below that taken-for-granted by non-Native populations. Embedded within the concept of control are not only fundamental questions of jurisdiction and governance but also critical questions of curriculum and curriculum development, teachers and teacher preparation, and resources and resource allocation that require simultaneous attention. The achievement of a satisfactory path to development around these issues poses major challenges not only for Indian people but for the whole of Canadian society.

For most Canadians, the public school is seen as the major social institution through which children, regardless of their family background, may enter, receive fair and equitable treatment, and leave with an appropriate body of learning experiences with which to begin to make their way in a society which similarly provides a relatively equitable share of life's chances and rewards. Few of Canada's status and treaty Indians[2] have reason to subscribe to either of these images of Canadian schools or Canadian society. Whatever indicators of educational well-being one wishes to choose — participation rates in post-secondary institutions of education, highest levels of formal education, high school completion rates, student attendance, drop-out rates and age-grade retardation, or more subjective measures of community and parental satisfaction — the picture that is consistently painted across the country, with few exceptions, is of a public school system that, in spite of some significant developments over the last decade and a half, continues to serve Canada's Indian population dramatically less well than the Canadian population as a whole.[3]

Contemporary efforts to understand and redress this situation and to respond appropriately to questions about the aims, methods and resources of Indian education inevitably hinge upon prior questions of the place of Indian people within Canadian society and the Canadian state — both at the present time and in an historical context. These two sets of questions are inextricably linked and at the present time both sets of questions are characterized by a high degree of uncertainty and disagreement amongst those people who have the most power to influence their outcome. Aboriginal peoples claim a very different relationship with the Canadian state than that of any other ethnic group in the country. Their specific status arises out of their ancestral claim to the vast landmass of contemporary Canada.

Section 35 of the *Canadian Constitution Act* (1982) acknowledges that Indian, Inuit and Metis people have peculiar rights. For their part, Canadian Indians argue that their particular claim is nothing short of sovereign self-government. However, constitutional talks between aboriginal peoples and the federal and provincial governments have consistently failed to reach agreement as to how self-government is to be defined and to demarcate the boundaries of Indian jurisdiction. The urgency of this concern for Indians and their frustration at the lack of progress in constitutional talks was clearly evident in the speech delivered by Georges Erasmus, National Chief of the Assembly of First Nations to the body's 1988 annual meeting when he stated:

> Canada, if you do not deal with this generation of leaders, we cannot promise that you are going to like the kind of violent political action that we can just about guarantee that the next generation is going to bring.[4]

Central to the Indian claim to self-government is jurisdiction over all aspects of the education of their children. This position has recently found expression in a large-scale survey of Indian views on education produced by the Assembly of First Nations (AFN) and released at the same 1988 assembly. This survey, entitled *Tradition and Education: Towards a Vision of Our Future,*[5] represents the first significant national report on Indian education since the landmark *Indian Control of Indian Education*[6] paper was forwarded by the National Indian Brotherhood to the federal government in 1972. The arguments presented in support of *Indian Control of Indian Education* (1972) were based upon extending to Indians those rights taken for granted by other Canadians, namely local control and parental responsibility.[7] The 1988 survey draws substantially on the earlier policy position but extends the basis of the argument:

> Education is one of the most important issues in the struggle for self-government and must contribute towards the objective of self-government. First Nations' governments have the right to exercise their authority in all areas of First Nation education. Until First Nations' education institutions are recognized and controlled by First Nations' governments, no real First

Nations' education exists. The essential principles are that each First Nation government should make its own decisions and arguments and apply its own values and standards rather than having them imposed from outside.[8]

The latter position is qualitatively different from the earlier one. The descriptive self-identification of the term "Indian" has taken a political connotation through the use of First Nation. The more limited meaning of control is replaced by the broader jurisdictional claim to self-government.

These changes are important; they represent a much more sophisticated notion of identity, one which has an explicit sense of its own power, and of the concept of education. Two components of the concept of education — "self-knowledge" or "identity," and "empowerment" — are central to this discussion of contemporary struggles over Indian education and Indian schools. Symons, in his report on Canadian Studies at the university level, *To Know Ourselves*, maintained forcefully that self-knowledge lies close to the heart of what it means to be truly educated: knowing and understanding ourselves; who we are; where we are in time and space; where we have been; where we are going; and what our responsibilities are to ourselves and to others.[9] Nor, from this perspective, can individual self-knowledge or identity be separated from an awareness of the community and society within which one lives, the two kinds of knowledge being not merely mutually dependent but "ultimately one and the same."[10]

Related to this is a second dimension of education, that of "empowerment": that is, education informs action and provides the knowledge and skills that enable people "to exert more control over the way in which [they] live."[11] While such conceptualizations of the meaning of education are clearly too broad to be confined to the formal practices of schools, few people have argued that such ideals are inappropriate as primary goals for public schools. For Indian people, they are central to the question of Indian jurisdiction over Indian schooling.

## History of Indian Schooling

For much of Canadian history, Indians have been treated as colonized peoples by the more powerful European elements of a Canadian society. That relationship has been characterized as one of internal colonization:

> Internal colonialism implies the absorption of the colony into the nation-state, controlled by the colonizer. As the colonizer expropriates more and more, the issue becomes eradication by the colonizer. . . . The peoples of internal colonization become termed "minorities," "ethnics," or "lower classes" rather than peoples, nations, or cultures.[12]

However, it would be wrong to assume that this relationship has been unchanging since first contact.[13] Colonization was not official policy from the beginning of the Indian-European relationships; the Royal Proclamation of 1763, for example, recognized Indian sovereignty in "Indian territory." Settlement by Europeans on Indian land was expressly forbidden until after treaty negotiations between the British Crown and representative aboriginal leaders had extinguished Indian land claims. However, following the War of 1812 when Indians ceased to have value as military allies and were no longer perceived as a threat to settlement, a policy of colonization began in earnest. Treaties were imposed upon aboriginal groups until well into the twentieth century (although not all lands in Canada have been ceded through treaty). In this process of colonization, the reserve system served as the laboratory for the "civilizing" of Indians. The *Indian Act* passed in 1876 legally defined who an Indian was, and made those registered as Indian virtual wards of the federal state. The intent of this legislation was, according to Tobias,[14] to isolate and protect Indian people until such time that those so identified were prepared for the duties of citizenship.

Very early in this colonization period, schooling was recognized as central to this process of colonization. Kelly and Altbach have succinctly described its administration and function:

> Education under colonialism lay beyond the control of persons or groups being educated. The content, medium, format, and uses of education were determined by the colonizer, not the colonized. The schools, regardless of the motive force behind their establishment — bureaucratic manpower needs, the missionary desire to do good works and save souls, exploitation of the resources of the colony, or a simple desire to bring progress to so-called backward areas — were set up by the colonizer on his own terms to meet the needs the colonizer, not the colonized, perceived.[15]

The Canadian parliament, like the British authorities and colonial legislatures before it, enlisted the services of the churches to operate schools among the aboriginal peoples. A number of institutional forms were experimented with over the years ranging from local day schools to residential schools often specializing in preparation for industrial and agricultural pursuits.[16] These schools generally aimed at christianizing ("civilizing") Indians and assimilating them into the lower strata of the dominant capitalist society.[17] It was not until the 1950s that the federal government began to take direct charge of Indian education. Indian people themselves gained no new authority through this transition — internal colonialism remained, albeit in an altered guise.[18]

For many Indian children, the residential school brought about a painful alienation. Bob Overvald described the impact which his experience at one such school had on him:

> ... I have become almost totally conditioned to fit into southern society. On the other hand, what these many years have taken away from me has caused irrevocable damage to me as a Dene: it has caused a split between my parents and myself that may never be healed; it has caused me to lose my Dene language; and, most significantly, it has left me in somewhat of a limbo — not quite fitting into Dene society and not quite fitting into white society. These are just some of the many by-products of the system. God knows I would not wish them on anyone.[19]

The federal government's new vision for Indian education was one which saw the client schooled in the various provincial education systems of the country. The province was the constitutional home of education in Canada; thus, there were compelling arguments for the province to oversee schooling for Indians as well. The provinces were seen to offer superior instruction through competent teaching staffs; there was an existing capacity to produce curriculum; and the standards of the physical plants were generally superior to federal institutions. That the integration of Indian children into the provincial school systems might hasten the ending of "the Indian problem" was implicit in the federal policy.

The policy of integration received support during the 1960s through the *Hawthorn Report*, a comprehensive study of Indian conditions in Canada. Hawthorn detailed a litany of social and economic problems for Indians: among them, substandard housing, poor health, and high unemployment rates. Indian children were compelled to attend school but "their stay there is often marked by [age-grade] retardation and terminated by dropping out; although ever more Indian children attend school and stay longer, the increasing national educational levels provide another receding horizon."[20]

Indeed, statistics show that while the national rate for children completing high school went from 50 to over 70 percent between 1965 and 1972, the Indian completion rate rose from a low of 10 to a high of only 15 percent.[21] The solution, according to the report, was to extend provincial services to Indians, including educational services. Because the Department of Indian Affairs would no longer be responsible for providing services to Indian people, it could, and in fact should, become an advocate on their behalf. The document, which saw their people described as "citizens plus" because of their special status, was well received by many Indian leaders.[22]

Indian attitudes toward those in control of the Canadian state changed quickly in 1969, however, with the release of the federal *White Paper on Indian Policy*. A product of a period which was deeply committed to the liberal tenet of equal opportunity for all individuals in society, this document proposed that the discrimination suffered by Indians over the course of Canadian history could be wiped away at a single stroke. The *Indian Act* would be legislated away; the special group relationship Indians had with the federal state would end; and Indians would become full members of Canadian society, free to enjoy the individual equality that membership was said to provide. Indian leaders were outraged by the proposal. Spokespersons such as Harold Cardinal claimed that aspirations to have their historic aboriginal and treaty rights recognized and honored were being dismissed as unrealistic and they, as peoples, were simply historical relics. In fact, reaction was so negative that the *White Paper* was withdrawn in 1971.[23] The following year, the National Indian Brotherhood released its *Indian Control of Indian Education* which was very specific about where power in education should lie. Indian parents should oversee the education of their children directly and so an emphasis was placed on the assumption of control at the local or band level.

Despite the changes that occurred in Indian schooling under European influence, much did not change prior to the 1970s. First, as already noted, the structure and content of Indian schools and their curricula was *always* defined and controlled by non-Indians. Second, and closely related, in that definition of school knowledge, Indian culture and identity were regarded as essentially irrelevant. Third, Indian schooling was, by almost *any* definition generally unsuccessful.

The significance of all this to the discussion of contemporary developments in Indian education is not simply to document an unfortunate and depressing past. Rather, its importance lies in the context that it provides for understanding the present, and preparing for a future. People — individually and collectively — cannot easily walk away from the material and psychological legacy of their history, and for Canada's contemporary Indian population that legacy has most often been one of structural and material deprivation and "socio-psychological wreckage."[24] For educators attempting to provide quality school experiences for Indian children, this legacy may not only include sub-standard facilities[25] but also a variety of social and psychological tensions that work against educational achievement in school.[26]

## The Governance of Indian Education

Introduced in 1876, the *Indian Act* with its several revisions has remained to the present day the authority defining and regulating Indian relations with the Canadian state. It was this legislation which the Trudeau government found so undemocratic and discriminatory in 1969 that it felt compelled to attempt its complete removal. The *Act* contains a number of clauses relating to education; some address the issue of compulsory schooling and others the right to separate education of Catholic and Protestant children. But what is of concern here is control over the schools and this is addressed in section 114 of the *Indian Act*.[27] It states:

(1) The Governor in Council may authorize the Minister [of Indian Affairs] in accordance with this *Act*, to enter into agreements on behalf of Her Majesty for the education in accordance with this Act of Indian children, with

(a) the government of a province;

(b) the Commissioner of the Northwest Territories;

(c) the Commissioner of the Yukon Territory;

(d) a public or separate school board; and

(e) a religious or charitable organization.

(2) The Minister may, in accordance with this *Act*, establish, operate and maintain schools for Indian children.

The most striking aspect of this list of potential purveyors of education is not their diversity, but that there is no mention of an Indian consultation mechanism nor is there any reference to band-controlled schools. Despite the apparent support that the Canadian government gave to this aspiration in 1973, the contemporary situation would seem to contradict the policy and there has been a lack of agreement between the Department of Indian and Northern Affairs Canada (INAC)[28] and Indian leaders over what control has actually meant; nor had a clear implementation plan been put into place. INAC has always maintained that the Minister must retain ultimate decision-making authority because it is so stated in the *Indian Act*. Moreover, the 1973 affirmation on the part of the federal government contained the debilitating proviso that Indian control would cost no more than if INAC continued to administer Indian schooling. Cardinal described the upshot of the policy in the following terms:

> We [INAC] agree to you controlling Indian education, but not Indian education as you define it. The only thing we agree to is that you run our educational programs as long as you run them the way we've always run them.[29]

According to Cardinal, bands which have taken over the management of their schools have operated them for INAC, rather than for themselves. The local school committees, many of which have existed since the 1960s, have had only advisory power. As Kirkness has stated more recently, "Indian people were and are permitted involvement but no control."[30]

The contemporary development of the educational structure among Canada's 575 bands has hardly been consistent across the country although most now control some areas of reserve-school administration.[31] About half of the Indian children who live on reserves in Canada attend provincially operated schools off the reserve; on-reserve schools are administered by either the federal government or the band.

## Table 1. Enrolment of Registered Indian Students in Teacher Education Programs, 1957/8-1978/9.

| 1957-58 | 21 | 1968-69 | 38 |
|---------|----|---------|----|
| 1958-59 | 33 | 1969-70 | 49 |
| 1959-60 | 33 | 1970-71 | 48 |
| 1960-61 | 13 | 1971-72 | 63 |
| 1961-62 | 25 | 1972-73 | 104 |
| 1962-63 | 20 | 1973-74 | 115 |
| 1963-64 | 14 | 1974-75 | 195 |
| 1964-65 | 24 | 1975-76 | 421 |
| 1965-66 | 18 | 1976-77 | 570 |
| 1966-67 | 13 | 1977-78 | 602 |
| 1967-68 | 23 | 1978-79 | 602 |

Source: Statistics Division Program Services
Branch, Indian and Inuit Affairs.

The high proportion of Indian children in provincial schools is in part due to the legacy of the integration policy as of the 1960s and 1970s. Through the policies, INAC signed a number of service purchase agreements with provinces and school boards on a per-pupil cost basis. In many instances, negotiations were conducted without Indian involvement and a number of long-term agreements were entered into, effectively blocking any alternative arrangement Indian communities might wish to undertake.[32] In addition, a number of capital cost-sharing arrangements were entered into for the construction of schools and facilities; invariably these were off-reserve arrangements which created additional difficulties for parents seeking to have a voice in overseeing their children's schooling. Some jurisdictions have made arrangements so that some seats on the school board might be occupied by Indians, allocations which Paquette has suggested are inadequate: "At best, the current representation of Native people on provincial boards of Education is a limited and flawed presence."[33] It should be acknowledged, however, that some bands prefer the connections which they have with provincial schools to alternative arrangements.

On-reserve schooling is conducted by either INAC or by the local band authority; together, they educate approximately half of the Indian children in Canada. The difference between these two types of administrative structures insofar as local input is concerned may be seen currently as essentially one of degree rather than kind. Band schools are nominally operated by local people, but INAC intervention is always a possibility should they not adequately perform their administrative tasks according to guidelines established by the federal authority. Many bands have chosen to retain the administrative services of INAC because they believe that they are more likely to receive a higher level of service than would be possible if they were to take control. In the meantime, INAC has been anxious to turn as much as possible of the day-to-day responsibilities of operating the schools over to the bands so that some of the burden of accountability can be transferred and lodged at the local level. Through its most recent policy, Alternative Funding Arrangements (AFA), INAC intends to turn much greater authority over a whole series of community services to Indian bands. Before briefly discussing what measures it contains it should first be placed in the context of the Indian self-government issue which it seeks to address at least partially.

Since the proclamation of the *Constitution Act*, 1982,[34] Indian leaders have been compelled to focus attention on the broad issue of Indian self-determination, and education has been folded into that struggle. The failure of the three constitutional conferences on aboriginal matters and, more recently, the absence of any reference to aboriginal concerns in the Meech Lake Accord have generally been viewed as major setbacks to Indian aspirations. There has, however, been an ongoing lobby on behalf of them among the Canadian populace and in the House of Commons itself.

Among the most significant public documents released since 1982, perhaps none has been more supportive than the *Report of the Special Committee on Indian Self-Government*[35] — the *Penner Report*. This Parliamentary investigation recommended three far-reaching changes to the aboriginal-Canadian state relationship. First, it supported constitutional inclusion of aboriginal self-government and the beginning of meaningful negotiations leading to fairly concluded aboriginal land claim settlements; second, it called for a massive revision of the *Indian Act*; and third, it suggested shifts in policy on the part of the federal government agencies in their dealings with aboriginal peoples in the direction of greater self-government. Since neither of the former two recommendations have been adopted, INAC has proclaimed that within its constricted frame of reference, it is taking its lead from the third proposal of the *Penner Report*. It is to this end that the Alternative Funding Arrangement is said to be directed.[36]

According to the department guide to AFA, the federal government has attempted to re-establish Indian control over the affairs of their communities since the 1970s but that until recently, the process consisted largely of transferring the responsibility for administering government programs and services to Indian councils. While this process made the delivery of program services more responsive to community needs and helped to develop administrative and management skills in Indian communities, it only provided limited real authority and flexibility in designing and managing programs and services.[37]

INAC claims that AFA will provide much greater control to Indian Councils (Band and Tribal) by placing in their hands the financial resources to conduct education, social assistance, housing, community development and other community services so that they might manage their own affairs according to the priorities established at the local level. Funding for capital construction remains the prerogative of INAC, but money provided through a data based formula and on a separate-program basis will not be tied as tightly, as is currently the case, to particular programs. So long as they maintain standard levels of service for each program, councils can divert funds to favored projects. There are restrictions and auditing procedures which must be followed, but within the policy guidelines there appears to be considerable freedom for communities to set their own direction in those programs included under AFA, although the Treasury Board agreement specifically states that there will be no additional cost to the federal government.[38]

INAC has generally been more comfortable dealing with bands on an individual basis than with provincial, regional or national organizations[39] so it is not surprising that it believes that it can deliver "a specific number of agreements annually for their [Treasury Board] review."[40] The Assembly of First Nations' report, *Tradition and Education*, suggested that the impact of AFA on the funding and control of Indian education "will be substantial."[41] It is unlikely that bands will be able to resist the offer to enter AFA because it adds much more opportunity to meet their needs, both long and short-term. However, since funding will largely be based on population statistics, it is very probable that smaller reserves will lack the ability to maintain the level of service that larger ones will be capable of delivering. Moreover, heavily funded programs like education may actually receive less support under this program since the temptation will be there to shift money into other programs.

The AFA requirement established by the Treasury Board states that schools must "provide educational standards which would allow students freedom of transfer within respective provincial systems."[42] This statement would seem to suggest that some form of quality control over the processes of schooling will be maintained. There is, however, a prior concern which educators of Indian children must also address and that is that Indian education be different. Central to the development of any unique forms of Indian education is the ability to control and develop unique curriculum

## Curriculum Control

A curriculum is not an archaic, inert vehicle for transmitting knowledge. It is a precise instrument which can and should be shaped to exact specifications for a particular purpose.[43]

Clearly, at the heart of the issue of Indian jurisdiction over education is the struggle for control of the school curriculum. It is a struggle which concerns the opportunity for Indians to determine the nature of the experiences (formal and informal, overt and hidden) to which Indian children will be exposed to during their school careers, and to determine the qualities necessary in those teachers charged with directing those experiences. Equally clearly, the struggle is about curriculum change. It represents a rejection of a pre-existing curriculum that virtually without exception has come to be dismissed as massively inadequate and inappropriate, and is concerned with the establishment of appropriate mechanisms for developing new curricula and new ways of recruiting and preparing teachers. While there is considerable debate as to what quality education might look like in different Indian contexts,[44] the inadequacy of existing Indian schooling represents an area of agreement amongst virtually everyone, Indian and non-Indian, associated with Indian education.[45]

For the National Indian Brotherhood and the Assembly of First Nations, there has been a clear understanding that schooling controlled and directed by Indians provides the opportunity and necessary pre-conditions to develop curricula that is not only qualitatively better but also substantively different than that currently in existence: a curriculum that could provide an appropriate balance between Indian and non-Indian content and experiences and which could offer the promise of both "cultural continuity and occupational freedom."[46] The National Indian Brotherhood has stated this unequivocally:

> The time has come for a radical change in Indian education. Our aim is to make education relevant to the philosophy and needs of the Indian people.

We want education to give our children a strong sense of identity, with confidence in their personal worth and ability. We believe in education: as a preparation for total living; as a means of free choice of where to live and work; and, as a means of enabling us to participate fully in our own social, economic, political and educational advancement. We do not regard the educational process as an "either/or" operation. We must have the freedom to choose among many options and alternatives. Decisions on specific issues can be made only in the context of local control of education.[47]

Efforts at making this ideal a reality have been reflected in the development over the last two decades of a variety of different educational programs. These programs range from those that have made minimal additions of Indian content to existing school programs to fully bilingual/bicultural programs that seek an equal balance between Indian and non-Indian content.[48] Defining the search for an appropriate balance between Native and non-Native curriculum content as "at once one of the most elusive and most crucial questions in native education today," Paquette suggests that several factors have tended to tilt the balance "overwhelmingly in the direction of non-Native content."[49] Included in these factors, he suggests, are the vested interests of existing school administrators and teachers and a "crisis of purpose among aboriginal parents and the organizations that represent them that counterpoises the goal of parity with the provincial system with the goal of distinctiveness."[50] It is his conclusion that:

> With rare exception, the curriculum response to these community realities continues to be an attempt to "do what they do in the public schools," to teach provincially mandated curricula without systematic modification to recognize the cultural and linguistic milieu students come from. . . . Authentic bilingual education, while much talked about, is virtually non-existent; only in the rarest cases has a jurisdiction attempted to implement a bilingual model in the aboriginal area (Tanner, 1981) — though the Northwest Territories appear to be moving in that direction.[51]

## Curriculum Development and Implementation

Debates over the importance of Indian languages — their preservation and revitalization — within an Indian education system not only serve to draw attention to the existence of different convictions as to what constitutes a viable cultural essence among and within different Indian populations,[52] but also highlights the extensive curriculum development and implementation challenges associated with the ideal of locally controlled and culturally relevant Indian schooling.[53] As with any situation of de-colonization, where for a prolonged period of time a particular minority group perspective has been suppressed and de-legitimated, the task for curriculum developers is not simply to develop curriculum materials that reflect a precisely defined and taken-for-granted Indian identity. Rather, in a fundamental way, those developing curricula become a part of the process of creating that positive identity.

Until recently, INAC has paid only minimal attention to questions of educational programing and curriculum content.[54] During the time that the agenda for Indian schooling was that of assimilation, the development of culturally and linguistically relevant materials was seen not simply to be unnecessary but indeed quite undesirable, and provincial curricula designed to reflect the needs of non-Indian populations, quite appropriate to the task at hand. Curriculum development costs were minimal. To move in short order from this reality to a recognized need for locally relevant, authentic, Indian curricula that legitimate Indian history, language, and cultures (present and past) is a formidable undertaking — one that has to begin in large part without an existing curriculum development infrastructure to make use of, and with a critical shortage of available personnel who can combine a cultural congruence with locally evolving Indian communities with a degree of expertise in the area of curriculum development and implementation.

Despite these obstacles, significant developments are occurring in a number of different jurisdictions. Several provinces with substantial Indian student populations have begun the process of developing — usually in consultation with Indian communities — materials, sourcebooks, courses and programs targeted primarily at Indian students.[55] The Northwest Territories, with two-thirds of its population Native and with a long history of curriculum development,[56] has in the 1980s placed considerable emphasis on curriculum development and program support for bilingual education at the elementary level, committing some $3 million to indigenous language program development in the early 1980s.[57] Similarly, Paquette draws attention to considerable curriculum development projects that have occurred within some of the larger reserves in eastern Canada and the potential that such projects hold for future developments.

The ability to adapt, develop and implement curricula is a central (and as yet unresolved) issue in Indian education without which locally "controlled" schools will have little choice but to implement other curricula. Usually, this curricula has been developed provincially and is designed for students in other cultural contexts. Funding questions are obviously important here, but equally important are funding mechanisms. What appears clear in the current situation is that, with few exceptions, individual bands are likely to prove too small to constitute a viable foci for effective curriculum development activities, and block funding at the band level is unlikely to facilitate this activity.[58]

## Teachers and Teacher Preparation

If the discussion of curriculum is shifted to what actually takes place in classrooms and the meanings that these activities hold for Indian children, then the centrality of the teacher as the agent of curriculum implementation is clearly highlighted. Once again, without a cadre of teachers committed to the goals of a locally relevant curriculum and with the professional capabilities to translate policy into practice, the ideal of local control is in essence an empty concept.

**Table 2. Distribution of Indian Children by School Type (1984)**

| | | |
|---|---|---|
| Provincial Schools | 36,053 | 49.8 percent |
| Federal Schools | 20,916 | 28.9 percent |
| Band Schools | 15,434 | 21.3 percent |

Source: Barman, Hebert and McKaskill (1986, p.22).

**Table 3. Native and Non-Native Teachers in Federal and Band Operated Schools by Region (1982-1983).**

| Region | Students | Teachers | | |
|---|---|---|---|---|
| | | Native | Non-Native | Total |
| Atlantic | 1,774 | 27 | 82 | 109 |
| Quebec | 3,219 | 110 | 108 | 218 |
| Ontario | 7,624 | 121 | 263 | 384 |
| Manitoba | 10,037 | 168 | 405 | 573 |
| Saskatchewan | 7,078 | 111 | 320 | 431 |
| Alberta | 4,777 | 60 | 193 | 253 |
| Yukon | - | - | - | - |
| British Columbia | 3,218 | 87 | 161 | 248 |
| TOTAL | 37,727 | 684 | 1,532 | 2,216 |

Source: Education Directorate, Indian and Inuit Affairs Program, September, 1983.

Without dismissing the possibility that non-Indian teachers may be capable of contributing effectively to the education of Indian children[59] or suggesting that cultural congruency of itself constitutes an adequate qualification to teach Indian children, the critical importance of the increased involvement of Indian teachers in the education of Indian children is in large part unchallenged.[60]

Attempts to meet these needs have seen the development of approximately 20 Native/Indian teacher education programs across the country, starting in 1961 in the University of Saskatchewan.[61] A major consequence of these programs has been a dramatic increase in the number of registered Indians preparing to become teachers and a similar increase in practicing Indian teachers. (See Tables 2 and 3).

While all of these programs have as a primary goal the increased representation of Indian or Native people in the teaching profession, they vary considerably in their specific characteristics — for example, their duration, final level of certification, and amount of Indian/Native content. While their success in increasing the numbers of Indian teachers is obvious, the different program characteristics have produced different levels of praise and criticism. Allison, for example, argues that since the goal of any Native teacher education program is to improve the education of Native children, the objective should be to "graduate specialized, extra-competent teachers, well prepared to both comprehend and cope with the legitimate demands of Native communities, parents and children."[62] However, he contends that few of the current programs conform to this model and instead argues that

> the majority of current Native teacher education programs are essentially Native teacher certification projects which graduate students at a lower level of professional preparation than that gained by their contemporaries in regular pre-service programs. As such they are special, rather than specialized, programs that appear to be primarily concerned with increasing the number of Native teachers rather than preparing outstanding teachers of Native children.[63]

The challenge for governments, universities and Indian groups in the 1980s is to move further toward the ideals of specialized Indian teacher education programs and not merely toward special programs that "train teachers who just happen to be Native."[64]

# Conclusion

In examining some of the issues that surround the contemporary struggle by Indians in Canada to gain increased control over the schooling of their children and attempting to locate that struggle within a broader historical and social context, we have argued that it is, and always has been, at once a structural and an ideological struggle. It is concerned not only with questions of governance, but also with fundamental concerns of substance about curriculum, practice, and Indian identity. Implicit in the concept of control is the ability to institute policy in the face of opposition; to chart directions (be they traditional or innovative) and see those directions put into practice. In elaborating on this we have focused attention on four key issues:

(1) The control of appropriate systems of governance that allow for representation and a sense of ownership at the local level;

(2) The control of adequate levels of funding for Indian schools;

(3) The control of curriculum and the capacity to develop and implement curriculum, and

(4) The availability and utilization of appropriately skilled teachers.

It is our contention that it is only when these distinct dimensions come together in a specific school setting that it is possible to talk of meaningful Indian control over Indian education. Control of the governance of Indian schools without adequate funding and the ability to allocate funds to meet locally defined needs is not really control. Control of governance of Indian schools in the absence of the capabilities to produce, adapt and implement new curricula is not really control. Control of the governance of Indian schools in the absence of a cadre of qualified teachers and administrators capable of operationalizing a vision of Indian education is not really control.

Important developments have occurred in various locations across Canada in each of these areas. Yet where it is detectable, progress has been accomplished almost entirely without benefit of constitutional or legislative change — the *Indian Act* remains intact and aboriginal rights and treaty entitlement issues (including land claims) have yet to be fully addressed. Meanwhile, in the national context, successive governments have paradoxically recognized a history of inadequate funding at the same time they sought to restrict future allocations.[65] There is a recognition of a poorly developed curriculum development infrastructure and a teacher education system that, while effective in increasing the number of Indian teachers, has been criticized for failing to provide them with the specialized skills necessary to most effectively function in that context.

In this political reality, meaningful forms of control over their children's schooling, and the significant improvement in the quality of education that might accompany such developments, remain for many Indian communities promises in an uncertain future.

## *Notes*

[1]We would like to acknowledge and thank Rod Clifton, Agnes Grant and Bob Gustafson for their helpful comments and criticisms of earlier drafts of this chapter and Eileen Repeta without whose careful retyping of the many drafts this chapter went through to the end-product would, in our opinion at least, be significantly less well developed.

[2]As used in this paper, the term "Indian" is strictly a legal definition wherein it means an individual who is registered as an Indian through the *Indian Act* and accordingly, has a special status in Canada. Federal government services provided to those holding status is usually restricted only to those Indians who live on reserves. This chapter is restricted to a discussion of education for this group. For greater detail, see Frideres (1988).

[3]H.B. Hawthorn, ed., *A Survey of the Contemporary Indians of Canada* (Ottawa: Queen's Printer, 1966-67). Two decades ago the Hawthorne Report documented the following state of Indian education: nation-wide, 57 Indians were attending university out of a population of 45,309 (p. 130); the attrition rate for Indian students between Grade 1 and Grade 12 was 94 percent (p. 130); approximately 80 percent of Indian children repeated Grade 1 at least once (p. 131); the average Indian student was 2.5 years behind the average non-Indian student by the end of Grade 8 (p. 132); and the average absentee rate among Indian children was 40 days per year. These figures have changed substantially in the 1970s and the 1980s but large discrepancies between Indian and non-Indian levels of educational attainment persist, and for most observers they are not adequately explained in terms of differences in Indian needs and aspirations. J.S. Frideres, *Native People in Canada: Contemporary Conflicts*, 3rd edition (Scarborough: Prentice Hall, Canada, 1988), p. 185, notes that "in 1981 fewer than 1 percent of Natives attended university compared to 7 percent of the general population." This divergence from the national average is compounded when one considers graduation rates. "University graduation as a success indicator was estimated at 25.8 percent for Indians and 72.6 percent nationally in 1983" according to the Neilson Report, Canada, *Taskforce on Program Review: Education and Research* (Ottawa: Minister of Supply and Services, 1986), p. 154. In 1981, 41 percent of Native People had less than Grade 9 as their highest level of schooling (the Canadian Association for Adult Education's definition of functional illiteracy) compared to 22 percent of the non-Native population, and 71 percent of the Native population had less than a high school diploma compared to 47 percent of the non-Native population. (See Canada, Statistics Canada, *Canada's Native People*, Ottawa: Minister of Supply and Services, 1984.) Frideres, (p. 181) notes that successful school completion to Grade 12 or 13 remains less than one-quarter of the national average. At the provincial level, it was reported that in Manitoba nearly half of the Indian children enroled in school have been held back at least two years [Assembly of Manitoba Chiefs, *Our Tomorrows . . . Today* (Winnipeg: Assembly of Manitoba Chiefs, 1984), p. 70)]. Other more localized studies document the same sorts of challenges in varying degrees. See J.A. Riffel and D.B. Sealey, *Easterville Education Review, A Report to the Easterville Education Authority* (Easterville, Manitoba, 1984); Riffel and Sealey, *The Development of Education in Fairford: A Community Manual* (Fairford Education Authority, Fairford, Manitoba, 1986); and Riffel and Sealey, *Education in Norway House, A Report Submitted to the Norway House Education Authority* (Norway House, Manitoba, 1987).

[4]Quoted in M.A. Janigan, "A Prophecy of Violence," *Maclean's Magazine* (13 June 1988): 13.

[5] Assembly of First Nations, *Traditions and Education: Towards a Vision of Our Future—National Review of First Nations' Education*, 3 vols (Ottawa: Assembly of First Nations, 1988).

[6] National Indian Brotherhood, *Indian Control of Indian Education* (Ottawa: National Indian Brotherhood, 1972). The National Indian Brotherhood (NIB) was organized in 1968 to speak for registered Indians in Canada. In 1981, the organization was reconstituted and the name was changed to the Assembly of First Nations (AFN). It should be noted that this is not the only organization which claims to speak for Canadian Indians at the national level.

[7] National Indian Brotherhood, p. 3.

[8] Assembly of First Nations, vol. 1, p. 47.

[9] T. Symons, *Report of the Commission on Canadian Studies: To Know Ourselves*, vol. 1 (Ottawa: Association of Universities and Colleges of Canada, 1975), p. 12.

[10] Symons, p. 14.

[11] A. Manicom, "Curriculum as Material: A Discussion," in J. Young, ed., *Breaking the Mosaic: Ethnic Identities in Canadian Schools* (Toronto: Garamond Press, 198)7, p. 158.

[12] G.P. Kelly and P.G. Altbach, "Introduction" in P.G. Altbach and G.P. Kelly, eds., *Education and Colonialism* (New York: Longman, 1978), p. 23.

[13] E.P. Patterson, *The Canadian Indians: A History Since 1500* (Don Mills, Ontario: Collier MacMillan Canada, 1972).

[14] J.L. Tobias, "Protection, Civilization, Assimilation: An Outline History of Canada's Indian Policy," in A.L. Getty and A.S. Lussier, eds., *As Long as the Sun Shines and Water Flows* (Vancouver: University of British Columbia Press, 1983).

[15] Kelly and Altbach, p. 19.

[16] For examples, see J. Barman, Y. Hebert and D. McCaskill, eds., *Indian Education in Canada*, vol. 1, *The Legacy* (Vancouver: University of British Columbia Press, 1986); and E.B. Titley, "Indian Industrial Schools in Western Canada," in N.M. Sheehan, J.D. Wilson and D.C. Janis, eds., *Schools in the West* (Calgary: Detselig Enterprises, 1986).

[17] G. Kellough, "From Colonialism to Imperialism: The Experiences of the Canadian Indians," in J. Harp and J. Hufley, eds., *Structural Inequalities in Canada.* (Scarborough: Prentice-Hall, Canada, 1980).

[18] R.M. Bienvenue, "Colonial Status: The Case of Canadian Indies," in R.M. Bienvenue and J.E. Goldstein, eds., *Ethnicity and Ethnic Relations in Canada*, 2nd. ed. (Toronto: Butterworth (Canada), 1985).

[19] B. Overwald, "The Schools," in M. Watkins, ed., *Dene Nation — The Colony Within* (Toronto: University of Toronto Press, 1977).

[20] Hawthorn, p. 5.

[21]Canada, Department of Indian Affairs and Northern Development (DIAND), *Indian Conditions: A Survey* (Ottawa: DIAND, 1980), p. 49.

[22]For a discussion, see S.M. Weaver, *Making Canadian Indian Policy* (Toronto: University of Toronto Press, 1981), pp. 20-24.

[23]See Weaver, pp. 20-24; and J.R. Ponting and R.Gibbins, *Out of Irrelevance* (Toronto: Butterworth (Canada), 1980), pp. 25-29.

[24]M. Foster, "Native People and the Demand for Self-Government," *Currents,* 4, 2 (1987): 9.

[25]Canada, *Taskforce on Program Review.* See note 3.

[26]J. Paquette, *Aboriginal Self-Government and Education in Canada* (Kingston: Queen's University, Institute of Government Relations, 1986).

[27]Canada, *Indian Act* (Ottawa: Minister of Supply and Services, 1985). In recent years, the *Indian Act* has been amended a number of times. Perhaps the most significant change has come about through Bill C-31 which was introduced to remove the sexual bias that all were agreed the *Indian Act* contained. As a result, there are now distinctions among registered Indians on the basis of degree of status. This has effectively placed restrictions on some Indians who cannot pass their status on to succeeding generations. This will have serious implications for the survival of Status Indians over the long term. For a discussion, see J. Holmes, *Bill C-31 Equality or Disparity? The Effects of the New Indian Act on Native Women* (Ottawa: Canadian Advisory Council on the Status of Women, 1987).

[28]The task of naming the federal government agency is somewhat confusing at this time. The Department of Indian Affairs and Northern Development (DIAND) has recently changed its title to Indian and Northern Affairs Canada (INAC) but the two names continue to be used interchangeably, even by the federal government itself.

[29]H. Cardinal, *The Rebirth of Canada's Indians* (Edmonton: Hurtig, 1977), p. 84.

[30]V.J. Kirkness, "Indian Control of Indian Education: Over a Decade Later," in H.A. McCue, ed., *Mokakit* (Vancouver: Mokakit Indian Education Research Association, 1986), p. 77.

[31]In 1983, INAC released a Capital Management Plan which laid out the financial obligations of the Department for the operation and maintenance of community capital structures, including schools. Funding levels are data-based and band councils are responsible for providing acceptable levels of service. This may be considered the forerunner to the new Alternative Funding Arrangements which are discussed in this chapter (Canada, INAC, Capital Management Internal Department Policy Statement, December 1983).

[32]Canada, *Report of the Special Committee on Indian Self-Government in Canada* (The Penner Report) (Ottawa: Government of Canada, 1983), pp. 28-29.

[33]Paquette, p. 11.

[34]Canada, *The Constitutional Act,* 1982 (Ottawa: Minister of Supply and Services, 1986).

[35]Canada, *The Constitutional Act.*

[36]Canada, DIAND, *Alternative Funding Arrangements: A Guide* (Ottawa: Minister of Supply and Services, 1986), p. 5.

[37]Canada, DIAND, p. 4.

[38]Canada, DIAND, *Alternative Funding Arrangements (AFA) - Treasury Board Submission*, 30 May 1986, p. 4.

[39]Cardinal, p.84.

[40]Canada, *AFA — Treasury Board Submission*, p. 12.

[41]AFN, p. 130.

[42]Canada: *AFA — Treasury Board Submission*, p. 9.

[43]NIB, p. 9.

[44]See, for example, A. More, "Quality of Education of Native Indian Students in Canada," in H.A. McCue, *Makakit*; and Canada, DIAND, *National Overview of Elementary/Secondary Evaluation Projects* (Ottawa: DIAND, 1984).

[45]Assembly of Manitoba Chiefs, p. 70; Canada, DIAND, *Indian Education Paper: Phase 1* (Ottawa: DIAND, 1982); and Canada, *Report of the Special Committee on Indian Self-Government in Canada.*

[46]J. Barman, Y. Hebert and D. McCaskill, eds., *Indian Education in Canada, Volume 2: The Challenge* (Vancouver: University of British Columbia Press, 1987), p. 5.

[47]NIB, p. 3.

[48]J. Archibald, "Locally Developed Native Studies Curriculum: A Historical and Philosophical Rationale," in H.A. McCue, *Mokakit*; A. More, S. Purcell and C. Mirehouse, *Indian Education Project in British Columbia Schools* (Vancouver: University of British Columbia Press, 1981); and J. Barman, Y. Hebert and D. McCaskill, p. 5.

[49]Paquette, p. 45.

[50]Paquette, p. 52.

[51]Paquette, p. 45.

[52]Paquette, p. 45; B. Burnaby, "1981 Census Perspective Planning for Native Language Programs," in H.A. McCue, *Mokakit*; B. Burnaby and N. Elson, *Language Development in Native Education, Final Report* (TESL Canada (Mines), 1982); and M. Foster, "Canada's Indigenous Languages: Present and Future," *Language and Society*, 7 (1982).

[53]See the following table. Burnaby uses a special analysis of the 1981 census to highlight some of the complexities associated with the teaching of Native languages. With 11 native language families and 53 officially designated languages to be taken into account (only three of which — Cree, Ojibwe and Inuktitut — meet Foster's (1982) criteria of having 5,000 speakers as a necessary prerequisite for a truly good chance of survival under modern North American conditions), geographically dispersed, serviced by three different types of school system, and suffering considerable erosion, the problems are obvious. Nevertheless, it is her conclusion that "these realities will continue to exist, but they

## Mother Tongue

| Part 1 | Canada | Nfld | PEI | N.S. | N.B. | Que. | Ont. |
|---|---|---|---|---|---|---|---|
| Cree | 67,495 | 5 | - | 15 | 5 | 8,010 | 7,310 |
| Ojibwe | 19,765 | - | - | 5 | 5 | 5 | 7,560 |
| Other Algonquian | 15,640 | 345 | 50 | 2,730 | 1,210 | 6,345 | 110 |
| Athapaskan | 11,655 | - | - | 10 | - | 2- | 140 |
| Haida | 295 | - | - | - | - | - | 60 |
| Iroquoian | 6,075 | - | - | - | - | 5,510 | 540 |
| Kootenai | 100 | - | - | - | - | - | 5 |
| Salishan | 895 | - | - | - | - | 5 | 15 |
| Siouan | 2,975 | - | - | - | - | 5 | 10 |
| Tlingit | 135 | - | - | - | - | - | - |
| Tsimshian | 1,435 | - | - | 5 | - | - | 10 |
| Wakashan | 975 | - | - | - | - | - | 10 |
| Inuktitut | 18,840 | 840 | - | 10 | 5 | 4,540 | 95 |
| unspecified | 20,285 | 415 | 40 | 285 | 890 | 3,625 | 6,330 |

| Part 2 | Man. | Sask. | Alta. | B.C. | Yukon | NWT |
|---|---|---|---|---|---|---|
| Cree | 15,880 | 17,680 | 17,200 | 1,165 | 10 | 15 |
| Ojibwe | 8,090 | 3,310 | 570 | 105 | - | 105 |
| Other Algonquian | 15 | 10 | 4,810 | 20 | - | 105 |
| Athapaskan | 475 | 2,390 | 1,870 | 2,445 | 225 | 4,091 |
| Haida | - | - | - | - | - | - |
| Iroquoian | - | - | 10 | 5 | - | - |
| Kootenai | - | - | 10 | 90 | - | - |
| Salishan | - | - | 10 | 865 | - | - |
| Siouan | 720 | 180 | 2,040 | 15 | - | - |
| Tlingit | - | - | 5 | 10 | 125 | - |
| Tsimshian | 5 | - | 5 | 1,415 | - | - |
| Wakashan | - | - | 20 | 930 | - | - |
| Inuktitut | 45 | 15 | 60 | 30 | 10 | 13,200 |
| Unspecified | 1,945 | 680 | 950 | 4,135 | 460 | 530 |

Mother Tongue Speakers of Amerindian and Inuit Languages, Canada and the Provinces, 1981.

do not provide sufficient cause for pessimism regarding the potential for broad-scale initiatives to plan, rationalize, and develop facilities which can support individual Native language programs within the context of their local needs and characteristics" (p. 36). The following taken from the 1981 census, indicates the linguistic and geographical diversity of mother tongue speakers of Amerindian and Inuit languages in Canada.

[54]Canada, DIAND, *Indian Education Paper: Phase 1.*

[55]Canadian Education Association, *Recent Developments in Indian Education* (Toronto: Canadian Education Association, 1984).

[56]P. Robinson, "Curriculum Development," in J.R. Mallea and J.C. Young, eds., *Cultural Diversity and Canadian Education* (Ottawa: Oxford University Press, 1984).

[57]Canadian Education Association, *Indian Education.* The calculations currently used by INAC provide for $43 per student annually for "Curriculum and Adaptation" in band-operated schools. Most do not have the student population to generate the funds necessary for meaningful local level curriculum development. Under AFA, the education budget will not be itemized and it may prove difficult to establish a proper funding procedure for needed curriculum development. Canada, INAC, Resourcing Formula, Telex (16 July 1987).

[58]J. Paquette; Canada, *Report of the Special Committee on Indian Self-Government in Canada*; and M. Wand,"Indian Education: Policy and Politics 1972-82", *Canadian Journal of Native Education*, 13, 2 (1986), pp. 10-21.

[59]J. Kleinfield, "Effective Teachers of Eskimo and Indian Students," *School Review* (February 1975): 301-344.

[60]Kirkness; D. Allison, "Fourth World Education in Canada and the Faltering Promise of Native Teacher Education Programs," *Journal of Canadian Studies,* 18, 3 (Fall, 1983): 102-118; and J. Wyatt, "Native Involvement in Curriculum Development: The Native Teacher as Cultural Broker," *Interchange*, 9, 1 (1978-79): 17-28.

[61]D. Allison, pp. 102-118; and J. Friesen, "The Preparation of Teachers for Native Students," in R. Patterson and C. Urion, eds., *Native Schools in Transition: Yearbook of the Canadian Society for the Study of Education*, vol. 1 (Edmonton: CSSE, 1974).

[62]Allison, p. 112.

[63]Allison, p. 112.

[64]Wyatt, p. 27.

[65]Canada, *Taskforce on Program Review,* Education and Research.

# Section 3:
# Future Prospects for Canadian Education

# 12

# Future Clientele for Public Schools: Some Postulations

*Y.L. Jack Lam*


As we begin to examine the problems confronting public education in this country, we are overwhelmed by the chilling fact of intense political struggle for resource allocation, financial restraints, negotiation deadlock, teacher militancy, program consolidation, legal complexities of operating the school, and public demands for quality education. Indeed, the symptoms of "malfunction" associated with the public school system operation that became apparent in the late seventies[1] seem to have intensified rather than diminished over the past ten years.

All measures adopted to resolve thorny issues in the past decade have proven to be ineffective and, at best, provide only temporary relief. The federal government's six-five guidelines have lowered salary demands but they have failed to contain educational expenditure. Job-protection pursued by teachers' organizations in a period of enrolment decline by means of "seniority clause" has resulted in the rapid aging of the teaching force. Job-sharing has received lukewarm support within and without the teaching profession. The proposals for reduction of class size have rekindled fear of uncontrollable educational costs and have been strongly resisted by provincial governments. The absence of new resources and the lack of improvement in the working conditions for teachers have precipitated annual confrontations between teachers and the school boards in the bargaining session with no solution in sight. Changes in the curriculum in response to social changes and expanded roles for teachers continue to tax their repertoire and energy to the extreme. A growing number of cases of teacher job-stress, distress and burnout have been reported.

As one scrutinizes the solutions advanced by governments, teachers' organizations, school boards and other concerned individuals and groups, one can readily accept the fact that most solutions are short-term, stop-gap measures to bandage the observable cracks and flaws without even touching the root problem. The end result is further procrastination in dealing head-on with the real issue; meanwhile, symptoms of maladjustment of the school system multiply and become more menacing every day.

## Fundamental Problem: Social Demographic Shift

The fundamental problem behind the many signs of breakdown in the school system lies in the slow but dramatic demographic shift which has radically transformed the structure of Canadian society. According to the projection of Zsigmond,[2] the proportion of children in the age-range of 5-17 in Canada is expected to rise from 1970 into the 1990s with some fluctuation in between. Taking a global perspective of the current sub-zero population growth and the longevity of an aging population, the proportion of the traditional school-age population will continue to shrink. Enrolment decline in the mid-seventies, with massive teacher lay offs demoralizing the front-line educators, and subsequent school closures triggering bitter community-school board confrontation, are a foretaste of what is to come when the system clings to the traditional format of operation in the face of rapid social change.

With the proportion of the population served by the public school undergoing steady decline, the solid political backing that the public school system enjoys may weaken. Old questions concerning the need to channel limited resources into the public school system will resurface. The clamor for a voucher system or a user-fee, familiar demands in the United States especially in the medical field, will be echoed in the Canadian education scene. Taxpayers with no children or grandchildren in the system who constitute the majority might even stage a revolt similar in kind to that identified with Proposition 13 in California.[3] Indeed, with the shrinkage of clientele that the public school serves, there is some degree of certainty that the political and economic foundation of the educational system, as we know it today, will be shaken.

## Toward a Final Solution

It becomes only too obvious that continued entrenchment of the present jurisdiction, which some of the conservative education leaders jealously defend, can only render the system archaic, magnifying the institutional lag in meeting the social needs of a changing environment. Renewal of mandate will require the public education system to reach out to new clientele in order to broaden and consolidate its basis of support in the years to come.

Scanning the global scene we note some of the interesting developments in two domains traditionally peripheric to public education. Recent trends in early childhood and basic adult education strongly suggest that their merger with the public education system is a logical outcome whose time has come. A closer examination of these trends seems to be in order.

# Early Childhood Education
## *Social and Political changes*

The initiation of a plan for the early education for the very young had a rocky start. The idea of placing children in an educational setting away from their mothers was frowned upon as hearsay. There was also a time when rural communities conducted a widespread "witch-hunt" for proponents of early childhood education. Nonetheless, with more and more women joining the work-force in the sixties, daycare centres, some well-equipped, some crudely furnished, began to mushroom. Such social changes were readily transformed into a visible political force with women's organizations pressuring for quality daycare and universal services.

While the demand of universal support to such social services has yet to materialize, many of the provincial governments have now in place acts and statutes defining the minimum standards daycare centres should meet before they are allowed to operate. More significant is the fact that classification of daycare workers, a vivid reminder of the classification of public school teachers in the early days, is now in effect; detailed prescriptions of the qualifications a daycare worker should possess for advancement from one class to the next are available. Parallel to the established legislation is a growing demand on post-secondary institutions, community colleges and universities alike, to have programs in place for the professionalization of the daycare workers who once were made up solely of untrained housewives. Currently, available daycare training programs, housed either in the community colleges or in the departments of family studies, social work or faculties of education at the universities, range from one-to-two years of training up to graduate studies. These are likely the combined outcomes of the subtle influences and interactions among the forces below.

## *Educational Research*

The educational evaluation of early childhood programs undertaken mostly in the States, as Brown observed,[4] has gone through three interesting phases. In the "dismal" period, the evaluation projects, notably those conducted by Westinghouse Learning Corporation and Ohio University,[5] in response to the demands of the Johnson administration, came to a sad conclusion that the summer Head Start program was totally ineffective and even had a negative impact while the full-year program was only marginally effective. In reviewing the design of the Westinghouse Report, four glaring weaknesses may be identified: the timing of data collection, the choice of the control group, the criterion measures and the variables selected.

In the "latency" period of the early seventies, the comprehensive early intervention model established by the Head Start program continued to spread.

Under the leadership of Edward Zigler, the Office of Child Development initiated a series of experimental Head Start programs with substantial progress in administration, training, and service programs. Performance standards were developed.

In the "watershed" period, more sophisticated and all-encompassing analytic techniques became available. With the arrival of meta-analytic technique,[6] data from the major studies were pooled together (each by itself provided too few data) for a new round of data analysis. Notable among the efforts in this direction was the Consortium for Longitudinal Studies,[7] the product of collaboration amongst 12 investigators. From this set of data, four important findings emerged:

(1) Early education programs significantly reduce the number of children assigned to special education classes.

(2) Early education programs significantly reduce the number of children retained in grade.

(3) Preschool programs produce a significant increase in the IQ and school achievement of low income children through at least the critical early primary years.

(4) Children who attend preschool are more likely to give achievement-related reasons for being proud of themselves. Their mothers also have high vocational aspirations for them.

That subsequent research[8] tends to confirm these results should reinforce our conviction in the efficacy of early intervention programs.

Drawing on extensive works recently completed in this area, Woodhead,[9] perhaps more than others, makes some insightful interpretations which link the manifested evidence with the less tangible extrapolations. Dismissing "critical period theory" and "sleeper effects" as the sole context for examining the long-term impact early intervention programs have upon the young, he stresses the social skills, achievement motivation and the momentum of parental interests in children's school performance as some of the potent variables that have the carry-over effects on children's later success. He accurately identifies that it was the moderately disadvantaged section of the population who benefited most from taking part in an early intervention program. In terms of the design of an intervention program, he indicates that a high level of professional support, a low ratio of children to staff, and a carefully planned curriculum aimed primarily at enhancing cognitive abilities are some of the critical characteristics to assure success in the early intervention program. In sum, he believes:

> The power of pre-school intervention to engender, reinforce and sustain parental aspirations and interest in their children's education appears to be a significant part of the transactional process which converts short-term cognitive and motivational change into long-term educational and social competence.

Further, if one consults the work of Berrueta-Clement and her colleagues,[10] which traces the effects of early education into the early adulthood, and the longitudinal study Lam[11] conducted linking high school achievement to university performance and occupational outcomes, one has a tentative empirical basis from which to project the ripple-effects of the preschool experience to post-higher education development.

## Moral and ethical considerations

If Woodhead's assertion[12] is correct, there are a number of moral and ethical issues that should draw the attention of public educators. Foremost among these is the observation that disadvantaged children will benefit most from early intervention programs. Implicit in this statement is the fact that without the government's direct intervention in funding quality preschool for the disadvantaged, the basis of inequality of opportunity between the rich and the poor children will be well-ingrained in the system. This makes later intervention even more costly and often too late to be effective. If public educators profess equal opportunities for *all*, is there not a moral obligation on our part to ensure that quality preschool is available for the disadvantaged?

In examining the characteristics of successful early intervention programs, one should readily acknowledge that carefully planned curriculum aiming primarily to enhance cognitive abilities can hardly be developed in ordinary households under the care of semi-professionals. Neither should that type of program be available only in the high-priced private nursery accessible only the children of affluent parents. The question to be raised to public educators is: Isn't it along the traditional line of duty for teachers to provide quality education to their children, and isn't it the jurisdiction of the public school to assure this quality program be universally accessible to all?

## Economic Reassessments

One of the most common arguments against extending the public school system to children younger than five-years-old is the immense cost the public will shoulder if the extension takes place. There are five aspects that, typically, people have forgotten to take into consideration when asserting the argument. In the first place, the cost projection is usually based on the gross estimation of the number of *all* eligible children from the census. The reality of the situation is that as long as we allow private preschools to continue to operate, as we always do with the dual school system, that number is certain to be vastly exaggerated and, correspondingly, the estimate cost will be unrealistically high.[13]

The second aspect is that a substantial amount of subsidy has already been given by social welfare and child care departments to the poor for their daycare expenses. The proposed integration of a daycare program with the public school system is simply a readjustment of the source of support from one government department to another so that the end cost of implementation should be further revised.

If an early intervention program reduces the number of referrals to special education classes and trims the rate of dropouts, as research indicates, opponents of integration have definitely missed another aspect in their deliberations. In Manitoba, for instance, the compensatory grant in 1984 for assisting children from disadvantaged socioeconomic backgrounds reached $13 million or 2 percent of the total budget.[14] The amount devoted to the categorical grants in support of education with special needs exceeded $32 million (5 percent of the total budget).

With respect to the problem of school dropouts, we know that the problem of school attendance today is a problem of illiterate or functionally illiterate adults tomorrow. This has serious economic repercussions that will be further scrutinized in the latter part of this chapter. If public educators recognize the severity of this issue and are prepared to adopt what Boston and a few other American cities have pioneered, the provision of incentive grants for students, the amount will be even more staggering.

If one is ready to proceed another step forward by examining social and indirect economic externalities which are frequently ignored by opponents of integration but become an aspect to be scrutinized by more researchers,[15] the beneficial effects can be more readily identified. Indeed, it has been estimated that early intervention programs, through prevention of delinquency, teenage pregnancy and improved likelihood of employment, manage to generate, through cost-benefit analyses, a net benefit to society at a rate of seven to one for one year of investment in preschool. Although some of us might look at the analyses with a grain of salt, we should be fully aware of the existence of externalities generated by extending education to younger children that are usually forgotten in projecting the cost of extending educational services.

Lastly, within the general context of economics of education, where the relationship between education and economic development of individuals and societies are closely studied, and where school reforms are viewed as investments for maximizing rates of return,[16] the proposed integration of early intervention programs with regular schooling should be deemed a landmark step in achieving congruency between providing equality of educational opportunity for all and maximizing our resource allocation. In the face of intensified international competitiveness, when the quality of our educational products are under closer scrutiny,[17] the proposed integration should represent a decent strategic choice in attaining our economic, social and educational objectives.

The time has indeed come for a more aggressive and research-verified step to revamp the public school system through infusion of new elements.

# Basic Adult Education

Turning to the other end of the demographic structure, we note that Canada, like many other industrialized countries in the world, faces the aging of a noticeable portion of the population. Indeed, it has been estimated that for every ten years, there will be an increase of 1 percent of the total population in Canada that constitutes the "senior citizen" category.[18] Accompanying this basic change in the demographic makeup is a shifting of the political power base and the growing responsibilities of welfare — pension, medical insurance and perhaps education of the adult population, which were at one time of marginal importance to society. In terms of public education, however, one clear message needs to be registered in the mind: the foundation of public education, to continue strongly, must rest on its ability to reach the major segment of the population, the senior adults which constitute a growing proportion.

Without dwelling in depth on life-long education, a topic which has saturated literature pertaining to adult education for the past two decades, and which embraces a domain far greater than this chapter can handle, we should remember one particular aspect that has an immediate implication for 'he public school system, namely, there is a substantial proportion of adults who are unable to function effectively, owing to their inadequacies in education. Available data[19] indicate that close to 25 percent of the Canadian population is either illiterate or functionally illiterate, a situation quite comparable to that in the United States. While such a phenomenon has greatly shaken educators and politicians (including the President)[20] in the United States, the response among Canadian counterparts, on the other hand, seems unusually calm and moderate. It is feared that unless the gravity of the situation is clearly understood, we might be lured into a state of inertia with consequences that will adversely affect the various aspects of the individual's welfare as well as the welfare of the country as a whole.

## *Significance of Adult literacy*

The significance of adult literacy is perhaps best reflected in President Reagan's 1983 speech to a gathering of American citizens concerned with adult literacy problems in the United States. He said,

> In this decade, America faces serious challenges on many fronts: to our National security, our economic prosperity, and our ability to compete in the international marketplace. If we're to renew our economy, protect our freedom, we must sharpen the skills of every American mind and enlarge the potential of every individual American life. Unfortunately, the hidden problem of adult illiteracy holds back too many of our citizens, and as a nation, we, too, pay a price.

It seems evident that undertaking adult literacy development is not so much a provision for a catch-up opportunity for individual adults to gain equality in academic skills, but a means for national survival in an era of great technological advancement and intense international economic competition. Brock,[21] in projecting the requirement of the work-force in the future, suggests three interesting developments. First, by 1995, about 90 percent of the new jobs will be in the service-producing sector, with a predominant proportion requiring post-secondary high school skills. Second, technological advances and industrial restructuring will require flexibility in the work force, a characteristic closely associated with individual cognitive and reasoning skills. Third, any job presently done by a functional illiterate could be done better, cheaper and faster by a machine.

If such predictions are correct, and if we do little to reduce the number of illiterate adults, we run into the risk of creating a queer class society, socially speaking, consisting of one group employed and another group unemployable. The social tension of such a society would be intolerable and unimaginable.

### Responsibility of Public Education.

In view of its economic, social and national implications, the task of educating adults with educational deficiencies is too important to be treated either as a peripheric or an *ad hoc* service of education institutions. Additionally, when we critically examine the current operations which consist of some night schools sponsored by the public school system, basic adult education programs housed in the community colleges, and special mature programs initiated by the extension departments of universities, all of which attempt to reach the same clientele, we sense the utter confusion of the jurisdiction of the various education institutions. Such a marked and disjointed fragmentation of responsibilities and overlapping programs, indeed, perpetuates the wasteful utilization of public funds and generates much unwanted inter-institutional jealousy and hostility.

Through a cooperative dialogue among the various concerned institutions, an all-encompassing model of adult education with some fundamental restructuring can start to take shape.[22] Under a cooperative scheme, it is rational to envision that the major role of the public school system will be assigned to the upgrading of the adults' basic academic skills as well as some basic business and vocational training. What is proposed is essentially an extension of the existing and presently available comprehensive programs to the adult clientele. Through this dual system, with the regular students in the day-time and adult students in the evenings, the facilities of the public school system will be utilized to the maximum. In so doing, the public school has freed the community and the university resources to engage in the urgent task of providing the nation with more technical and professional manpower to compete in the international marketplace of the twenty-first century.

Prerequisite to the success of such an undertaking is a revamping of the overall curriculum to ensure articulated progression from one level to another, from the basic core of education to the diversified pursuit of different career preparations. The insertion of adult education into the general public education system will indeed provide impetus for one of the most logical and rational approaches for redesigning school curriculum.

## *Some Basic Questions and Spontaneous Answers*

Questions similar to those raised in conjunction with the integration of early intervention programs might be posed again by conservative educators about the feasibility of mainstreaming adults into the public school system. Foremost in the list is the funding of such an enterprise. The cost in this case is readily estimated from the existing operation in different types and levels of institution. By concentrating basic adult education in the hands of public educators, the savings from the elimination of overlapping programs in community colleges and universities should be substantial. The increase of public education expenditure is more than compensated by the reduction of duplicate services at the post-secondary level.

To carry the financial analysis one step further, it is noted that using a reported figure of 6 million illiterates and functional illiterates, and using a teacher-student ratio of 1 to 30, some 200,000 teaching jobs will be instantly required to eliminate the illiteracy problem in Canada. Based on a gradual recognition that unemployment and social welfare pose a far heavier burden on society than engaging people on the job, the mainstreaming of adult learners into the public education system resolves quite readily the oversupply of teachers in the current market and ensures in the long run, a broader and more secure basis for teacher retention.

In the final analysis, as the literature on the economics of education stresses again and again, schooling is the best form of investment. Education returns more to the economy than it takes out. Aside from ensuring a higher rate of return, education, by lowering the likelihood of unemployment and generating higher fringe benefits, sometimes defies tangible quantitative analyses.

The second type of question posed is likely to be concerned with the inter-institutional jealousy and intra-institutional inertia relating to the implementation of the bold venture. The magnitude of the political forces and the resistance likely to be engendered against any infringement on an existing parameter of operation should certainly not be underestimated. On the other hand, if no drastic change has taken place, it becomes only too obvious that all institutions are heading on a collision course and the scramble for the adult clientele will begin to intensify correspondent to the slow but steady demographic changes in our society. In the foreseeable future, the political entanglement will be far more complex and the inter-institutional animosity will be far more intense as long as each party continues to consolidate and expand its scope of operation without clarifying its jurisdictional boundaries.

## Conclusion

The problems currently confronting public education are very much a reflection of symptoms of malfunction in a system that has catered to a selected narrow range of clientele for the past 80 years. With the dramatic changes in the demographic structure resulting from smaller family size and from medical and nutritional advancement, the once unquestionable political and social support for public education is undergoing subtle changes and the future utility and the omnipotent function public education performs become murkier than before.

At the same time, however, the impact of an early intervention program on children's long-term performance, and the economic and social implications for the inclusion of a basic adult literacy program into the public school curriculum become better understood. Evidently, the merger of these two marginal enterprises with the mainstream is not merely a distant possibility, but a logical and sensible measure to take.

Granted that there is much debate about the economic ramifications of steering toward this radical course, much concern about intra-organizational inertia and much uncertainty about redefinition of territorial jurisdiction, it remains clear that inaction leads to the obsolescence of a system from which a nation draws its leadership and its professional and technical pool of manpower. Certainly, for the sake of the future well-being of the nation, the suggested merger should deserve a trial.

### Notes

[1] Y.L.J. Lam, "Adult Education, Implications in a Period of Social Change," *Canadian Education Association Newsletter* (1988).

[2] Zoltan Zsigmond, *Population and Enrolment Trends: 1961-2001* (1976).

[3] S.J. Mushkin, (ed), *Proposition 13 and its Consequences for Public Management*, The Council for Applied Social Research (1979).

[4] B. Brown, "Head Start, How Research Changed Public Policy," *Young Children* (1985): 9-13.

[5] V.G. Cicirelli, J.W. Evans and J.S. Schiller, *The Impact of Head Start: An Evaluation of the Effects of Head Start on Children's Cognitive and Affective Development 1-2* (Athens, Ohio: Westinghouse Learning Corporation and Ohio University, 1969).

[6] G.V. Glass, B. McGaw and M.L. Smith, *Meta-analysis in Social Research* (Beverly Hills, Ca.: Sage Publications, 1981).

[7] Consortium on Developmental Continuity, *The Persistence of Pre-school Effects* (Washington, ACYF: Consortium for Longitudinal Studies, 1979); *Lasting Effects after Pre-school* (Washington, ACYF: Consortium for Longitudinal Studies, 1983); and *As the Twig is Bent* (New York: Erlbaum Associates).

[8] For example, E. Zigler, W.D. Abelson, P.K. Trickett and V. Seitz, "Is an Intervention Program Necessary in Order to Improve Economically Disadvantaged Children's IQ Scores?" *Child Development*, 53 (1982): 340-348; M.B. Bronson, D.E. Pierson and T. Tivnan, "The Effects of Early Education on Children's Competence in Elementary School," *Evaluation Review*, 8 (1984): 615-629; and E.B. Goldring and L.S. Presbrey, "Evaluating Preschool Programs: A Meta-analytic Approach," *Educational Evaluation and Policy Analysis*, 8 (1986): 179-188.

[9] M. Woodhead, "Pre-school Education has Long-Term Effects: But Can They be Generalized?" *Oxford Review of Education*, 11 (1885): 133-155.

[10] J.R. Berrueta-Clement, L.J. Schweinhart, W.S. Barnett, A.S. Espstein and D.P. Weikart, "Changed Lives: the Effects of the Perry Preschool Program on Youths through Age 19," *Monograph of the High/Scope Education Research Foundation*, 8 (1984).

[11] Y.L.J. Lam, "Occupational Attainments of University Graduates: A Case Comparison of Men and Women," *Educational Research and Perspectives*, 10 (1983): 23-40.

[12] Woodhead, p. 133-35.

[13] For example, the estimation done by Mass. governor's official for possible integration of preschool into the public school system is two billion (or 1/5 of the total public school budget). This estimation is based on all the eligible children derived from the census and is therefore on the high side.

[14] G. Nicholl, *Enhancing Equity in Manitoba Schools* (Winnipeg, Manitoba: Government press, 1983).

[15] C. Breedlove and L.J. Schweinhart, *The Cost Effectiveness of High Quality Early Childhoold Programs*, report for the 1982 Southern Governors' Conference (Ypsilanti, Mich.: High Scope, 1982).

[16] D.H. Saks, "A Legacy for the Twenty-First Century: Investment Opportunities in Our Children's Schooling," *Peabody Journal of Education*, 63 (1986): 27-69.

[17] Y.L.J. Lam, "Tracking by Student Competency Performance: An Economic, Legal and Educational Concern," *National Forum of Educational Administration and Supervision Journal*, 5 (1988): 14-24.

[18] L.O. Stone and S. Fletcher, *A Profile of Canada's Older Population* (Montreal: The Institute for Research on Public Policy, 1982)

[19] Data released by Statistics Canada, 1986.

[20] T.G. Sticht, "Strategies for Adult Literacy Development" *ERIC Ed* (1984): 240-300.

[21] W.E. Brock, "The American Work Force in the Year 2000," *Community, Junior and Technical College Journal*, 57 (1987): 25-26.

[22] Y.L.J. Lam, "Tracking by Student Competency," pp. 14-24.

# 13

# The Funding of Independent Schools

## Mark Holmes

The context of the Canadian independent school is beset by centrifugal trends; these trends favor the independent school, but make for interesting times. Meech Lake, the increasing power of the provinces, the *Charter or Rights and Freedoms*, bilingualism, and multiculturalism, all diminish the ideal of a centralized, homogeneous, consensual culture in which an essentially common school could be nurtured.

There are nevertheless, compelling and generally popular arguments for the common school. To a certain degree, almost every Canadian will endorse the notion that schools should serve, at least partially, the following five purposes: the continuation of our culture; the socialization of the young for harmonious living with others; the provision of equal opportunities in an open, democratic society; and the development of some sense of common moral purpose so that the country may stand behind abiding principles.

In fact, however, the common school, never strong in many provinces, is in severe decline for several reasons. Constitutional protection has assured the survival of minority Catholic or Protestant school systems in most provinces, with the results that Canada has never built a strong common school tradition. Residential segregation on the basis of socioeconomic status has become much more common as the population changes from being rural and small town to being urban, suburban and "exurban." Heterogeneous schools enroling everyone in town are replaced by homogeneous schools enroling those who can afford to live in a particular subdivision. Program differentiation, often involving segregation in different schools, increases rapidly, with French immersion being particularly popular across the country. The persistence of faith in Deweyan, progressive educational ideas by dominant educators causes a rift in many provinces between the majority of the public and the neighborhood schools; that rift increases parental demands for alternatives.

The status quo is unfair in that some religious and interest groups are publicly supported, while others are not. As Canada increasingly embraces the idea of different regions and cultures, the idea of a common school (where none exists in fact) becomes an improbable paradox. Compounding this, in an age of individualism, there is strong feeling that individual parents should have the right to full participation in the education of their children, particularly when public and private values are in flux. Finally, there is empirical evidence that schools representing shared values are more successful than those trying to represent a variety of competing and incompatible interests.

A strong case can be made for the funding of those independent schools which meet the appropriate standards of a pluralistic and divided society.

## Background

The image of the independent school that most readily springs to mind, certainly among public school teachers, is that of elite schools typified by Upper Canada College in Toronto. However, the elite private schools are scarcely relevant to the issue of funding for two reasons: first, they form a small minority of independent schools in Canada and, secondly, they are usually wealthy enough to be uninterested in direct funding from the government. The largest single group of private schools in Canada consists of those with a particular religious connection.[1]

Canada's treatment of religion in education is different from that found in either England or the United States, the countries with which we have the strongest educational connections. In England, there remains a state religion, the Church of England. There is thus no tradition of separation of church and state. In practice, most English schools, public and private, have incorporated religious rites and programs within their curriculum until recent times.[2] During the twentieth century, adherents of religious denominations have declined in number and influence, and the status of religion in the public schools has become more attenuate. An atheistic staff is unlikely to bring much religious fervor to Christian prayers. Nevertheless, in principle, England's public schools remain symbolically Christian. There is a long tradition too of publicly supported Catholic (as well as Church of England) schools, but Catholics are only a small minority in England and so there is no extensive dual system. (Elite private schools in England, however, which usually have some incidental religious connection have been and remain much more prominent than in Canada.)

In contrast, church and state are constitutionally separate in the U.S.A. This separation has led to the contentious banning of prayer in public school classrooms and the prohibition of unrestricted general grants to religious private schools, although there has been some limited indirect funding.

## Table 1. Private Elementary and Secondary Enrolment in Canada as a Percentage of Publicly Funded Enrolment 1974/75 - 1984/85

| | 1974/75 | 1980/81 | 1985/85 | % increase 1975/85 |
|---|---|---|---|---|
| | a | b | c | d |
| Canada | 3.23 | 4.30 | 5.11 | 58.0 |
| Newfoundland | - | - | - | - |
| Nova Scotia | .49 | .54 | 1.14 | 133.0 |
| New Brunswick | - | .65 | .70 | - |
| Quebec | 6.13 | 7.86 | 8.81 | 44.0 |
| Ontario | 2.56 | 4.03 | 4.95 | 93.0 |
| Manitoba | 3.04 | 3.92 | 4.52 | 49.0 |
| Saskatchewan | .89 | .98 | 1.49 | 67.0 |
| Alberta | 1.39 | 1.37 | 2.68 | 93.0 |
| B.C. | 4.10 | 5.10 | 6.11 | 49.0 |

Columns a, b and c show private enrolment as a percentage of public enrolment.
Column d shows the percentage increase of column c over column a.

Sources: Education in Canada 1978/79. Statistics Canada, 1980.
Education in Canada, 1984/85. Statistics Canada, 1986.

Canada, while closer to the British tradition, fits neither pattern exactly. There is no state religion but neither is there separation of church and state. Both Catholic and Protestant schools have been continuously operated in Quebec since Confederation as have public and Catholic schools in Ontario. Ontario's public schools were, and in rural Ontario sometimes remain, Protestant.[3] Neither New Brunswick nor Nova Scotia, the other two founding provinces, have constitutional protection for sectarian schools but both have operated Catholic schools. Newfoundland brought a full denominational school system into Confederation as late as 1949 and some other provinces have arrangements for the provision of Catholic education.[4] Thus, a principle related to the funding of private schools is integral to the constitutional and educational structure of Canada. Religion is taught in many publicly funded schools and must be taught, by law, in some.

Several provinces have moved to fund private schools. British Columbia and Alberta have the most far-reaching funding arrangements. Quebec provides as high a level of funding, but one which is not so easily accessible.

As in most things educational, Canada is a patchwork quilt with a variety of funding arrangements. However, there are few more universal fundamental issues in education today than choice in education. Put most simply, the question is the following: If provinces will fund Roman Catholic education (and most do), gifted classes, French immersion and alternative "free" schools, why should they refuse to fund Jewish, sectarian Christian or traditional schools? The force of the question varies geographically, with demand for choice being greatest in the largest population centres. This chapter bears most heavily on education in the densely populated areas of Canada, particularly in Quebec, Ontario, Alberta, and British Columbia, in those provinces where independent education is either most prevalent or growing fastest. In a less urbanized, less multicultural province like New Brunswick, there is little evidence of demand for educational alternatives (see Table 1).

## The Argument for the Common School

Certain assumptions must be made at the outset. Virtually all Canadians, whether or not they support the funding of private schools, share the view that the appropriate education of young people is desirable and that it should be compulsory. Similarly, nearly all believe that it should be paid for by the state. Perhaps less clearly expressed, but still generally accepted, is the notion that parents should not be compelled to send their children to a provincially operated school. Thus, law usually provides both for the education of children at home and for their education in private schools. It will be readily seen that these assumptions fit somewhat uncomfortably together. Education is good, is compulsory, should be paid for by the state, but may be provided independently at the parents' own expense. If it is so valuable and necessary, why is public education not mandatory? If alternative choices are reasonable, why is choice dependent on willingness and ability to pay?

There is no exact analogy for the service of schooling in contemporary society. Perhaps the closest is health care. It simply is not practical to make general health care for children compulsory. Some parents send their children to doctors very frequently, some scarcely at all. Only in extreme cases does the government intervene. Vaccination may be compulsory when children attend school, but for the protection of others rather than for the protection of the individual child. The government may intervene in some cases if there is reasonable belief that a child's life is at risk, but there is no government prescription for appropriate health care at home. Children may be and are fed according to quite inappropriate diets; supervision of very young children often borders on neglect and there is enormous variation in accepted styles of home care.

While children are provided by their parents with an enormous variety of general health care, it is only at considerable expense (private school fees) or very great trouble (approved and inspected education at home) that parents may avoid public education. This disparity becomes even greater if health care is expanded to involve psychological and spiritual care. Even if an elastic definition of adequate psychological and spiritual upbringing is used, it is clear that large numbers of children are brought up with inadequate love, support, encouragement, security, values and manners, leaving aside all those whose parents are guilty of neglect in a technical, legal sense. Society accepts enormous freedom of parents with respect to the upbringing but not the schooling of children.

Public health care and public schooling differ in another way. Within the health care system, patients have considerable choice. Most fundamentally, they choose their own doctor. Having chosen a doctor, they have significant choice with respect to treatment. Indeed, they may change their doctor if they do not like the kind of treatments provided. In contrast, many parents feel compelled to send their children to a local school where they have very little control over their treatment.

The main legitimating reason for this unique characteristic of public schooling is a belief, in most parts of the developed world, in the values of a common core, better still, a common curriculum — better still, a common school. There is no comparable belief in a common regimen of health. The point is not that there is less professional consensus about what constitutes good physical and psychological health than about what constitutes good education. (The reverse may in fact be true.) Rather, no belief has developed among the people that a single system of psychological and physical health is desirable in itself while there is strong belief in the values of a common education. In the past, it has also been more feasible to compel schooling than health and psychological care.

I shall show that one of the problems of the idea of the common school is a disagreement about what it should represent among those who believe in it. The distinction between the implicit assumption that there is a body of consensual enforceable common schooling and the assumption that there is no such body of common health care and child upbringing is crucial. Put more simply, the idea of the common school is dependent on there being some agreement on what it is. Its imposition is also dependent on its being enforceable.

There are five major reasons for supporting the idea of the common school. They are the desirability of (1) a common knowledge base for functioning citizens; (2) the continuance of a common culture; (3) a common socialization so that all citizens may live together harmoniously; (4) an equalizing experience so that all may have equal opportunity; and (5) a common moral or spiritual experience so that all will grow up with some common values and beliefs. I shall return to the philosophical underpinning of this doctrine when I state my own argument in the context of two contrasting doctrines.

**(1) A Common Knowledge Base.** The spread of mass education has usually been attributed, particularly outside the U.S.A., to a desire for an educated populace. In northern Europe, Protestants wanted all children to learn and read the Bible. European rulers wanted educated soldiers. Industrialists wanted workers who could read, write and manipulate numbers. Historically, when the population was mainly rural, a single common school was simply the only feasible arrangement.

In Canada, many communities in the nineteenth century were distinctively Protestant or Catholic so that the "common" school was in fact denominational. Twin Catholic and Protestant systems developed in some provinces largely as a response to the geographical distribution of immigrants of different backgrounds. In other words, it can be argued that the schools were either Protestant or Catholic largely because that was what the schools' occupants tended to be. This is still the case in many Newfoundland outposts. Thus it can be argued that religious separation developed simply as a function of more general linguistic and social separation and that the common, community school is more important today than any vestigial segregation.

Today, the fundamental functions that the school system must provide are the ABCs — allocation (i.e., social distribution among enormous numbers of different occupations requiring very different levels and types of education and training); the basics (i.e., the basic skills and competencies for survival in modern society); and custody (i.e., the safe supervision of children and adolescents at a time when, increasingly, either both parents or the single parent work).[5] A school system further fragmented by religion appears by this argument to make little sense in the face of the programatic diversity of French immersion, schools of the arts, and classes for the learning disabled, together with other real or imagined pedagogical needs. As we shall see, the argument is double-edged and perhaps even internally contradictory when applied to the contemporary Canadian scene. Nevertheless, its force is significant. Most Canadians believe there is a common base of knowledge and understanding to which all children should be exposed.[6]

(2) **A Common Culture.** The second argument is more ideological than practical. It reflects the view that the school should pass on the best of our culture to succeeding generations. The school's job is not so much to prepare young people for work as to introduce them to systems of knowledge, to significant ideas, to aesthetic expression. Clearly, if there is a powerful and valuable culture on which our society is based, it makes sense to capture it in our schools and pass it on to all our young, provided that we can agree on what it is.

This raises the significant question as to what kind of doctrine the common school should represent. This question will be addressed more fully later. Suffice it to say here that there is a big difference between a common school with low doctrine (some would even claim, fallaciously in my view, without values) and one representing key ideas in Canada's cultural heritage. There is a big difference between a minimal doctrine of tolerance (where every idea is accepted that does not directly lead to the physical or psychological degradation of others) and the doctrine of support for a strong consensual sense of mission. Moreover, not only is there dispute on the amount of doctrine; there is also disagreement about what the particular doctrine should be.

(3) **Socialization.** As our society becomes more complex and more heterogeneous, it is important for all children to learn some common beliefs, habits and norms, notably tolerance of and consideration for others, so that they will be able to live together harmoniously as adults. Thus, this argument implicitly suggests that in more cohesive and consensual times, the common school was actually less necessary. The more multicultural, multiracial and multi-faith our society becomes, the more we need the glue of the common school.

(4) **Equal Opportunity.** The fourth argument is usually characterized as being egalitarian. At the very least, we need a system of schooling that provides reasonable access so that all children, however unequal their home backgrounds, have a chance to make real choices in school. Many would go further and argue that it is important for all children to experience to a significant extent the same experiences in school and, finally, some would argue that it is a responsibility of the state to diminish the influence of social origin (by race, religion, ethnic background and gender) by ensuring a fairly equal distribution of different kinds of people in all areas of employment by means of affirmative action. A single integrated school system is helpful for, or compatible with, such outcomes.

(5) **Common Moral Experiences.** Finally, there is the moral or spiritual argument. If children are to grow up to value democratic principles and share

a consensual set of religious or moral beliefs and values, then it is necessary for the state to provide the required education in the schools. As families endorse different religious faiths, it is necessary for the school to produce some form of common base. It is evident that there are close links among the cultural, socialization and moral arguments.

It is likely that few common school supporters would endorse all these somewhat independent arguments. Moreover, all five can be interpreted in a number of different ways. Not everyone agrees the basic skills needed for modern society. There is not complete agreement on what does and does not constitute liberal culture (e.g., on the inclusion of computer studies or British history). There is not agreement on the values required for socialization. What are the limits of tolerance? What about other sometimes conflicting virtues? For example, is it tolerant to permit abortion or is it acquiescence in evil? There is considerable disagreement about what constitutes equality of educational opportunity. And there is decreasing belief that equality of educational opportunity will result in greater social equality.[7] As for the spiritual argument, it has become distinctly unfashionable to voice belief in a set of predetermined virtues.[8]

It is easy to become confused between arguments for a common school and arguments for monopolistic administrative control. Many supporters of the public monopoly actually do support a common school; in New Brunswick, for example, the two ideas merge; in Toronto and Edmonton, they do not. This chapter is not primarily concerned with administrative arrangements. The term independent is used to imply significant, but not necessarily total, autonomy. Thus, independent schools could vary from the many financially independent private schools in Ontario to the now defunct Logos (Christian) schools that once existed within the Calgary public system. Compromise arrangements can also be envisaged.[9] However, an important issue is the selection of criteria for qualification for funding, whether the independent school is inside or outside the public system.

My primary purpose here is to analyze the question of significantly funding schools, some of whose major purposes and directions are not established by majoritarian governmental authority. The argument for limiting alternatives to those approved by the public system is part sophistry and part job protection. If public school supporters concede that there should be alternatives according to public demand within the public system, there appears to be no conceptual reason for not funding all independent schools, providing such problems as standards and accessibility are dealt with. But if they argue that only "pedagogically" desirable alternatives should be permitted, they are not simply denying one of the principal motives for setting up alternative schools. They also manage to leave the "experts" (i.e., themselves) to determine what is "pedagogically" desirable. So this chapter is less about public or private administration of independent school than about common or differentiated schooling. My support for private operation is based more on practicality than principle. It is hard to believe that public monopolies will help and encourage independent schools which become more popular than their own "pedagogically" desirable creations.

Just as supporters of the common school do not necessarily accept all the arguments in its favor, so its opponents may use very different grounds for rejecting them. However, it would be fair to say that the proportion of the Canadian population that would reject all five arguments out of hand is quite small. That is to say, there are few avowed libertarians who believe as a starting principle that parents should have almost complete freedom to determine their children's education. Indeed, the arguments for a common school are quite similar to the major arguments for compulsory, free education — and that is favored by almost everyone, including private school supporters. So, it becomes important to consider the extent to which a Canadian system of public schools can substantiate those five broadly accepted justifications for the common school and to consider to what extent the funding of independent schools is inconsistent with them.

Before turning to the case in favor of funding independent schools, I shall outline the current state of the common school. A major argument for funding independent schools is that the ideals of the public, common schools are not and are not likely to be reflected in Canadian educational practice. If, as I suggest, the arguments for the common school are weakened by its decay, we are left with three choices: we can begin again with a renewed common school; we can continue to muddle through with a system that no longer reflects its guiding purposes; or we can design a new system that will better suit current cultural realities.

## The Decline of the Common School

I have suggested that there are few Canadians unimpressed by all five arguments for common schooling. However, if the common school is becoming less and less common, if it has actually died in parts of Canada without anyone mourning, the arguments lose their force. Yet how can the arguments seem so forceful as statements of principle and yet be so invalid as guides to practice? There are two explanations. First, some of the arguments for common schooling can be restated in amended form as arguments for compulsory education (public or private) with some common elements, with a common core for example. Second, although the five arguments constitute sound, if not universally accepted, bases for policy, they run into other principles, ones that are sometimes equally sound and sometimes ascendant.

There are five major factors which together account for the generally low state of the common school in Canada. The five factors vary in force geographically as does the strength of the common school itself. In Atlantic Canada,

Newfoundland's sectarian system is the antithesis of common schooling, but contrary to national trends, there are signs of its weakening as the mainstream Protestant groups come together in "integrated" school systems and as joint service agreements are made between them and some Catholic boards. Also, I have noted that in parts of Newfoundland, either the Protestant or the Catholic local school remains a de facto common school for that particular community. In the Maritimes, the common school remains strong, except in parts of New Brunswick where the French/English split intensifies. Outside Atlantic Canada, the decline of the common school is most marked in fast growing urban and suburban Vancouver, Calgary, Edmonton, greater Toronto and Montreal.[10]

The five generalizations explaining the weakness of the common school in Canada today are:

(1) There has never been a strong national tradition of the common school of the kind found in Scandinavia and the United States;

(2) Ever strengthening patterns of residential segregation related to differences in income, social class, ethnic origin and type of employment mean that even where there is a neighborhood "common" school, it is not common in the broader sense implied by the arguments for common schooling;

(3) Program differentiation has increased rapidly, partly at the instigation of educators, partly at the instigation of parents. This results in pull-out programs, segregated classes within schools and segregated schools. Thus, the common school gradually disappears, without its disappearance being noticed;

(4) Increasingly prevalent in some parts of Canada, particularly among educators, is the "progressive" philosophy that argues that education should serve the individual "needs" of children. This philosophy is generally inconsistent with the idea of a common curriculum and a strong set of common values for all; and

(5) Independent schools have grown in many parts of Canada as parents increasingly demand something different or better for their children.

## Absence of Tradition

A truly common school is constitutionally illegal in most of Canada. A key part of the compact that brought Upper Canada and Lower Canada together was the protection of Catholic schools in the former, Protestant schools in the latter, with the understanding that the school of the majority in each province would be Protestant and Catholic respectively. Analogous patterns are reflected in Saskatchewan, Alberta, Newfoundland and the federally governed Northwest Territories. Although minority Protestant schools have declined drastically in Quebec with the exodus of Anglophones from the province in the seventies, Catholic schools in Quebec have increased rapidly as a result of immigration from Catholic countries. In 1985, the implementation of a full, publicly funded Catholic secondary program in Ontario began.[11]

In 1987, the idea of a complete dual system in Canada's largest province was declared fully constitutional in a unanimous Supreme Court ruling.[12] The implication of this dual system is significant, for Ontario and for Canada. It means that, at least in the foreseeable future, there can be no support for the idea of a common school from the parents of that one-third of Ontario's pupil population that is Catholic.[13] Constitutionally mandated segregation by religion weakens the force of any moral argument against the development of Jewish and Christian sectarian schools whose supporters are often more distinctive in their beliefs than are, for example, Catholics from Anglicans.

However, precisely because Catholics are, in Canada, not readily distinguishable from many Protestants, it is arguable that the separation of children into Catholic and non-Catholic schools in Canada is less socially divisive than it is in, for example, Northern Ireland. Religion has tended to lose its divisive force in Canada in recent years, particularly in the urban and suburban regions where the educational segregation is most marked. Church attendance decreases, intermarriage among faiths increases and liberal Catholics become almost indistinguishable in their beliefs from liberal Protestants. In urban and suburban Canada, the obvious social divisions are by race, ethnic background and, above all, social class. Catholics and non-Catholics are both represented in high political office and in all sectors of the social spectrum; the traditional low social status of Catholics is becoming a thing of the past — at least for those coming from established families of British, Irish or French origin.[14]

Religious segregation is particularly important, insofar as the idea of the common school is concerned, for symbolic reasons. It provides legal and moral legitimacy for segregated patterns of education. However, as it is not possible to distinguish many Catholics from non-Catholics in the everyday discourse of work and play as it once was, such religious segregation probably has comparatively little bearing on later life. Society's leaders are typically educated in unsegregated university settings.

Tied closely to the tradition of religious segregation is the tradition of segregation by language, English and French. Indeed, in those parts of Canada where religious and linguistic differences coincide (e.g. Montreal, northern and eastern Ontario, northern and eastern New Brunswick, St. Boniface in Manitoba), it is language more than religion which divides. Segregation by language has increased rather than decreased in recent times, most notably in Ontario and New Brunswick where traditional bilingual schools are all but extinct.[15] Thus, while the Catholic/non-Catholic division is less socially divisive in most of Canada than it once was, the language division, with which it is sometimes associated, has become more marked. Indeed, Anglophone Quebecers see constitutionally protected Protestant schools as a bulwark protecting Anglophone schools rather than the Protestant religion.[16]

Thus, the traditional separation of Canadians is given new life by linguistic schisms in French-speaking parts of Canada and by immigrant Catholics in urban Ontario. Finally, cultural differences sometimes accompany the religious and linguistic differences, further cementing the legal divisions. The common school does not exist in law in most of Canada.

## *Residential Segregation*

Suppose there are two high schools, each with elementary feeder schools in a given region. One enrols students from an area occupationally characterized by an oil refinery, small business, government offices and a hospital. The other enrols students from a community with an automobile parts plant, outlying farms, a university and a community college. That situation is even less socially divisive than the Catholic/non-Catholic split in a modern, suburban unilingual neighborhood. The two populations are different, but not organizably so. Of the two types of social division, the religious split is more important symbolically, more real when it is joined to language or culture. Strictly speaking, neither situation (schools separated by religion or by differences in parental occupation) denotes a pure common school, but the spirit of the common school may survive. In other words, it would be unreasonable to imagine that there could be, in any country, a perfect set of common schools, each demographically indistinguishable from all the others.

Modern trends, however, are producing school populations that differ very noticeably on the basis of family income, reflected in clothing, life-style, leisure pursuits and friendship ties; of ethnic background, reflected in clothing, language and patterns of community; and of race.

The single most powerful trend destroying the common school in Canada, as in the U.S.A., is probably the growth of residential segregation by occupation and income. Such segregation has been characteristic of highly industrialized countries, notably of the U.S.A., for some time. It is in the last 20 years that the process has become obvious in Canada. The educational effect can be seen most clearly if one compares achievement test or examination results among schools, their best predictors being the average social status of the parents and average level of intelligence of the students. Canadian school boards are typically less open about the comparative standing of their schools than are their American counterparts, but the facts do sometimes come out. For example, in 1984, Winnipeg published the results of achievement tests at the elementary level and the dismally low standing of its "inner city" schools was well publicized.[17] In the United States, the educational status of the catchment area of a particular school is an established criterion in the purchase of family homes. In urban and suburban Canada, the same situation increasingly prevails.

Some cities, such as Toronto, deliberately try to counter this trend by planning socially mixed communities. Informal discussions with Toronto teachers and published and unpublished reports of different success rates of high schools lead me to believe that in Toronto too there are significant differences in achievement levels among both elementary and secondary schools. Published and unpublished accounts of movement from school to university show major differences between, for example, Northern Secondary School, which has more applicants than it has places, in affluent northern Toronto and Parkdale Collegiate Institute, situated in the much less affluent west end.[18] Increasing competition from private schools in urban centres provides a strong disincentive to mandatory social integration.

The proportion of Canadians living in small towns and remote rural areas is decreasing while the proportion living in suburbs and in the quasi-rural "exurbs" increases rapidly.[19] As the population becomes more socially diverse, (i.e., the proportion of very affluent families with two professional parents increases at the same time as proportion of very poor families with a single, non-working parent also increases), the rationale for residential segregation becomes stronger. That is to say, the choice of the suburbs and "exurbs" is made increasingly not only on the grounds of convenience or financial saving, but also on the grounds of a congenial social setting. Put crudely, the doctor and lawyer with two children destined for university choose not to live next door to a single parent on welfare with four children.

While the facts of changing demographic patterns and the resulting increase in residential segregation cannot be denied, it may be argued that the education experienced by children is the same wherever they happen to live. Programs, for example, available in urban and rural areas, are, it may be said, the same. Quite apart from the fact that programs in large and small schools are not necessarily the same, the educational experience is different even when the programs are the same.

Increasingly, research in effective schools suggests that climate or ethos is the most important differentiating factor among schools. The students themselves and the kind of community they come from are important influences on ethos.[20]

## Program Differentiation

Constitutional religious segregation stands as a symbol negating a truly common school in much of the country. Residential segregation makes a uniform common school ethos irreversible and impractical in most of Canada. But it is probably program differentiation that most clearly marks the fatal nature of the disease with which the common school is stricken because differentiation results not from historical tradition, not from sometimes individual choice of life-style with accompanying educational side effects, but from deliberate educational choice.

Those choices emanate from both parents and educators, sometimes but not always in agreement. By far the best example of parental choice of program is French immersion. It is probably the most significant, Canadian educational

## Table 2. Ontario Elementary Enrolment, 1971/72 - 1984/85

| | Pulic % | Separate % | Private % | Private and Separate Enrolment as a % of Total Enrolment |
|---|---|---|---|---|
| 1971/72 | 70.0 | 28.6 | 1.4 | 30.0 |
| 1977/78 | 67.0 | 31.1 | 1.9 | 33.0 |
| 1984/85 | 61.8 | 35.3 | 3.0 | 38.0 |

Notes:

(1) Estimated percentage of elementary students enroled in Ontario's public non-Catholic schools excluding French immersion programs in 1986/87 = 58%

(2) If those significantly segregated by residential patterns associated with social class or by enrolment in heritage language classes, gifted programs and programs for the disabled are excluded, probably fewer than one-third of the elementary population remains enrolled in a genuine common school, reasonably representative of the larger as distinct from the immediate community in which they live.

Source: Educational Statistics 1985, Ministry of Education, Toronto.

innovation, in terms of effects and acceptability, of the last 20 years. Without attempting to assess completely this very complex and controversial program, I note three characteristics of the innovation relevant to the idea of the common school:

(1) Immersion necessarily involves the segregation of children, usually from the age of five; the segregation is typically total or almost total for at least the first four or five years of school; there is evidence that immersion programs either develop distinct attitudes and ambitions or attract students with such characteristics;[21]

(2) The supporters of immersion assert the success of its graduates — well documented achievement in French is not paid for by any lack of academic progress in other subjects;

(3) In five years in the 1980s, enrolment in Canada is said to have doubled to 200,000.[22] This figure almost equals the total enrolment in private schools.

If enrolment in French immersion were randomly distributed by geography and social class, its effect on the common school would be slight, just as segregation between Catholics and non-Catholics and between different groups of parental occupational backgrounds in some circumstances may not be divisive. But that is not the case; French immersion programs are concentrated particularly in Anglophone Quebec, the Ottawa region and in major urban and suburban centres, in general in precisely those areas that are affected by residential segregation and by competing Catholic and non-Catholic schools.

In Ontario, I have conservatively calculated that by 1985 over 40 percent of Ontario's elementary students attended classes or schools significantly segregated by religion or program (see Table 2). If residential segregation is taken into account, it is doubtful if more than one-third of Ontario elementary pupils attend schools and classes unsegregated by social class, ethnicity or religion. Further, if one takes into account the possibility of an increasing gap between the beliefs and ideology of rural Ontario and those found in urban Ontario, those pupils in a genuine common school reasonably representing Ontario (let alone Canada) as a whole must be few indeed.

The point here is that a significant number of parents, including some of the most influential members of the community, do not in practice value the idea of the common school sufficiently to forgo a program they want for their child (e.g., French immersion).

Although French immersion is unique in its impact, it should not be seen as being an exceptional, deviant program running against contemporary trends. Another example of programatic differentiation is the policy of open enrolment. Although I am not aware of research into the effects of parental choice of public schools in Canada, it is reasonable to assume they include increased social separation. That is to say, it is to be expected that the parents who try to enrol their children in Toronto's oversubscribed Northern Secondary School on flexible boundaries are people who value an emphasis on academic excellence;

i.e., they are more like than unlike the school's other parents. Similarly, Jewish parents are more likely to try to get their child into rather than out of a school, such as Toronto's Forest Hill Collegiate, with a predominantly Jewish clientele. Open enrolment is in fact an admission that many parents do not like the social and academic character of the neighborhood school and that it is legitimate for them to choose something else. The proportion of students affected by open enrolment is probably quite small; but the policy indicates a general acceptance on the part of educators that the common school should not or cannot be sustained.

Educators have themselves fostered a number of program alternatives. The idea of "alternative" schools, originally of a "progressive," student-centred nature, has been endorsed by academics, teachers and administrators. Only when the alternatives have been broadened to include a wide range of schools representing a broader spectrum of public opinion, as in Calgary and Edmonton, have they been subject to criticism by educators.

Programs for the gifted and for the disabled under the aegis of special education have proliferated in most provinces. They are often prompted by public demand, but unlike French immersion which is sometimes opposed by Anglophone educators whose jobs are taken by Francophones, special education is often encouraged by educational administrators and either supported or tacitly accepted by teachers. "Experts" on special education have been known to claim that as much as one-third of the population should receive some form of special education service.

In recent years, there has been some reversal of the trend towards segregated special education (but not towards designated special education). Interestingly, the argument for desegregation is made on individualistic rather than communitarian grounds — that most disabled children will learn better in the mainstream than when segregated. Thus, mainstreaming has had little effect on segregated programs for the gifted, who, it is assumed, will not benefit from being mainstreamed.

French immersion, open enrolment, alternative schools and special education are major examples of program differentiation that have developed or expanded rapidly over the last 20 years. What is noteworthy about these changes is that they have rarely been subject to debate in terms of their effect on the common school or the larger community. A major exception is the system of Christian alternative schools developed in Calgary and then abandoned as a result of their success, specifically their effects on the availability of neighborhood schools. Public debate on the much more widespread and socially divisive French immersion has been muted and opposition to it has often been presented by the media as anti-French bigotry.

There are other examples. Secondary education has always been subject to some segregation. For example, no Canadian province has ever had a common secondary program participated in by all or nearly all young people. A recent attempt by the government of New Brunswick to introduce a common secondary school program quietly died with the defeat of the Hatfield government. However, even had the common program been implemented, New Brunswick students would still be segregated by language, in some instances by religion (even when the language is English) and, as suburban growth has accompanied rural decline, by residential segregation. Thus, even in New Brunswick, a province with a highly centralized educational system with negligible private enrolment, and with the political will to implement a common secondary program, there was no chance that young people in the Kennebecasis valley in Saint John's "exurbs" would receive essentially the same overall education as young people in the Restigouche valley in rural Francophone New Brunswick.

Two points stand out. First, program differentiation has had a significant segregation influence on Canada's more urban schools. Second, program differentiation, in one form or another, is accepted broadly by educators and parents.

## Children's Needs

The legitimacy of program differentiation is related to the idea that curriculum should be based on "children's needs." Very few teachers and fewer parents seriously intend to let children freely determine their own education, to let them choose between chocolate cookies and reading, ice cream and numbers, or sticking pins in small animals and scientific observation. The idea of curriculum based on "children's needs" is normally interpreted as letting children make very limited choices from a set determined by certain groups of expert adults.

However questionable the philosophical premise of giving children either genuine or artificial choice, the result is some program differentiation within the classroom. After all, if we acknowledge that children are different, it is easy to argue that their "needs" are different. Analogously, many educators will argue that of course schooling in the Restigouche valley should be different from that in the Kennebecasis valley because the children's "needs" are different. If children in Restigouche County "need" a different education from those in King's County, it is a short step to arguing that very different children within King's County should also have a different education because their "needs" are equally different. The implementation of "progressive" policies may inadvertently also lead to further differentiation among schools, as parents who oppose "progressive" ideas choose "different," including private, schools.

The important idea that education should respond to children's individual "needs" and coupled with that, the complementary idea that different children, because of their parents, background and interests, have different "needs" is, to a significant extent, antithetical to the idea of a common school. Four of those five involve the common treatment of all children in terms of knowledge, culture, opportunity and values. If the "progressive" idea is seriously accepted, those four types of common treatment become not only impractical but wrong, because all four assume that children ought to get much of the same stuff — either that they have the same "needs" or that, irrespective of their individual "needs," they will require one prescription. There remains the fifth argument — common socialization enabling different people to live together harmoniously. It is that last argument on which "progressive" proponents of the common school, and there are many, depend heavily.

So while it is not logically inconsistent for a "progressive" to favor a common school, "progressive" practice tends to make the common school less legitimate, less likely, and less viable for two reasons. Many parents do not want "progressive" education for their children;[23] therefore, the implementation of "progressive" ideas leads parents to look for alternatives. And, the educators' doctrine of individual "needs" implicitly, if unintentionally, reinforces the legitimacy of parents asserting their own particular definition of the child's "needs." Thus, once the individual becomes paramount, parents will counter educators' assessment of "pedagogical need" with their own assessment of their children's "need" for, perhaps, discipline, high academic expectations, and rigorous moral training.

The first two explanations for the decline of the common school are non-educational, in a sense unintended. It is doubtful that either the Fathers of Confederation or suburban developers have conspired against it. Even in the case of program differentiation, which appears to be a frontal attack on the common school, the debate rarely hinges on the common school principle. One reason for the absence of debate among educators as the common school is increasingly debilitated is the prevalence of "progressive" ideology. Teachers have been trained to believe that their job is to try to address the individual child's "needs," even when it is obvious that the reason they have sent Jim to sit outside the principal's office for an hour or so has little to do with Jim's unknown needs and everything to do with teachers' and other students' perfectly legitimate wants. So it becomes almost heretical to assert, "I don't care about Lynn's future advantages from learning fluent French. I am concerned about the others left behind who are disadvantaged"; or to state, "I don't know whether or not Joy would benefit from the gifted class. But in any case, it would be better for the class as a whole if she remained."

Moreover, the fundamental issues of the tension between society and individual that lie at the heart of compulsory education is obscured and diminished by the prevailing ideology[24] among educators which serves to legitimate only one side of the debate. Thus, public school employees appear hypocritical when they attack private school funding and the extension of Catholic education in the name of the common school.

## Private Schools

Even though taxation for public education is high, enrolment in private schools has rapidly increased.(See Table 1).

Probable reasons for this include:

(1) The belief that private education is superior;[25]

(2) Dissatisfaction with discipline and standards in public schools;[26]

(3) The increasing unionization and bureaucratization of public schools;[27]

(4) The increased "progressive" emphasis of public schools not favored by a majority of parents as already noted;

(5) A decline in public consensus about education;[28]

(6) Teachers' strikes in public schools;[29]

(7) Increased funding for private schools in Quebec, British Columbia and Alberta;[30]

(8) The belief among many religious sects that the public schools are determinedly secular, humanist, and hostile to their beliefs.

It is important to note the significance of the belief, which we know exists in British Columbia and which may exist elsewhere, that private schools are in fact better than public schools. This belief can only be enhanced by recent research suggesting there is a factual basis for the belief.[31] If it is true that schools are really much more effective if they reflect a community of consensual values, then the prospects for the public, common school in an age of multiculturalism and sharp religious and philosophical division are indeed bleak.

If independent schools are better and if they do not cost any more than public schools to operate, then the question arises: Why should they only be available to those willing and able to pay for them?

# The Argument for Independent School Funding

The fundamental argument for the funding of independent schools in the post-industrial age is not dependent upon a natural ascendancy of parental rights. A poll of popular opinion in Canada today would probably show that most people favor the idea of a common school. That is to say, there is no strong sympathy with the idea of parental rights, any more than there is sympathy with the funding of private schools. However, those in favor of the common school would likely include many parents of students in French immersion as well as, inevitably, employees of the public educational system.

Even so, there would be difference of opinion if those who favor the common school were then asked what the common institution should look like.[32] Should it teach Christianity? Should it teach virtue? Should it teach sexual equality? Should there be girls-only basketball teams? Should French be compulsory from first grade? Should progressive methods be introduced throughout the system? Should school be made truly common by carefully adjusting school zones and by transportation arrangements in order that every school reflect the social constitution of the larger community? Should segregated French immersion continue? I am not suggesting there are simple right answers to those complex questions. Quite the contrary, those questions would likely receive a variety of answers and qualifications for very good reasons. The fact is that urban, suburban and "exurban" Canada is so far removed from a common system of schooling that only a major act of revolutionary social engineering could impose it.

That is the first important argument in favor of funding independent schools. Most current demographic, educational and political trends are working against the common school in Canada. Indeed, an argument often used by public school supporters against private school funding is the fact that there is enormous differentiation of program within the public system. Besides the practical argument, there are four further arguments as to why funding independent schools is a sensible alternative policy to current chaos:

(1) The current system is manifestly unfair. Some interest groups are supported but others are not. Independent school funding would put all interest groups on the same footing and would force the public development of criteria for the acceptance and rejection of segregation;

(2) Canada is a decentralized country lacking a national and nationalist central focus. It is a community of communities;

(3) Parents should have a significant say in the education of their children, particularly in an age when public values are in flux; and

(4) There is increasing evidence that schools representing shared values are more successful in achieving their goals than are schools with vague and disparate goals.

## The Unfairness of the Current System.

I have already shown that certain interest groups are reflected in Canada's educational mosaic. Major examples of such groups are educators, the single most powerful special interest group in education, who exert an enormous influence on general educational patterns in the public schools. "Progressive" methods of instruction, the right of teachers to strike, lengthy collective agreements, and teachers' freedom of lifestyle, whereby they no longer are significantly expected to act as models of character to students, are examples of the salience of teachers' collective interests in many jurisdictions. Parents who choose residential segregation, French immersion and gifted education, are generally served by the publicly supported system, as are Catholics in most provinces. In contrast, parents who want traditional rather than "progressive" education are often not served in urban Canada. Orthodox Jews and Christians belonging to minority sects have to choose between paying for a private service and an abhorrent secular, relativist program.

## Canada as a Community of Communities.

Canada's federal governments over the last 20 years have systematically, if not always deliberately, set up a strongly decentralized state. Traditionally, Canada had two social systems living in relative harmony — a French culture based in Quebec and an English culture based outside Quebec. Federal bilingualism was initially an attempt to create a more unified bilingual country. The outcome in contrast has been the loss of the British tradition throughout Canada and an intensified French culture in Quebec. The earlier English presence in Quebec has been greatly weakened by emigration and by language law. Multiculturalism has officially replaced biculturalism.

The Meech Lake accord of 1987, whether or not it receives final approval, reflects the reality of late twentieth century Canada. Canada is a collection of communities whose main anchor is a perceived, if sometimes imaginary, difference from its southern neighbor. The communities are partially captured by provincial boundaries (e.g., Prince Edward Island and Nova Scotia). In contrast, Ontario contains numerous communities.

In the absence of any strong centripetal sentiment, schools based on community, defined in some parts of Canada by the province, make the best conceptual sense. To a significant extent, these forces are already at work. Inuit and Indian schools already exist in embryonic form. Jewish and sectarian Christian schools are already well established as private entities. Edmonton has gone some way to recognize the separate interests of the different communities within it, although it draws an arbitrary line against Christian minorities.

## Parental Rights

I am not prepared to argue that parents have a fundamental, universal right to select their children's form of schooling. Rights from my perspective are socially derived and, therefore, matters of both individual and societal value. However, in times when there is an evident lack of social consensus resulting in considerable variation in educational and family practice, it is reasonable to argue that parents should not have their children educated in ways they believe inappropriate, particularly when schools reflecting their wishes are readily available elsewhere to other parents. There is something odious about educators telling public school parents they cannot have the "old fashioned," traditional schooling they want at the same time as affluent citizens pay enormous fees for precisely that kind of schooling in elite private schools — without any apparent loss.

The traditional family structure is under attack from many sources. Parental authority is weakened by: other families, often non-traditional, where there is little surviving parental control; the pervasive and powerful media, particularly television; and peer group structures which fill the vacuum of weakened family and community values. It is understandable that many traditional parents want schools to foster rather than undermine the Judaeo-Christian heritage, the fundamental virtues of truth, justice, courage and compassion, conservative views of sexuality and marriage, firm discipline, industriousness and the acceptance of personal responsibility. Parents of this kind, who very likely form a majority in many parts of Canada, are understandably resentful when other, much smaller interest groups are accommodated, sometimes at the sacrifice of their majority values. In Toronto, for example, publicly funded alternative schools have been available for many years — but not one is a rigorous, disciplined, Christian or Jewish alternative.

## Value of the Consensual School.

The most effective schools are those that have a clear sense of purpose, a mission.[33] For many urban and suburban schools, a straightforward mission is the very thing that would tear them apart. They survive by ambiguity. The result is a value vacuum where teachers feel that it is inappropriate, even unethical, for them to preach their own values. Either their values are not those most parents would approve of or they are majority values which are still likely to offend many minorities. As this situation becomes more evident, caring, knowledgeable parents seek a way out — through French immersion, by enrolment out of zone, by moving to a different neighborhood more reflective of their own values, or by purchasing private education.

The common, public school, to the extent that it exists, faces a crucial problem. What will its core be? Will its doctrinal core be values, methodology, goals or program? There is some logic in having a minimal doctrine (essentially one of tolerance); one can argue then that no one should object too much. But that position has many conceptual as well as practical weaknesses. If there is very little doctrine, there appears to be little reason why it should be so important. If it does not matter what different values children learn, why should they not learn different values in different schools?

The ideal of tolerance and a low level of doctrine is itself far from being uncontroversial; those who hold to the doctrine that abortion is morally wrong do not view those who are tolerant of abortion on demand as being non-doctrinaire. In fact, one has to doubt the extent to which a low level of doctrine can be implemented. What is seen as non-doctrinaire by one person is highly doctrinaire to another. Some of those who object strongly, for example, to "indoctrinating" strong Christian values in school see no objection to programs of "peace education" which seem highly doctrinaire to others.[34] Finally, opinion polls suggest that parents want schools to provide a framework of values, in other words, a doctrine.

The more the common school builds up its common core of consensual doctrine in an attempt to build a genuine consensus of shared values, the more it conflicts with other opposing strong doctrines, and the more obviously unreasonable it is to force parents to have their children exposed to ideas in conflict with their own.

Simply, the common school either tries to be almost completely free of values, belief and bias — which pleases few people; or it tries to build up a solid consensual doctrine which is necessarily opposed by different doctrines. The situation, inevitably delicate and complex, is aggravated by the gap between the public and leading educators. The doctrinal core approved by educators differs from that wanted by the public. This is particularly apparent in Ontario and British Columbia.

## Other Perspectives

Before turning to a conclusion, it will be helpful to situate my arguments in the context of current philosophical debate on this important topic. Not being a philosopher, I have grounded my arguments so far in policy analysis based on public and private interests. That does not mean that there is no philosophical foundation for the ideas developed. The philosophy on which my arguments is based comes significantly from Alasdair MacIntyre who is a vigorous proponent of the importance of maintaining our cultural traditions.

Guttman[35] adopts a liberal collectivist perspective in a work designed to show how education in a liberal democracy should look. She rejects "liberal neutrality," whereby schools provide minimal doctrine so as to remain neutral; she rejects "moralism" whose explicit purpose is to "inculcate character," a high doctrine; and she rejects "amoralism," the notion that schools should try to stay away from morality altogether and stick to the formal academic curricula. She advocates instead the inculcation of democratic character and the application of moral reasoning to this kind of teaching. She distinguishes democratic liberals (whom I distinguish also from supporters of the generally accepted notion of liberal democracy) from sophists who argue cleverly without a moral base and from traditionalists "who invoke established authority to subordinate their own reason to unjust causes." She then goes on to argue that there is no prior right for parents to determine their children's education and that, therefore, it is a matter of examining the consequences of a public monopoly versus some constricted version of private choice. In the end, she concludes, it is public education that is a welfare right of children and it is public education that is most able to provide a genuine democratic education to suit state rather than private interests.

Crittenden argues that a liberal democracy (or at least a pluralist liberal democracy, and he assumes that liberal democracies either are or should be pluralist) must pay special attention to minority interests and should lean toward less government intervention rather than more.[36] He also argues that parents rather than the state have the prior right to educate the child. He concludes, therefore, that public schools should be imbued only with those limited values required of a pluralist liberal democracy (on the details of which he differs considerably from Amy Gutman), but that the state has the obligation to help support independent schools. Essentially then, Crittenden develops the classic liberal position that parents have constricted rights, which are contingent on their being applied in a way that is compatible with pluralist liberal democratic values.

My argument follows the lines of neither of these positions. Guttman and Crittenden both provide reasonable arguments which are intended to be universal — for those who believe in liberal democracy. But each tilts her or his interpretation of liberal democracy in a way that foreshadows the conclusion of each. Guttman, in the U.S.A., develops a universal plan very like the ideal American common school; Crittenden, in Australia, develops a universal plan very similar to the ideal towards which Australian states appear to be working; the one stresses "democratic participation," the other the importance of families being able to re-create their world view.

My proposals, in contrast, are based in the context of our society, our culture and our times. I do not argue that parents have a prior right to educate their children because I see rights as being traditional, cultural and emergent. Guttman stereotypes traditionalists unfairly when she says they use established authority to subordinate reason to unjust causes. One could argue equally as well that she uses the tyranny of "democratic participation" to reason unjustly that it is acceptable for the rich to pay for schooling to their liking but not for the poor to be supported in their wish for schooling to their liking. Shils explains tradition differently:

> ... not all traditions are benign; not all of them merit survival. Nonetheless, the fact that a practice or belief has persisted for an extended period is an argument for its retention.[37]

In countries which are pluralist, multicultural or multi-faith, a public monopoly with all schools administered by centrist experts will probably lead to a low common denominator, with a few additions made in the interests of the experts (i.e., leading educators) themselves. Traditional belief in all cultures and faiths is inevitably diminished — against the express wishes of many parents. Thus, my own argument is that neither the society nor the parent has a fundamental right to primacy (certainly not the state), but rather that what is right depends on the culture, the history and the current social fabric of society. Certainly, however, in a liberal democracy there must be some balance between the interests of parents and those of the larger society. In highly centralized, homogeneous societies (such as Japan) the survival of the homogeneous culture may be helped by tilting the schools towards a homogeneous, central system. In decentralized, highly pluralist countries such as Canada, the traditional beliefs and cultures not excluding the mainstream Judaeo-Christian tradition, can best be helped by giving them clear expression in the schools. Whereas Guttman prescribes a universal American solution from 1920, and Crittenden a more contemporary universal Australian solution, I attempt to provide a

Canadian solution which I believe could be broadly applied to other countries in a similar situation.

## Conclusion

The problem of the independent school is one of the most difficult political issues. The school, the agent that carries on our culture from one generation to the next, is in trouble precisely because we are not sure what our culture does mean or what we want it to mean. Although Canada's constitution and history are distinctive, many of the same difficulties beset the other western, democratic, affluent countries such as the U.S.A., Britain and Australia. Those countries that are ethnically, linguistically and culturally homogeneous with powerful centripetal traditions are least affected (e.g., Japan, West Germany, Denmark and Sweden). There are many Canadians outside Quebec who likely do believe there should be one strong, unified country with its own distinctive culture; unfortunately, they disagree profoundly on the basis for that strength, unity and culture! Nowhere is this disagreement more evident than in education. Do we want to be more individually competitive, like Japan? Or more socialistic, cooperative and ecologically aware, as we imagine Sweden and New Zealand to be? Do we want Canadians to be distinguishable from Americans? If so what should a Canadian be? A traditional Amish? An orthodox Jew? A Francophone Quebecois? All of the above? Or an American? It is because there is no consensual answer to these fundamental questions, as well as to most other value questions, that independent schools should be favored.

Some will answer that the common school should simply represent Canadian differences; the school should be multicultural, multi-faith, multi-ethnic. I have suggested that this is not and cannot be the case. Residential segregation together with educational choices made by educators and parents alike ensure that the ideal is rare indeed. In any case, many groups do not want to be assimilated in a single common school with very little formal doctrine. If there is minimal formal doctrine, informal doctrines (developed by the dominant peer group, by individual teachers) will soon fill the vacuum. Parents generally do not want schools to vacate the important areas of values and intellectual and aesthetic discrimination.

Some critics will fear the consequences of parental choice. Parents may make bad choices for their children, or their choices may be divisive. But many parents make choices now. It seems unlikely that future choices should be any worse than the current ones. And certainly the funding of independent schools should be accompanied by some accountability (more accountability, I would hope, than is generally expected now of many public schools). Social divisiveness is more difficult to forecast. No one knows. My own feeling is that more public choice and influence will lead to very little more division in the long run. The greatest effect of giving more emphasis to parental choice will be to make schools more reflective of the public will. As the public will may well be more consensual than many educators believe (as it is educators themselves who are often dissenters), there may even be less division over time as the different cultures come to accommodate one another.

Three factors that often loom large in discussion of funding independent schools, I shall deal with briefly — one technical, one speculative, and the other trivial. It is argued that funding private schools is tantamount to subsidizing the affluent to choose a different or better education. That raises an essentially technical question. It is perfectly possible to fund all independent schools and forbid at the same time "extrabilling" — as is done in the Netherlands. For example, one plan would pay private schools 90 percent of equivalent public school per pupil costs, limit tuition fees to say, 15 percent of government support, and make the availability of scholarship mandatory for those unable to pay.[38] Another plan, suggested by Crittenden, would see independent schools supported on a sliding scale depending on such factors as: the distinctiveness of their educational offerings; the level of their fees (those with low fees receiving more funding); and the proportion of hard-to-teach students and students in expensive programs.

It is argued that the funding of independent schools will leave the public schools with the residue of the hard to teach. This notion is hypothetical. It is possible but by no means certain that inept, public school bureaucracies, with their well placed vested interests, will be unable to respond to competition and to reflect the public will. If they do prove uncompetitive, then the result of increasing flight from public schools will result in a residual core of the hard-to-teach. The same argument is sometimes put in a slightly different form, "Yes, the proliferation of programs in schools is divisive enough already; funding independent schools will just make it worse." The flaw in this argument, apart from crocodile tears about current program differentiation to which there was no previous objection, is the assumption that the result will in fact be worse than the current situation for the hard-to-teach. Schools for the hard-to-teach in inner cities today are often particularly ineffective and the number of such schools might hypothetically increase. Conversely, parents of these children currently have no real choice. There is no reason why inner city schools of the future where alternatives are available will be worse than the ones at the moment where there is no choice. In most areas of life, we encourage, where it is possible, free articulation of choices because we believe the results will be beneficial.

Finally, it is argued that a divided school system will be more expensive as a result of duplication of services. The evidence is that, with the exception of the elite private schools, many private schools are less expensive to operate than public schools. There is no evidence that public monopolies generally provide cheaper service than private businesses — hence the drive to deregulation and privatization in most of the democratic world, including several countries with socialist governments. One area where duplication is an important issue is student transportation, but this is already an issue with the numerous differentiated programs now in existence. Some compromise must be found, with or without funded independent schools, between transportation costs and program accessibility. A strong case can be made for a centrally administered transportation service for all schools.

What we have now is a patchwork quilt of education where some special interest groups receive preferred treatment and where others with equally or more legitimate interests are ignored. Canada is and has recently reinforced its sense of being a decentralized country. Differentiated schooling is constitutionally established. The public school quasi-monopoly, like other public service monopolies, is ever more powerful and increasingly apt to educate still less of their parents. Indeed, the very existence of Catholic schools, private and alternative schools, and special programs may have made it easier for the quasi-monopoly to control what remains. It is easier to control the flock when the rebels and heretics have gone. Parents, facing increasing pressure and competition from their children's peer groups and the media, are unhappy when even schools no longer seem to reflect their own interests and values.

Certainly the funding of independent schools and the conversion of all but the most expensive private schools into fully or partially funded independent schools must be undertaken with care. There should be no insurmountable barriers in terms of parental ability to pay. There should be a common core basic program. There should be mandatory testing of learning outcomes (just as there should be at the moment in the many public systems that lack it). There should be no use of racial or ethnic origin as a criterion for admission, although schools should legitimately be able to demand strict compliance with a particular cultural or religious tradition. There should be no restriction of access to knowledge and no preaching of violence or racial or ethnic superiority. In a word, there should be standards.

The idea of the public, common school, perhaps unfortunately, has outlived its purpose in much of Canada. No longer is there a consensual spirit to convey; there is no longer a consensual sense of the virtues with which to imbue the nation's young; its prevailing philosophy is more likely that it should, contrarily, meet the "individual needs" of children. It is perverse to grant educators, public employees, the power to choose which "individual needs" they should serve. Should a secular teacher have the right to determine that a child "needs" more time in the play centre or watching television, or hands-on time on the computer, when parents may not select an education reflecting their fundamental and traditional values? The reason why independent schools should be an available choice to parents is that there is no central consensus on which to build a common school tradition. This may be bad; but tears will not erase the reality. That vacuum has been filled in much of Canada by the pedagogical and ideological preferences of educators.

The decline of the common school leaves us with three choices. First, we could begin again. But to begin again requires precisely that common purpose which we lack, and which has led to the common school's decay. Second, we could muddle through, as we continue to make accommodation for some groups but not for others on the basis of inconsistent and indefensible criteria, while leaving the public schools in a state of vacuous neutrality over fundamental values. Third, we could develop new public schools built on a strong consensual majority or plurality, and permit fully funded independent schools for dissenters.

The third option seems logical and sensible. Either the result would be strong, directed public schools competing with a healthy and substantial set of strong, directed independent schools, or it would be strong, directed public schools for most students with small minorities attending their own independent schools. Either way, the public would choose, without financial penalty. In a decentralized, multicultural democracy, that is as it should be.

## Notes

[1] B.J. Shapiro, Commissioner, *The Report of the Commission on Private Schools in Ontario* (1985) shows that three large groups, Christian, Jewish and Anglican schools in Ontario, enroled twice the number as those enroled in all the elite private schools.

[2] The Education Reform Bill of 1987 does not include religion in its "core" or "foundation" subjects, but the Minister responsible, Kenneth Baker, wrote that religion was already compulsory (*The Daily Telegraph*, November 11, 1987).

[3] This appears to be changing. The Ontario Court of Appeal has ruled that predominantly Christian opening exercises are unconstitutional. Religious education is under review in Ontario (*The Globe & Mail*, September 24, 1988).

[4] Publicly funded Roman Catholic schools exist in Alberta, Saskatchewan, Quebec, Newfoundland, the Northwest Territories and in a limited way in New Brunswick and Nova Scotia.

[5] This argument is developed further in: Mark Holmes,"The Fortress Monastery: the Future of the Common Core," in Ian Westbury and Alan Purves, eds., *Cultural Literacy and the Idea of General Education, Part II* (NSSE Yearbook 1988), (Chicago: University of Chicago Press, 1988).

[6] For example, a meeting of the Ontario Association of Alternative and Independent Schools (representing a large proportion of independent schools other than the elite group) consensually supported a draft statement of such a common base. Meeting held in Toronto, October 4, 1988.

[7] In a poll conducted among Ontario's directors of education and among a control group of university graduates of the same age not involved in education, both groups ranked the egalitarian philosophy sixth out of six, with a significant

minority refusing to rank it at all. Mark Holmes, *Ontario's CEOs: Their Values, Beliefs and Actions: An Interim Report* (Toronto: OISE, 1988).

[8]Scarborough Board of Education, serving a large relatively conservative suburban population, has approved a value statement which is merely "consistent" with traditional virtues; its own first ranked value being respect for self! *Ethics in Education*, 8, 3 (1989).

[9]The Shapiro Commission recommended fully funded "associated" status under existing school boards for independent schools that were willing to meet certain conditions. Edmonton, according to Professor John Bergen (Private correspondence Oct. 1988) comes very close to full funding of independent schools, including a *de facto* Jewish School.

[10]The fact that in some parts of Canada there is satisfaction with the public, common school and no great desire for alternatives does not support the thesis being developed. The question is whether significant public demand for independent schooling should be supported by public funding. No one argues that independent schools without clients should be funded.

[11]Premier William Davis announced in the Ontario Legislature on June 12, 1984, the gradual implementation of funding of a complete Catholic system of schools.

[12]The Supreme Court of Canada upheld in a unanimous judgement delivered June 24, 1987, the constitutionality of full funding for Roman Catholic separate high schools.

[13]Between 1971 and 1984, the proportion of all elementary students enroled in Roman Catholic Schools in Ontario increased from 30 percent to 35 percent. (Table 2).

[14]Before 1984, most Roman Catholics in Ontario attended public schools in the senior years of high school. Although there were some reports of conflict based on race, language and culture, religious conflict only surfaced after segregation was established (in the form of disputes over the sharing of existing secondary school buildings).

[15]In 1988, the Ontario government introduced legislation to set out for the first time a school district based on language as well as religion (to embrace the metropolitan Ottawa region). New Brunswick's school districts are today almost completely separate by language.

[16]In 1975, the North Island Regional School Board in suburban Montreal (now the Laurenval School Commission), although nominally Protestant, had an enrolment that was less than 50 percent Protestant (there were large Catholic and Jewish minorities). None of the schools taught Protestant religion, although Catholic religion was taught where there were sufficient numbers.

[17]*Maclean's* (May 28, 1984): 65-68.

[18]I am not implying that Northern Secondary is a more effective school than Parkdale Collegiate. To test that hypothesis one would have to examine the changes brought about in students in the two schools so sampled as to represent equivalent external factors, i.e., previous attainment, home culture and measured intelligence. At the same time, I am not implying that the public acts irrationally

in the light of its limited information. One factor that does seem to influence student performance is the academic climate of the school, which is likely to be more demanding in strongly academically oriented schools.

[19] The fastest growing school districts in Canada in 1988-89 were in the suburban and "exurban" areas encircling Toronto, notably Dufferin, Durham, Peel and the Region of York.

[20] This finding is evident in the effective school literature. A good recent example is in J.S.Coleman and T.R. Hoffer, *Private and Public High School* (New York: Basic Books, 1987).

[21] David Oborne recently completed a thesis investigating the different attitudinal characteristics of high school immersion and regular students in Manitoba, with similar home background characteristics. Oborne found that immersion students persisting through high school were of exceptional ability and came from advantaged homes. They were disproportionately female and favored post secondary education in the social sciences and disfavored engineering and mathematics, even allowing for the influence of gender. D. Oborne, "Academic and Career Aspiration of Students in Secondary French Immersion Schools," unpublished Ed. doctoral dissertation, *OISE* (1988).

[22] *OSTC Education Reports*, 11, 39 (1987): 1.

[23] See 3. The Canadian Gallup Poll Limited, *Let's Talk About Schools: Gallup Survey* (Victoria, British Columbia, 1985). It shows: 67 percent of the public believe that the education is better or much better in private schools than in public schools; 94 percent of the public but only 15 percent of the teachers believe that standardized methods of evaluation for public and independent school students are very or somewhat important.

[24] The British Columbia and SSHRC Polls (notes 23 and 7 respectively) illustrate greater preference for progressive ideas among educators than among the public.

[25] The Canadian Gallup Poll Limited, p .12.

[26] See for example, D.W. Livingstone, D.J. Hart and L.D. McLean, *Public Attitudes Toward Education in Ontario 1982* (Toronto: OISE Press, 1983), p.9. Only 32 percent of respondents were satisfied with discipline in elementary and secondary high school in that province.

[27] This argument is developed further in: Mark Holmes *Collective Bargaining: Its Relationship to Traditional and Non-Traditional School Models* (Toronto: OISE Press, 1987). Prepared on behalf of the British Columbia Department of the Attorney-General.

[28] "1986 OISE Survey — General Issues," *Orbit*, 17, 4 (1986): 20, 22. Satisfaction with Ontario elementary and secondary schools has dropped from 55 percent in 1982 to 42 percent in 1986. There is a major split of opinion as to which schools should be funded, 21 percent favoring public only, 12 percent favoring public and limited Catholic (the status quo in 1984) and 39 percent public and full Catholic (the 1987 status quo) and 26 percent favoring the inclusion as well of other religious or all other schools. British Columbia increased its funding for

independent schools and reduced the time of operation required for eligibility to one year in 1987.

[29]Livingstone et al., p. 35. Opposition to teachers' right to strike exceeded 50 percent in the U.S. by 1980. In Ontario, the majority had reached 63 percent by 1982. In Quebec, a majority of 85 percent was opposed in 1982.

[30]Shapiro, pp.11-15.

[31]Coleman and Hoffer.

[32]I recently polled Ontario's directors of education and a similarly educated sample of non-educators of the same age concerning educational policy. Neither group favored funding private schools but the two groups had entirely different consensual views of how the common school should look. See note 7.

[33]Coleman and Hoffer.

[34]See Evelyn Dodds "The Ethics of Peace Education," *Ethics in Education*, 8, 1 (1988).

[35]Amy Guttman, *Democratic Education* (Princeton, New Jersey: Princeton University Press, 1987), p. 51.

[36]Brian Crittenden, *The Parent, the State and the Right to Educate* (Melbourne: Melbourne University Press, 1988).

[37]Edward Shils, *Tradition* (Chicago: University of Chicago Press, 1981), p. 328.

[38]A discussion of different approaches to funding private schools is found in Mark Holmes, "The Funding of Private Schools in Ontario: Philosophy, Values and Implications for Funding." in Shapiro, pp. 109-152.

# 14

# The Future Funding of the Public Education System: Some Recommendations

*Peter Atherton*

In 1988-89, total expenditures on education in Canada will amount to $40.72 billion dollars. Of this amount, two-thirds or $25.8 billion will be expended for elementary and secondary education.[1] The raising of revenues to support this level of expenditure must therefore be seen as a major challenge for both government and individuals. It is the major purpose of this paper to explore the means by which these revenues may be raised and distributed.

In this exploration, an attempt is made to focus on the general problems which may arise in connection with revenue raising and distribution rather than on the more specific details of taxes and grant structures themselves. It is hoped that the reason for this approach will become clear as the discussion develops. Generally speaking, however, it must be argued initially that there is no "one best way" of financing education. Each province administers its responsibility for a provincial education system in the light of its own circumstances with respect to historical traditions, economic structures, and most importantly a set of social priorities as they may be manifest through the political system.

The autonomy of each province in legislative matters is guaranteed by section 93 of the *British North America Act*. Nevertheless, it is true to say that each of the different systems of educational finance in Canada reflects concern for the values of equity, efficiency and autonomy which tend to act as a common denominator in discussions of education of finance generally.

Although there are three ways in which revenue for education may be obtained — by charging fees, by borrowing, or by levying taxes — Canadians have opted for a publicly supported elementary and secondary school system supported in the main by government grants provided from provincial tax sources. In some provinces, these grants are accompanied by provisions for local authorities to raise money from local tax bases identified by the province for that purpose.

While some provinces permit school boards to levy fees, usually in the form of user charges, such charges do not provide significant contribution to overall revenues. Provisions for local school boards to borrow money also exist in some provinces, but such provisions are usually restricted to borrowing for capital purposes and not for operating costs. Furthermore, conditions of borrowing are usually closely regulated by the province and the amounts themselves frequently are guaranteed by the province.

Although in the past it was customary to deal with taxation for educational purposes as a special subject, the significance of educational expenditures and the increasing competition from other services in the public sector, particularly at the provincial level, requires that problems of raising revenue for public education be considered in the general context of public finance.

## The Legal Framework

It is worth noting that the exclusive power allocated to the provinces to legislate in educational matters by section 93 of the *British North America Act* is not matched by such freedom in matters of revenue raising.

The *Act* granted the Dominion Government the right to make laws relating to "the raising of money by any mode or system of taxation." It limited the power of the provinces to the right to raise direct taxes and only then for the purpose of "raising a revenue for provincial purposes."

The classic definition of a direct tax is one which is paid directly, by the person upon whom the tax is levied, to the government. It might first appear, therefore, that the retail sales tax which is used widely by provincial governments across Canada under different names such as "hospital tax," "education tax," "gasoline tax," etc., would be *ultral vires* (beyond their powers). A legal case in 1935 established the terms under which these taxes could be considered "direct." A newly elected government in Alberta in 1935 moved to introduce a retail gasoline tax. The Dominion Government charged that such a gasoline tax would be indirect under the classic definition and, therefore, *ultra vires* the provincial government's power. The Government of Alberta defended its position to the Supreme Court of Canada by stating that the amount of the tax was announced at the point of sale (and therefore not "hidden" as is normally the case with a sales tax). It further held that the retailer, in collecting and remitting the amount of the tax, was acting as an agent for the provincial government. Alberta's position was sustained.

Since the personal income tax, property tax and retail sales tax, as legally defined, are all direct taxes, it becomes apparent that provincial governments now have legal claim to all three very substantial sources of revenue.

It should be noted at this point that constitutional allocation of powers of taxation makes no reference to municipal governments. Each province has the legal power to create whatever municipal structures it so decides. A province may decide to allocate whatever power it legally possesses to a municipal structure. The same legal authority is applicable to taxation and revenue sources. Legally, therefore, a province could permit both income and retail sales taxes at the municipal level. Although in the past this has been done, no province in Canada currently does so.

Thus, the existence of school boards and the role of the property tax in the financing of education reflects traditional, administrative and political considerations at the provincial level rather than any constitutional or legal requirement. The province of New Brunswick has demonstrated its power in this respect. In 1967, the provincial government elected to shift the basis of finance and administration from the municipal realm to the provincial realm. In doing so, it designated the residential property as a provincial tax. Similarly, the provincial power in matters of local government has been demonstrated in British Columbia. Among the changes made to accommodate the fiscal crisis of 1981-82 were the shift of the taxation of non-residential property from the local level to the provincial level and a temporary suspension of the right of school boards to levy taxes to raise revenue above the level determined by the province.

This preeminence of the provincial government's responsibility in matters generally affecting educational finance was made explicit some years earlier in the so-called "Salmon Arm" case in 1952.[2] The Court found that where a province had legislated compulsory attendance, it was the ultimate responsibility of the province to provide adequate funding. In this context it seems appropriate, therefore, to separate, conceptually at any rate, the problems of revenue raising (taxation) from the problems of distributing revenues (grant systems).

## Federal-Provincial Relations

Although the provinces have legal access to the main taxation bases, the sovereignty of provincial governments within this sphere has produced a number of fiscal problems for both levels of government. These problems include the lack of correlation between expenditure responsibilities and revenue sources, difference in fiscal capacities of different provinces, the joint occupancy of the major tax fields, and problems arising out of possible conflicts between federal and provincial governments over the implementation of fiscal policies. Stresses and strains arising out of these problems have led to the development of a number of mechanisms which have become the subject of annual federal-provincial finance conferences. The setting of levels of unconditional transfers (grants) from the federal to the provincial government is of considerable significance; these transfers attempt to recognize both the high cost of social programs and regional inequalities of wealth and have the effect of providing a substantial source of non-tax revenue, particularly to the poorer provinces to finance their programs. Provinces are able to allocate these funds to programs as they wish.

In addition to the general purpose of unconditional grants, transfers are made by the federal government to the provinces which reflect specific purposes such as bilingualism. Although these payments were originally provided for special purposes including post-secondary funding, their allocation is not tied to any specific expenditure level and so to some extent they are considered as making a contribution to provincial general revenue.

## Sources of Provincial Revenue

Table 1 provides a breakdown of the major sources of provincial revenues. The table provides the basis for a number of observations.

First, it may be noted that all provinces assess both income and sales taxes to varying degrees. It should also be noted that four provinces also assess the property tax base to provide a source of provincial revenue.

A second observation is the extent to which the personal income tax and the consumption or sales tax are the major source of the provinces' own revenue. Except for Alberta where the major single source of provincial revenue is derived from natural resources, personal income and consumption taxes account for well over half the provincial revenue (excluding general purpose transfers from the federal government).

Newfoundland, Prince Edward Island, Nova Scotia and New Brunswick all depend on intergovernmental transfers for just over 50 percent of their annual revenues. Quebec and Manitoba each receive close to 25 percent of their annual revenues from the federal government. The size of these payments together with the fact that they are transferred to the provincial government, suggests that some degree of centralization of school finance in these provinces is both logical and necessary both from an efficiency and an equity standpoint.

Many would go further and argue that the size of transfer payments renders unnecessary the development of any specific federal aid plan for elementary and secondary education such as exists in the United States and other democratic countries. Others[3] contend that the need for specific assistance is still required.

Table 1 provides details of provincial revenues. It does not provide details of school revenues. Table 2 provides details of the revenues for elementary and secondary education in Canada. One of the most striking aspects of Table 2 is the difference in the proportions of total educational revenues derived from the provincial and municipal levels of government.

In the provinces of Newfoundland, Prince Edward Island, New Brunswick and Quebec, the municipal contribution is less than 5 percent. In Ontario,

**Table 1. Selected Revenue Sources of Canadian Provinces (1983) and Sub-Total (Percentages).**

| Revenue Source | Nfld. | PEI | N.B. | Que. | Man. | Sask. | Alta. | B.C. | Sub-Total |
|---|---|---|---|---|---|---|---|---|---|
| Personal Income Tax | 12.69 | 10.94 | 17.51 | 26.75 | 26.45 | 17.66 | 15.73 | 11.51 | 18.90 |
| Corporation Income Tax | 1.72 | 1.76 | 2.65 | 1.73 | .88 | 5.17 | 3.35 | 3.79 | 5.84 |
| Total Income Taxes | 14.41 | 12.71 | 20.20 | 16.90 | 27.64 | 31.63 | 21.02 | 19.52 | 17.37 |
| Real Property Tax | - | 3.86 | .01 | 5.10 | - | 1.14 | 7.30 | 1.30 | |
| Consumption Taxes (Including Sales and Fuel) | 21.72 | 18.95 | 18.76 | 20.07 | 16.08 | 23.87 | 16.91 | 11.32 | .85 |
| Health and Social Insurance Levies | 1.34 | 1.03 | 1.14 | 1.80 | 12.39 | 9.69 | 3.97 | 1.63 | 3.52 |
| Natural Resource Revenue | 1.32 | .11 | .47 | .90 | .61 | 2.20 | 21.11 | 42.30 | 7.69 |
| Licences and Permits (Including Motor Vehicle) | 2.75 | .86 | .28 | 1.39 | 2.80 | 2.69 | 1.19 | 1.64 | .82 |
| Total Gross Revenue from Provincial Sources | 53.39 | 51.65 | 57.45 | 56.19 | 76.01 | 82.76 | 72.28 | 82.60 | 90.81 |
| General Purpose Transfers-Federal Government | 28.47 | 30.65 | 24.34 | 23.67 | 11.88 | 0.25 | 13.92 | .64 | 1.90 |
| Special Purpose Transfers Federal Government (Including Health, Social Services and Education) | 18.10 | 17.68 | 18.15 | 19.90 | 11.78 | 16.56 | 13.50 | 16.62 | 7.22 |

Source: From Statistics Canada: Provincial Government Finances; Revenue and Expenditure 1983, Ottawa, Statistics Canada, 1986.

**Table 2. Direct Source of Funds for Elementary and Secondary Education, Canadian Provinces, 1983-84 (Percentages)**

| Province | Federal | Provincial | Municipal | Sub-Total | Fees and Other |
|----------|---------|------------|-----------|-----------|----------------|
| Newfoundland | - | 93.1 | 3.4 | 96.7 | 3.3 |
| P.E.I. | 2.1 | 95.7 | - | 2.2 | |
| Nova Scotia | 1.9 | 81.7 | 13.9 | 97.5 | 2.5 |
| New Brunswick | 2.0 | 97.2 | - | 99.2 | 0.8 |
| Quebec | 1.5 | 90.0 | 3.5 | 95.0 | 5.0 |
| Ontario | 1.4 | 50.3 | 43.1 | 94.8 | 5.2 |
| Manitoba | 9.3 | 49.7 | 35.6 | 94.6 | 3.4 |
| Saskatchewan | 10.1 | 50.8 | 36.5 | 97.4 | 2.5 |
| Alberta | 3.7 | 57.1 | 35.0 | 96.1 | 3.9 |
| British Columbia | 3.1 | 84.9 | 8.1 | 96.1 | 3.9 |

Source: Statistics Canada, *Financial Statistics of Education*, 1983-84 (81-208), Ottawa 1987 (p.45).

Manitoba, Saskatchewan and Alberta, the proportion of revenue derived from municipal sources exceeds 30 percent. Nova Scotia and British Columbia fall between the two groups at 8.2 and 14.2 percent respectively.

Since municipal taxation is based primarily on the residential and non-residential property tax, it would appear at first glance that the difference between the two major groups is a function of the emphasis placed by the western provinces on property taxation as a direct source of school revenue. This conclusion is not altogether unwarranted but needs further explanation in the light of the traditional approaches to the reform of educational finance at the provincial level.

In Canada, as the provinces of New Brunswick and Prince Edward Island have demonstrated, the issue of reform of the property tax and reform of educational finance can be easily separated. The provincial governments merely redesignated the local property tax as a provincial tax. More recently, both Manitoba and Nova Scotia have taken similar action by instituting a provincially mandated property tax levy. By provincializing the property tax and sharing the proceeds through the grant structure, the issue of educational finance reforms is clarified to some extent. The issues of equity, adequacy and efficiency, insofar as educational systems are concerned, become more visible.

Indeed it may be argued that one of the major difficulties in the analysis of problems in educational finance is the tendency to associate considerations of educational finance reform with considerations of property tax reform or municipal taxation reform. The reports of the MacDonald Commission in Ontario in 1985 and the Sullivan Commission in British Columbia in 1987 particularly provide evidence of these difficulties.

## The Property Tax

There is little question that the levying of the property tax is in need of reform. Virtually every writer in the area of public finance has condemned, and continues to condemn, the administration of the property tax with respect to problems of flexibility in assessment, lack of relationship between property tax-base and income, the failure of yields to respond to increases in income without changes in the rate (lack of tax elasticity) and, discriminatory assessment practices among classes of property, to mention but a few. These concerns are echoed by writers in the area of educational finance particularly in the United States. For example, in publications such as *The Journal of Educational Finance,* probably the major journal in the field, well over 80 percent of the papers published have their basis in varying approaches to reform of the property tax.

The reliance on the property tax was also common in Canada. Up until the early 1960s, the provinces allocated the property tax to school boards as their primary source of non-grant revenue. This allocation seemed reasonable at the time because education was seen primarily as a service offered to local residents. There was little concern with the spill-over benefit of education to the wider community. Since the costs of the service were not excessive, a local tax-base capable of local administration seemed appropriate. There was a vast increase in the quantity of service required in the 1960s and 1970s to meet the increasing birth rate and wider concept of the role of elementary and secondary education.

### Future Prospects for the Property Tax

The Canadian Tax Foundation reported that in 1981 Canada collected $11.1 billion in property tax. In that same year, the provinces derived $16.5 billion in personal income tax, $8.5 billion in general sales tax and a further $2.6 billion in gasoline tax.[4] It is clear from the provincial point of view that it would be difficult to eliminate the property tax altogether, particularly in those provinces which do not receive federal unconditional grants, without such massive increase in other forms of taxation as to be politically and economically unrealistic.

We may assume, therefore, that the property tax will continue to be a major source of provincial income (depending on designation). Reform of the administration of the property tax through reassessment, redistribution of the base among different classes of property, and provision of tax-credits to offset regressivity, may well shift the incidence of the tax but not diminish the total burden appreciably.

Furthermore, it is unlikely that competition for the property tax from municipal governments will decline. Growing priorities in such areas as publicly subsidized housing, municipal transit, old age care facilities and the environment are likely to increase the amount of competition for the property tax. It is, therefore, likely that there will be increasing demands from municipal governments to restrict the access of the schools to property tax. At the same time, provincial governments faced with the equally intense competition for tax revenues are unlikely to abandon such a legislated source of revenue they can escape a large measure of political responsibility for raising.

## Revenues from Grants

The revenues of any school or school board are derived from at least four sources:

(1) Provincial grants.
(2) Proceeds of a mandatory tax levy.
(3) Proceeds of a supplementary tax levy.
(4) Proceeds from fees and voluntary donations.

However, this classification as a basis for the discussion of revenues involves a "definitional problem."

For instance, it is customary in statistical reporting to report as grants to school boards only that money which is paid from provincial consolidated revenue to school boards. In the cases of Prince Edward Island, New Brunswick, Newfoundland, Quebec and Alberta where there is no compulsory levy at the local level on the property tax, the reported amounts reflect the actual revenue derived from grants. Ontario on the other hand uses a grant system in which the school board receives an amount of money which, together with the proceeds of a mandatory levy on assessment determined by the province and a rate also determined by province, is equal to that defined as necessary to support a "basic" level of education. The mandatory tax level is never entered into the provincial accounts and is, therefore, never counted as a grant. This approach, however, serves to conceal the fact that the province is determining a much larger share of total revenue for education than the reported statistics would suggest. If in fact the proceeds of the mandatory levy on local property were to be considered as a provincial tax, (which, since municipalities have no control over the amount levied, it really is) then the provincial contribution to school board revenues would appear much higher. No comparative estimates of "real" contribution have been made but, given the attempts of school boards to live within the grant provisions so as to avoid the financial penalties of paying 100 percent of any supplementary costs themselves, one might argue that across Canada, grants and mandatory revenue might account for as much as 80-100 percent of school board revenue.

The significance of this introductory comment may become apparent only after discussion of Canadian grant structures.

## General Principles of Grant Structures

Writing in the early 1920s in the United States, Strayer and Haig formulated the twin pillars of educational support programs as being "equalization of educational opportunity" and "equalization of school support," and they identified two major conditions which would need to be met to attain these goals. They were:

(1) To establish schools or make other arrangements sufficient to furnish the children in every locality within the state with equal educational opportunities up to some prescribed minimum; and

(2) To raise the funds necessary for this purpose by local or state taxation adjusted in such manner as to bear upon the people in all localities at the same rate in relation to their taxpaying ability.[5]

That these are still the major thrust of educational grant structures may be verified by reference to the systems of grants currently in operation in Canada.

Before examining these structures, however, it is necessary to examine the term "equalization of opportunity" in more detail. It is also necessary to provide a discussion of the issues which attend the concepts of efficiency and adequacy and their relationship to the design of grant structures.

## Equality of Opportunity

While, generally speaking, there is little disagreement that all young people, within the limits set by compulsory attendance laws and the availability of resources, should have equal educational opportunity, there is frequent disagreement as to what this means or how to implement it.

Historically, the emphasis in educational finance has been on the provision of horizontal equity which may be defined as the equal treatment of equals. Within this definition, a number of approaches are possible. One can, for instance, approach the problem by providing each student with free access to a basic program of studies, the cost of which is mandated by the province.

An extension of this approach is to provide equal resources to all students in attendance in the system without any attempt to distinguish between basic and additional levels of education. This approach is characteristic of those provinces which provide full funding for school programs from provincial sources, such as Quebec, New Brunswick, and Prince Edward Island. It was also characteristic of the percentage equalizing grant structure provided in Ontario from 1969-1977. In this case, the definition of adequate programing was left up to school boards with the province providing support for a percentage of total expenditure which was inversely proportional to the wealth of the board.

In the 1950s and 1960s, and largely as a result of the recognition of racial and social inequality in society as a whole, attention focused on the inadequacy of defining resource allocation on the assumption that equal dollars would purchase equal educational opportunity. It became clear that unequal treatment of unequals would be necessary to meet the goals of equal educational opportunity. This approach was defined as the vertical equity approach. In solving problems associated with the achievement of vertical equity, it is necessary to focus on the needs of the student and to provide resources necessary to meet these needs.

In the context of a homogeneous society with relatively simple expectations from the educational system, the need to provide vertical equity was seen largely in terms of providing weightings for geographic, demographic and economic factors which had cost implications. The need to provide for a programatic adjustment to achieve vertical equity was not seen as critical since high drop out rates and legal exclusion of students with special physical or other handicaps was acceptable.

For a variety of reasons, there is now a heavy emphasis on individual differences, compensatory education and the special needs of handicapped children. This shift in emphasis suggests that there is now a much greater need to provide for vertical equity in the system.

The concern with vertical equity may be heightened with the coming into effect of section 15 of the *Constitutional Act* of 1982. This so-called "equity rights" section of the *Act* guarantees everyone equal protection of the law without discrimination and in particular "without discrimination based on race, national or ethnic origin, color, religion, sex, age or mental or physical condition." While the impact of this legislation has not yet become fully apparent, it obviously implies that greater provision will need to be made for special and compensatory education of all kinds. Moreover, it is also clear that since it is now possible to launch court action to support cases of what are perceived as discriminatory practices in education, the courts will now become involved in directing some educational expenditure to remedy these practices.[6] These will have consequences for the revenue of schools.

## Efficiency

There are also different ways of looking at what is meant by *efficiency*. The first and most common approach to efficiency is to consider it as cost minimization. Thus, an efficient school unit may be viewed as one with the lowest cost per student. It is also frequently assumed that provision for local autonomy is one effective way of ensuring efficiency at the local level through the close supervision of costs. In the distribution of grants it is assumed that the formulae through which the grants are calculated and administered will ensure efficiency.

It is also possible to look at efficiency as the least costly method of combining resources to meet a given level of effectiveness. Such an approach requires considerable freedom on the part of administrators to combine alternative forms of labor and capital in addition to the establishment of a desirable level of effectiveness. While there is no question of the desirability of approaching efficiency through this latter approach, there is little evidence that is practicable at this time. For one thing, the collective bargaining process tends to restrict alternative approaches to the combination of resources. Thus, the introduction of teacher aides ( a form of lower cost labor ) or capital ( computers, etc.) is seldom seen as an *alternative* way of combining resources, but usually as a *supplement* to resources which will make the work of the teacher more effective. A further discussion of the efficiency issue is provided below in the context of factors which effect total education costs.

## Adequacy

The adequacy question may also be examined from two approaches. The first approach requires an answer to the question "Are we spending an adequate amount on education?" While clearly of primary significance, this question is inappropriate in the context of a paper addressing the revenue issue.

However, in the context of revenues, this question resolves itself into the question of the adequacy of grants. Adequacy, from this perspective, may be examined from at least two standpoints:

(1) The adequacy of the grants to provide support for the educational programs decided upon by the province; and

(2) The adequacy of year to year adjustments to maintain the level of support decided upon by the province.

## Approaches to Canadian Grant Plans

There are, in Canada, essentially two approaches to the design of grant plans: the foundation plan approach and the budget control approach. The following discussion attempts to characterize the systems of providing revenues into one or the other category. It must be admitted, however, that this approach perhaps oversimplifies the structure existing in each province.[7]

### *The Foundation Plan*

This term originated in the U.S.A. in the 1920s and reflects the thinking embodied in the definition provided by Strayer and Haig discussed above. This approach is most frequently used in jurisdictions in which the cost of the educational program is shared between the province, the source of grants, and the local government, the source of local contribution. Canadian provinces which adopt this approach include Alberta, Saskatchewan, Manitoba, Ontario and Nova Scotia.

In the foundation approach, the province determines a level of expenditure which constitutes the estimated cost of the "prescribed minimum" or foundation level of education. This level of expenditure is usually defined as "x" dollars per pupil or, as it has been in the past, "y" dollars per classroom unit (a classroom unit being defined in term of the number of students in a classroom). Usually the "x" dollars receive a weighting factor which will reflect the additional costs of differing levels of education, and sometimes a weighting factor which reflects the differential costs associated with geographical factors. Saskatchewan, for instance, provides a weighting for cities, whereas Ontario provides a weighting factor for school boards which lie in Northern Ontario. Some provinces set the per student figure at a sufficiently high level to include other aspects of the total cost of operating schools, such as plant operation, maintenance and central office administration, while others reduce the per pupil allowance and provide separate formulae for calculation of entitlement. In practice, the per pupil allowance is a reflection of the average cost per student as it is in the time immediately preceding the introduction of the plan, or it may reflect a more recent average in the case of a revision of the plan

The cost per student is then used to calculate the total cost of providing the foundation plan by multiplying the cost per pupil by total enrolment. This total cost is given different names in different provinces. In Saskatchewan, it is designated as "total recognized ordinary expenditure"; in Manitoba, it is defined as "supportable expenditure"; and in Alberta, it is described as the "foundation level."

# The Future Funding of the Public Education System 273

Having determined the cost of providing the foundation level, the next step is the determination of the proportion of total cost to be provided through provincial grants and the proportion to be raised through local contribution.

In the determination of the local contribution, the concept of "equal effort" is used. That is to say, attempts are made to equalize the approach to property assessment across the province so that assessed values are comparable among jurisdictions. The provincial government then sets a rate on this equalized assessment so that in all jurisdictions the mill rate will be the same. Obviously, the same tax rate for all the assessments in a rich jurisdiction area will raise more than it will in a poor jurisdiction. When the local contribution has been calculated, the provincial grant may then be determined. The calculation is:

**Provincial Grant = Cost of Basic Program - Local Contribution**

In provinces using the foundation plan approach, any jurisdiction in which board expenditures exceed the foundation or recognized level must rely on property tax levies added on to the mandated one for additional revenue.

The essential simplicity of this approach is confounded when the differing methods of computing the cost of the foundation program and the equally varying terminology associated with the methodology in use in each province is introduced. Furthermore, each province approaches the equalization of assessment differently and so attempts to contrast and compare the variety of grant plans is made almost impossible.

In the foundation approach, the efficiency problem is assumed to be met by requiring a board to levy its own revenues for expenditures beyond the foundation level. It is assumed that a board which is inefficient in its bargaining with teachers or resource allocation will pay the penalty of levying additional property taxes. It will, therefore, control costs to avoid this consequence. However, the central problem here is that of distinguishing the "inefficient" boards from those who wish to exercise their prerogative to meet "local demands" for service beyond the minimum.

Distinguishing between "inefficient" boards who experience additional costs, and boards who wish to provide "more than the minimum" by increasing cost, is complicated when the problem of adequacy is brought into the discussion. It is possible that the use of average data to compute the cost of a "foundation plan" may result in a foundation plan which is barely adequate for some boards who because of demographic, geographic or social characteristics, face higher than average costs. While many systems do attempt to take such problems into account in deciding the per pupil cost, it is inevitable that some characteristics may not be accurately accounted for. Alternatively, some boards for the same reasons may receive more than adequate amounts. There are always boards above and below "average."

Even if the initial setting of the foundation level of expenditure is adequate, problems will arise unless the adequacy of this basic figure reflects any necessary change in the year to year adjustments of the foundation level. Theoretically, such adjustments should be made in the light of the changing levels of prices for educational inputs such as those measured by the Canadian Education Price Index compiled by Statistics Canada. More often than not, however, the year to year adjustments are made on the basis of monies available to the government and may, for sound economic or political reasons, lag behind the levels of prices. Frequently, too, provincial authorities will mandate new educational programs or increased requirements of existing educational programs which are seldom accompanied by accurate costing.

Any inadequacies in the year to year level of provincial identification of foundation costs will, under this type of plan, be transferred as cost increases to be levied on local ratepayers. Without frequent revision, such problems will multiply over time.

It, therefore, becomes almost impossible for one to distinguish whether tax levies to support education at the local level are the result of local desires to provide above average "quality of education"; inefficiency on the part of the board in operation; or increases in the cost of the "foundation program" which have not been recognized by the province in its year to year adjustments of grants. This difficulty is also one which makes more vexatious any analysis of the adequacy of the degree of equity, vertical or horizontal, provided by basic grants under the foundation approach.

## The Budget Control Approach

When the budget control approach is used, the province decides on a level of expenditure necessary to provide the educational program, and the revenues for the required program of education are met almost entirely from provincial revenues. This approach is used in Newfoundland, Prince Edward Island, New Brunswick and Quebec.

It should be pointed out, however, that in the computation of the cost of the basic level of education, a number of formulae are used which in many cases are very similar to those used in provinces which utilize the foundation approach.

One of the major differences between the two approaches lies in the variability of the amount approved as the budget for jurisdictions operating under this system. In the computation of the typical foundation program, the province is obliged to define a figure beyond which it will provide no support. In provinces using the budget approval system, each jurisdiction must prepare a budget which will reflect provisions for its own circumstances. Thus, in New Brunswick, the budget provides for variation in the size and socioeconomic characteristics of the area. In Quebec, budgets are determined using the specific characteristics and historical experience with strict rules, whereas budgets in provinces using the foundation approach tend to follow only general requirements. Thus, control by the provinces using the budget control approach becomes much greater. Since boards receive their funding entirely from the province through budgetary requests, the opportunity to spend money beyond the limits determined by the province is extremely limited.

The institution of full provincial funding and budget control in Quebec, New Brunswick and Prince Island resulted from provincial concern over the difficulty of providing horizontal equity in circumstances of major inequalities in the distribution of wealth. To the extent that reducing inequalities in expenditure per pupil may be regarded as providing equality of educational opportunity, there is evidence that the centralization of revenue has been successful in meeting this objective. Nevertheless, the difficulties arising from the need to provide vertical equity are similar to those faced by provinces using a foundation approach. The problems include the accurate identification of specific costs necessary to provide additional levels of service for specific populations. The problems of cost may be the same, but the need for accuracy is increased since the system of budget approval makes it difficult to switch categories of expenditure, and so the budget flexibility afforded to local administration under the foundation plan approach is lost. The difficulties associated with very strict budget control were recognized in a new system of allocation in Quebec in 1986 whereby provision was made to transfer funds between budget categories and, thus, provide some measure of control at the local level.

## Other Approaches
### *Percentage Equalizing Grants*

A variation in the foundation approach was attempted in Ontario early in the 1970s. The major difference between the Percentage Equalization Grant, as it was named, and the foundation plan approach was that the foundation level of expenditure was not set by the province and was allowed to vary in each jurisdiction. The province agreed to pay a proportion of a board's total cost which varied inversely with the board's wealth as measured by local assessment. While the virtue of this system lay in the implicit recognition that a board's expenditure would reflect the needs of students in its jurisdiction and, thus, strengthen local autonomy, the financial implications of providing local boards with virtually a blank cheque soon became obvious at the provincial level.

### *Resource Cost Approach*

Another variation of the foundation approach is the so-called resource cost approach. In this approach, the foundation level is identified through provincially mandated education programs and level of service. It is in theory, therefore, more defensible in educational terms. The cost of providing the programs are then translated into budget terms by combining enrolment data from the school system and converting them into costs by means of an index which reflects the market price of inputs. Grants are based on the foundation approach as described above.

This approach to revenue stresses both equity and efficiency. Equity, both horizontal and vertical, may be strengthened by building into the programs appropriate standards and levels of service. The approach also encourages efficiency. For instance, a board which is able to obtain inputs at less than the market price reflected by the index, gains revenue which may be applied to the reduction of the local tax-rate. A board which pays higher prices than those provided in the index is forced to pass along this "extravagance" to tax-payers.

The province of British Columbia implemented such an approach in 1982. The program was introduced as part of the "Fiscal Framework" which was introduced following the recession of 1981-82. It is not clear whether the fiscal framework was intended to improve the problem of resource allocation in the system or merely to hold down expenditures. For instance, in the selling of "service" levels, an essential ingredient of the resource cost model, the province decreed that the level of service in terms of pupil-teacher ratio for Grades 1-7 should be 25:1, one of the highest in Canada. It is worth noting that this level of service implied a return to the level of pupil-teacher ratios for 1976 with a consequent reduction in overall cost.

## Expenditures in Education

As was pointed out initially, grant structures whether they be of the foundation variety or the centralized revenue distribution approach, have a common basis in the aim of achieving equity, efficiency and adequacy. In the assessment of the degree to which those revenue structures attain these objectives, one is forced to examine their effect on expenditure patterns. Since each province approaches these issues with differing social and economic values, any comparison is made difficult.

Given the somewhat complex picture of revenue sources relating to education, it might be useful, therefore, to provide some indication of the relationship between expenditures on education and their relationship to certain socioeconomic indicators. Expenditures in education, after all, correspond directly to revenue.

Details of expenditure by school boards as they are related to the Gross National Product, a measure of the value of all goods and services produced in Canada, and as they are related to total personal income are provided in Table 3. Personal income statistics are particularly useful since personal income is the base for educational revenue whether it be through taxation of income, expenditure or wealth or whether it be through fees.

Personal income reflects the total wage, salary and incorporated business income (farm, professional and small business net income) received by individuals in Canada.

The picture presented in Table 3 is one of remarkable stability. The stable relationship between Gross National Product and educational expenditures suggests that in Canada as a whole, the revenues from whatever source they may be derived have kept pace with increases in Canada's wealth.

The same can be said about expenditures related to personal income. There is indeed some decline of the proportion of personal income devoted to educational expenditures since 1980, but this should be viewed in the context of a declining enrolment particularly in the elementary and secondary school system. Elementary and secondary education account for something like two-thirds of all expenditure on education, and the decline in enrolments (assuming the consistently strong relationship between education prices and the movement of prices in the economy as a whole) would be reflected in a decline in total burden.

The relationship between total expenditures on education and total personal income in the provinces is shown in Table 4. It will be noted that the picture of stability reflected above, for Canada as a whole, is also representative of the provinces. It should also be remembered that the picture of relative stability has been maintained during a period which has seen numerous changes in approach to financing education in many provinces.

**Table 3. Expenditures of School Boards in Canada as a Percentage of Gross National Product and Total Personal Income Canada (Excluding Adult Education) 1980-84.**

| Year | Percentage of G.N.P. | Percentage of Personal Income |
|------|------|------|
| 1980 | 4.5 | 5.4 |
| 1981 | 4.4 | 5.2 |
| 1982 | 4.7 | 5.3 |
| 1983 | 4.6 | 5.4 |
| 1984 | 4.5 | 5.2 |

Source: Statistics Canada, *Financial Statistics of Education*, Ottawa, Statistics Canada (81-229), p. 57.

**Table 4. School Board Expenditures as a Percentage of Personal Income in the Canadian Provinces, 1980-84**

|                   | 1980 | 1981 | 1982 | 1983 | 1984 |
|-------------------|------|------|------|------|------|
| Newfoundland      | 7.7  | 7.4  | 7.6  | 7.4  | 8.0  |
| P.E.I.            | 6.3  | 6.3  | 6.2  | 5.9  | 6.1  |
| Nova Scotia       | 6.0  | 6.0  | 6.0  | 6.2  | 6.4  |
| New Brunswick     | 6.3  | 5.9  | 6.5  | 6.7  | 6.9  |
| Quebec            | 6.4  | 6.1  | 6.0  | 5.9  | 6.3  |
| Ontario           | 5.1  | 4.9  | 4.9  | 5.0  | 5.3  |
| Manitoba          | 5.4  | 5.0  | 5.1  | 5.4  | 5.8  |
| Saskatchewan      | 5.6  | 5.0  | 5.4  | 5.8  | 6.2  |
| Alberta           | 4.6  | 4.6  | 4.9  | 5.1  | 5.3  |
| British Columbia  | 4.5  | 4.6  | 4.8  | 4.7  | 4.7  |

Source: Statistics Canada, 81-208, p. 56.

It will be noted that the percentages for the provinces east of Ontario are higher than those to the west. To some extent, these percentages must be viewed in the context of the substantial unconditional and conditional transfers from the federal government to these provinces. Nevertheless, it must be emphasized that although these transfers reflect provincial revenue which does not need to be derived from the provincial tax-base, they do form part of the revenue pool which *all* provinces have at their disposal to meet provincial priorities. Moreover, the existence of these unconditional transfers is a reflection of the lower tax-bases available to the recipient provinces. The lower percentages shown for Ontario and the western provinces may well reflect the higher proportion of education expenditures/revenues derived from the province's own resources. It is also worth noting that those provinces which rely most heavily on property taxation for the support of elementary and secondary education also spend a lower proportion of personal income on education (Table 2).

These observations must be accompanied by a cautionary note: this data ignores the question of burden (the number of students in each system) and comparative cost per student. Nevertheless, even with the limitations posed by this caveat, the data does provide the basis for some interesting questions which include:

(1) Does the lower visibility of general taxation (particularly property taxation) in some provinces permit the allocation of a greater proportion of provincial resources to education?

(2) Does the greater visibility of the property tax in some provinces inhibit the allocation of a greater proportion of provincial resources to education?

(3) To what extent does the higher visibility of revenue sources particularly related to elementary and secondary education provide a greater degree of cost control than in provinces with a low degree of visibility of revenue sources?

## Efficiency and Total Expenditures on Education

It will be recalled that the discussion of the relationship between total expenditure and socioeconomic indicators ignored questions of burden (the number of students) and the comparative cost per student. It also ignored the question of internal efficiency.

In spite of the stability of patterns of revenue generation demonstrated in the section, the discussion did little to answer concerns about levels of expenditure *per se*. Much of the concern with respect to revenue raising is a reflection of a public perception that costs in elementary and secondary schools are out of control. At the same time, there appears to be a contrary but, nevertheless, substantial indication that the public is prepared to spend more on education but wants guarantees that the extra money will be well spent.

The response to the second concern is in a large part the reason for the existence of the first concern. If this seems paradoxical, the following analysis should provide some insights.

Between 1970 and 1975, total expenditures on elementary and secondary education in Canada increased by an average annual rate of 10.77 percent.[8] Awareness of the increase, coupled with a similar awareness of declining enrolments, caused a great deal of unease among the public. The media wasted no time in pointing out that the average annual rate of increase in expenditure per pupil over the same period was 12.39 percent.[9] The facts provided a substantial base for the argument that the educational cost structure was out of control. However, what received less direct acknowledgement was that the period 1975-1981 was also characterized by a high rate of inflation in the economy as a whole. In fact, when the rate of increase in expenditure per pupil is deflated by the Canadian Education Price Index produced by Statistics Canada, the rate of annual increase is reduced substantially. It is estimated that *real* expenditure per pupil in Canada in the period 1975-1981 was 0.53 percent per year.[10] Clearly the major factor leading to the rapid annual increase in expenditure per student was inflation. This analysis was inadequate to calm public concern over education costs and so cost control became a continuing public concern.

Demand for cost control led to the identification of the two most significant variables in the determination of educational cost: teachers salaries and pupil-teacher ratios. The average teacher's salary increased between 1976 and 1982 from $16,085 to $26,720 for elementary teachers, and from $19,495 to $31,470 for secondary teachers, and pupil-teacher ratios declined by some 15 percent. The increase in salary of approximately 60 percent for both elementary and secondary teachers is the subject of much public concern. However, it should be pointed out that much of the increase in real salary can be accounted for by increases in qualifications and regular teaching experience in the teaching force. Both qualifications and experience tend to be regarded positively by the public.

The assumptions that lower teacher-student ratios and more qualified and experienced teachers provide "higher" quality education have been attacked increasingly since Coleman in his famous study, *Equality of Educational Opportunity*,[11] showed very little association between student performance in schools and these critical cost factors. It should be also noted that, by and large, increases in cost, rising out of declining pupil-teacher ratios, are not generally viewed as totally bad by the public since the conventional wisdom assumes that smaller classes are better than larger ones for instructional purposes. It may be noted, for instance, that the guarantee of small classes always seems to loom large in advertising for private schools.

A recent analysis summarizes the results of 144 studies made since 1966 on the relationship between teacher qualifications, experience and class size, and student performance as follows:

(a) There is no consistent evidence that class sizes affect student performance.

(b) There is no consistent evidence that degree level of the teacher affects student performance.

(c) There is some but not overwhelming evidence that teacher experience might be related to student performance.[12]

While the writer goes on to point out that his evidence should not be interpreted to mean that all teachers and schools are the same or that some teachers and schools are not more successful than others, it does suggest that "the typical school or school system is economically inefficient — it is paying for things that are not consistently related to student's performance."

Given this lack of consistent relationship between cost and quality in public education, it seems apparent that the question which should be asked, "How much should we be paying for education?" instead becomes "How much are we willing to pay?"

## Alternate Sources of Revenue of Elementary and Secondary Education

The provision of revenues for elementary and secondary education in Canada is viewed primarily as a public responsibility. Some of the historical reasons for this view have been examined by Lawton.[13] In economic terms, elementary and secondary education have been regarded in Musgraves terms as a "merit want."[14] A merit want is defined as a service which, although it may be provided for adequately (in economic terms) through the private sector, has for reasons of social and political concern been made a "public" good to be provided through government.

Inherent in the discussion of public education as a "merit want" is an assessment of the extent to which the benefits conveyed by education constitute a private or a social benefit. Elementary social justice would suggest that governments should not use public monies to provide services which are accessible only to a limited part of the population. Variations of this argument may be used to support the case for toll-bridges, fees for freeways, high admission fees to national parks and the whole range of services from which one can exclude from benefit anyone who is unprepared to pay the cost. Schools may be subject to this so-called "exclusion principle."

The economic justification for providing free public education is that the benefits conveyed by education accrue to society as a whole and should, therefore, be financed by society as a whole. An individual who fails to complete elementary, or in these days secondary education, is not likely to be able to make a major contribution to the economy and is, in fact, likely (depending on the array of social support services) to represent a net cost to the community as a whole. On the other hand, an individual who completes a secondary academic program and who proceeds to university to complete a professional education is likely (if the secondary and university program is highly subsidized) to reap a return on his investment. The benefit which society may derive may be limited to the additional amount of tax which such an individual might pay as a result of moving into the higher income bracket.

The analysis of who benefits economically from education and to what extent, is a major focus of the field of economics of education and is beyond the scope of this discussion. As a broad generalization, the case for public benefit is strongest at the elementary level, less strong at the secondary level particularly insofar as narrowly defined academic vocational and specialist technical education is concerned, and even less strong for post-secondary education. It seems reasonable, therefore, that the case for public subsidy would follow this order.

If one accepts that any program of education would convey a combination of both private and social benefits, then the question of whether the individual should pay a higher or lower proportion of the total cost becomes a matter of deciding whether or not the program provides a higher degree of private than public benefit. Since many of the benefits of education are difficult or impossible to qualify, the issue is an open one.

Nevertheless, proponents of privatization (through unsubsidized private schools) or partial privatization (through the voucher system) of schools are, whether consciously or unconsciously, reflecting a view that the benefits conveyed by education constitute to some extent a private benefit, whereas those who advocate a totally funded public school system are reflecting the view that education constitutes a wholly social benefit.

Notwithstanding the above discussion, there is, in the western world, ample evidence of an increasing trend towards the re-evaluation of the role of government in all sectors of the economy. The trend toward the privatization of crown corporations and the deregulation of markets are the most obvious examples. The trend is also clear in the re-evaluation of the role of governments in the provision of goods and services traditionally provided as "merit" wants. Education is one such service undergoing such re-evaluation.

While, in Canada, no radical proposals for privatization have as yet advanced seriously the existence of a large element of the population with no children in school, a wide-spread perception that control over educational costs is impossible under current mechanisms, and a general feeling of dissatisfaction with the content and administration of elementary and secondary education has led to the development of a growing interest in private schools. Statistics Canada reports that in 1960-61 just over 4 percent of total enrolment was in private schools. By 1985-86, the proportion had risen to just under 5 percent. However, the same statistics can be put in another way to show a steady growth of interest in private education. Thus, while enrolment in the total system of elementary and secondary schools had increased between 1960-61 from

4,201,607 to 4,646,474, enrolment in private schools had increased from 168,163 to 234,219 — an increase of 82 percent.

# Future Directions

While to some extent the growth in private education in Canada may be attributed to an increasing interest in denominational and religious issues as distinct from the social, philosophical and political issues which characterize the increased size of the private education sector in Great Britain and the United States, it may be anticipated that the question of fees and private funding will become of increasing interest.

## *Voucher Systems*

The current form of providing aid to private schools is that of providing subsidy to the institution through grants. There are those who would argue that subsidy should be provided to individuals who would then be free to buy education in the "market" place. The advocates of the "voucher" system base their case on freedom of choice and concerns of economic efficiency and reflect an alternative system of providing public revenue to private schools.

In addition to providing parental choice and the possibility of providing substantial inputs of non-tax revenue, the voucher system can be viewed as a means of imposing a regimen of "market" discipline over cost through competition.

It may be questioned whether the apparent popularity of voucher systems is due to their potential to provide real parental choice, or to provide a market in which teachers and educational organizations must compete with each other to control costs.

To some extent the voucher proposal reflects a faith in the power of the competitive system to reduce costs. It may be argued, however, that the role of market forces in assuring economic efficiency is limited by the degree to which the market is really "free." It is not necessary to enter into a lengthy discussion of the economic requirements of a perfectly competitive market system to suggest that deregulation of education will not automatically ensure lower costs. The level of educational costs are to a large extent "controlled" by two factors: the average salary of teachers and the pupil-teacher ratio.

The voucher system and its variation are a reflection of a move to privatize the public school system. There have been proposed, however, systems of revenue generating compatible with a fully publicly funded system. One such scheme is tax-targeting.

## *Tax-Targeting*

All voucher plans assume a public contribution from tax-payers at large including those without children. They also assume that only those with children should bear any cost additional to those provided for by the voucher. As a consequence, the debate around the case for vouchers is not only one of parental choice and efficiency but as we have seen, it also is a debate about the public and social benefits of education and concern for an appropriate approach to horizontal and vertical equity. To some extent, the tax-targeting plan avoids these issues.[15]

The essential part of any tax-targeting plan is the identification of, initially, a small proportion of the local (normally the supplementary portion) tax bill which would be "targeted" by individual tax-payers to a public school of their choice in the jurisdiction. While undoubtedly, parents of children in school would identify their local school as the primary target for the receipt of such revenues, non-parents would have a wider choice of recipients. Obviously under this plan, schools would have an incentive to develop and market programs which would be responsive to tax-payer and client needs.

## Non-Tax Sources of Revenue

Currently, there exist fairly extensive provisions concerning non-tax revenues for schools. The provisions may be described as user-pay options. For instance, many schools, particularly secondary schools, raise fairly substantial sums of money to supplement tax and grant receipts. There is general acceptance of the role of schools in raising funds to support school athletics and cultural programs through the sale of goods and services. There also appears to be widespread acceptance of the role of schools in raising revenues for the purchase of capital items in the form of sports and gymnasium equipment and even computers, library and audio-visual equipment.

These sums of money do in fact reflect a form of non-tax revenue and considerably more study of their extent and variety is required before any analysis can be undertaken. Nevertheless, it would be possible to systematize the conditions and purposes for which such non-tax revenues could be raised. Such a formalized system would in fact become a form of voucher system.

It seems likely that extension of the role of such revenues would raise substantial political and social questions which might include the extent to which this type of revenue raising will serve to compound the difficulties of accessing public revenues, the degree to which equality of educational opportunity may be threatened, the degree to which the methods used to raise such revenues are acceptable by the general public and the question of accountability for the raising and expenditure of the funds.

Current practice also seems to be tending towards an increase in user-pay provisions in the form of incidental fees for special subjects (e.g., music, art, and vocational education) as well as the reduction of programs of textbook rental and the provision of free supplies in elementary schools. Again the question of equity must be raised when considering the impact of such user-pay fees on parents of lower socioeconomic status. On the other hand, it is also fair to raise the issue of whether the system of school financing should be held responsible for rectifying the perceived inadequacies of the distribution of income in our society.

## Conclusion

Canadians, for a variety of historical, social and cultural reasons, have prided themselves on the creation of elementary and secondary schools which provide for universal access and provision for a wide range of needs and an immense variety of programs. Moreover, they have elected to do so almost exclusively through publicly financed and administered systems.

Economists have long been aware that one of the major problems of financing public sector activities is that the demands for service frequently exceed the willingness to pay for that service. As long as Canadians continue to expect an increasing range and improved quality of educational service funded through the public purse, the pressure on revenue sources of all kinds will increase accordingly.

There are only two ways of reducing this pressure: by reducing costs through improving efficiency, or by reducing the demand for educational services. Neither of these solutions has much direct appeal for publicly elected officials since both solutions involve conflict with the organized teaching profession, with the public or with both. We have attempted to show the extent to which the public and the profession share the assumptions upon which claims for improvement in the "quality" of education may be based, and further, that these assumptions tend to result in open-ended demands for increased expenditures. As a result, it would appear that the public appetite for education and its attendant higher cost is likely to be unabated.

For this reason, the major problem associated with revenue raising is essentially one of distributing the burden of cost. In a democratic society, the question of distribution of cost is largely a political matter in which current concepts of equity need to be balanced against political feasibility.

### Notes

[1] Statistics Canada, *Advance Statistics of Education 1988-89* (Ottawa: Statistics Canada) (81-220), p. 17.

[2] McLeod vs. Salmon Arm School Trustees, 4WWR (YS) 385 (1952)2 DLR 562 (BCCA).

[3] See for instance, Wilfred Brown, *Education Finance in Canada* (Ottawa: C.T.F., 1981), Chart 1.

[4] Brown, p. 34.

[5] George D. Strayer, and Robert Haig, *Financing of Education in the State of New York* (New York: The MacMillan Company, 1923), pp. 174-75.

[6] Joseph E. Magnet, "The Canadian Constitution: Implications for Education," *The Canadian School Executive, 2* (September 1982): 16.

[7] A full description for each provincial system is provided in *The Financing of Elementary and Secondary Education* (Toronto: Council of Ministers of Education in Canada, 1985).

[8] Wilfred Brown, "The Educational Toll of the Great Recession," in *The Costs of Controlling the Costs of Education in Canada*, proceedings of a Symposium on Educational Finance (Toronto: OISE, 1983), p. 10.

[9] Brown, "Educational Toll", p. 12.

[10] Brown, "Educational Toll," p. 13.

[11] J.S. Coleman et al., *Equality of Educational Opportunity* (Washington D.C.: Government Printing Office, 1966).

[12] E.A. Hanushek, "Educational Production Functions" in G. Pasacharopoulous, ed., *Economics of Education* (Oxford, England: Permagon Press, 1987), p. 41.

[13] Steven B. Lawton, "Political Values in Educational Finance in Canada and the United States," *Journal of Educational Finance, 5, 1* (Summer 1979): 1-18.

[14] Richard A.Musgrave, *The Theory of Public Finance* (New York: McGraw Hill Book Company, 1959), p. 147.

[15] For a fuller description of tax targeting see Daniel Brown, "The Case for Tax-Target Plans," *Journal of Educational Finance, 5, 2* (Fall, 1979).

# 15

# The Emerging Role of the Lobbyist in Canadian Education

## *Pat Renihan*

For numerous reasons — the resurgence of participatory democracy, the impact of human resources philosophy, the rise of mobility, changing expectations for key administrative roles — lobbying in its various forms is an emerging phenomenon in Canadian educational governance. Lobbying is manifest in both formal and informal influence strategies, through a variety of power bases and tools, in overt and covert ways and in the exertion of pressure downward as well as upward.

Contrary to its reputation as a subversive force, the lobby provides for balance in the political culture, a healthy "reconstruction of preferences," a clarification of positions and a valuable source of information for policy-makers. As a political activity, it demands an understanding of political intricacies at local and central levels. Consequently, school organizations would benefit greatly from a deliberate, planned study of interest groups, political elites and community power structures in order to work intelligently and supportively with the political environment.

In addition, such formal groups as municipal associations and teacher associations have sustained a long-term interest in political activity at the local level. The emergence of such groups as strong political actors would seem to call for serious examination of policies of public relations and involvement on the part of educational government at all levels. It also demands serious consideration of the advantages of formal lobbying and the impact of such factors as exchange, sanction, organization, persuasion and hard numbers in determining the success of lobbying attempts.

A healthy, constructive and proactive approach to lobbying can provide educational leaders with a potent and valuable resource in their efforts to provide the best possible educational services for Canadian youth.

## The Emerging Role of the Lobbyist in Canadian Public Education

Lobbying is a political activity. For those who have significant dealings with government at any level, the act of lobbying board members, provincial MLA's, civil servants or federal MP's is a crucial and potentially effective means by which one might attain the best possible service for one's children, one's schools, one's programs and so on.

A considerable body of research and learned opinion has accumulated during the past 30 years, providing perspective directly and indirectly related to the lobbying process. This has served also to remove much of the mystique associated with the lobbying phenomenon, and has provided enrichment to the arsenal of strategies from which the lobbyist can select. But to what extent have these been utilized in the educational context? Which have most potential for educational lobbyists? More generally, what are some of the more significant forms of political activity at the local level? What are the prospects for the lobbying process in educational governance? These questions demand consideration of the variety of forms which lobbying takes, and at least an understanding the variety of circumstances under which the process is conducted.

## Problems of Definition

The original use of the term "lobby" referred to the act of frequenting the lobby of a legislative assembly for the purpose of influencing members' votes. It originated in the United States in the early 1830s. Since that time, the term has been utilized in a variety of circumstances. It has come to relate to a variety of political realities, and it has been applied in interpretations far more liberal than the circumstances to which it originally applied.

Several factors, most notably the power which has accrued to various levels of government, the realization of the presence of a variety of targets for influence and the emergence of a variety of potential lobbyists, both inside as well as outside government and administrative circles, have prompted this writer to select the liberal interpretation of the term. Unfortunately, this involves obvious problems which defy attempts at drawing parameters, even for discussion purposes.

Consider the following vignettes:

-A new deputy minister of Education is appointed. He has been given the mandate to make sweeping changes to the education system.

Representatives of several groups and associations have requested meetings with him.

-The school board of a large urban system meets with its local members of the Legislative Assembly in order to apprise them of the current status of the system, (enrolment trends, recent program initiatives, and related financial and facility needs projected for the future).

-A Francophone group in a predominantly English-speaking Canadian province is striving to break from the regular system and to form their own publicly funded, independent boards of Education. They pursue meetings with the Minister of Education and with the Catholic Bishops of the province.

-A committee of concerned parents is formed as a reaction to the decision by a board of education to close a school. The committee has requested permission to make representation at a forthcoming meeting of the board.

-Individual boards, together with provincial and national trustee associations, combine to react to the implications of a proposed federal taxation bill which has negative economic implications for school boards.

Assuming, as this writer does, that each of these represents a lobbying activity suggests that our liberal interpretation of the definition be sufficiently wide to encompass formal and informal influence strategies, the use of a variety of power bases and tools, the exertion of pressure downward, as well as upward, and the use of covert, as well as overt strategies of influence. An additional point of definition lies in the distinction between lobbying efforts which are a "reaction" to activities and decisions in government, and those which constitute an expression of interests and needs in a more proactive sense. In the foregoing vignettes, the reactive variety predominated, and this would seem to be the norm in Canadian educational contracts.

At the risk of repetition, we need, therefore, to dispense with two major misconceptions stemming from the traditional view of lobbying. I will do this by making two statements:

(1) It is not necessarily a one-way process, involving influence attempts "upward" to senior levels of government; and

(2) It can largely be a covert process with elements of bargaining, conducted predominantly outside of the public purview, between political elites.

In regard to the first point, Hennessy observed that administrative officials and agencies occasionally direct their influence at public opinion, in that they shape public opinion intentionally through information programs and through subtle feedback to voluntary associations that tailor their demands and strategies accordingly.[1] This is reminiscent of Lindblom's notion of "reconstruction of preferences" which suggests that, although citizens send upward their opinions and preferences, a downward influence is also felt when at each rung of the ladder, a more informed participant in policy-making is sending downward information which ultimately helps citizenry to understand and better express their own desires and needs.[2]

Associated with the second point, the lobbying effort need not be an overt approach to government or a governmental elite. It may represent an attempt (possibly fairly long-term) to socialize an elite. Take for example the vignette relating to the new deputy minister. By their reactions, communications and influence attempts, key political elites in the educational sector sought to bring the individual into line with the political culture with its policy making norms, rules for collaboration, interagency cooperation and so forth.

The parameters for definition, given the liberal stance which has been taken in this discussion, are as broad as the variety of means at lobbyists' disposal for the expression of opinion and the exertion of influence. Perhaps the common definitive thread, regardless of power base, power tools, or strategies of influence, is that lobbying is the process by which an individual, group or organization exerts influence in order to promote governmental action which is favorable to the self-fulfillment of the lobbyist, favorable to "the public good," and/or favorable to the pursuit of justice.

# The Value of Lobby

Once we have removed several common misconceptions about lobbying (that it is a narrow concept, that it is subversive and confrontational, that it pertains only to the upward exertion of influence by privileged elites), some of the more significant and constructive aspects of the process can be illustrated. These constructive aspects have prompted this writer to argue for the formal acceptance of lobbying activity as a means of improving educational policy-making, on one hand, and citizenship participation on the other. Four major arguments which serve to justify the existence of the lobbying process are presented here:

(1) **Balance in the Political Culture.** The influence of those who lobby for their positions has been identified as a means of adjusting conflicting claims upon government, thereby maintaining balance in the political culture. The existence of lobbying activity (and its recognition as a legitimate and worthy activity) is one mechanism which provides, in the words of Moodie and Studdert-Kennedy, a "guarantee of good behaviour."[3]

(2) **The Reconstruction of Preferences.** Enough has been said above of the nature of this process, but it should also be perceived a viable end in itself. The lobbying process, in providing for an airing of positions, does open the door for counterargument, comparison and the injection of new information. In so doing, it provides an opportunity for educational leaders to assume a key educative and reconstructive role.

**(3) The Clarification of Position.** Lobbying, when conducted in an open and conducive environment, provides a forum for the clarification of positions on key issues, elucidating who supports what in the political culture.

**(4) The Provision of Policy-making Information.** Lobbyists are important instruments for decision-makers, helping them to make policy choices. Paraphrasing Lindblom, the policy-maker is "busy," whereas the lobbyist has the advantage of taking an in-depth (though one-sided) look at a policy issue, and can study and present issues concisely, removed from the distractions of multitudinous additional tasks and pressures.[4] Finer made the point more vehemently when he observed that, "without the lobby the ruling party would be a rigid and ignorant tyranny and its civil servants a rigid and stupid bureaucracy."[5]

## The Protagonists

The problem with taking a liberal approach to the definition of the process is that it necessitates an equally liberal interpretation when it comes to identifying the major actors and describing their roles. On the basis of my discussion to date, the lobbyist may be identified as an internal or an external, an appointed official, an elected official or member of an interested public, perhaps even as an organization with a stake in governmental policy.

In this context, the term "stakeholder" has much to recommend it, for it implies the existence of that interest which will drive the efforts of both the active and the latent lobbyist. Mitroff raised a valuable point relating to stakeholders when he observed that stakeholders do not exist by themselves or in isolation from one another.[6] The significance of this for the lobbying process should not be lost, for it implies that lobbyists also have *a significant potential influence on one another.* One special wrinkle in the lobbying process over the long-term, therefore, is that lobbyists and lobby groups can shape one anothers' preferences through exposure (directly and indirectly) to one another's viewpoints and arguments. Consequently, the "reconstruction of preferences" may be as much horizontally influenced as it is vertically.

Lobbying is a political activity, and the stakeholders referred to above may be referred to as "the political public."[7] The protagonists are those members of the general public who participate, however irregularly or infrequently, in the political life of their society.[8] This is the broad base from which lobbyist is defined. However, a meaningful discussion of prospects for lobbying as a viable process in educational governance requires a more detailed explication of the nature of the beast.

The logical starting point is within the mechanisms of government itself. Government elected officials, administrative officials and agencies are, by virtue of their active involvement in the mainstream of policy-making action, potent lobbyists at the legislative level. Related to their role, however, is the recurring dilemma of whether elected officials should follow their own conscience and best judgement or be bound by the demands and instructions of their own constituents. Burke's philosophy was clear on this point when he suggested that "your representative owes you, not his industry only, but his judgement; and he betrays instead of serving you, if he sacrifices it to your opinion."[9] The role of the legislator, therefore, may be seen as one of maintaining balance: listening to opinions, listening to information and weighing all according to his own judgement in examining the viability of alternative courses of action.

A vital consideration for administrative and legislative officials, at any level, is the need for a realization that the "political public" is not necessarily confined to a few involved "elites." Numerous school boards have found to their chagrin, for example, that groups can emerge from nowhere and, even in the most placid of communities, fight with unprecedented tenacity and mobilize resources with amazing speed, given the "right" issues and the "right" cause. Those within government circles, therefore, have a very large stake in channeling lobbying activity, managing it through liaison programs, public relations, public discussion forums and interagency networks. More important is the inculcation of an attitude (within government) that lobbying activity is valuable, not only from the perspective of the self-interest of the lobbyist and what he represents, but also from the perspective of government as a source of information and a means of tapping the "complex of preferences"[10] which exists among stakeholders to the enterprise. This point was also underscored by Moodie and Studdert-Kennedy who observed that various lobby and pressure groups are the bridges between the decision-making elite and the general public, adding that "their importance lies in their contribution to the discussion process."[11]

Of course, such groups are varied in nature and purpose, and any attempt at categorization will not do full justice to the complex phenomenon. As suitable as any is Pross's differentiation between issue-oriented pressure groups and institutionalized pressure groups, and (in terms of the temporal consideration) between mature groups and fledgling groups. The implications for lobby are, essentially, that institutionalized groups, to paraphrase Pross, will have greater continuity and cohesion, more knowledge of government and administration, a more stable membership and a broader focus than will issue-oriented groups.[12] The Committee of Concerned Parents (in reference to the earlier vignettes) probably had less initial credibility, less resources from which to draw, and less understanding of the intricacies of government action than did the trustees associations who lobbied for changes to the taxation bill.

To conclude this discussion of protagonists in the lobbying process, some consideration needs to be given to the relative influence of *minority* and *majority* as lobby group sources of power. The natural assumption is that majorities, by virtue of number and base of support, have the upper hand. Those who have had experience with educational policy-making at any level of government in education would, however, be able to draw upon many experiences to refute this argument. Majorities do not necessarily control policies. Minority coalitions often have significant input into public policy. Neither, of course, is "majority" always synonymous with "right." There are many examples scattered throughout history where minority opinion has prevailed in the face of widespread intolerance, bigotry and injustice regarding such ideals as civil liberty. Lawrence noted that "a democratic system can survive the intolerant attitudes of the masses as long as they are balanced by the tolerant attitudes of the politically active."[13] As Hennessy puts it, "in the democratic community, as in other kinds of political communities, power makes policy."[14] This is due in no small part to the general apathy of the citizenry concerning day-to-day political concerns.

In the educational arena, the same phenomenon holds, in that the vast majority of stakeholders in the educational enterprise are passive, and leave matters relating to educational policy to a minority comprised of interested "representatives" of stakeholder groups. In the local governance of education, this phenomenon of passivity has been apparently much more marked in Canadian systems than in their U.S. counterparts; there being, in the Canadian context, less dependence upon public referenda around key educational and budget issues, less active public involvement, and more control by key appointed officials. For this reason, the lobbying instinct has been much more successfully cultivated in the American psyche, and is less a natural instinct among Canadian educational publics.

## Other Forms of Political Activity at the Local Level

An understanding of political activity at the local level demands an appreciation of where the major sources of influence lie in regard to the educational system. As Beare has noted, although the conservative view is that the schools' internals are the prime movers, the view has changed in recent years to an appreciation that:

(1) Parents are one of the most powerful determinants of the educational achievement of the child, outweighing in their impact and influence (some researchers claim) all the inputs which schools and teachers can provide.

(2) The community provides resources for education far in excess of what the school can provide.

(3) Community values, community ethos and tone dominate educational influences.[15]

He summarizes by noting that "the paying public is a participant in public education: they have an inalienable part of the action."[16]

Consequently, political activity at the local level has been broadened in recent years to include the negotiation, debate, application of force, persuasion, etc., entered into by parents and the local community. Of course, the typical community is organized around groups with special interests, with varying degrees of compatibility with the purposes and programs of the school system. Many, such as the service organizations (the Legion, the Rotary clubs, etc.), serve a supportive function and as an invaluable resource for the school. Other groups have, as their goal, a specific change or set of changes to school policy and are often as much in conflict with other interest groups as with the school board. The task for school authorities is to identify the philosophies and strategies of these groups and to weigh these in terms of the broader community interest.

In addition, the school system should be able to deal effectively with the power structure in the community. This presupposes a knowledge of the characteristics peculiar to power structures. Paraphrasing Kindred, Bagin and Gallagher:

(1) Power structures are controlled by people of influence who try to shape community decisions in ways that protect their own interests.

(2) Members of power structures are drawn from a wide cross-section of community life (business executives, bankers, newspaper publishers, etc.).

(3) Many members of power structures have numerous contacts in the community where they can spend propaganda and mobilize support.

(4) Members of power structures are most frequently sincerely concerned with the well-being of the community especially from an economic point of view.

(5) Members of power structures find it advantageous to align themselves with political parties and holders of public office.[17]

According to Kindred and others, perhaps the best protection the school has against power-structure pressure on financial and other decisions is a well planned and carefully implemented program in school and community relations:

> By taking parents and other citizens into complete confidence about the institution, its policies, its needs, its operating procedures, its problems and its accomplishments, the school can develop sufficiently intelligent and supportive public opinion to offset the influence of the power wielders.
>
> It has been apparent in recent years that properly organized citizens and advisory committees have had a constructive effect upon power groups.[18]

Apart from the informal power structure, several more formal structures have a significant and very powerful impact. Two of these, the municipal association and the teachers' professional organization have emerged as crucial actors who loom large in the local political environment.

In regard to the municipal associations (by way of an example), in Saskatchewan, school boards are holding their own in the face of a strong and persistent lobby from urban and rural municipal associations to have the property tax removed as a basis for school funding. The trustees' position is purposes is crucial for board autonomy. This view appears to have an impact; however, the continued lobby by the municipalities is forcing a sustained counter-lobby on the part of trustees. How long the trustees' position will prevail will depend upon the continued strength of their lobby relative to that of the municipalities.[19]

In regard to the teachers' professional organization, some of the more traumatic tensions have their roots in the bargaining procedure, and the negotiation process has always had the potential to influence the political tone of the school system and its community. This is particularly apparent in times of economic scarcity when board spending is viewed with a critical eye by communities faced with decreased earning power and increased income taxation and property taxation. The escalation of concern among the community groups can, in this case, manifest itself in increased demand for school system accountability, greater vocal disagreement on the part of groups and individuals with the policies of the system, and can be reflected in the results of school board elections where alternative factions compete for power, and incumbency weakens drastically as a predictor of re-election to their school board.

In Saskatchewan, bargaining with teachers is conducted under a "two-tier" system. In other words, some items are bargained provincially, while others are bargained locally. Provincial level bargaining, which includes, among other items, teacher salaries, provides a classic example of the potential of the teachers' organization to influence political relationships at all levels. The move by the government to a two-tier system won the teachers' federation more influence, for they were now able to bargain and be heard as one voice.

The professional organization did not stop there. They were astute enough in their quickening growth to buy the expertise and time of enough people to form a strong provincial organization. Having made the provincial cabinet their target, they were quick to seize the initiative to fight for and win membership on curriculum committees, on advisory committees, on ad hoc ministerial committees and on provincial policy-making committees.[20] From their once tenuous position as a junior member, they grew by using the political arena to sound advantage. They have in many respects pre-empted in importance school boards and the provincial trustees' association as an influence in the provincial educational arena.[21]

This example underscores Moodie and Studdert-Kennedy's conviction regarding a major factor in political activity and in the work of pressure groups.[22] In addition, provincial and local policy should likewise have an impact upon political activity at the local level in years to come. Perhaps most significant will be the policies of participation which many governments are employing in their own policy-development processes. This is an optimistic scenario, but governments in recent history have learned that an open-system philosophy is a far better alternative to that in which hidden agendas, misinterpretations, and mismanagement are bared periodically by a media misinterpretations, and mismanagement are bared periodically by a media which has become incrementally more powerful and sophisticated in its ability to reveal and disclose.

## Rules of the Game: Prescriptions for Effectiveness

Several variables would seem to be key considerations in the planning of lobbying strategies. From these, the educational lobbyist can select ideas and weigh alternatives when deciding how best to get what his/her schools need. This list of considerations makes no claim to comprehensiveness, neither is it presented in any particular order of significance or preference.

(1) **The Quid Pro Quo.** A fairly good predictor of the success of a lobby attempt arises when a government body for some reason discovers that it wants something from the group in question. Several concepts prominent in exchange theories[23] would appear to have relevance for the degree of success which can be attained. These relate to the *rewards* of the exchange, the *costs* to the organization, the *perceived outcomes* (profit and loss), and *comparison levels* involving previous experiences, perceptions of the *value of alternative projects*, etc.[24] It goes without saying that the degree to which each of these are planned and carefully conveyed to government will dictate the success of the lobby.

(2) **Sanction Capability.** The ability of a group to impose sanctions upon government is also a significant factor where it relates, for example, to influencing support near an election period. Other sanctions, of course, demand attention where they have implication for the removal of expertise, the creation of uncertainty, the removal of key resources and so on. Groups and organizations which have multiple powerful sanctions upon which to draw, do tend to "bend the ear" of government and government officials more frequently, if not necessarily more effectively, than most others.

(3) **Legitimation.** Why do some groups appear to be heeded more than others? While this question relates to the above points, it also illustrates an initial need among prospective lobbyists to establish legitimacy and a significant claim to credibility in the eyes of those to whom influence attempts are directed. At times of major changes in government and in civil-service personnel, such as occurred recently in this writer's province, the need arises for even the more established agencies to reassert themselves and to concern themselves with the task of reaffirming their image and agenda in the minds of policy-makers.

(4) **Organization.** It appears trite to state that the better organized a group is, the more effective it is likely to be, and yet the propensity of key representatives of agencies to make public statements on vital issues *contrary* to their organization's stance has been a common source of embarrassment for government and non-government agencies alike. However the sugges-

what our left hand is doing," the point remains that organization, and its concomitant consistency and coordination of goals and strategies, is a crucial criterion for effectiveness.

(5) **Numbers.** The ability to mobilize and demonstrate the interest and active support of large numbers of people (particularly constituents) is a significant, though also quite obvious, factor. Though individual opinion, and the opinion of minorities[25] are weighed, and do indeed matter very much, there are times when the *logic* of a school board's argument in lobbying provincial government, is given considerable weight when government can be convinced of the massive public support behind their position.[26]

(6) **Ideals and Beliefs.** Lobbyists for groups whose ideals and objectives are quite far removed from those widely held by the community at large, usually have a tougher struggle in winning concessions from policy-makers. Yet history is replete with examples of minority opinions succeeding in the face of majority opposition. The key to success seems to rest in the *nature* of the ideals in question, the *educational ability* of the minority group in changing public opinion (and the opinions of elites), the *strength* of their own commitment and, of course, the *fervor* with which they pursue the issues in question.

(7) **Persuasion.** The persuasive ability of the lobbyist is undoubtedly a major criterion for success, and it calls into play a variety of techniques which draw significantly upon one's leadership, motivational, communicative, educative and influential capabilities. As Lindblom observed, these combine to go beyond mere tricks:

> Is that all? you may ask. No pressure? No tricks? No clever machinations? All these are possible — some officials, for example, are simply bribed, or seduced by the prospects of a high-paid job on their retirement from government. The big engine of interest-group participation in the play of power, however, is persuasion, and it is powerful indeed.[27]

Those who have had the experience of political interaction in the educational arena within Canadian provinces would agree that much of this persuasion is conducted through *informal* interaction. Several key "gatherings" provide opportunities for political elites to interact. One of the more significant in this writer's province, is the annual convention of the School Trustees' Association. Always well attended by elected and appointed officials at various levels of government, the informal political interplays and interactions are very much in evidence. This largely informal channel is one of the major sources of access to, and persuasion of, policy-makers.

There is no shortage of literature advocating specific "persuasion tactics" for the lobbyist. Park, for example, suggested that the lobbyist pay attention to *listening, loitering, information-giving, choosing co-workers,* the tendency to slip into the *persecution syndrome* and the tendency to *create adversaries* where *they don't exist* as considerations in the contemplation of lobbying strategies.[28]

# Emerging Prospects for Lobby

To this point in the chapter, the nature of the lobbying process, the major actors involved and guiding factors associated with lobbying effectiveness have been discussed on the basis of a liberal interpretation of the concept of lobby.

The discussion now turns to an explanation of this writer's view that the lobby is an emerging force in educational governance, one which should play a significant role in the shape of educational structure and delivery. Eight contextual trends, (which may be variously described as organizational, political and societal in nature) would seem to support this contention. They are outlined briefly below.

(1) **The dramatic sophistication in the use of the news media as a power tool of the lobbyist** has provided the opportunity for arguments and issues to be brought forcefully into the wider arena, thereby gaining a greater proportion of public support, and additional committed allies for the lobbyist and the issue at hand.

(2) It might be argued that **human resources thinking** has had impacts far beyond the limits of intraorganizational life, and has made itself felt in the philosophy that the community is a "reservoir of untapped resources." This line of thinking has manifested itself in the inclination of some governments to go through a prolonged (and sometimes painful) public phase in the examination of an educational issue, or in the introduction of a discussion paper preparatory to the parliamentary phase.

This spirit of collaboration has had the added effect of opening channels of communication between potential lobbyists and government. Once individuals and groups have been formally involved in deliberations concerning government action, lines of communication to elites become clearer.

(3) People are less career-bound and, probably, less place-bound than they have ever been before. Economic uncertainty, come-and-go resource crises, technological change and changing societal expectations regarding quality of life-style, have probably been the more significant contributory factors in this regard. These **mobility factors** have had the combined effect of producing a greater proportion of the "body politic" with a broad base of organizational and governmental understanding.

(4) Fueled by a media which has been giving prominence to the treatment of societal issues, human rights, and governmental responses to community and group action, there would seem to have been, in recent years, **an escalation in political-legal expertise and "rights consciousness" among the population at large**. In the Canadian context, such knowledge has been promoted by the prominence given to the *Charter of Rights and Freedoms*, the Constitution, and a host of concerns relating to employment equity, language rights, and native self-governance.

The political public, at least, would seem to have had ample opportunity to become more aware of, first, the options relating to lobby, second, at whom to direct lobbying attempts and, third, the more effective lobbying strategies at their disposal. Success is a powerful motivator and it might be argued that exposure to successful lobby, combined with the clarification of individual and group rights, will have the effect of increasing the incidence of lobbying attempts.

(5) **The Humanization of Authority.** There have always been loyal opponents to those in positions of authority — particularly in governmental circles. Policy-makers, elected officials, even royalty have been scrutinized, opposed, criticized, ridiculed, depicted in grotesque shapes and situations by the humorists. The media have become more and more adept at capturing the private and public lives of these people for all to see. This has had the effect of at least reducing the mystique of "public figures," humanizing them in the eyes of the public. In turn, of course, this makes them more approachable. The would-be lobbyist, it would seem, has much less cause to fear in lobbying an official who has been portrayed in such stark humanness by media and public scrutiny.

(6) **Impact of the Involvement Ethos and the Rise of Participatory Democracy.** Representative democracy served a useful function in its day, but for several reasons, some of which have been outlined above, it can no longer serve as the sole model by which government is run. Representatives, no matter who they are, become elites and, in many cases, once they become socialized to their respective government levels, become farther and farther removed from their constituents.

For some years now, *participatory* democracy has enjoyed favor. This has had the added effect of elevating pressure groups from a status somewhere below subversive and sinister forces of evil to that of legitimate and, indeed, valuable tools of government. Needless to say, the lobbying process, and its formal acceptance in government circles, is one powerful means of exercising participatory democracy.

(7) The popular view of the role of the chief executive officer, and **the role of the school administrator in general has shifted in recent years to encompass the political environment.** Recent discussions of the aspects of these roles in the Canadian context have shed light on demands associated with the shift in the tide away from rationality toward power politics in the CEO's role[29] and the stresses associated with the emergence of a host of political demands in the principalship — including the demand for lobbying.[30] There is strong evidence of increased expectation that boards, superintendents and other personnel actively engage in lobbying activity. In the light of the above comments there is no sign that this expectation will ebb in the foreseeable future.

# Conclusion

Lobbyists shape policy. The formal lobbyists, the informal lobbyists, the newcomers, the institutions, all contribute in their own way to the discussion process and, consequently, improve policy-making and the opportunity for citizen participation. The potential of lobby for ensuring balance in the political culture, providing for meaningful reconstruction of preferences, clarifying positions, and assisting policy-makers, constitutes a sound argument for its formal recognition and acceptance in educational contexts.

For numerous reasons — the resurgence of participatory democracy, the spread of the human resources philosophy, the humanization of public figures, the rise of mobility, changing expectations concerning administrative roles in educational organizations — lobby is an emerging phenomenon in educational governance. Its presence should be even more pronounced at those times and in those places where education enjoys a high level of priority on the public agenda. In addition, schools and school systems seem to be breaking from that "institutional shyness" which has been a common point of contrast between the educational and the private sectors. The break has been due, in no small part, to the impact of the trend toward marketing schools and to the high profile of school effectiveness research. In terms of its potential dividends, these factors have provided lobby with a considerable degree of legitimacy and respectability.

As we approach the final decade of the twentieth century, what forms will lobbying take in educational governance? By way of conclusion, five simple prognostications for the Canadian context are suggested:

(1) Lobby will manifest itself more formally and more overtly in our educational agencies and government institutions, and will demand a greater number of individuals with responsibilities specifically directed at legislative and government affairs.

(2) While the provinces continue to be the major partners in educational governance in Canada, lobbying activity in the Canadian educational context will be predominantly targeted at the provincial level.

(3) There will be an increased level of attention, among intermediate levels of government, to both sides of the lobbying process:

    (a) in dealing with the lobbying efforts of constituents; and

    (b) in planning and implementing the effective lobby of senior levels of government.

(4) Experience will bring about an increase in *proactive* and *educative* lobby, as opposed to *reactive* (why are they doing this to us?) lobby, particularly among *institutions* in their relationship to government.

(5) The increase in lobbying activity by one major actor in the educational sector will bring about an increase in the lobbying efforts and capabilities of other actors competing for government resources.

With a healthy, constructive and proactive approach to the lobby, and with a deeper understanding of its wider value in the educational sector, governments can rise far above the unfortunate, sometimes undeserved, stamp of "ignorant tyranny" with which they have at times been branded. More important, educational leaders will have one more tool, a potent tool, at their disposal in their efforts to provide the best possible educational service for Canadian youth.

## Notes

[1] B. Hennessy, *Public Opinion* (Monterey, Ca.: Brooks/Cole, 1981).

[2] C.E. Lindblom, *The Policy-Making Process* (Englewood Cliffs, N.J.: Prentice Hall, 1968).

[3] G.C. Moodie and G. Studdert-Kennedy, *Opinions, Publics and Pressure Groups* (London: Allen and Unwin, 1970), p. 71.

[4] Lindblom, *Policy-making*.

[5] S.E. Finer, *The Anonymous Empire* (London: Pall Mall, 1966), p. 113.

[6] I.I. Mitroff, *Stakeholders of the Organizational Mind* (San Francisco: Jossey-Bass, 1983), p. 11.

[7] Moodie, p.71.

[8] Moodie, p. 110.

[9] Hennessy.

[10] Lindblom.

[11] Moodie, p. 110.

[12] A.P. Pross, *Pressure Group Behaviour in Canadian Politics* (New York: Mc-Graw-Hill, 1975).

[13] D.G. Lawrence, "Procedural Norms and Tolerance: A Reassessment," *American Political Science Review*, 70 (1976): 82.

[14] Hennessy.

[15] H. Beare, "School and Community as Educational Partners" in J.E. Watson,ed., *Policies for Participation* (Wellington: Deslandes Ltd., 1977).

[16] Beare, p. 162

[17] L.W. Kindred, D. Bagin, and D.R. Gallagher, *The School and Community Relations* (3rd ed.) (Englewood Cliffs, N.J.: Prentice-Hall, 1984).

[18] Kindred et al, p.26

[19] Patrick J. Renihan, "Notes on the Realities of the Local-Provincial Relationship," *The Yellow Papers*, 4, 1 (December, 1984).

[20] E.D. Hodgson, "Control Over Local Control" in E. Hodgson, J. Bergen and B. Bryce, eds.,*The Organization and Administration of Public Education in Canada* (Edmonton: University of Alberta, 1980).

[21]Renihan, "Notes."

[22]Moodie, p. 110.

[23]J.S. Adams, "Inequity in Social Exchange" in J. Berkowitz, ed., *Advances in Experimental Social Psychology* (New York: Academic Press, 1965).

[24]W.G. Scott and T.R. Mitchell, *Organization Theory: A Structural and Behavioural Analysis* (Homewood, Illinois: Dorsey Press, 1972).

[25]Hennessy.

[26]Renihan, "Notes."

[27]Lindblom.

[28]G. Park, "Review the Twelve Rules of Lobbying and Get What You Want for Schools," *American School Board Journal*, 171 (December, 1984): 39.

[29]G.B. Isherwood, "The C.E.O. Speaks," *Education Canada*, 24 (Spring, 1984): 1.

[30]T.R. Williams, "Politics and Principals," *The Canadian School Executive*, 2 (1983): 11.

# 16

# The Process and Substance of Curriculum Reform in Canada

*K. A. Leithwood, J. B. Cousins and D.M.A. Trider*


How does curriculum reform typically occur in Canada? What have been the processes and substance of reform in the recent past? In the near future, at least, what types of reforms might be expected? These are the questions addressed in this chapter. To answer, we adopted a broad view of the curriculum and what constitutes reform: "planned experiences for students in school" adequately captures our meaning of curriculum (this definition does not include the "hidden" curriculum). As a verb, we use the term *reform* to mean "any systematic set of initiatives undertaken to alter the curriculum in a direction valued by an identifiable group of people" (the process of reform). The term *reform* is also used as a noun; in such cases reference is made to the desired result of the reform process (the substance of reform).

The time frame within which reforms were considered spanned approximately 1976 to 1987: the beginning of this period corresponded with the publication of a review of Canada's education system by the Organization for Economic Cooperation and Development[1] (OECD). In this review, Canada's public school systems were seen to be at a watershed in their development. They were, it was asserted,

> ... [at] the end of a period of exceptional expansion — an expansion which has allowed for higher expectations, widespread experimentation, and perhaps over-idealized hopes for the social transformation that could be brought about through education. (p. 15)

The review goes on to suggest that, in 1976, Canada faced

> ... new era of recognizing realistic limitations of education, a time of bringing education close to concommitant social policies which must be developed in parallel with education for its promises to come anywhere near to the realization of the objectives that it could be expected to serve ...

major educational issues . . . require treatment within the framework of larger political and social concerns. (p. 15)

An interesting supplement to the question of reform substance is suggested by the OECD review: to what extent have reforms since 1976 been expressions of larger social and political concerns? We take up this question in the final section of the chapter.

# The Process of Curriculum Reform in Canada

Our definition of curriculum reform admits initiatives for change ranging from those associated with a small group of teachers or even a single teacher within a school (a largely apolitical source) through proposals by the Council of Ministers of Education acting on behalf of all the provinces and territories in Canada (a highly political source). Processes for reform look quite different depending on which group initiates the reform, how distant the initiators are from the classroom and how much designated authority they have. As well, processes may vary depending on the breadth of the discrepancy between the desired results of a reform and the practices it is designed to alter or replace, the scale of the reform or the numbers of people whose practices are to be changed.

In the face of such variables which argue for variety if not uniqueness in reform processes, we accept the claim made by Connelly, Crocker and Kass[2] that " . . . within Canada, curriculum reform has traditionally been a matter of revising [provincial] government curriculum policy." This type of reform initiative is in contrast with, for example, U.S. federal reform efforts in the 1960s which included the development of extensive curriculum materials, or more recent European initiatives which take the form of staff development: it is the type of reform process described in this section of the chapter.

In addition, it should be noted that this process of revising government curriculum policy in Canada is typically stimulated in one of two ways. One way involves cyclical reform of curriculum policy initiated by ministries of Education. Under these circumstances, curriculum revisions are often modest in size (although not necessarily unimportant), largely controlled by education professionals, and in response to professional concerns. A second way in which revisions to government curriculum policy are stimulated is through initiatives by those other than education professionals, what would typically be referred to as political initiatives. Such initiatives are often intended to result in significant change. This second "political" way in which curriculum reform occurs in Canada is the focus of this section of the paper.

Our understanding of the process of provincial, government-sponsored, politically stimulated curriculum reform has emerged from, and is grounded in, large scale studies of two cases of reform in Ontario. Processes used in these two cases are believed to be similar in many respects to reform processes in other provinces. Our studies, undertaken over the past six years, have examined processes used to introduce new special education legislation[3] and changes to both the organizational structure and the curriculum of secondary schools. The second of these reforms, centred on a policy entitled "Ontario Schools: Intermediate and Senior Division - 1984 (OSIS)," provides an especially productive case to use in illustrating "typical" reform efforts. We were able to study this reform effort from its earliest initiation through subsequent development and ultimate implementation in schools and classrooms;[4] the substance of this reform was also similar to reforms underway at the same time in provinces other than Ontario — for example, New Brunswick and Nova Scotia.

As compared with the policy it replaced (Circular HS1, 1979-81)[5], the substance of the OSIS policy called for increased equality of educational opportunity and greater control by central authorities. More specifically, the policy demonstrated a greater concern for the relationship between the school and the workplace and for the nurturing of students. It provided an expanded concept of sex equity and called on schools to give more attention to the needs of non-university bound students. More attention was also to be given to the needs of cultural and linguistic minorities and there was a shift in the number and nature of compulsory courses that corresponded to tougher rules for graduation. Finally, the policy was somewhat more prescriptive than its predecessor.

Our conception of the curriculum reform process is a product not only of our own research but also of systematic reviews[6] of research by others concerning both policy development and policy implementation[7] (we will use "policy" and our substantive view of "reform" interchangeably). Based on these sources of information, we view the process as involving three phases of partially distinct activity:

(1) An initiation phase which ends with a decision to develop a policy;

(2) A development phase, the product of which is a set of policy specifications; and

(3) An implementation phase which includes alterations in peoples' practices, organizational structures and possibly other aspects of the educational environment in response to the policy.

The implementation phase also includes efforts to ensure that policy-related changes "stick" — that is, become routine or institutionalized. Although generally sequential, there is often considerable interaction among activities across phases about which little is known. Research has typically not distinguished initiation from development and has examined development and implementation quite independently.

## The Initiation Phase

Four components included in our conception of the initiation phase are summarized in Figure 1. A variety of individuals and groups (component 2) are actively involved in trying to make sense of conditions in their environment (component 1). Given their unique, as well as shared, beliefs, values and goals, they interpret the meaning of such conditions as problems requiring some type of action. Because conditions in the environment do not present people with well-defined problems, it is possible for individuals and groups to find (or define) quite different problems in the same set of conditions. In spite of such variation in the results of problem finding, these individuals and groups nevertheless see government policy-making as part of the solution to their problems and exert pressure for action on those in policy-making roles. Given enough pressure, in concert with other precipitating factors (e.g., strong governmental leadership), policy makers decide to initiate the policy development process.

Problematic conditions in the environment (component 1) may include demographic, economic, social and technological changes; they may also include changes in professional "know-how" and shifts in both professional and public assessments of the adequacy of the education system at the time. In the case of OSIS, the following examples of such conditions included:

- Demographic changes — declining student enrolments;
- Economic changes — increased youth unemployment resulting from a period of economic instability and eventually recession;
- Social changes — greater interest in such matters as sex equity, individuals with special needs, bilingualism and cultural diversity;
- Technological changes — burgeoning of many new information technologies requiring specific operational skills;
- Change in professional "know-how" — development of technologies for measuring student achievement in relation to at least a portion of the curricular objectives in the province;
- Shifts in public views of education — publication of opinion polls indicating major concerns about student attitudes and discipline; a belief that schools were too permissive; a belief that academic standards were dropping or at unacceptably low levels;
- Shifts in professional views of education — surveys showing teacher concern for the number and type of credits required for graduation.

Conditions such as these impact differently on different people and groups (those outside the system, those inside, and those with narrowly specialized interests), depending upon their own beliefs, goals and values. Such differences in impact produce different definitions of the problem. In the case of OSIS, for example, people outside the secondary school system were preoccupied with youth unemployment and the pressures it placed on the post-secondary system: they (especially colleges, employers) were also concerned with a perceived lack of basic literacy skills. People inside the system, on the other hand, focused on inadequacies in the organization of secondary education, course requirements, and variations in assessment standards. Those people with narrowly specialized interests aligned themselves around their favored issue (e.g., sex equity, special education).

Different groups bring pressure on policy makers for action in quite different ways (which we do not try to describe here). In order for a decision to be made to develop policy, however, in addition to exercising such pressure, there appears to be a need for the emergence of precipitating events or factors. In the case of OSIS, one such factor was substantial agreement among Ministry of Education officials that major changes were needed (somewhat ironic in light of the final results after the implementation of OSIS)[8] in secondary school organization and that simply fine-tuning existing policy would not be sufficient.

## *The Development Phase*[9]

Figure 2 summarizes the components involved in the development of a reform — in this instance, a government policy. Reforms likely to emerge as policy specifications from the development phase are bound by a widely shared set of ideas, values, theories, and beliefs (component 1). Such a "culture" constrains and shapes what are considered desirable and feasible consequences of the development phase (in the case of OSIS, for example, no one seriously considered doing away with secondary schools or privatizing public education).

The development phase involves a process of making decisions about the nature of the reform or policy (component 5). This process is influenced by previous development practices and policies (component 2) as well as the actions taken by interest groups (component 4) and members of the Ministry or Department of Education (component 3).

Political structures and procedures (component 2) can have a powerful influence on policy by acting as guidelines for decision making. Such guidelines direct and constrain how policies are developed, depending upon the extent to which those in authority insist on adherence to them. There are usually options available within such guidelines ranging from those in which only members of the government bureaucracy participate to the establishment of a royal commission.

In the case of OSIS, the influence exercised by this component was minimal with one exception: the Minister of Education exercised her authority in relation to both substance and process in a pervasive fashion. In terms of substance, she reflected the concerns of the public generally and, in particular, insisted that attention be given to the needs of the non-university bound student. The Minister's role was also pivotal in selecting the process used to develop the policy. She rejected existing structures for reviewing secondary education as well as the establishment of a royal commission (because it would have taken too long, would have been too costly, could have deviated from its mandate, and might have produced difficult-to-implement recommendations).

Members of the government bureaucracy (component 3) normally influence policy (1) through a shared set of values relevant to the substance of the policy, (2) through a commitment to the established procedures for policy development and practice and (3) through their direct participation in the policy development process, often in key roles. They are sometimes able to garner sufficient power through these avenues to fashion policies which do not reflect public preferences. Stamp's review of educational policy development in Ontario from 1876 to 1976 suggests, however, that such policies usually encounter serious opposition and are eventually overturned.[10]

OSIS was significantly influenced by members of the Ministry of Education: the values which they shared from the outset are widely reflected in the policy and help account for its relatively modest departure from the policy it replaced. They were able to exercise such influence because they designed the decision-making processes which were used and then played key roles in the process, serving as the secretariat for the decision-making committees that were more broadly representative. In these key roles, members of the bureaucracy exercised influence by keeping more radical proposals for change out of the deliberations and deflecting proposals of which they did not approve.

Major reforms of the sort described in this chapter are initiated, as we have discussed, out of the efforts of many groups with at least partly different interests (component 4). Their efforts are typically sustained through the development phase and often into the implementation phase, as well. Many of the groups which actively attempted to influence the nature of OSIS during its development are likely to be quite similar to the groups one might expect to be active in relation to many educational reforms in any province: they included colleges, universities, business and industry, teacher federations, the secondary school principals' association and subject-matter groups. In addition, groups with more specialized interests (e.g., separate school supporters, affirmative action groups, Franco-Ontarians, multicultural groups) also participated. While the particular special interest groups will vary depending on the policy to be developed, it is likely that some such groups will choose to participate.

The extent to which a group is able to have its values and preferences reflected in the policy which emerges from the development phase seems to depend on two factors: the actions of other groups with which it competes and the decision-making processes followed in the process of determining the nature of the policy or reform (component 5). Interest groups have greatest influence when they are unopposed. In OSIS, their influence was relatively weak because the Minister took steps to ensure that all groups were heard. The effect was that groups tended to cancel one another out. The Minister also acted as a spokesperson for the general public's interest (as she understood it) throughout the development phase.

The decision-making processes used in formulating the policy (component 5) also determine the extent of influence a group is able to exercise. Such processes vary along two dimensions relevant to our purposes: their degree of rationalism and democratization. Highly rational forms of decision-making require extensive knowledge of policy alternatives and relevant criteria for judging their appropriateness, information about consequences and methods for choice-making. Hammond has suggested six possible levels of rationalism, the higher levels of which are remote from the real world of policy-making.[11] Indeed "incrementalism," one of the less rational forms of decision-making, appears to best capture typical policy-making practice. Incrementalism assumes the availability of very little information, generally, the choice of action from very few alternatives and a trial and error stance toward selected alternatives usually involving only marginal departures from the status quo.

OSIS development processes were atypically rational in a number of respects. For example, an open-ended search for issues, concerns, data and solutions led to a report which included as close to a definitive set of issues as could be identified. This report became the agenda for subsequent deliberation. The effect of such rational approaches was to favor proposals that had broad support and insist on explicit, written reasons for either accepting or rejecting recommendations.

The second dimension of the development process relevant to our purposes is its degree of democratization — the extent to which all those with a stake in the policy have an opportunity to present their case and have it carefully weighed. Greater democratization generally decreases the chances of any particular group exercising disproportionate influence during the policy development phase. This appeared to be the case in OSIS. In addition to ways already discussed, relatively high levels of democratization were also achieved by seeking out appointments to decision-making structures of people who were willing and capable of thinking independently of their organizations. Committee members were told to represent themselves not their interest groups and they tended to do so.

## *The Implementation Phase*[12]

In order to implement and institutionalize reforms which require a change in their practices, implementors may need to overcome a variety of obstacles, such as lack of policy-related knowledge or skill, disincentives to change, inconsistent organizational arrangements, or inadequate resources. The extent to which such obstacles are overcome depends largely on the conditions, broadly conceived, within which reforms must be implemented.

Our conception of the implementation phase uses the term "factors" to encompass both the obstacles encountered by implementors and the conditions, including change strategies, which prevent or permit the overcoming of such obstacles. A factor may exist in a condition ranging from highly supportive to quite unsupportive of implementation and institutionalization. For example, the policy or reform may be written in forms ranging from clear and precise to obtuse and highly ambiguous. Implementation is usually fostered by the former condition and hampered by the latter. The large number of factors potentially affecting the implementation process can be classified as either policy specification factors, political and organizational context factors, or personal and professional context factors.

In Figure 3, the main components of the implementation phase are summarized: outcomes of implementation (component 5) are a function of the actions of individuals acting in the role of implementor (component 4). The conception is grounded on the assumption that actions are taken by individual implementors on the basis of their information-processing activities. These are, in turn, strongly affected by a wide range of factors emerging from the development process, from personal, political, and organizational contexts (components 2 and 3), and from the policy specifications (component 1). That is, what people do depends on what they think. The outcomes themselves, once directly experienced, are fed back to implementors as political, organizational and personal context factors, and have the potential for influencing their continuing information-processing and further actions. The outcomes also have the potential for influencing, over time, the development process and the policy specifications themselves.

The implementation process involves gradual change over time in the actions (i.e., practices and behaviours) of implementors toward those increasingly likely to realize reform goals. All changes can be described as actions taken by individuals in various roles who are involved in policy development, implementation and the outcomes of those actions. For example, changes in school system policies over time, in response to OSIS, can be described in terms of changes in the actions taken by school system policy developers, and associated outcomes; similarly, changes in human resources can be described in terms of changes in the actions taken by those distributing resources. The consequences or outcomes of policy implementation actions may be positive or negative, intended or unintended; they may impact on people in some or all roles associated with policy including, of course, the student, as in the case of OSIS. A policy-stimulated change is viewed as more or less institutionalized as the changed actions of people become endorsed and supported by the school and school system's standard operating procedures. For example, one indicator of institutionalization of a practice would occur when performance appraisal procedures explicitly recognized use of the policy-related practice as a criterion for judging performance.

Policy specifications (component 1) are the responsibilities or actions explicitly identified for an implementor in the policy itself or its subsequent regulations. About a half dozen factors or characteristics of such specifications appear to influence implementation generally. In the case of OSIS, a perception held by school staffs concerning the centrality of the policy to the core activities of the school appeared the greatest stimulant to implementation of this type. The clarity of the policy and its adaptability also fostered implementation.

Political and organizational content factors (of which there appear to be about a dozen) include characteristics of the school and broader political environments in which implementation must take place and which are likely to affect implementation processes and outcomes. Such characteristics include norms and roles with the school and broader environments and relationships among them (component 2). Within this category, quality of working relationships in the school system, resource allocation, school system capacity to implement, and public support for the policy are examples of factors which influenced OSIS implementation.

Component 3 in Figure 3 refers to the personal and professional beliefs, experiences, knowledge and skills held by implementors both in general and in policy-specific terms. Our research has identified seven such factors as especially important. In the case of OSIS, beliefs about the contribution of OSIS to what was best for students, agreement with the goals of OSIS and beliefs about whether or not one possessed the necessary knowledge and skill to implement the policy are examples of such factors which influenced implementation.

Examples of factors linked to component 4 in the implementation phase, "actions, behaviours, practices," include political support (e.g., from trustees), leadership at all levels (e.g., problem solving, communicating), quality of in-service training, and involving staff in implementation decisions and monitoring the implementation process. Each of these factors appeared to be significant influences on OSIS implementation.

The final component to be examined in the implementation phase is outcomes. In addition to recognizing that there usually are both intended and unintended outcomes, our research concerning OSIS suggests that there may be a way of classifying such outcomes which helps predict their likely level of implementation. We found that the large numbers of regulatory and administrative outcomes specified by OSIS (e.g., compulsory courses) were fully implemented rather quickly; policy specificity, strong leadership and political support were examples of factors that seemed to foster implementation of such outcomes particularly. In addition, OSIS included a number of outcomes that reflected major social trends (e.g., sex equity, multiculturalism). Such outcomes were also implemented to a relatively high degree but OSIS was not credited with making a large contribution to them. The centrality of the OSIS policy to the ongoing activities of the school was a factor fostering such outcomes.

A third category of intended outcome desired by OSIS was changing the basic services being delivered to the client (e.g., meeting the needs of non-university bound students). These outcomes were poorly implemented and, in fact, we refer to OSIS elsewhere[13] as a "fatal remedy" for the problems of non-university bound students; that is, the policy appeared to exacerbate problems it was intended to solve. In the face of multiple, potential outcomes, implementors make choices. These choices depend on their understanding of fundamental purposes (poorly understood in the case of OSIS), as well as the letter of the policy; they also depend on the ease of accomplishing different policy outcomes in the face of competing demands.

## The Substance of Curriculum Reform in Canada

The initiation, development and implementation of OSIS has been used to illustrate a "typical" process for bringing about curricular reform in Canada: some of the most common sources of influence outside the school ("political" influence) on curriculum are also evident in this case. In this section, we turn from the process to the substance of reform. What were the purposes for reforms undertaken during the 1976-87 period, and what has been their apparent impact to date? Out of what contexts did these reforms arise? What forces initiated and fostered these reforms?

A wide ranging analysis of relevant literature suggested that most major curriculum reforms have been undertaken to accomplish one or more of four purposes:

(1) To reshape the goals of education for individual students;

(2) To increase equality of educational opportunity;

(3) To increase the effectiveness of schools in accomplishing their goals; and

(4) To foster closer linkages between the school and real-life contexts, in particular, the workplace.

An analysis of two curricular reforms aimed at each purpose illustrates what we suggest was the substance of a large proportion of the reform in Canada between 1976 and 1987.[14] Our choices of reforms to analyze resulted, in part, from brief interviews with selected senior school system curriculum administrators, Ministry or Department of Education officials and university faculties in eastern, central, and western Canada. We also looked for evidence of reform initiatives, over the 11 year period, in the *Canadian Journal of Education*, publications of the *Canadian Association for Curriculum Studies*, and in descriptions of educational initiatives within each province (provided by Connelly and his associates)[15] and a wide array of provincial policy documents. The eight reform initiatives which were selected reflect considerable variation in curriculum area, level of schooling, and assumptions about the nature of change and sources of initiation. Each reform was also sufficiently widespread (e.g., pursuit of the reform in three or more provinces) to be considered a "national" reform. Each of the reforms is summarized in a common framework in Table 1.

This purpose for curriculum reform is probably the most fundamental of the four identified. Such reforms are of two sorts: direct attempts to state or restate educational goals; and the development of approaches to instruction which are likely to accomplish such redefined educational goals. One example of each type of reform is discussed here.

## Direct Attempts to Specify Educational Goals

Provincial departments or ministries of Education attempt to influence the nature of school curricula, in part, by the preparation and distribution of curriculum guidelines to schools. A pervasive feature of virtually all such guidelines is a statement concerning the goals of education for the province along with objectives specific to the curriculum area and reflecting provincial goals. Results of Robinson's study of Ontario curriculum guidelines[16] indicated that goals of education typically offered vague and ambiguous direction for practice. Furthermore, objectives for specific areas of the curriculum often appeared related in unclear ways to broader goals of education. Such an indictment could be made, safely, in reference to jurisdictions other than Ontario.

Several provinces are considering or have undertaken activities designed to clarify the nature of their goals of education and to transform them into more helpful instruments for curriculum and instructional decision-making.[17] Although still underway at this writing, the prototype reform effort of this sort was being carried out by the Curriculum Branch of British Columbia's Ministry of Education.[18] The immediate impetus for this reform came from a desire to help curriculum development committees do their jobs more efficiently. In particular, this initiative was to remedy such problems as biased treatment of teacher feedback by committees and lack of clear directions for new committees. It is not clear the extent to which this initiative was an indirect response to the demands for accountability and rationalization placed on the province's education system. These demands were a direct outgrowth of fiscal restraint policies established by the government as a means of coping with economic recession.[19] In a mission statement issued by the Ministry,[20] it declared its role to be ensuring that the province's education system gives students an opportunity to receive a quality education in a cost-effective manner.

Through a careful procedure for analyzing existing statements of goals, the Branch identified an image of the educated person as follows:

> The educated person is one who is a thinking individual, capable of making independent decisions based on analysis and reason. The individual is curious, capable of and interested in learning, capable of acquiring and imparting information, and able to draw from a broad knowledge base. The individual appreciates and is able to contribute to creative expression. The individual is self motivated, has a sense of self worth, pursues excellence, strives to be physically healthy and is able to achieve satisfaction through achievement. The individual has sound interpersonal skills, morals and values, and respects others who may be different, understands the rights and

achievement. The individual has sound interpersonal skills, morals and values, and respects others who may be different, understands the rights and responsibilities of an individual within the family, community, nation and the world and is aware of Canada's cultural heritage. The individual is flexible, has skills necessary to function in and contribute to the world of work. (p. 2).

This statement served as the basis for developing a detailed framework for generating curriculum objectives. A conception of growth within objectives was also developed and applied to the expectations for student development in the primary, junior, intermediate and senior grades. As a follow-up to such goal setting, given the importance attached to the development of students' intellectual processes, the Branch has also begun to describe what is known about the teaching of thinking.

The image of the educated person as a self directed problem solver put forth in British Columbia is very similar to the image statement issued by Ontario's Ministry of Education.[21] Indeed, an analysis of goal statements from most Canadian provinces suggests a growing national consensus on this crucial matter. British Columbia was unique, at the point of this writing, however, in applying a systematic procedure (developed by Robinson, and his colleagues)[22] for generating specific objectives linked to this image. In doing so, the Province appears to have taken a big step toward eliminating problems with goal statements discussed at the outset of this section.

## Whole Language Instruction

Efforts to reform the teaching of first language were undertaken in the face of an overwhelming accumulation of research evidence suggesting that traditional forms of instruction (transmission-oriented in nature) contributed little to communicative competence. Whole language instruction, as an alternative, was initiated largely by the university community and fostered by teachers. In Nova Scotia, for example, professors in faculties of education advocated such instruction to their pre-service and in-service students. These students, in turn, formed study groups throughout the province to explore whole language instruction further and to determine how to implement it in their classrooms. Such "grassroots" interest eventually was captured in provincial policy[23] and by 1987 all but a handful of school boards in the province had made considerable efforts to implement whole language instruction.

The context and forces for this change in Nova Scotia were essentially similar to those found in many other provinces and territories. Virtually all Canadian language arts guidelines and other publications supported the whole language reform effort by 1987.

Whole language instruction was selected as an example of what the adoption of an image of the educated person as a self-directed problem-solver would mean in practice. Such instruction builds on theories of learning drawn from contemporary cognitive psychology which ascribe central importance to the learner's active construction of meaning through the use of prior experience. Examples of what this means, in practice, are illustrated by several of the ten "Principles of the Language Arts Program" contained in Nova Scotia's *Language Arts in the Elementary School* (published in 1986):

(1) The learner's construction of meaning from written or spoken language is central to all learning.

(3) Language is learned from whole to part. Language is more than a series of words strung together. We understand what a series of words means before we know what the individual words are.

(5) Children learn language by using language; that is, they learn to read and write from reading, writing, and talking, not from a series of "readiness" activities.

Teachers are also viewed, for example, as responders and models to act merely as purveyors of facts and evaluators (p. 8).

# Increasing Equality of Educational Opportunity
## *Secondary School Reform*

An example of this type of reform (in Ontario) was used as the case for illustrating the process of curriculum reform outlined in the first section of the paper. In Table 1, aspects of this reform (as it was carried out in Ontario) are summarized relevant to our present purposes. Readers of the first section of this chapter will require no further explanation of this summary.

## *French Immersion Programs*

"Immersion" refers to the teaching of second language skills and conducting instruction through most or all of the school day in that second language. Maxwell Yalden, a former Commissioner of Official Languages, has characterized French immersion as "a Canadian success story"(p.3).[24] The proliferation of French immersion programs across Canada was part of a response to increased tensions among English and French-speaking Canadians. These tensions, experienced most dramatically in Quebec, resulted from concerns about cultural assimilation — specifically assimilation of the French culture by the English. A policy responding to these tensions was developed by the federal government in the late 1960s guided by the *Report of the Royal Commission on Bilingualism and Biculturalism* in 1967. These policies were viewed as instruments for increasing educational, social, and legal equality for French-speaking minorities in all parts of the country. In addition, these policies created public expectations of significant economic advantages in the future for bilingual Canadians through access to broader job opportunities.

As part of the move toward official languages equality, French immersion programs were initiated at the grass roots level. The first immersion program began in 1965 in St. Lambert near Montreal.[25] It was the result of two years of discussion by parent groups, education officials and researchers interested in improving French second language instruction. From these modest beginnings, French immersion programs have become a part of the public education system in all of Canada's provinces and territories. By 1977-78 more than 45,000 students were enroled in such programs: this number had increased to almost 180,000 students (about 5 percent of the total school population) by 1985-86 — even more remarkable was that this period was one of overall decline in school enrolment across Canada.[26]

Such growth in the availability of French immersion programs has often been the product of hard won political battles at the local level. Burns claims that local advocate groups had to exert considerable pressure on trustees and board administrators to have immersion programs adopted or expanded.[27] These programs can be political quagmires as non-supporters fight the loss of scarce resources to them: they can also create particularly intractable administrative problems, such as the need to bus students extraordinary distances (a problem which has found its way into the courts) and the need to find many more well-trained teachers than are available. Local groups have been substantially supported in their battles by provincial and national parent groups such as the New Brunswick Parents for Early Immersion and the Canadian Parents for French.

This reform is noteworthy in the unusually direct and aggressive role that has been played by research and the universities.[28] McGill researchers were involved in the initial program implemented in St. Lambert. In part as a result of government funding (Secretary of State, Provincial Ministry of Education), researchers have continued to inquire into questions of policy and practice as immersion has grown and come under increased scrutiny regarding its value.[29] For example, Stern[30] explored policy issues for the New Brunswick government; other faculty from the Ontario Institute for Studies in Education's Modern Language Centre engaged in a major research program in applied linguistics which furnished a steady stream of data relevant to immersion issues.[31] More recently, explorations of the wider social and curricular consequences of French immersion have suggested unintended effects. In particular, Burns[32] raises the possibility of children with higher socioeconomic family backgrounds being enroled in disproportionately large numbers thus furthering the equality of opportunity gap between themselves and children from lower socioeconomic family backgrounds. There seems little doubt, however, that students enroled in French immersion programs make impressive gains in French language competence with no corresponding losses in achievement in any other areas.[33]

# Increasing Effectiveness of Schools in Achieving Traditional Objectives

*Large-Scale Assessment of Student Achievement Prior to 1967*

All provinces in Canada had compulsory (usually exit) examinations that were used primarily as requirements for graduation, yardsticks for educational attainment, and admission criteria into post-secondary institutions. In the late 1960s, these examinations were either discontinued or drastically modified. Only two provinces, Quebec and Newfoundland, maintained the practice of province-wide individual achievement testing through the 15 year period to follow.

A swing to the assessment of the performance of educational systems was commonly observed in other provinces. This was manifest in a shift from year-end examinations to the evaluation of objectives typically beyond the scope of such examinations. Test development was based on provincial needs and many provinces used achievement and ability tests that had been standardized elsewhere. The thrust of the movement was from individual testing to the testing of samples of students. Individual student evaluation and assessment for graduation purposes was left to teachers. Testing practices were focused on assessing program quality and development.[34]

Changes in provincial government testing practices over the 1976-87 period were in response to increased political concern regarding educational quality. The effect of such concern was movement back to province-wide achievement testing. By 1987, there were six provinces (British Columbia, Alberta, Quebec, New Brunswick, Nova Scotia, and Newfoundland) engaged in such practice. Saskatchewan was also engaged in similar practices but only where teachers were not accredited to teach particular subjects. Typically, tests were administered in basic skills and core curriculum areas of mathematics, English (first language), French (first language) and science. In most cases, scores on exit examinations made up a substantial portion (e.g., 50 percent) of students' graduation marks with teacher assigned grades accounting for the remainder.

There were two especially influential forces accounting for the trend. First, universities expressed dissatisfaction with what they believed was high variability in educational standards across high schools which in turn posed problems for admission committees.[35] Concerns were also expressed by universities about what was believed to be a significant drop in standards. The second related force was growing public demand for accountability in conjunction with, for example, high teacher salaries and reform efforts in the U.S. stimulated by apparent drops in student achievement.[36]

By 1987, most provinces responded to these forces with a return to (or maintenance of) individual testing practices. Ontario, however, adopted a model of assessment that in theory allows for both accountability and program improvement objectives to be addressed. With the development of the Ontario

Assessment Instrument Pool (OAIP) and related item bank development, and the use of multi-matrix sampling procedures Ontario planned to test, on a cyclic basis, samples of students on selected subjects. Using a model that prescribes the collection of information on the intended, implemented and observed curriculum, and sampling on a representative basis for the province, the Ministry intends to provide information that would be suitable for estimating educational attainment (accountability) and for making decisions about program and instructional change. The Ontario model is not only more cost-effective than individual student achievement testings, but also allows for a much wider range of curriculum objectives to be tested.[37]

Not all forces brought to bear on education in the 1976-87 decade supported the province-wide testing movement. Technological innovations such as microcomputers, for example, promoted a more individualized curriculum and ran counter to the notion of a core curriculum and common examinations.[38] It is premature to estimate with confidence the impact of the return to province-wide exam initiators in any comprehensive fashion. However, preliminary evidence[39] suggests that one effect has been narrowing of the curriculum. Teachers appear to be "teaching to the tests." Due to the greater specificity as compared with objectives found in many curriculum guidelines, such tests were becoming the operational objectives for instruction. On the other hand, few would agree that such tests adequately reflect the range of objectives aspired to by curriculum policy.

## *Performance Appraisal of Teachers and School Administrators*

By performance appraisal we mean relatively formal policies and procedures designed to describe and make judgments about the value of teacher and principal practices. Unlike other reforms examined in this chapter, performance appraisal of teachers and school administrators does not have direct effects on the curriculum. Nevertheless, it fits our definition of reform since it is aimed, at least much of the time, at improving schools' delivery of curriculum.

In their comprehensive review of literature, Ondrack and Oliver[40] identify legal, economic, social, and demographic trends which define the context in which performance appraisal was developed over the 1976-87 period: they also suggest how such trends impacted on appraisal policies and practices. Canada's efforts to promote human rights have created a context in which school systems' judgements about employee performance are increasingly open to challenge in the courts. This trend accelerated the adoption of formal performance appraisal systems and the search for more objective and valid appraisal methods. The same effect was promoted by economic trends. Overall, the 1976-87 period was one of economic downturn and restraint in public sector spending, although by 1987 this trend was easing. Such restraint increased demands on school systems, often through the influence of cost-conscious trustees, to justify and utilize human resources as efficiently as possible.

Social and demographic trends, in particular, fostered development of more growth-oriented (or formative) as distinct from judgmental (or summative) appraisal practices. Ondrack and Oliver[41] point to a social environment in which professional educators desired greater participation in decision-making generally and wanted and demanded more information about themselves. Furthermore, the relative stability of the education labor force during the 1976-87 period created a need for appraisal systems which could assist with human resource planning, the motivation of "plateaued" teachers and school administrators and the identification of in-service education needs.

Although by 1986, ministries of Education (for example, in Ontario and New Brunswick) had begun to consider what policy initiatives might be taken at a provincial level concerning appraisal, the main forces driving development of performance appraisal systems appear to have been local.[42] School board trustees saw appraisal practices as a route to greater accountability. Senior school administrators viewed appraisal as a potentially useful instrument for ensuring that effort was devoted, at the school level, to goals established by the school system.

Evidence concerning the objectives for performance appraisal actually pursued in school systems, as well as estimates of the impact of this reform, were based on a study carried out in Ontario by Lawton and his colleagues[43] in 1986. Combining evidence concerning teacher and principal appraisal practices suggests that board appraisal systems were perceived by the appraisees, at least, to be pursuing three immediate objectives: (1) to comply with Ministry and board policy; (2) to identify weaknesses in practice and stimulate improvement in such areas; and (3) to reassure staffs that they were doing a good job and to help build or maintain their self-confidence. Clearly, the long term objective was to increase the effectiveness of schools in achieving whatever goals they had in mind for students; presumably, the three short-term goals were viewed as means to this long term end.

To judge the impact of appraisal practices, Lawton and his associates[44] collected perceptions of teachers, principals and others which suggested that typical appraisal practices achieve their perceived goals to a modest degree (although more for principals than teachers). For example:
- About 87 percent of teachers and principals felt that they received honest sincere praise from their appraisals and about 70 percent felt good about their appraisals (thus contributing to self-confidence);
- A similar 87 percent of both groups felt judgments made about their performance by evaluators were fair (this was important given the legal context for appraisal discussed above);
- 84 percent of the teachers and 70 percent of the principals, however, judged the degree of improvement in their performance resulting from their last appraisal to be non-existent or very small.

# Strengthening the Links between School
# and Real-Life Contexts
## Science Education

Efforts to examine and alter science curricula have a history which predates the period of our study by many decades. At the national level, however, five inquiries related to science and education were conducted following the OECD[45] report up to 1984.[46] Virtually all provinces and territories engaged in science curriculum revision during that period, as well. Berg and Mac-Keracher[47] suggest that such pervasive issues as economic recession, increased unemployment, declining school enrolments, environmental concern, technological lag, and the like, created pressure on science education and were a part of the context in which such revision took place. More specifically, at the senior secondary level, provincial efforts were stimulated by pressures to expand the francophone science curriculum and to accommodate substantial changes in other areas of the school system. Changing theories of learning and child development were among the stronger forces for change in elementary and lower secondary school curricula (e.g., inferences for instruction drawn from Piaget's theory of intellectual development along a concrete to abstract dimension).

Changes to science curricula across Canada have been undertaken to serve all four goals for reform which we have identified. However, initiatives undertaken by the Science Council of Canada provide particularly good examples of reforms aimed at strengthening links between school and real-life contexts.[48] The Science Council of Canada's initiatives first took the form of a series of integrated research studies stimulated by several criticisms of science education in Canada. T.H.B. Symon's report, *To Know Ourselves* (1978), claimed that Canadian students were being taught nothing about the impact of science in their own country. This claim was reinforced and widely espoused by a prominent scientist-broadcaster (David Suzuki); members of the public, in his view, were ignorant of the effects of science and technology on their lives. At the same time, challenges to the way science was being taught were emanating from Quebec. The Science Council, in the face of these claims, concluded that " . . . a public with little or no understanding of science and its impact on society is at the mercy of technological change"(p.23).[49]

The Science Council of Canada studies included analyses of curricula, surveys of opinion concerning the nature of science education and case studies of science teaching. The goals of the studies were to document the purposes and characteristics of science teaching, conduct a historical analysis of science education in Canada and to stimulate active deliberation concerning future options for science education. The Council's final report[50] consisted of 12 basic recommendations along with an extensive set of proposals for how the recommendations might be implemented. Five of the 12 recommendations are related to the goal of increasing links between the school and real-life contexts:

guaranteeing science in every elementary school, increasing participation of young women in science education, presenting a more authentic view of science, emphasizing the science-technology-society connection and setting science in a Canadian context.

While it is too soon to estimate the consequences of the Science Council's activities on curricula and students in Canada, some impact is already evident. For example, Ontario's Ministry of Education has recently issued a new policy on science teaching in elementary schools. This policy grew directly out of Council's recommendations and was formulated with the assistance of the senior author of the Council's report (Graham Orpwood).

## Cooperative Education

Educational programs that offer work experience in real work settings have been operating since the early 1900s in North America. It has only been comparatively recently, however, that they have been offered as diploma credit courses; this feature distinguishes cooperative education from other related activities such as "field training," "on-the-job training," "experiential learning" and "work experience".[51]

Cooperative education in Canada began in Ontario at the post secondary level and quickly spread to the secondary schools in the early 1970s. Early initiatives were in business and technical education and were primarily spearheaded by groups of teachers who recognized the potential value of field-based educational opportunities. At this time, Canadians were faced with a competitive job market coupled with rising unemployment. Corresponding claims that public education lacked relevance to the real problems of contemporary society were heard with increasing frequency. Also, enrolments were declining and the student dropout rate was high. These conditions prompted school systems to give serious consideration to alternative modes of education that were more relevant and attractive to both students in school and those who had dropped out.

Cooperative education usually aims to provide students with an opportunity in a practical setting to develop skills, improve problem-solving abilities and acquire positive work habits. In contrast to the U.S., cooperative education in Canada has been largely "educationally driven." Typically, students receive little or no remuneration for their efforts in the work setting. As a consequence, education systems have been able to maintain control of the programming and monitoring. Programs are designed for students at all levels and streams and is not intended only for students bound for the work force. In Atlantic Canada, programs were initially developed in the context of vocational education and serving the educationally disadvantaged. By 1987, particularly in Nova Scotia, this focus had broadened substantially.

Cooperative education has grown rapidly over the past 15 years and there are no signs that the rate of growth will level off in the near future. From 1985 to 1986 in Ontario, for example, there was an increased enrolment in cooperative education of almost 40 percent in publicly funded secondary schools. By the end of 1987, there were cooperative education associations in all provinces and territories in Canada and some 70,000 students were involved in cooperative education programs (about 50 percent of these students were in Ontario). Some of the more influential factors that stimulated increased growth of cooperative education were federal and provincial government funding incentives, commitment and sanction from provincial governments, a broad base of public support, and the establishment of provincial and national cooperative education associations. A national association, called the Cooperative Career Work Education Association of Canada, was formed in 1984.

Because some of the objectives of cooperative education are highly congruent with youth employment, job training and skills development, Employment and Immigration Canada has provided financial support since the mid-1970s. Commitment of provincial governments also had considerable influence on cooperative education by providing, for example, access to grants by school systems for the establishment of cooperative education co-ordinator/consultant positions, professional development, and various operational expenses such as transportation to and from work sites for students. In addition to financial incentives, provincial policies have supported cooperative education through such actions as granting diploma credit (e.g., Ontario, Alberta) and specialist training in some provinces. On the other hand, secondary education reform processes in New Brunswick in 1987 appeared to favor more traditional academic educational processes.

The potential benefits of cooperative education have been heavily promoted, particularly by local and provincial associations, but a paucity of data is available to demonstrate that cooperative programs are achieving their objectives. Most available research took the form of surveys (usually questionnaires) of educators, students, parents and supervisors involved in cooperative education or work experience programs. Such surveys conducted in Ontario, British Columbia and Alberta[52] showed high levels of satisfaction with cooperative education and work experience programs. Cognitive and affective benefits were also attributed to the programs but this was not the case concerning work-related skills development according to Hughes and King.[53] Two small-scale Ontario studies[54] suggested that cooperative education programs promoted increases in personal skills such as empathy, decision making, time management and self-esteem.

# Conclusion
## *The Reform Process*
Using the 1976 to 1987 period as an approximate boundary, the process and substance of curriculum reform in Canada has been examined through the use of eight selected cases. The beginning of this period corresponded with a

review of education in Canada by OECD[55] which suggested that future educational reform ought to be treated "within the framework of larger political and social concerns" (p. 5). Analysis of at least the eight reforms selected for attention in this chapter suggests, unequivocally, that this usually has been the case.

Forces initiating and fostering most of the reforms were responding in part, at least, to such political and social problems as high youth unemployment, federal government language and cultural policies, fiscal accountability demands and human rights concerns. But is this strong relationship between education reform efforts and broader political and social issues really new? Tomkins' review of the history of curriculum development in Canada suggests that it is not.[56] Indeed, the OECD review seems to have been based on a misreading of how Canadian curricula have been shaped historically. Even in the absence of a national education system, Tomkins' analysis concludes, national issues have usually become curriculum issues. Education policies have been, and appear to remain, responsive to larger political and social problems because the very existence of Canada was and is problematical given the pervasive influence of the U.S. on most facets of Canadian life.[57] Such responsiveness is more likely given the high degree of centralized control over curriculum policy by provincial governments and the indirect but growing influence on such policy by the federal government.[58]

In the face of broad political and social issues and problems, often translated into proposals for change in educational policy and practice by groups outside the school system, the major role of public school educators has been to veto (by inaction rather than by active opposition), modify and/or find ways to implement such proposals. Processes used to bring about change, such as the example used in the first section of this chapter, frequently involve public school educators in providing feasability information about proposals for change. But rarely, it seems, are such educators, themselves, initiators of the change.

In our view, these processes for reform are unlikely to change significantly over the next 15 years. The process of secondary school reform (OSIS) in Ontario (discussed at the outset) was generally more rational (more careful to identify and weigh alternatives, more concerned with reliable information, more concerned with representing the views of all those with a stake in the outcome including education professionals) than is typical of provincial policy-making processes: this seems to have had generally positive effects on the outcome, leading us to expect (and advocate) more attention to increased rationality in the future.[59] Aside from such change, however, there seems little reason to expect major shifts in the forces for change or the processes used in response to such forces.

The only exception to our general conclusions regarding reform processes, concerns the role of the educational research community: in five of the eight cases of reform, there is considerable evidence of its influence either quite directly (French immersion, whole language, science education, student achievement testing) or more subtly and indirectly (e.g., refining the goals of education). We suspect that this degree of influence would not have been found in earlier periods of reform in Canada and that this influence is symptomatic of the maturing of the educational research enterprise in Canada. The next 15 years may well see an increase in reforms stimulated by educational research, fostered directly by its main consumers (educational practitioners) and subsequently sanctioned by policy. During this period, non-research based advocates of reform may also make greater use of research to strengthen their claims. As well, policy makers seem likely to become more sensitive to research as a more helpful source of information than has been the case, in the past.

## *The Substance of Reform*

Our approach to the substance of curriculum reform in Canada over the next 15 years is structured by the four reform goals illustrated in the preceding section of this chapter. In the case of each goal, extrapolations are made of plausible future solutions or initiatives to current problems or practices. We make few claims for the originality of these extrapolations — only their reasonableness.

Reshaping the goals of education was one purpose for reform during the 1976-87 period: British Columbia's project to define the image of the educated person and whole language instruction exemplified initiatives designed for this purpose. There appears to be a growing consensus across Canada about the importance of self-directed problem solving as the core of what it will mean to be educated in the future.[60] Only a few provinces and school systems, however, have begun to systematically and comprehensively grapple with the curricular and instructional implications of such an image. British Columbia's project seems likely to result in a set of curriculum objectives that may serve as a model for other jurisdictions; whole language as compared with traditional language instruction illustrates the changes in teaching implied by a focus on self-directed problem solving.

Most current curricula and the instruction required for their implementation are based still on "transmission" assumptions; the role of the teacher is to convey knowledge and skill to students with very little interaction or opportunity for students to impose personal meaning. To develop self-directed problem-solving, on the other hand, will require the design and implementation of "transactional" curricula; fostering experiences with students which empower them with the ability to shape their own lives in a personally and socially meaningful fashion. More intense, systematic and skillful effort toward transactional curricula may consume a significant amount of reform effort over the next 15 years.

Fostering equality of opportunity was a second reform goal pursued during the 1976-87 period. The two examples used of efforts to accomplish this goal make quite different assumptions about how equality could be fostered by educational policy. In the case of secondary school reorganization (specifically the Ontario version) the route to equality was assumed to be through the imposition of a uniform policy on all schools in a province. All schools, for example, were expected to offer programs at three levels of difficulty, to have uniform credit requirements and to offer the same range of credits to students. Elsewhere we point out how such uniform policies seriously detract from the possibility of some schools offering the best programs of which they are capable and some students learning as much as they are capable of learning.[61]

More generally, Diorio[65] argues that:

> . . . policies which impose uniform schooling practices on persons who do not want them involve an illegitimate devaluation by government of the worth of the lives of some citizens. (p. 147)

Equality of opportunity, in other words, is a function of both the purposes of a policy and its effectiveness in accomplishing those purposes with all those who are intended to benefit. French immersion programs nicely illustrate an approach to educational policy which assumes that not everyone values the purposes such policies are intended to accomplish. Obstacles encountered at the local level in implementing French immersion programs also may be symptomatic of difficulties associated with the pursuit of differentiated educational policies.

Nevertheless, given the ever increasing linguistic and cultural diversity to be found among Canadians, we are likely to witness many more efforts to develop and implement differentiated educational policies in the future. At some point, of course, further differentiation will seriously threaten the social fabric and administrative viability of schools as we know them. The next 15 years may see us testing the limits of institutionalized education and determining whether or not such limits are able to accommodate our needs for policy differentiation in the service of equality.

The two examples used to illustrate reforms designed to improve the effectiveness of schools were large scale assessment of student achievement, and performance appraisal of teachers and administrators. Both examples assume that better information about the nature and effects of current schooling practices is a prerequisite for improving such practices. The problem in both cases, however, is the extremely limited conception of either student achievement or schooling practices on which they are based. Provincial assessment programs rarely measure the extent to which students have acquired core qualities associated with self-directed problem solving. Similarly, performance appraisal systems most often look for practices associated with the implementation of transmission curricula. Indeed, teachers implementing transactional curricula in order to foster self-directed problem-solving in the context of many current appraisal systems, may be punished for so doing.

A trend, much to be wished for over the next 15 years, is a significant shift in the focus of both student achievement testing and performance appraisal of staff. At present, the two examples used to illustrate reforms to increase effectiveness seem largely reactionary in their efforts: since Egerton Ryerson's days, examination policies, for example, have served as instruments of stability and control[62] rather than change and this still seems to be the case. Because these reforms have such a powerful steering effect on school practices, however, it seems especially important to reshape them in the service of educational goals more directly reflecting curriculum policies.

Reform efforts aimed at strengthening the links between the school and real-life contexts were illustrated using the cases of science education and cooperative education. The goal itself has been a prominant theme in much of the writing of those concerned more with the education of adults than of children — for example, the concept of lifelong learning in which movement between work settings and formal education settings is relatively easy, socially acceptable and something which occurs throughout one's adult life as one's needs and interests change and mature.

Other examples of efforts to pursue closer links between school and real life contexts abound: recent efforts to more closely link "high tech." industry with relevant university research programs to the benefit of both; the variety of applied courses offered by colleges; "adopt-a-school" arrangements in which corporations undertake to sponsor special activities within schools and open their doors to staff and students who wish to learn more about their operation. The potential exists in many of these examples for a narrowing of educational goals to the applied and vocational with diminished attention devoted to cultural, moral, aesthetic and higher order intellectual goals. But this is far from inevitable.

Indeed, we see in these specific efforts a powerful general strategy for the development of self-directed problem-solving through a curriculum which has a much richer transactional character than the school alone is capable of providing. More actively developing links between the school and real life contexts over the·next 15 years may be a way of realistically expanding the limits of institutionalized education (change is most likely when it can happen incrementally) without the necessity of de-schooling society and losing the many valued supports that schools provide.

Table 2. The Substance of Curriculum Reform in Canada: Selected Cases

| Goals for Reform and Selected Cases | The Context for Reform | Objectives for Reform | Forces Initiating and Fostering Reform | Impact |
|---|---|---|---|---|
| 1. Reshaping the Goals of Education 1.1 Direct Attempts to Specify Education Goals (e.g., British Columbia). | -economic recession education funding reductions. -demand for accountability. -vague and ambiguous statements of educational objectives. -clearer direction needed for curriculum development. | -provide students with a "quality education in a cost-effective manner." -clarify goals of education and provide framework for provincial curriculum develop't. -increase effectiveness in teaching thinking skills. | -Ministry of Education (Curriculum Branch). -initiative of key individual in collaboration with university. -a well developed procedure for developing educational goals and related curricula. | -too early to determine. |
| 1.2 Whole Language Instruction (e.g., Nova Scotia). | -overwhelming accumulation of research evidence supporting view that traditional forms of language arts instruction contribute little to communicative competence. | -to improve the language competency of students by implementing forms of instruction consistent with contemporary models of the learner. | -university professors and students enroled in their courses. -"study groups" of language arts teachers. | In Nova Scotia all but 4 of 5 boards actively attempting to implement the form of instruction. |

| Goals for Reform and Selected Cases | The Context for Reform | Objectives for Reform | Forces Initiating and Fostering Reform | Impact |
|---|---|---|---|---|
| 2. Increasing Equality of Educational Opportunity | -declining student enrolments. -increased youth unemployment. -availability of new student testing instruments. -public concerns about student attitudes and discipline. -teacher concerns for numbers and types of credit required for graduation. | -enhanced opportunities for non university-bound students. -enhanced concerns for sex equity and needs of cultural and linguistic minorities. -increased graduation standards. -closer links between the school and the workplace. -greater nurturing of students (e.g.,counselling, discipline). | -employers. -colleges and universities. -educators. -a variety of special interest groups (e.g., Franco-Ontarians, special education, separate school supporters). -government bureaucrats. -politicians. | -altered requirements for graduation. -changes in patterns of student course choices. -modest increases in attention to sex equity, needs of cultural and linguistic minorities. -more explicit discipline policies. -decreased opportunities for non university-bound students |
| 2.2 French Immersion | -Report of the Royal Commission on Bilingualism and Biculturalism(1967) and resulting federal government olicies. -Charter of Rights and Freedoms -British North American Act (Section 133). -increased public awareness of Canada's cultural diversity and concerns regarding cultural assimilation. | -to promote Canadian bilingualism outside as well as inside Quebec. -to foster greater appreciation of the French culture. -to produce a high level of proficiency in French with no accompanying loss in any area of educational development, including first languages. -enhance chances of child's success in a future labor market governed by bilingual policies. | -community-basd parent groups (e.g. Cowichan Valley Parents for French). -provincial and national parent organizations (e.g. Canadian parents for French). -Teacher associations (e.g., Canadian association for Second Language Teachers). -educational researchers -governments: federal (e.g. Secretary of State) and provincial (Ministry of Education). -Courts and Laws | -native or near-native language proficiency (at least in reading & writing) among a significant proportion of immersion program graduates. -greatly increased participation in French immersion in all parts of the country. -possible creation of opportunities for developing high status knowledge in which largely middle class students take part. |

| Goals for Reform and Selected Cases | The Context for Reform | Objectives for Reform | Forces Initiating and Fostering Reform | Impact |
|---|---|---|---|---|
| 3. Increasing Effectiveness of Schools<br>3.1 Large Scale Assessment of Student Achievement | -public dissatisfaction with educational quality and demands for accountability.<br>-university dissatisfaction with secondary school standards.<br>-test score decline in U.S. accompanied by reform movement.<br>-neo Conservative politics raising in Canada. | Student examination: monitor educational standards.<br>-provide baseline data from which future comparisons could be made (e.g., provincial norms).<br>-descriptive information for educational policy.<br>-requirements for graduation.<br>-admission criteria for universities.<br>Student assessment: assessment of educational achievement at provincial, system, school, class levels.<br>-provide data for program change and improvement of instruction. | University councils desire data from common exams and core curriculum<br>-public demands for accountability<br>-dissatisfaction with current practice. Negative forces include: technical inovations which allow for more individualized instruction and run counter to notion of core curriculum; enormous costs associated with province-wide exams. | -narrowing of curriculum.<br>-measurement driven.<br>-very little use of data for improvement of instruction. |
| 3.2 Performance Appraisal of Teachers and School | Legal trends: increased need to ensure protection of human rights.<br>-Economic trends: downturn in economy and resulting constraints increase demands to utilize human resources efficiently.<br>-Social trends: employee demands for greater satisfaction and participation in their work.<br>-Demographic trends: lack of turnover among staff. | Short term:<br>-to comply with Ministry and Board policies.<br>-to identify aspects of teaching and administration in need of improvement and to stimulate such improvement.<br>-to reassure and develop self-confidence.<br>Long term:<br>-to improve student learning. | -school trustees<br>-senior school administrators | -increase or help maintain self-confidence of teachers and principals.<br>-contribute in modest ways to improving teacher and principal performance.<br>-unknown effects on students. |

| Goals for Reform and Selected Cases | The Context for Reform | Objectives for Reform | Forces Initiating and Fostering Reform | Impact |
|---|---|---|---|---|
| **4. Strengthening the Links Between School and Real-Life Contexts** **4.1 Science Education (Science Council of Canada Research Initiatives)** | -criticism of science education as not teaching about impact of science on Canadian society. -claims that Canadian public ignorant of impact of science and technology on their lives. -criticisms of the nature of science teaching. | -guarantee science teaching in every elementary classroom. -increase participation of women in science education. -present more authentic view of science in schools. -emphasize connections among science, technology and society and set science in a Canadian context. | -Organization for Economic Cooperation and Development (1975 report). -Federal government report (Symons, 1978). -research reports produced by the Science Council of Canada. -communications network developed among researchers and policy-makers. -theories of learning and child development. | -changes in provincial curriculum policies. |
| **4.2 Cooperative Education** | -competitive job market (rising unemployment). -claims that public education is not relevant to the real problems of current society. -declining enrolment patterns. -high dropout rate. | -to allow students to gain valuable work experience in a real work setting which is related to their in-school studies. -provide practical opportunities for: skill development; improved problem solving abilities; acquisition of positive work habits; provide opportunity for a structurally different mode of teaching and of learning | -broad base of support from students, parents, educators, unions, business/industries. -federal and provincial funding initiatives. -provincial commitment and sanction. -provincial and national cooperative education associations. | -rapid growth of cooperative education programs across the country. -improved personal skills of students. -"energized" educational system |

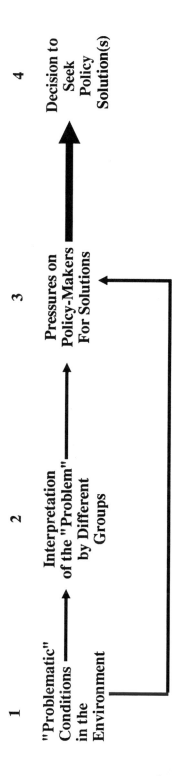

Figure 1. Components of the Policy Initiation Process

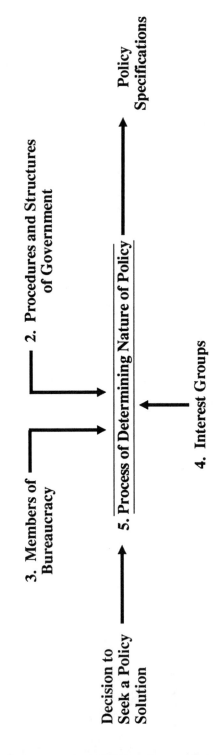

Figure 2.  Components of the Reform or Policy Development Phase

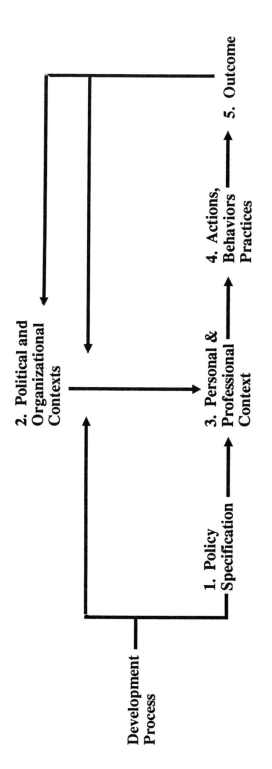

Figure 3. Components of the Implementation Phase

## Notes

[1] Organization for Economic Cooperation and Development, *Reviews of National Policies for Education: Canada* (Paris: OCED, 1976).

[2] F.M. Connelly, R.K. Crocker and H. Kass, *Science Education in Canada, Volume 1: Policies, Practices,and Perceptions* (Toronto: OISE Press, 1985), p. 1.

[3] K.A. Leithwood et al., *The Implementation of Bill 82 in Ontario*, mimeographed paper (Toronto: OISE, 1985); D. Trider and K.A. Leithwood,"Exploring Influences in Principals' Practices," *Curriculum Inquiry* (1988).

[4] K.A. Leithwood et al., *The Develpment of Ontario Schools: Intermediate and Senior Divisions — 1984 (OSIS) and the Initial Phase of its Implementation* (Toronto: OISE Press, 1987b); K.A. Leithwood et al., *The Nature and Consequences of Selected Processes for Developing, Implementing and Institutionalizing Major Educational Policies*, technical report (Toronto: OISE Press, 1987a).

[5] See Ontario Ministry of Education, Circular HS1 (Toronto: Ministry of Education, Ontario, 1979).

[6] This literature is reviewed in Leithwood et al., *Ontario Schools*, Chapter 4.

[7] We have reviewed this literature in a segmented fashion. For relevant non-education literature see K.A. Leithwood and S. Anderson, *Evaluating Policy Implementation*, mimeo (Toronto: OISE Press, 1985). For relevant education literature see D.M.A. Trider, *Factors Influencing the Policy Implementation Behavior of Principals*, doctoral dissertation (Toronto: University of Toronto, 1985).

[8] See for example, Leithwood et al., *Nature and Consequences*.

[9] In addition to our own research, this section is based on conceptions of policy development offered by T.R. Dye, Understanding Public Policy (Englewood Cliffs, N.J.: Prentice-Hall, 1972); R. Simeon, "Studying Public Policy," Canadian Journal of Political Science, 9 (December 1976): 548-580; K. Hammond, "Toward Increasing Competence of Thought in Public Policy Formation," in B.H. Raven, ed., *Policy Studies Review Annual*, Volume 4 (Beverly Hills, Ca.: Sage, 1980); and others. These were reviewed in some detail by Leithwood et al. in *Ontario Schools*.

[10] R. Stamp, *The Schools of Ontario, 1876-1976* (Toronto: University of Toronto Press, 1982).

[11] Hammond, "Increasing Competency of Thought.".

[12] This section has been adapted from Leithwood et al., *Nature and Consequences*.

[13] Leithwood and Cousins, *Fostering Inequality*; Leithwood et al., *Nature and Consequences*.

[14] A more comprehensive identification of reforms may be found in Connelly et al., *Science Education*; and M.G. Fullan, *School Improvement Efforts in Canada*, prepared for the Council of Ministers of Education, Canada, mimeographed paper (Toronto: OISE Press, 1986).

[15] See note 14 above.

[16] F.G. Robinson, *The Influence of Guidelines on Local Curriculum Planning* (Toronto: Commission on Declining School Enrolments in Ontario, 1978).

[17] For example, in 1987 Prince Edward Island's formal answer to a review commission on educational reform (Paquette Report) called for a long range statement of the province's educational goals.

[18] Information concerning this project was obtained from V. Overgaard, *Curriculum Goals and Perceptions, a Position Paper* (Victoria: Ministry of Education, British Columbia, 1987); and Bitish Columbia Ministry of Education, *Let's Talk about Schools: Discussion Paper* (Victoria Ministry of Education, British Columbia, 1985).

[19] Sometimes referred to as "The Great Recession".

[20] British Columbia Ministry of Education, *Mission Statement* (Victoria: Ministry of Education, British Columbia, 1985).

[21] Ontario Ministry of Education, "Issues and Directions," response to the final report of the Commission on Declining Enrolments in Ontario (Toronto: Ministry of Education, Ontario, 1980).

[22] F.G. Robinson, J.A. Ross and F. White, *Curriculum Development for Effective Instruction,* monograph, series 17 (Toronto: OISE Press, 1985).

[23] Nova Scotia Department of Education, *Language Arts in the Elementary School*, Curriculum Teaching Guide, No. 86 (Halifax: Department of Education, Nova Scotia, 1986).

[24] M. Yalden, "French Immersion — A Canadian Experience," *Language and Society,* 12 (Winter 1984).

[25] F. Genesee, "Bilingual Education of Majority Language Children: The Immersion Experiments in Review," *Applied Linguistics*, 4, 1 (1983): 1-46.

[26] The Canadian Parents for French, *The CPF Immersion Registry 1986/1987.*

[27] Burns, "French Immersion Implementation in Ontario: Some Theoretical, Policy and Applied Issues," *The Canadian Modern Language Review*, 42, 3 (1986): 572-591.

[28] J. Cummins, "Immersion Programs: Cuurent Issues and Future Directions," in L.L. Stewin and S.J.H. McCann, eds., *The Canadian Mosaic* (Toronto: Copp Clark Pitman, 1987).

[29] M. Swain, ed., "Bilingualism in Canadian Education: Issues and Research," *Canadian Society for Studies in Education Yearbook,* 1976.

[30] H.H. Stern, "The Immersion Phenomenon," *Language and Society*, 12 (Winter 1984): 48-54.

[31] For example, see S. Lapkin and M. Swain, "Research Update," *Language and Society,* 12 (Winter 1984):47; and Genesee, pp. 1-46.

[32] See Note 31 above.

[33] Cummins, *Immersion Programs.*

[34]R.K. Crocker, " Science Student Assessment Practices," in F.M. Connelly, R.K. Crocker and H. Kass, *Science Education in Canada, Volume 1: Policies, Practices and Perceptions* (Toronto: OISE Press, 1986); and H. Schulz, *Summary of Provincial Practices in Canadian Public Education* (Toronto: Council of Ministers of Education, 1985).

[35]G. Fitzsimmons, "Advances in Achievement Testing: Some Implications for the Classroom," in L.L. Stewin and S.J.H. McCann, eds., *Contemporary Educational Issues: The Canadian Mosaic* (Toronto: Copp Clark Pitman Ltd., 1987) pp.137-145; L.D. McLean, *The Craft of Student Evaluation in Canada* (Toronto: Canadian Education Association (1985); and R.E. Traub and L.D. McLean, *A Rosey View — University Admission Officers' Preferences and Expectations for Provincial Examinations,* mimeographed paper (Toronto: OISE Press, 1987).

[36]V.R. Nyberg, "Educational Standards in Canada," in Stewin and McCann, *The Canadian Mosaic,* pp. 109-125.

[37]P. Nagy, R.E. Traub and K. MacRury *Strategies for Evaluating the Impact of Province-Wide Testing* (Toronto: The Queen's Printer for Ontario, 1986).

[38]Fitzsimmons, pp. 137-145; and L.D. McClean, *The Craft of Student Evaluation in Canada* (Toronto: Canadian Education Association, 1985).

[39]McLean; C.S. Ungerleider, "Testing: Fine Tuning the Politics of Inequality," in Stewin and McCann, *The Canadian Mosaic.*

[40]D.A. Ondrack and C. Oliver, *A Review and Analysis of Performance Appraisal Processes,* Volume 1 (Toronto: The Queen's Printer for Ontario, 1986).

[41]Ondrack and Oliver.

[42]We based his conclusion on data from interviews with senior Ministry and board officials as well as with university-based consultants working with school systems to develop appraisal policies and practices.

[43]Data for this study included (a) an analysis of relevant policies from 119 of Ontario's 187 school boards (b) a survey of school and school system staff in a sample of 30 boards and (c) case studies conducted in seven boards. Our direct contacts with many school systems outside Ontario suggest that data from the Ontario study may overestimate the general level of sophistication of appraisal practices in Canada.

[44]Ondrack and Oliver.

[45]Ondrack and Oliver.

[46]D. Mackeracher, "Science Education in a Changing Society," in Connelly, Crocker and Kass, *Science Education in Canada.*

[47]L. Berg and D.MacKeracher, "Science Education: Past Contexts," in Connelly, Crocker and Kass, *Science Education in Canada.*

[48]Information about these initiatives was taken from G.W.F. Orpwood and J.P. Souque, *Science Education in Canadian Schools, Volume 1: Introduction and Curriculum Analysis* (Ottawa: Science Council of Canada, 1984); G.W.F. Orpwood and I. Alam, *Science Education in Canadian Schools, Volume II, Statistical Database for Canadian Science Education* (Ottawa: Science Council

of Canada, 1984); J. Olson and T. Russell, eds., *Science Education in Canadian Schools: Volume III: Case Studies of Science Teaching* (Ottawa: Science Council of Canada, 1984); Science Council of Canada, *Science for Every Student: Educationg Canadians for Tomorrow's World* (Ottawa: Science Council of Canada, 1984).

[49]Orpwood and Souque.

[50]Science Council of Canada.

[51]J. Hughs and A.J.C. King, *A Study of Cooperative Education in Ontario's Secondary Schools: Summary Report* (Toronto: Ontario's Secondary Schools Teacher's Federation, 1982).

[52]See Hughs and King: R.S Stevens, "An Evaluation of Work Education Programs," research report 78-04 (Vancouver: Board of School Trustees, 1978).

[53]See note 51 above.

[54]P. Shaughnessy, "Personal Skills Development of Cooperative Education Students in Two Secondary Schools in the City of York: A Preliminary Study," mimeographed paper (Toronto: Board of Education for the City of York, 1985); E. Stressman, "A Study of Personal Skills of Cooperative Education Students," *Ontario Cooperative Education Assocation Newsletter* (Fall 1987): 16-17.

[55]See note 54 above.

[56]G. Tomkins, "The Moral, Cultural and Intellectual Foundations of the Canadian Curriculum," in D. Roberts and J. Fritz, eds., *Curriculum Canada* (Vancouver: Centre for the Study of Curriculum and Instruction, 1984).

[57]S.D. Clark, *Canadian Society in Historical Perspective* (Toronto: McGraw-Hill Ryerson Limited, 1976). Quoted in Tomkins, 1984.

[58]J.J. Bergen, "Council of Ministers of Education in Canada: At a Political Juncture?" in J.H.A. Wallin, ed., *The Politics of Canadian Education*, 1977 Yearbook of the Canadian Society for the Study of Education, Volume 4.

[59]What this might look like is described in Leithwood et al., *Development of Ontario Schools*.

[60]Tomkins has described a decline in consensus, beginning about 1960, concerning what purposes the school curriculum should serve. It is, however, a decline in moral and social values — historically, a crucial part of the foundation of the Canadian curriculum. Perhaps what we are witnessing at present is the rebuilding of consensus on different grounds.

[61]Leithwood and Cousins, *Fostering Inequality*, pp. 1-10.

[62]Tomkins.